THE HABITUAL CRIMINAL

THE HABITUAL CRIMINAL

BY

NORVAL MORRIS, LL.M. (Melbourne), Ph.D. (London)

Senior Lecturer in Law, University of Melbourne

GREENWOOD PRESS, PUBLISHERS

WESTPORT, CONNECTICUT

Library of Congress Cataloging in Publication Data

Morris, Norval.
  The habitual criminal.

  Reprint of the 1951 ed., issued in series:
Publications of the London School of Economics.
  Based on the author's thesis, University of London,
1949.
  Includes bibliographies.
  1. Recidivists. I. Title. II. Series:
London School of Economics and Political Science.
Publications.
[HV6049.M6 1973]   364.3'2   72-9831
ISBN 0-8371-6601-2

A Greenwood Archival Edition—reprint editions of classic works in their respective fields, printed in extremely limited quantities, and manufactured to the most stringent specifications.

Originally published in 1951 by Longmans, Green and Co., New York

Reprinted with the permission of Norval Morris

Reprinted in 1973 by Greenwood Press
A division of Congressional Information Service, Inc.
88 Post Road West, Westport, Connecticut 06881

Library of Congress Catalog Card Number 72-9831

ISBN 0-8371-6601-2

Printed in the United States of America

10 9 8 7 6 5 4 3 2

TO MY PARENTS

ACKNOWLEDGEMENTS

The text of this book formed the substance of a thesis accepted for the degree of Ph.D. by the University of London in October, 1949.

I wish to express my thanks to Mr. L. W. Fox, C.B., M.C., Chairman of the Prison Commission, to Sir Theobald Mathew, K.B.E., M.C., Director of Public Prosecutions, and to the Assistant Director, Mr. E. Clayton. On the facilities they made available much of this work depends. The continuing interest of the Governors of the penal institutions I visited, and the friendly co-operation of their staffs, made my work pleasant and gave it what practical truth it may possess.

Professor D. Hughes Parry and Dr. Hermann Mannheim, both of the London School of Economics and Political Science, supervised the development of this book. The benefits to be gained from wise and intellectually generous supervisors are inestimable. Here I was most´ fortunate.

Professor Glanville Williams and Mr. George Benson, M.P., read the proofs and made several suggestions which I gratefully accepted.

Mrs. Adela Harris struggled with my turgid style and saved me from numberless unhappy turns of phrase: those that remain must be attributed to my stubbornness.

Finally, I would like to thank the prisoners themselves for their instructive, amused scepticism.

NORVAL MORRIS

London School of Economics
and Political Science
January 1950

TABLE OF CONTENTS

CHAPTER ONE

INTRODUCTION

1. CLASSIFICATION AND DEFINITION

SCIENTIFIC progress in criminology, as in other disciplines, depends on analysis and artificial isolation. For many centuries the consideration of " crime " as distinct from the consideration of " criminals " inhibited the development of criminology and confined discussion on criminal law and its place in society to ethical and philosophical homilies. This condition was analogous to pre-Darwinian evolution and pre-Newtonian physics. It was owing largely to the influence of Lombroso that the criminal became a subject of scientific observation; the necessity for notional classification followed.

Lombroso's classification (adopted by many later writers, including Havelock Ellis and Enrico Ferri) incorporated the following groups: the born criminal, the insane criminal, criminals by passion, occasional criminals, and habitual criminals. The progress of research has established that several of these groups are of no scientific value and has, of course, varied their content considerably. Nevertheless, the insane criminal and the habitual criminal are two of these groups that have stood the test of analytic investigation and remain in the forefront of any modern objective classification of asocial individuals.[1] In particular, the " habitual criminal " has remained the title of a separate group, a group distinguished both legally and theoretically from the mass of criminals. There are very few modern legal systems which do not treat the habitual criminal as a criminal requiring either additional or special sanctions. Similarly, there is no theorist of any standing who has not recognised that however successful the measures he advocates for the majority of criminals may prove, there will be a group with whom all these measures will fail. Normally the term " habitual " is applied to such criminals.

---

[1] I say " objective classification " because psychiatric and psychological research increasingly stresses the importance and significance of the classification of all criminals and delinquents into psychological types—a classification in which the offence, which was the fundamental of objective classification, is regarded as but a symptom for purposes of subjective psychological classification.

Who, then, are " habitual criminals " ? There is much support for the view that " only jurists ask for definitions. Everybody else knows that a definition can only be properly given at the end of an investigation—and even then only perhaps—because it will of necessity be incorrect. For, as a matter of fact, the science on which the definition is based is never complete."[1] Such a view rests on a fundamental confusion between *nominal* definitions, by which temporary agreement is reached, a practical working resolution made concerning a verbal symbol, and *real* definitions which seek to incorporate an analysis of the verbal symbol. Unless ostensive definition is possible, which is rarely the case in criminology, some sort of nominal or verbal definition of one's basic terms is necessary. Admittedly every such nominal definition " depends necessarily upon one's perspective, i.e. it contains within itself the whole system of thought representing the position of the thinker in question."[2] But this must not prevent us from reaching some working agreement on the terms which are fundamental to this study, the whole purport of which is the search for a real definition of "habitual criminal". As Aristotle affirmed, " the basic premises of demonstrations are definitions."[3] In seeking nominal or verbal definitions, however, we must endeavour to relate them to the actual forces that condition them in reality, so that at the end of our investigation the real definitions that emerge are amplifications, reconstructions and analyses of our nominal definitions.

Fundamental to this study are the terms " recidivist " and " habitual criminal "; but also important and worthy of considera-tion are several other terms whose purport we will consider in developing nominal definitions of the above two terms.

" Crime " and "offence", and " criminal " and "offender", are used throughout to refer respectively to any breach of the existing criminal law of the country under whose jurisdiction the offending person falls, and to one who so breaks that existing criminal law; they are used interchangeably for the sake of variety, though it is clear that there will be stronger emotional overtones attached to " crime " and " criminal " than to " offence " and "offender". Such purely formal definitions of these terms are inadequate jurisprudentially, but suffice for purposes of this work in

[1] Winkler, quoted by Bonger : *An Introduction to Criminology.*
[2] K. Mannheim : *Ideology and Utopia,* p. 177.
[3] Aristotle : *Posterior Analyticus,* in *Works,* ed. by W. D. Ross, Vol. I, 1928, p. 90 *b.*

which those offences on the borderline of the law of delict or torts will not concern us.[1]

The nouns " recidivist " and " recidivism " are in some legal systems used as terms of art, in others as merely descriptive of a condition in itself having no legal significance. They are terms of very general application and much importance. The recidivist constitutes a generic class, one species of which is the habitual criminal.[2] Let us consider some of the senses in which the term " recidivist " is used. The Oxford English Dictionary defines " recidivism " as " the habit of relapsing into crime " and hence " recidivist " as " one who habitually relapses into crime." How, then, does it define " relapse "? As " a falling back into error, heresy or wrongdoing—the fact of falling back again into illness after a partial recovery—to fall again into heresy after recantation." The dictionary definition thus involves an idea of temporary cure or amelioration. Similarly, H. M. Metcalf defines " recidivism " as a " falling back or relapse into prior criminal habits, especially after punishment,"[3] which also implies a conception of cure. It seems clear that both in popular and technical usage only previous punishment and not necessarily any temporary cure is required before subsequent commission of crime. The Prison Commissioners in their annual reports,[4] under the heading "recidivism", present information as to those criminals received into prison during the year who have been in prison before. Some writers append the term " recidivist " to one who has been previously convicted by the criminal courts, but not necessarily sentenced to any term of punitive custody, which renders the whole conception too wide to

---

[1] The criminals whose records have qualified them for inclusion in this study have built up those records on wrongs so manifestly breaches of the criminal law that they are but rarely tried as torts, or by actions at the suit of a common informer. Though our case-records include many hundreds of convictions for the crime of larceny there is no record of any action on the tort of conversion. Nor are traffic offences, nor the so-called " public welfare " offences, breaches of pure food orders, price-fixing regulations and kindred manifestations of the paternal state of the type with which we shall be concerned. We can, therefore, accept Kenny's well-known real definition of crimes as " wrongs whose sanction is punitive, and is in no way remissible by any private person, but is remissible by the Crown alone, if remissible at all," and make but passing reference to the criticisms of this definition to be found in Winfield, *The Province of the Law of Tort*, Ch. VIII ; Allen, *Legal Duties*, pp. 221-52 ; and Paton, *A Textbook of Jurisprudence*, pp. 145-8.
[2] This is not true in U.S.A. where "recidivist" and "habitual criminal" are wholly interchangeable terms in both law and literature.
[3] H. M. Metcalf : *Recidivism and the Courts*, Journal of Criminal Law and Criminology, Vol. 26, No. 3, p. 367.
[4] For example, *Report for the Year 1947*, Cmd. 7475, pp. 41 and 42.

be serviceable. It seems to be generally agreed that a recidivist is one who has previously been in punitive custody (thus excluding remand and on-trial prisoners), but it is rarely clear whether previous committal to an Approved School or Borstal Institution constitutes previous punitive custody in this context.[1] Let us adhere to the lowest serviceable common denominator of the above views and nominally define a recidivist as *one who having previously served a term of penal servitude, imprisonment, or Borstal training, is sentenced to a term of penal servitude or imprisonment.*[2] When applying that term to a foreign legal system it will be necessary to substitute for penal servitude, imprisonment and Borstal training, similar punishments imposed by that legal system; for most countries this presents no difficulties.

The term " Persistent Offender " frequently appears in English literature. Its connotation is very similar to that of " recidivist " as we have defined it, but there is the added element of a larger number of offences and punishments than are necessary to constitute a recidivist. Thus it lies somewhere between " recidivist " and "confirmed recidivist", a conception to which we will return. The usage of " persistent offender " is well illustrated in the Report of the Departmental Committee on Persistent Offenders, 1932, Cmd. 4090, throughout which " recidivist " is sedulously avoided and the term " persistent offender " is used as descriptive of a genus of which " habitual criminal " is one species. Because of its international application and more general usage it seems better to adhere to " recidivist " in this work.

Before leaving the genus " recidivist " and considering the differentia of the "habitual criminal", examples of legal systems using " recidivist " as a term of art are worth mentioning. Articles 56 and 57 of the French Penal Code are outstanding in this respect, giving a precise yet complex meaning to "le récidivisme", which we shall consider in detail later in this work. Similarly the Polish Penal Code uses " recidivist " as a technical concept and defines such a person as " a delinquent who, after having undergone at home or abroad at least three sentences of imprisonment, or else having been released from a prison implementing a " mesure de sûreté " (anglice, preventive detention), commits, within five years, another crime

---

[1] For the definition of this term by the staff of an American prison see Clemmer, *The Prison Community*, pp. 56-7.
[2] The term " penal servitude " is abolished by the Criminal Justice Act, 1948. This does not affect the applicability of our definition.

inspired by the same motives or a crime of the same category as the preceding infraction."[1] Whenever " recidivist " is used in such a technical fashion this fact will be noted.

Persistent Offender, Professional Criminal, Incorrigible Offender, Dangerous Recidivist (Finnish law of 1932), Hardened Offender, Rélegable, Habitual Criminal, and many similar terms are used to define certain groups of recidivists against whom various countries are prepared to take special measures to protect themselves,—measures usually involving their protracted segregation from society. Except when considering in detail the law of a specific country, when that country's terminology will be used, I shall use " Habitual Criminal " to represent all these terms. On grounds of logic there is much to be said for the term " incorrigible " as used in the Polish Penal Code,[2] but as " habitual criminal " has been popularised in this country by Part II of the Prevention of Crime Act, 1908, I have adhered to it.

Women are very rarely in any country sentenced as habitual criminals, and the problem presented by the recidivist woman is for various reasons quite unlike that posed by the male recidivist.[3] Therefore, this study is confined to an examination of habitual criminality amongst males.

Those countries which make use of this conception of the habitual criminal, define its scope in relation to some or all of the following factors:—

1. Number of crimes committed by an offender (sometimes over a certain period or since a certain age).
2. Type(s) of crimes committed by an offender (sometimes over a certain period or since a certain age).

[1] *Recueil de documents en matière pénale et pénitentiaire*, Vol. XIII, Book 1, September, 1947, pp. 54-6. Article by T. Krychowski, then Director of the Penal Department, Ministry of Justice, Warsaw.

[2] This contention will be supported later in this work, but at this stage the term " incorrigible " as used by Michael and Adler at p. 363 of *Crime, Law and Social Science* should be noticed : " What type of offenders is it justifiable to incapacitate ? In terms of the social good, it must be answered that it is justifiable to incapacitate only incorrigible offenders. To remove from society an individual who can be reclaimed as a social agent is injurious to the welfare of society. While this is clear the determination of incorrigibility is not clear. Moreover, it is difficult to decide what risks society should take, that is, whether it should take the chance of incapacitating individuals who are not incorrigible rather than the chance of returning incorrigibles to society." Thus " incorrigibility " is a very convenient term and one which leads rapidly to the root problems of our subject.

[3] Lombroso's contention that women cannot be classified under his heading, " the born criminal," does seem to receive some support from habitual criminal statistics in which female criminals are but rarely found.

3. Seriousness of offender's last crime(s) (and sometimes period since commission of previous crime).
4. Number and type(s) of punishments he has undergone (sometimes over a certain period or since a certain age).
5. Extent of danger to public presented by such type(s) of crime.
6. Extent of danger to public presented by such an offender.
7. Age of the offender.
8. Mental condition of the offender.
9. Biological and social background of the offender.
10. Susceptibility of the offender to reformation.

A nominal definition would be too unwieldy were it to include all such factors. Let us, therefore, while bearing these factors in mind, seek the principal conceptions that go to the composition of the species "habitual criminal". The Oxford English Dictionary defines "habitual" as "inherent or latent in the mental constitution" and also defines it as " existing as a settled practice or condition; constantly repeated or continued", and thus includes subjective as well as objective elements, or to put it more bluntly and less accurately, a mental pattern plus conditioning experiences. We shall use "habitual criminal" to include both these elements, and add one more; that the offences with which the community is threatened, when such a criminal is not segregated, are regarded by that community as of appreciable danger to its ordered existence.

The three elements which we include in " habitual criminal " are, then,

(a) criminal qualities inherent or latent in the mental constitution;
(b) settled practice in crime;
(c) public danger.

It will be seen that the ten factors listed above can be divided amongst these three elements.

Before leaving these problems in semantics it is necessary to comment briefly on the three elements in our nominal definition of " habitual criminal".

First, it is important that by the use of the words " inherent or latent in the mental constitution " there is no implication of pre-judgment on the relative importance of inherited and environmental factors in conditioning those "criminal qualities". This phrase refers to a condition and seeks to avoid any decision as to the ætiology of that condition. Quite arbitrarily let us exclude from the conception " habitual criminal " those certifiable under English law as insane or mentally deficient.

Secondly, there is some support for the view that " settled practice in crime " is not a necessary element of habitual criminality and need not therefore appear in its definition. Supporters of this view hold that we may well be able to recognise and to isolate the " habitual virus " even before that " virus " has been involved in an appreciable number of offences and punishments, or even before the criminal possessing it has become a recidivist, or indeed even before he has faced a criminal court. "Habitual criminal", then, should be defined only in terms of the elements (a) and (c) above. This is the extreme position taken up by certain modern Positivists adopting a medical approach to criminology and basing treatment-punishment exclusively on the social dangerousness of an offender or potential offender. It completely excludes the conception of *nulla poena sine lege* and would appear to exaggerate the adequacy of our existing knowledge. We shall hereafter examine in detail and for various countries the different minimal requirements of actual crimes for the classification of a criminal as habitual, but for the present it is sufficient to affirm that this is such a general element in the criminological approach of all countries that we must include it in our definition, even if, on grounds of abstract theory as distinct from empirical knowledge, a case for its exclusion can be made.

Thirdly, it must be appreciated that the danger any particular offence or type of offender is thought to present to the community will vary from one legal system to another. However, for convenience let us exclude, again quite arbitrarily, prostitutes, vagrants, habitual drunkards and other habitual offenders regarded by English criminal law as petty delinquents.[1]

[1] The exclusion of " habitual petty delinquents " from our nominal definition is necessary for clarity of exposition. Frequently, however, many countries, including England, declare offenders whom one would evaluate as petty offenders, to be habitual criminals. That this is so will appear later in this work. The difficulty is again a semasiological one, the term " petty delinquent " being a high-level abstraction, nowhere rigidly defined, and with no clear referent. Its purport is, however, unambiguous, and greater clarity cannot be achieved over the large number of legal systems for which we will use the concept of habitual criminality, given the variations between the definitions of offences in different legal systems, the seriousness with which they regard different offences, and consequently the " petty " nature of a " delinquency ".

To recapitulate: an " habitual criminal " is " *one who possesses criminal qualities inherent or latent in his mental constitution (but who is not insane or mentally deficient); who has manifested a settled practice in crime; and who presents a danger to the society in which he lives (but is not merely a prostitute, vagrant, habitual drunkard or habitual petty delinquent)*".

2. THEORIES OF PUNISHMENT

No one theory explains the different punitive measures to be found in Anglo-American criminal law. They can be explained only by the existence of different conceptions, conscious and unconscious, at the time when they were respectively introduced.[1] This is not an adverse criticism of such measures, for frequently subsequent rationalization of practical experience tends more to true justice than any rigid adherence to theoretical preconceptions. On the other hand it might be expected that there would, at the present time, be widespread agreement as to the end we now hope to achieve by our penal sanctions. The contrary is the case. One can still agree with Kenny who wrote that " it cannot be said that the theories of criminal punishment current amongst either our judges or legislators have assumed . . . either a coherent or even a stable form."[2]

Nor is this condition peculiar to our society. Malinowski, considering the reactions to this same problem of the Melanesian inhabitants of a part of the Trobriand Archipelago, wrote: " We have found that the principles according to which crime is punished are very vague," and that this was so because " all the legally effective institutions . . . are . . . means of cutting short an illegal or intolerable state of affairs, of restoring the equilibrium in social life and of giving vent to the feelings of oppression and injustice felt by individuals."[3]

But because neither the primitive tribe nor a highly complex civilised society seek any single conscious purpose through their penal sanctions, we must not suppose that we are facing an academic and impractical problem. When a court decides what sentence to impose on the criminal convicted before it, even though limited by

---

[1] " The influence of any doctrine or idea depends on the extent to which it appeals to psychic needs in the character structure of those to whom it is addressed. Only if the idea answers powerful psychological needs of certain social groups will it become a potent force in history." Fromm, *The Fear of Freedom*, p. 54.

[2] Kenny, *Outlines of Criminal Law*, 15th ed, p. 38. Kenny wrote this in 1902 in the first edition of his book, and it has remained unaltered throughout all editions to the revised 15th in 1947. It is still an incontrovertible contention.

[3] B. Malinowski, *Crime and Custom in Savage Society*, pp. 98 and 99.

maximum and minimum punishments fixed by the legislature, it must so decide with reference to some purpose or purposes, conscious or unconscious, articulate or inarticulate. To refuse to define an aim for the sanction imposed is to make Pilate's choice, and to give way to the emotions of others, or indeed to one's own emotional motivations. Herein lies one of the most deep-rooted causes of the fortuitousness of penal sentences by which bigamist A will serve a term of six months' imprisonment, while bigamist B (who adduces equally mitigating circumstances, is of a similar psychological type, but appears before a different bench) will serve a term of three years. My readers will be familiar with many such examples, of which a multiplicity will be found in the case records analysed in Part II of this work. For the legislator, and everyone connected with the penal system, this is a fundamental and challenging problem.

In considering " punishment " one is faced immediately by a semasiological difficulty; there are few words more heavily charged with subjective emotional and intellectual overtones. Let me avoid this by insisting that " punishment " is here used as a symbol for society's official reaction to crime, and does not necessarily connote either the swish of lashes or the soft dripping of sentimental tears. Hanging, imprisonment, Borstal detention, approved school training, probation, fine—these are all "punishment".

Prevention, reformation, deterrence, retribution, expiation, the Kantian argument that punishment is an end in itself, all these mingle in the wild semantic and dialectic confusion which constitutes most discussions on the purposes of punishment. Legislators, judges, prison administrators, wardens, interested members of the public, and prisoners themselves, all express their own particular and widely varying rationalizations of punishment. But to point to this diversity is not to advance a demand for ultimate truth, and " it is doubtful that a wholly satisfactory explanation of the existence of punishment can be made "[1]; it is merely suggested that a compass is desirable by which to guide oneself, even if only for a short distance and over a particular part of the journey. It is this desire that has prompted philosophers and jurists, at least since Plato and Aristotle, to give a great deal of their attention to this problem.

The aim of punishment is concealed by its relationship with the vexed issue of determinism and free-will, " which finds no end, in wandering mazes lost ". Certainly the increasing adherence to a

[1] Reckless, *Criminal Behaviour*, p. 257.

determinist philosophy has been contemporaneous with a movement away from a retributive-expiative theory and towards a utilitarian conception of the purpose of punishment. Vengeance, retribution, expiation, atonement have lost much of their conscious influence, but, as I shall show, their present emotional power is great. In an excellent brief survey of theories of punishment Professor Paton contends that " to-day the usual legal approach is utilitarian, for it is recognised that the law cannot attempt to carry out all the dictates of religion or morality, but can enforce only that minimum standard of conduct without which social life would be impossible."[1] For the time being let us accept this conclusion.

However, within a broadly utilitarian approach there are many subsidiary purposes receiving general support and which fall conveniently under three main headings—deterrence, prevention, and reformation. It is clear that even those who seek a utilitarian purpose through punishment are far from agreed concerning these sub-headings. The contrasting views of some eminent thinkers will prove this point:

Sir John Salmond : " The ends of criminal justice are four in number, and in respect of the purposes so served by it, punishment may be distinguished as (1) Deterrent, (2) Preventive, (3) Reformative and (4) Retributive. Of these aspects the first is the essential and all-important one, the others being merely accessory. Punishment is before all things deterrent, and the chief end of the law of crime is to make the evil-doer an example and a warning to all that are like-minded with him."[2]

The Most Reverend William Temple, speaking of the deterrent aspect of penal action, affirmed that " it is morally justifiable provided that it is subordinate."[3]

Oliver Wendell Holmes, Jr. : " Most English-speaking lawyers would accept the preventive theory without hesitation," and later, " prevention would accordingly seem to be the chief and only universal purpose of punishment."[4]

S. and E. Glueck : " For the vast majority of the general run of traditional crimes and criminals, the corrective theory (reformation) . . . should predominate."[5]

[1] G. W. Paton, *A Textbook of Jurisprudence*, p. 348.
[2] Salmond, *Jurisprudence*, 10th ed., p. 111.
[3] In 1934, as Archbishop of York, in the first Clarke Hall Lecture, published as *The Ethics of Penal Action*, p. 34.
[4] Holmes, *The Common Law*, pp. 43 and 46. It is worth noting that many leading jurists have subscribed to this view, as Kenny says in his *Outlines of Criminal Law*, 15th ed., p. 32 : " According to the most generally accepted writers—as for instance Beccaria, Blackstone, Romilly, Paley, Feuerbach—this hope of preventing the repetition of the offence is not only a main object, but the sole permissible object, of inflicting a criminal punishment."
[5] S. and E. Glueck : *After-Conduct of Discharged Offenders*, p. 97.

Not only is the juxtaposition of these views startling, but their existence is of great significance for legislative, judicial and administrative practice.[1] For practical purposes there is supposed to be an antithesis between deterrence and reformation, and there has been a tendency to contend that " there is thus a conflict in each case between the needs of a particular prisoner and the social interest in enforcing the law. What may be the best treatment for a criminal may conflict with the necessity of deterring others. The real problem is therefore to combine the deterrent and reformative theories in due proportions."[2]   Sir John Salmond doubted the feasibility of this, contending that " it is plain that there is a necessary conflict between the deterrent and the reformative theories of punishment."[3]

There is a frequent confusion between means and ends. Deterrence *per se* can never fully justify punishment, nor indeed can reformation outside Utopia. The end, as it is frequently stated, is the protection of society. Punishment is certainly not the only social force working towards this end, but it is an important one of them.[4]   There is a dichotomy in the means punishment uses towards this end, for it functions both in the macrocosm of society and in the microcosm of criminals within society. First, in society as a whole, though its function has not been fully explored, it would seem safe to say that the individual's super-ego, his inner tribunal or conscience, is reinforced, and to a certain extent conditioned, by the existence of formal punishments imposed by society; further, for some people and for some crimes the existence of punishment prevents them as potential offenders from becoming actual offenders, thus having a generally deterrent effect. Secondly, in its relations to criminals, it becomes the function of punishment to reform where possible, to deter where possible, and generally to work on the offending criminal with the aim of rendering society safe from his depredations; in effect, of removing him from the microcosm into the macrocosm.

In fact, " deterrence " is used in two senses: as one of the methods

---

[1] " Il règne donc une grande complexité dans les buts de la peine ; c'est elle qui explique l'extrême variété des moyens répressifs." Donnedieu de Vabres, *Traité de Droit Criminel et de Législation Pénale Comparée*, 3rd ed., p. 276, Paris, 1947.
[2] G. W. Paton, *A Textbook of Jurisprudence*, p. 351.
[3] Salmond, *Jurisprudence*, 10th ed., p. 112.
[4] In their acidulous book, *Crime Law and Social Science*, Michael and Adler state a similar conclusion in an inverted way : " Punishment can be justified only as an intermediate means to the ends of deterrence and reformation which, in turn, are means for increasing and preserving the welfare of society," p. 352.

of rendering society free from the criminal activities of an individual who has been convicted of crime, and in the wider sense of its operation on the minds of society at large.[1] It is primarily in the latter sense that Professor Paton and many others have suggested that there is a conflict between deterrence and reformation, though this conflict is also alleged to exist in relation to the treatment accorded those who have offended against the criminal law.

It is my contention that the only reason that there appears to be a conflict between reformation and deterrence is that the former is a relatively recent arrival on the scene. By quoting the heritage of the repressive systems of the past it is possible to make apparent nonsense of the reformative aim, especially as until now it has drawn its experience only from work with, and research on, the most malleable group of criminals, the youthful offenders. To most youths, Borstal training holds a great deal more deterrence than the shorter prison term that might alternatively be imposed.[2] The point implicit in that statement holds true of many of our reformative techinques, and is reinforced by the fact that all such techniques involve individualization, so that the threat of what appears to him to be the most severe punishment will always hang over the potential offender and the potential recidivist. Reformative techniques, with their necessary corollary of individualization of punishment and the abandonment of the " price-list " system (by which the offender if he is so minded can, with reasonable accuracy, estimate his punishment should he be convicted of a crime), will if anything strengthen what deterrent effect punishment has on society and on the criminal. Frequently it is the unpredictable quality of punishment that conditions its deterrent force.

The whole answer to this suggested conflict must be sought in classification of offenders and in an attack upon the problem of crime on a wide front, suiting our weapons to their task. Then, indeed, there is no necessary antithesis between deterrence and reform, and we may perhaps slowly exorcise from our conception of punishment its primitive heritage of vengeance. But to do this we shall need greater knowledge of reformative methods, and a greater understanding of the rôle that deterrence plays in the life of society.

[1] The distinction here drawn is the same as that between " special prevention " and " general prevention " as these terms are used in Continental literature. It is unfortunate that such a useful terminological distinction has not gained currency in this country.

[2] Every asylum for the insane gives manifest proof of the deterrent quality of even the most advanced reformative techniques.

Tentatively I would say that the effectiveness of deterrence varies in inverse proportion to the moral seriousness of the offence ; such ideas, however, must be put to the proof of future research.

The real difficulty lies not in the reconciliation of deterrence and reformation, but in blending into our utilitarian pragmatic approach to punishment the emotional requirements of the community. If our task is, as was suggested above, the protection of society, then we are undertaking to influence men's actions by means of the threat and actuality of punishment, which involves the exercise of control over the emotional instinctual forces that condition such actions. We must then include amongst those instinctual subjects of our control a very deep-rooted hatred of the criminal, and a very great reliance on him as the butt of aggressive outbursts. Writing shortly after the controversies that surrounded the debates on the Criminal Justice Act of 1948, one need hardly stress this point. As Dean Roscoe Pound said : " Anglo-American lawyers commonly regard the satisfaction of public desires for vengeance both as a legitimate, and a practically necessary, end of penal treatment."[1] Undoubtedly there is almost universal inconsistency between the ends of social protection and punitive retribution.

Our instinctual reactions to crime are two-edged in their operation. They condition the group's opposition to the criminal and thus provide the emotional prop on which punishment rests, and they form the polarities of leniency and severity outside of which the punishing authorities cannot safely proceed. Thus Julius Stone writes : " Failure to visit *what group-members regard* as an adequate evil on violators, intensifies the retributive impulse, sometimes to the point of lynch justice. Conversely excessive severity in relation to the supporting group attitudes tends to place the violator in the light of a martyr. The frequent impossibility of getting juries to convict when the number of capital offences in England was 160, in the early nineteenth century, is well known."[2] These instinctual reactions to the criminal are not even modified by the *lex talionis* and are only controlled by a repression which attaches significance to the façade of a legal system in which the punishment of the criminal has been taken out of the hands of the wronged individual, his family or tribe, and given to a central authority. The punishments this central

---

[1] *Criminal Justice in Cleveland*, 1922 ed., p. 575.
[2] *The Province and Function of Law*, p. 684. It may well be that Part II of the Prevention of Crime Act, 1908, exceeded what group-members regarded as the pole of severity, and that this in no small measure accounted for the failure of this legislation.

authority imposes are, however, emotionally tolerable to the community only so long as they do not fall below an inarticulate but nevertheless perceptible pole of leniency.

We are but on the threshold of an understanding of this aspect of punishment, and an adequate psychological investigation of the function of judicial punishment in the lives of those who never come before a criminal court is desperately needed. *Inter alia*, it might well throw an entirely new light on our almost unchallenged conception of punishment as a potent deterrent force. Those psychoanalysts who have interested themselves in criminology have begun to open up this field of the psychology of the punishing community, but until recently only sporadically.[1] A start has been made, however, and a considerable step forward taken by Paul Reiwald's *Society and Its Criminals*.[2]

Though our " idea of punishment has deep irrational roots ", and though " psychology claims to detect unconscious motives for the demand for punishment in man's fear, in his insecurity, and even in a sense of guilt which seeks satisfaction in the vicarious suffering of the convicted criminal,"[3] there is no reason why we cannot logically examine the conscious superstructure of our punitive system. There is indeed one other purpose of punishment which we cannot overlook. It was presented most forcefully by Malinowski, who found amongst the Melanesians that punishment was used quite consciously to serve the needs of social cohesion within the group. This has been supported as an important aim of punishment by many other thinkers, for example, Sutherland, who contends

[1] For example, K. Friedlander, in the *Psychoanalytical Approach to Juvenile Delinquency*, writes (p. 192) : " If progress is to be made in the treatment of offenders it is important to recognise the strength of the unconscious trends which hinder any loosening of the connection between crime and punishment. It is also important to realise that ' common sense ' alone is not an adequate weapon against these unconscious tendencies. Common sense is very valuable in all those instances where intellectual judgment is unhampered by unconscious emotions. But it is helpless against influences arising out of our own unconscious. History, not in the field of criminal research alone, is full of examples showing that only expert knowledge can remove prejudice based on unconscious motives. The treatment of the insane before the emergence of psychiatric knowledge is but one example of the crass error of judgment committed by ' common sense '." With this in mind it is interesting to consider Mr. Justice Stable's advice to the new magistrates assembled at Dolgelley on January 4th, 1949 : " Have confidence in yourselves. Do not imagine you have to be learned in the law. Do not worry about the law but use your common sense. If you use it and find that it does not tally with the law, then there must be something wrong with the law, because common sense cannot be wrong." I tremble for the sexual offender coming before a magistrate who has accepted this advice and who finds such a case emotionally disturbing.

[2] Translated by T. E. James and published by Heinemann, London, 1949.

[3] M. Grünhut, *Penal Reform*, p. 2.

that " respect for law grows largely out of opposition to those who violate the law. The public hates the criminal, and this hatred is expressed in the form of punishment. In standing together against the enemy of their values, they develop group solidarity and respect for the orders of the group."[1]

There is at present in criminology a conflict between philosophy and psychology, between law and medicine, between ethics and empirical knowledge—a conflict based frequently on ignorance of one another's disciplines. For example, Dr. John Bowlby writes that as weapons against crime " exhortation and punishment are relatively fruitless and, indeed, unnecessary, since in every man's heart there is as strong a drive to co-operate with others as there is in his body a drive towards health,"[2] and Mr. Nigel Bridge replies affirming that " by speaking as he does . . . Dr. Bowlby betrays his distaste for the problems of good and evil, right and wrong. But these problems are eternal and inescapable."[3] Truly, it is not yet appreciated that " sciences are of a sociable disposition, and flourish best in the neighbourhood of each other."[4] But the reconciliation of this unfortunate conflict is beyond the scope of our subject. It is, however, necessary to point to it before breaking off that section of the problem particularly relevant to the treatment of confirmed recidivists and habitual criminals.

Punishment under the ægis of the criminal law is a jurisprudential problem. It has all too frequently been regarded solely as a problem in ethics.

Professor Julius Stone in his monumental work, *The Province and Function of Law*, defines jurisprudence as " the lawyer's extraversion. It is the lawyer's examination of the precepts, ideals and techniques of the law in the light derived from present knowledge in disciplines other than the law."[5] There is a remarkably close analogy between the conflicting schools of jurisprudence and the conflicting theories of punishment; and understanding will never illumine either conflict while systematization, for its own sake, has such influence, and knowledge gathered from other disciplines is so hesitantly allowed to obtrude. When to theories of punishment the criminologist brings an extraverted interest based on adequate knowledge of

[1] Sutherland, *Principles of Criminology*, 4th ed., p. 358.
[2] *The Times*, letter to the editor, December 20th, 1948.
[3] *The Times*, letter to the editor, December 24th, 1948.
[4] Blackstone, 1. Comm. 33.
[5] *The Province and Function of Law*, p. 25.

those sciences in the light of which such theories must finally be resolved, then perhaps order will emerge from the present chaos in which it is necessary for virtually every writer of a criminological work to make his testament, to propound his approach to the problem of punishment, and to relate his conclusions on this point to the plan of his work. At present the psychiatrist regards society's official reaction to crime as ideally a therapeutic endeavour, the lawyer as *inter alia* vindicating the law and preserving the King's Peace, the writer on juvenile delinquency as a pedagogic problem, and so on. There is a nexus between all such people, but it is far from defined, and it will never be defined while practitioners of diverse disciplines approach the problem of punishment from their own particular premises.[1]

I realise that my contention that theories of punishment must become the criminologist's extraversion demands a definition of the discipline of " criminology " if it is to be a practically useful suggestion. This is a problem beyond the scope of my present purpose. But the minimum requirement for a " criminologist " who animadverts to the purpose of punishment, and uses information gathered from other disciplines, is a full, personal, emotional and intellectual understanding of the actual functioning of the existing penal sanctions, and of their effect on the individual subjected to them—a much rarer understanding than one might suspect.

In the light of the above definition of the problem of punishment, let us now consider the particular relationship between habitual criminals and the purposes to be served by punishing them.[2]

---

[1] A good example of this is to be found in Dr. A. C. Ewing's brilliant book, *The Morality of Punishment*, a summary of part of which was published by Dr. Ewing in the Cambridge Pamphlet Series, *English Studies in Criminal Science*, under the title of *A Study on Punishment*. Here the philosopher delves in an incisive and comprehensive fashion into the problem we have been considering ; but the influence of his work has not matched its worth. It is the specialist considering punishment from outside as it were, and as such seems unlikely to have much effect until it is related to existing conditions by receiving an extensive admixture of criminological understanding of the problem it considers.

[2] Hardly a criminological or penological work fails to incorporate a chapter on the theories of punishment. There is much in common between them. The most complete English study on this subject is that of Dr. A. C. Ewing, referred to above, while the most readable was written by George Bernard Shaw and published as a preface to Sidney and Beatrice Webb's *English Prisons Under Local Government* (1922). Jerome Hall in his incisive *General Principles of the Criminal Law* adopts what is to my mind the wisest course for the time being in considering the theories of punishment. He relates his analysis of them separately to each fundamental principle of the criminal law which he examines, and does not attempt to define his standpoint generally. Thus, for example, he considers the purpose of punishment in relation to criminal attempt and then later in relation to strict liability, and so on. By doing this he is able to find for each topic a wider area of general agreement than he could were he to define his ethical approach to the whole field of criminal law.

3. THEORIES OF PUNISHMENT AND THE HABITUAL CRIMINAL

Aristotle's theory of moral accountability, developed in the fourth century B.C., was formally introduced into jurisprudence as a technical concept by Pufendorf who, in his *Elementia Jurisprudentiae Universalis* published in 1660, used the term " imputability " (or " accountability "), the essence of which was that for punishment to be just it must be rationally related to moral culpability. The close links between such a justification of punishment and an indeterministic freedom of will are sufficiently obvious, and the conception of a free choice between various possible courses of action was the essential condition for, and the philosophic basic of, moral accountability, of imputability, and therefore of penal responsibility.[1] " Imputability " was the fundamental tenet of the Classical School of Criminology, and constituted its intellectual rationalization of the emotional force of retribution. The will being free, the criminal's offence being imputable to him, each offence must be regarded as a single event, the result of a distinct and individual choice between the alternatives of keeping and breaking the law. Reinforcing this conception was the force of religious belief which regarded the criminal's offence as a sin to be purged before God and man—to be expiated by punishment. The identification of imputability with sin was achieved often with difficulty, as for example in the case of lunatics who, being " *demens et furiosus, non per feloniam*",[2] were not regarded as imputable or accountable to the law for their crime, owing to their manifest incapacity to make an intellectual choice between alternative courses, and who were regarded by the Church as possessed of evil spirits or of the devil, and therefore not necessarily burdened with sin for the offences they committed whilst so possessed.

If he were imputable and capable of sin, then expiation was at once the criminal's right and heavenly duty, and it was society's task to overcome any hesitancy on the part of the criminal in accepting his expiatory suffering. Such an approach to punishment excluded any classification of imputable sinful offenders for purposes of punishment, and hence recidivism never arose as a problem in punishment.

Later, when the Classical School of Criminology predominated,

---

[1] An excellent account of " imputability " is given by O. Kinberg in his *Criminology*, pp. 37-49.
[2] Kentish Eyre of 1313 (Selden Society), I, 81.

punishments were intended to be at once retributive and expiative, and habitual criminality was no problem for a new reason. Punishments tended by their very nature to exclude a subsequent commission of any but the most trifling offences. If the larceny of twelve pence is met by hanging, or, if the court is leniently inclined, by transportation, there is remarkably little scope for the development of any class of habitual recidivists. One might commit many serious offences and in that sense be habituated to crime, but once the ponderous and unsubtle mechanism of the criminal law had one within its grasp there was little likelihood of the continuance of such criminality. Theory fitted practice, for it will be noted that the Classical School concerned itself predominantly with the justification of punishment, not its purpose, and if it were necessary to inflict a second expiatory punishment on the same individual that did not suggest any failure of the punitive mechanisms.

In course of time sentences became less severe. In consequence of diverse factors—the spread of humanitarian ideas; a slight shift of the focus of attention from a preoccupation with the moral gravity of the offence towards the particular offender; the emergence of psychological and sociological thought; and above all, the realisation that an amelioration of punishment was not followed by an increase of crime—criminal law in England, as in other countries, has resorted less and less to extreme punishments. Thus habitual recidivism has become a practical possibility.

This amelioration of the severity of penal sanctions has not ostensibly developed from the idea embodied in the phrase " *tout savoir, c'est tout pardonner*", but has resulted rather from new moral conceptions, which themselves spring from our increasingly teleological approach to punishment and our increased understanding of the sources of human conduct. The beliefs that have gone to the formation of this approach " whether they appear to the particular judge . . . as correct or incorrect, or even if he is not conscious of them, have still influenced his opinion, consciously or unconsciously, directly or indirectly. And whereas to understand the crime does not mean to forgive the crime, a healthy and necessary striving after understanding has led, with psychological compunction, to milder and milder sentences."[1]

The theoretical developments accompanying and conditioning the teleological approach to punishment were initiated by Lombroso

[1] Exner, *Studien über die Strafzumessungspraxis der deutschen Gerichte*, Leipzig, pp. 27-8.

and his disciples of the Italian School. They introduced into criminology a new method, induction based on scientific research, and a new interest, the criminal instead of the crime. Though the criminal stigmata that Lombroso sought to define have been disproved by later workers, notably Dr. Goring in England,[1] and were quite possibly nothing but prison stigmata, it is to Lombroso's everlasting credit that his work turned men's minds to the consideration of the criminal as an individual requiring scientific investigation. The shift of attention from this to the consideration of the purpose and the function of the penal sanctions which pressed upon him followed logically. This incursion of psychiatry into criminology and the insistence that the efficiency of a social institution could only be tested by its beneficial effect on that society, led inexorably to the death of the Classical School of Criminology. In its place there arose from this teleological scientific approach to criminology a School that has come to be called Positivist. In order to complete this sketch of the broad lines of division on the theoretical plane, it is worth noting that from the embers of the Classical School there was born, in the neo-Classical School, a conception of punishment and an approach to criminology posited on deterrence.

Since the Positivist School of Criminology was, unlike its predecessor, scientifically interested in the criminal, it was very much concerned to classify him, one inevitable classificatory rubric being the recidivist. And, again unlike its predecessor, being interested in the purpose of punishment and its function within society, the Positivist School saw in the recidivist a manifest failure of that purpose.

Thus it was that the incorrigible offender, the habitual offender, the confirmed recidivist, and the recidivist imposed on a society which regarded its penal sanctions as teleological instruments (and it must be remembered that this was common both to positivists and neo-classicists) the intellectual necessity of inventing special measures to deal with them; and since punishments had become of such a nature that recidivism was physically impossible, this intellectual necessity developed into the practical necessity of introducing such measures into the criminal law so that " a modern criminal code cannot be conceived without (them)."[2]

---

[1] The writings of the American anthropologist, Dr. E. A. Hooton, though tending to revivify much of the substance of Lombroso's basic contention, have not supported his conception of criminal stigmata.

[2] Timasheff, *The Treatment of Persistent Offenders Outside the U.S.A,,* Journal of Criminal Law and Criminology, Vol. 30, No. 4, p. 459.

We thus return to the utilitarian conception of the protection of society as the purpose of punishment. By definition society is not protected from the habitual criminal by normal criminal sanctions. Something more is needed, and we shall in Part I of this study consider the special sanctions that are applied in different countries. In so doing it will be helpful to keep in mind that no penal system has ever rationally pursued its aims, and this for three reasons. First, the rationality of an aim is directly connected with the state of our knowledge (so that, for instance, a group which believes that fire is divine acts rationally in feeding that fire with human sacrifice to avert divine wrath). Seeing errors of " knowledge " in the past, we are naturally sceptical of the true wisdom of our present aims, doubting as we do the accuracy of the " knowledge " on which they are based. Secondly, there is within all of us an attachment to old customs, a reluctance to abandon at least the façade of an institution to which we have adhered in the past. Thirdly, there are hidden personal desires, unconscious motive forces, which masquerade as being for the benefit of society but which distract us from the pursuit of a rational aim.[1] Providing society had expended its best efforts to protect itself from an habitual criminal and had used all the practical means within its power to make him live a life that society was prepared to tolerate, it would be rational to destroy him.[2] It would certainly be rational to keep him from again entering society. But for the above three reasons, and because, in George Bernard Shaw's phrase, we lack " the ruthlessness of the pure heart " we but rarely proceed to such logically complete conclusions.[3]

Nevertheless, we must strive to protect society from habitual criminals. What, then, are the tools which lie to hand for labour in this field ?

[1] Thus to complete the analogy of the fire-worshippers : the three reasons adduced in the text why social aims are not rationally pursued will gradually lessen the frequency of human sacrifice, will make those who are sacrificed be of a type or group not desired by the society, and will lead eventually to symbolic sacrifice of animals instead of humans, and in similar fashion will continue to be modified.

[2] However, the German law of September 4th, 1941, which provided capital punishment for certain habitual criminals, was not even a " rational " measure, for the two conditions precedent we have specified had not been fulfilled.

[3] Another factor limiting completely logical measures is well and concisely stated by Professor Julius Stone : " Even the punishment of the criminal, it is recognised, must stop short of denying his humanity, for that denial draws with it the denial of that of members of society generally." (*The Province and Function of Law*, p. 598.)

4. The Indeterminate Sentence

There is much confusion between the *indeterminate* and the *indefinite* sentence. When a criminal lunatic is committed to Broadmoor the period for which he will be detained is indeterminate; when a youth is committed to a Borstal Institution the period for which he will be detained is indefinite. To the former is set no bounds but administrative decision; the latter though also governed by administrative decision functions within limits determined by the legislature and the court—limits which control both the maximum and minimum periods for which youths so sentenced can be detained. A sentence fixing only either the minimum or the maximum term, and leaving the exact date of release to an administrative authority, is likewise indefinite.[1]

The Inquisition occasionally imposed sentences " for such time as seems expedient to the Church,"[2] but it would seem that this idea was not publicly advanced until 1787 when, at the home of Benjamin Franklin, Dr. Rush of Philadelphia read a pamphlet on punishment in which he advocated an indeterminate sentence for all criminals.[3] In the early nineteenth century the work of Obermaier in Germany and Montesinos in Spain proved that the indefinite sentence could indeed function, whilst Archbishop Whately of Dublin, and Livingstone, the author of the Criminal Code of Louisiana, both published works supporting the indeterminate sentence. In 1840, Captain Alexander Maconochie took the first practical steps to implement the indeterminate sentence for adult criminals in the penal colony on Norfolk Island,[4] and his plan was copied and modified by Sir Walter Crofton in Ireland. Though both these experiments eventually collapsed under the weight of official prejudice, they had great influence on subsequent penological developments.

---

[1] The terms " absolutely indeterminate " and " relatively indeterminate " are commonly used to represent the distinction we have drawn between indeterminate and indefinite sentences. On etymological grounds the indeterminate-indefinite usage is preferable and is adopted by many American writers, notably by Barnes and Teeters in *New Horizons in Criminology*.

[2] Chrysostom : " I require not continuance of time, but the correction of your soul ; demonstrate your contrition, demonstrate your reformation, and all is done." Quoted by George Ives, *A History of Penal Methods*, London, 1914, p. 38.

[3] See Barnes and Teeters, *New Horizons in Criminology*, p. 488.

[4] Maconochie, in arguing for an indeterminate sentence, contended that " when a man keeps the key of his own prison he is soon persuaded to fit it to the lock." Quoted in Barnes and Teeters, *ibid.*, p. 548.

Thus neither the theory nor the practice of the indeterminate sentence is novel. Indeed, for the last seventy years it has been in the forefront of criminological controversy. A huge literature has been built up, and no useful purpose would be served by canvassing the details of the arguments advanced. The broad lines of cleavage are, however, worth mentioning as they have a bearing on the problems of the indefinite sentence with which we shall be confronted throughout this work.

It is argued, in support of the indeterminate sentence, that at the end of a trial the judge can have scant knowledge of the criminal he has convicted, and none of his probable reactions to reformative treatment. Therefore, the determination of the sentence to which the criminal will be subjected should pass out of the judge's hands, and the offender should not be released until, in the opinion of those who have observed his demeanour in prison and considered his background and the environment into which he will be conditionally discharged, there is some likelihood that he will not again endanger the community. This argument is frequently linked with a demand for the establishment of Treatment Tribunals.[1] Many prison administrators as well as theorists have supported these contentions. For example, the well-known Declaration of Principles of the American National Prison Congress in 1870 contained the recommendation that indeterminate sentences should replace peremptory sentences, and in 1925 at the International Prison Congress held in London, the following resolution was carried: "(i, 3) Indeterminate sentences are the necessary consequence of individualisation of punishment and one of the most effective means for the social defence against criminality."

The main point made by those resisting the introduction of the indeterminate sentence is that only by adhering to the conception of *nulla poena sine lege* in its application to punishment can any defence against official abuse be guaranteed to the individual; and to support this they point to the development in criminology under totalitarian régimes where " scientific criminology " was perverted to political ends. In the absence of legal control of punishments they fear administrative arbitrariness. Thus Jerome Hall contends that " the insight of the common lawyer on these vital issues reflects the informed knowledge of Western civilisation. In the choice of alternatives, he knows the value of legal control of official conduct,

[1] H. Mannheim, *Criminal Justice and Social Reconstruction*, pp. 226-37.

especially when the personal rights of weak individuals are at stake."[1]

We need not concern ourselves here with the relative merits of the above contentions. Even for habitual criminals indeterminate sentences are rarely applied, and have been tested in Europe only by Denmark and Germany. Thus " the indeterminate sentence . . . has been a goal rather than an achievement of criminal reform."[2] On the other hand, the indefinite sentence, which is a *via media* between judicially determined sentences and the indeterminate sentence, has found general acceptance for certain types of offenders in many modern legal systems, in particular for juvenile offenders and habitual criminals. In the comparative law study which follows we shall examine the application of indeterminate and indefinite sentences to habitual criminals, but we will not revert to the general problem of the indeterminate sentence.

5. Capital Punishment

We do not possess " the ruthlessness of the pure heart ". We are not prepared to carry our ideas to their logical conclusion. We do not painlessly destroy the incurably insane. For the sake of society we are prepared to destroy a mad dog but not a dangerous criminal who has proved incorrigible. Incorrigibility is, after all, a concept relative to our knowledge; and since the protection of society can be achieved by alternative and less absolute means of dealing with habitual criminals, we are not forced to challenge the sanctity we ascribe to human life.

6. Transportation

In theory, transportation is the perfect solution to the problem the habitual criminal poses to society. In practice it has been a complete failure. Transportation has been tried and abandoned by England, France, Russia, Portugal, Spain, Italy, Holland, Denmark,

---

[1] *Principles of Criminal Law*, p. 53. Similarly, L. Radzinowicz in his article, " The Persistent Offender ", at p. 167 of *The Modern Approach to Criminal Law*, writes that "unless indeterminate sentences are awarded with great care, there is a grave risk that this measure, designed to ensure the better protection of society, may become an instrument of social aggression and weaken the basic principle of individual liberty."

[2] Grünhut, *Penal Reform*, p. 114. Two Bills providing indeterminate sentences for certain habitual criminals have been modified by the respective legislatures and have emerged as inaugurating indefinite sentences—in New York in 1877, and in England in 1908.

Chile and Equador. This does not, of course, mean that a successful penal colony for habitual criminals could not be established, but it does entitle one to disregard transportation as a presently practical solution of the problem of habitual criminality.

Only France has applied transportation specifically to habitual criminals, and in the comparative law study we shall consider the French law of May 27th, 1885 (which instituted a system of lifelong transportation of certain recidivists to Guiana or New Caledonia), and the later developments in this punishment, which is called " relégation ".

7. CASTRATION AND STERILIZATION

There is a frequent notional confusion between these measures and the problem of the habitual criminal. There may well be good reasons for the castration of habitual sexual criminals (as, for example, is practised in Denmark and in certain States of America, notably California), but this is a group which only incidentally overlaps the habitual criminal group. There may be other good reasons for sterilizing certain inferior types capable of transmitting their inferiority,[1] but again only some members of the group who should be sterilized will chance to be habitual criminals. In other words, castration and sterilization are not measures applicable to habitual criminals as such, and their consideration is therefore excluded from this study.[2]

8. AGGRAVATION OF PUNISHMENT AND PREVENTIVE DETENTION

There remain, then, two methods of combating the habitual facet of habitual criminality. First, the sentence for the last crime may be increased or continued indefinitely, the conditions under which this increased term is served remaining both in theory and practice unchanged—this process we will call " aggravation of punishment ". Secondly, the sentence for the last crime may be followed or supplanted by a different type of punishment applicable to habitual criminals as such—this punishment we will call

---

[1] See H. Mannheim, *Criminal Justice and Social Reconstruction*, pp. 19-36, and also the *Report of the Departmental Committee on Sterilisation*, 1933, Cmd. 4485.

[2] The protracted detention of habitual criminals may well tend to have a eugenically selective effect—this is an interesting, and possibly scientifically fruitful, indirect consequence of such detention.

"preventive detention". In Part I of this work we shall examine aggravation of punishment and preventive detention.

9. EXTENT OF RECIDIVISM AND HABITUAL CRIMINALITY

Recidivism, as we have defined it, is a concept applicable to every country, and is the most accurate available yardstick for measuring the incidence of a country's legislation against habitual criminals; and this because such legislation is aimed at a species of the genus recidivist.

Let us consider some statistics of recidivism in England as an illustration of the practical nature of our problem.

Table A[1] (page 26) shows the extent of recidivism in England and Wales during the last eighteen years for which figures have been published. It does not include people on remand for trial, those committed to prison for civil process (e.g. failure to pay maintenance orders), nor those whose convictions relate solely to offences against the Intoxicating Liquor Laws.

It shows that of all such men received into prison over this period, an average of 46·1 per cent. (standard deviation 4·44 per cent.) were recidivists. This fact, though of interest in itself, does not throw much light on the question of habitual criminality, nor, indeed, does the last column on the right of Table A showing the number of recidivists who had been sentenced to imprisonment or penal servitude on six or more previous occasions. It does give us one element of our definition of the habitual criminal—a settled practice in crime—but tells us nothing about the other two elements—subjective criminal qualities and public danger. Table B (page 27) endeavours to rectify this defect to a certain extent by including the concept of public danger.

The Annual Volumes of Criminal Statistics adopt, for certain purposes, a threefold classification of offences, namely Indictable Offences, Non-Indictable Offences akin to Indictable Offences, and Other Non-Indictable Offences. Since 1931 this classification has been followed in Table VII(A) of the Annual Reports of the Commissioners of Prisoners and Directors of Convict Prisons. Table B (page 27) is based on those tables, and includes all men received into prison on conviction of indictable offences and non-indictable offences akin to indictable offences, but excludes those convicted of

[1] Figures extracted from the annual reports of the Commissioners of Prisons and Directors of Convict Prisons, Appendices VIII.

TABLE A
Receptions of Men on Conviction (exceptions as above)

Year	Total (a) Receptions	Recidivists (b)		Recidivists with Six or More Previous Sentences
		Total	Percentage of Receptions	
1931	27,353	13,839	50·6	4,587
1932	30,773	14,928	48·5	4,813
1933	29,504	14,818	50·2	4,772
1934	28,242	14,496	51·3	4,886
1935	25,533	12,761	50	4,311
1936	23,231	11,696	50·3	4,092
1937	23,211	11,592	49·9	3,851
1938	23,625	11,760	49·8	3,972
1939	21,926	10,494	47·9	3,439
1940	18,887	8,024	42·5	2,468
1941	24,062	8,796	36·6	2,362
1942	26,836	9,637	35·9	2,519
1943	25,101	10,168	40·5	2,615
1944	23,872	10,214	42·8	2,679
1945	25,673	11,295	44	2,767
1946	25,923	11,991	46·3	2,956
1947	28,970	13,733	47·4	3,390

(a) In the words of the Prison Commissioners, frequently repeated throughout their reports : " The number of receptions is always greater than the number of different persons received into prison, since some persons after finishing one sentence are sent to prison again in the course of the same year."

(b) This slightly underestimates the actual number of " recidivists " as it does not include those whose only previous sentence was one of Borstal detention, nor those who have previously been sentenced only for offences against the Intoxicating Liquor Laws.

other non-indictable offences. Also excluded are those received into prison for non-payment of fines. Thus only those convicted of offences generally regarded as of a more serious nature appear in this table.

It shows that when we consider only men convicted of more serious offences, we find that an average of 48·7 per cent. of them (standard deviation 4·48 per cent.) are recidivists. Of these recidivists, 29·2 per cent. (standard deviation 3·47 per cent.) were those whom we can term " confirmed recidivists ", having been sentenced previously on six or more occasions for these more serious offences.

From a comparison of Tables A and B it appears that there is little relationship between recidivism and gravity of offences (46·1 per cent. as compared with 48·7 per cent.), but what relationship there is gives even more force to the two columns on the right of Table B.

TABLE B

Adult Male Receptions on Conviction of Indictable Offences and Non-Indictable Offences akin to Indictable Offences

Year	Total Receptions	RECIDIVISTS (a) (b)		RECIDIVISTS WITH SIX OR MORE PREVIOUS SENTENCES (b)	
		Total	Percentage of Receptions	Total	Percentage of Recidivists
1931	19,692	10,403	52·8	3,397	32·6
1932	22,161	11,266	50·8	3,637	32·3
1933	20,837	11,029	52·9	3,508	31·8
1934	19,989	10,897	54·5	3,603	33·1
1935	18,366	9,817	53·5	3,213	32·7
1936	17,304	9,155	52·9	3,058	33·4
1937	17,561	9,091	51·8	2,868	31·5
1938	17,884	9,166	51·2	2,945	32·1
1939	16,704	8,541	51·1	2,720	31·8
1940	15,247	6,850	44·9	2,047	29·9
1941	19,578	7,779	39·7	2,041	26·2
1942	20,583	8,273	40·2	2,151	26
1943	19,771	8,736	44·2	2,214	25·3
1944	19,216	8,820	45·9	2,268	25·7
1945	21,752	9,990	45·9	2,395	24
1946	23,163	10,945	47·3	2,607	23·8
1947	26,120	12,571	48·1	3,001	23·9

(a) Does not include recidivists whose only previous sentence was one of Borstal detention.

(b) These columns do not include sentences to prison for non-payment of fines.

It will be seen that the average yearly number of such men was 2,804. These figures of confirmed recidivists—men who fulfil two of the three elements of habitual criminality as we have defined it—do give some idea of the extent of habitual criminality in England and Wales, and prove that we are not dealing with an insignificant portion of the prison population.

Not only is the habitual criminal a statistically significant member of the prison population, but he is a part of that population relatively untouched by the legislation intended to combat him. During this very period, the years 1931 to 1947, an average of no more than 12·9 men were declared habitual criminals each year.[1]

[1] This figure of 12·9 does not include men sentenced as habitual criminals whose sentences were subsequently quashed by the Court of Criminal Appeal.

10. PLAN OF THIS STUDY

Multiple-factor analysis of causation is the only scientifically valid method, and the vogue of ascribing crime solely to any particular social condition or phenomenon is long past.[1] Rejecting, therefore, any single-factor ætiology of crime, it is safe to assume that the ætiology of recidivism will include all those factors tending towards crime, and that the ætiology of habitual criminality will include all those factors tending towards recidivism and crime. Successively more factors must be considered, for it is unlikely that any factors contributing significantly towards crime will not have contributed also to habitual criminality. In a study of the habitual criminal it is, therefore, impossible to reach any fundamental ætiological conclusion, the ætiology of crime itself not having been charted. We may be able to isolate some of the causative differentia of habitual criminality, but we shall certainly not reach any understanding of the " cause " of habitual criminality. Indirectly, however, isolating such differentia may throw some light on the question of causation when they are related to other more general investigations of the ætiology of crime, especially amongst young offenders. Understanding the differentia of the species " habitual " will more readily enable this segment of criminals to be fitted into the pattern created by ætiological studies, but such a result is an offshoot of this study, and not its chief purpose.

For convenience, this work is divided into two parts. In the first, an analysis is made of the laws adopted by many countries to combat the habitual criminal. An endeavour is made to evaluate the relative success of these laws, and to distil their essence by analysing the differences between them. Special prominence is given to English legislation and practice, and it is hoped that by comparing it with that of other countries, we may learn from their mistakes and profit by their successes. In the second part, the records of some three hundred confirmed recidivists and habitual criminals are analysed. Here the approach is empirical, and the purpose of this part is to establish some knowledge in the light of which the chief problems created by the existence of habitual criminals can be considered in relation to the characteristics of those criminals. Until we understand more completely than we do at present the individuals on whom our criminal law presses, it is unlikely that we shall make

[1] On this point see Sir Cyril Burt's *The Young Delinquent*, 4th ed., 1948, p. 590

much progress towards a rational sentencing policy or wise penological methods. An important by-product of this examination of case records is the preparation of the ground for a follow-up study into the later careers of those criminals who are here considered. Such a follow-up study would be of inestimable value in many respects, not the least of which would be the creation of Prediction Tables[1] for the guidance of those authorities whose task it is to decide when such criminals shall be conditionally discharged from prison.

To epitomise the purpose of this work: we must protect society from the habitual criminal, and this will not be achieved until we comprehend the characteristics of habitual criminals, and the various means the criminal law (of this and other countries) can contrive to this end. Progress in criminology must be founded on an understanding of the criminal and his relation to society. It is hoped that this work will provide a factual basis for an understanding of habitual criminals.

[1] Prediction tables have not, as yet, been constructed in England. In the United States of America such tables have been prepared and tested in the light of experience, and it is certain that they are more efficient prognostic instruments than the " magic eye " of " sound common sense " on which we rely. In this field Sheldon and Eleanor Glueck have been eminent workers, and have developed—and statistically validated—methods of preparing prediction tables. The present work forms a base on which follow-up studies could be used to construct such tables for English conditions, and it is to be hoped that the opportunity will not be allowed to pass. The problem of method will be considered in Chapter IX.

PART I

CHAPTER TWO

PART II OF THE PREVENTION OF CRIME ACT, 1908

THE FORTY YEARS EXPERIMENT

FOR forty years the sole means by which the English courts could deal with the problem of habitual criminality was Part II of the Prevention of Crime Act, 1908.[1] In 1949, with the promulgation of Section 21 of the Criminal Justice Act, 1948, the already moribund experiment embodied in the earlier Act was finally buried—there were no mourners.

This unanimity did not extend to any agreement as to the cause of the Act's failure. For this and several other reasons a detailed examination of the Act should be valuable. In implementing a new habitual criminal law, it would be regrettable if we did not learn from the mistakes we made in applying previous habitual criminal legislation, but we cannot do this until we have diagnosed our previous errors with precision.

We shall do well, for another reason, to devote some attention to the Act. In itself, the analysis of the successive phases, legislative, judicial and administrative, of an important criminological measure is of considerable interest from the point of view of the technique of drafting criminal legislation; for there is all too frequently, as in this Act, a great disparity between legislative aims and administrative effects.

For convenience, our treatment of the Act will be subdivided as follows:

1. Genesis and form of the Act;
2. Judicial interpretation of parts of the Act;
3. Function of the Director of Public Prosecutions under the Act;
4. Details of preventive detainees sentenced pursuant to the Act;
5. Function of the Advisory Committees under the Act;
6. Conditions in preventive detention; and
7. A general evaluation of the Act and its implementation.

---

[1] Part II of the Prevention of Crime Act, 1908, will be referred to in this chapter as " the Act ".

1. THE GENESIS AND FORM OF THE ACT

The history of criminological thought in relation to the segregation of habitual criminals has already been discussed; and we shall now limit ourselves to an investigation of the intention of the legislature in 1908 by reviewing the relevant administrative, judicial and legislative official publications.

Let us begin with the year 1894. In that year a strong committee under the chairmanship of Mr. Herbert Gladstone was formed to inquire into the state of the prisons. They adverted to the problem of the habitual criminal, and on this subject reported:[1]

> " There is evidently a large class of habitual criminals—who live by robbery and thieving and petty larceny—who run the risk of comparatively short sentences with comparative indifference. They make money rapidly by crime, they enjoy life after their fashion, and then, on detection and conviction, serve their time quietly, with the full determination to revert to crime when they come out. We are inclined to believe that the bulk of habitual criminals at large are composed of men of this class. When an offender has been convicted a fourth time or more he or she is pretty sure to have taken to crime as a profession and sooner or later to return to prison. We are, therefore, of opinion that further corrective measures are desirable for these persons. When under sentence they complicate prison management —when at large they are responsible for the commission of the greater part of the undetected crime ; they are a nuisance to the community. To punish them for the particular offence is almost useless; the real offence is the wilful persistence in the deliberately acquired habit of crime. We venture to offer the opinion that a new form of sentence should be placed at the disposal of the judges by which offenders might be segregated for long periods of detention, during which they would not be treated with the severity of first-class hard labour or penal servitude, but would be forced to work under less onerous conditions. As loss of liberty would to them prove eventually the chief deterrent, so by their being removed from the opportunity of doing wrong, the community would gain."

With a just appreciation of the problem before them, the Gladstone Committee laid down the strategic plan of an appropriate remedy; they did not give this plan any detailed tactical formulation, which indeed could hardly be expected under their wide terms of reference. Mr. Gladstone's Committee officially sowed the seed; it was left to others to nurture it and bring it to fruition.

[1] *Report of the Committee on Prisons*, 1895, p. 31. This committee met shortly after Oscar Wilde's *Ballad of Reading Gaol* had so stirred public opinion.

In 1901, the Judges of the King's Bench Division agreed on the following resolution:

" That, in the opinion of His Majesty's Judges exercising criminal jurisdiction, the time has arrived when inquiry may profitably be held whether some modification of the discipline of penal servitude may not safely be made, especially in respect of long sentences and into the best way of dealing with habitual and professional criminals."

The next step towards the Act was taken by the Prison Commissioners who, in their annual report for the year 1902, stated that they had considered the Gladstone Committee's recommendations, that by means of a census of the prison population they had proved the truth of the contention that there was " a large class of habitual criminals ", and continued:

" We believe that the time has now come when a special form of detention should be devised under which prisoners, shown by their records to belong to this . . . class, might be segregated by order of the court for long periods of time, say, for the legal maximum of their last particular offence, subject only to conditional liberation by the Secretary of State, when he is satisfied, on the report of the prison authority, that there is a reasonable ground to believe that the prisoner can be released without danger to society."

Pursuant to the above advice of the Prison Commissioners, and to several statements made by Mr. Justice Phillimore stressing the need for such legislation, several questions were asked in the House of Commons.[1] In August, 1903, the " Penal Servitude Bill "[2] was brought down by the Home Secretary, Mr. Akers-Douglas, and ordered to be read a second time and printed. This Bill was withdrawn before Second Reading, the sole purpose of its presentation to the House in 1903 being that ample opportunity should be given for informed public opinion to express itself. In February, 1904, substantially the same Bill was brought down,[3] and in June it was given a Second Reading by the House of Commons.[4]

Clause 1 (i) of both the above Bills reads as follows:

" Where any person who has previously been convicted more than twice of an indictable offence is convicted on indictment of an offence punishable with penal servitude, and it appears to the court—

(a) that at the time when he committed the offence for which he is to be sentenced, he was leading a persistently dishonest or criminal life ; and

---

[1] *Parliamentary Debates*, 4th Series, Vol. 123, Col. 121 and Vol. 125, Col. 850.
[2] Bill No. 318 of 1903.   [3] Bill No. 86 of 1904.
[4] *Parliamentary Debates*, 4th Series, Vol. 135, Cols. 722-70.

(b) that by reason of his criminal antecedents and mode of life, it is expedient for the protection of the public that he should be kept in detention for a lengthened period of years,

the court may, if it thinks fit, in passing a sentence of penal servitude for any term of not less than seven years, direct that, after serving a portion of his sentence under the general rules relating to sentences of penal servitude, he shall serve the residue thereof in the habitual offender division."

The other clauses of the Bill provide the details for the implementation of this new power which was to be given to the courts.

By this Bill the Judge was to be empowered to order detention of seven years or more, of which the first quarter (or such longer period as he might direct) would be served under the general rules governing penal servitude, and the remainder under milder circumstances " which would amount really to little more than restraint."[1] A maximum period of fourteen years was specified (for example, three years and six months ordinary penal servitude, and ten years and six months under ameliorated penal conditions); but the Judge could fix any period between seven and fourteen years for such a sentence without making any formal declaration of habitual criminality. Though the sentence imposed was for a fixed term, a discretion was given to the Secretary of State to discharge such prisoners conditionally before the expiration of the term imposed on them.

In the debates on the Second Reading of this Bill, it was argued that the allegation of habitual criminality should be the subject of a separate legal charge with a separate verdict. The Under-Secretary of State for the Home Department endeavoured to answer this contention by recounting that the Judges of the King's Bench Division exercising criminal jurisdiction had considered this point at a special meeting at which their advice was solicited, and had expressed an almost unanimous opinion that the matters to be considered regarding habitual criminality should not be the subject of formal proof, but that the Judge should continue to act as when dealing with a prisoner's antecedents.

The Government was not prepared to force the Penal Servitude Bill through Parliament as a party measure, and agreement was lacking for its acceptance as a non-party issue.[2] Therefore, in August 1904 this Bill was withdrawn.

[1] Mr. Akers-Douglas, in introducing the Penal Servitude Bill in June, 1904. *Parliamentary Debates*, 4th Series, Vol. 135, Col. 722.
[2] It was given a second reading by 181 votes to 71.

The next important step was taken in May 1908, when the then Home Secretary, Mr. Gladstone, introduced the Prevention of Crime Bill.[1] Having dwelt on the advantages to be expected from Part I of the Bill in its inauguration of the Borstal System for the treatment of certain young offenders, he adverted to Part II of the Bill and outlined the plan it embodied by which habitual criminals would be held in preventive detention " during His Majesty's pleasure ". In two sentences he caught the essence of these provisions:

> " A court, on the finding of a jury, is to have power to sentence an habitual criminal to a term of preventive detention, which will continue until the man gives bona fide and sufficient assurance that he will take to an honest life, or until by age or infirmity he becomes physically incapable of resuming a life of crime. . . .[2] We propose that the prison discipline should be less rigorous than that now prevailing, alike as regards hours, talking, recreative occupations, and food."[3]

The Prevention of Crime Bill was dealt with throughout as a non-party measure, and there was no doubt as to the general approval it received and that it would be given a Second Reading. Speaking immediately after Mr. Gladstone, Mr. Akers-Douglas, the previous Home Secretary, pledged the Opposition's support for this Bill now introduced by a Liberal Government. Soon, however, it became clear that though the general policy of the Bill as it dealt with habitual criminals was acceptable to the House, there was violent opposition to the potentially perpetual quality of the punishment it introduced, and a general feeling that no individual's liberty should be committed so exclusively to the care of the Prison Commissioners.

Thus, the Second Reading debate was concerned primarily with the question of the penological wisdom of the indefinite sentence subject to no legal maximum term; and Lord Robert Cecil epitomised the feeling of the House in the suggestion that " at this experimental stage there is something to be said in favour of a sentence not exceeding ten or fifteen years."[4]

One other major objection to these provisions was raised in the House. It was argued that more discretion should be given to the Judge in the imposition of preventive detention and that, in particular, he should be allowed to order preventive detention in lieu of, as well as in addition to, a sentence of penal servitude; in

---

[1] *Parliamentary Debates*, 4th Series, Vol. 189.   [2] *Ibid.*, Col. 1122.
[3] *Ibid.*, Col. 1123.   [4] *Ibid.*, Vol. 190, Col. 513.

other words, that preventive detention should be a single-track or dual-track measure at the discretion of the trial Judge. In a speech of remarkable prescience, Mr. A. C. Salter made that point and also objected to the indefinite quality of preventive detention, predicting that " whatever the facts might be, juries would hesitate or refuse to find a verdict that a man was an habitual criminal, because they would anticipate and dislike the consequence of such a verdict."[1]

The House of Commons gave the Bill a Second Reading by 133 votes to 11, leaving its objections to certain details of the Bill to be ironed out by Standing Committee C, to which the Bill was committed, and during the later stages of its passage through Parliament.

Only one issue of any importance to our study of this Bill arose at the Committee Stage: amendments were moved to the effect that the words " during His Majesty's pleasure " be omitted and the words " for a further period not exceeding (three) (ten) years " be inserted in their place. These amendments were rejected by the Committee, who preferred to retain preventive detention as an indefinite punishment. They accepted, however, an amendment providing a parliamentary safeguard of the detainee's right to freedom, by which the Secretary of State was directed to discharge a preventive detainee at the expiration of ten years from the commencement of the term of preventive detention unless he had definite reason to believe that, if released, the prisoner would relapse into crime. If this was the Secretary of State's opinion, and if he did not then release the preventive detainee, he was to be statutorily obliged to make a special report to Parliament, stating the grounds upon which he had decided not to discharge the detainee.

Thus the Bill emerged from the Committee Stage with preventive detention as an indefinite punishment, but with a parliamentary safeguard after the detainee had served ten years. However, when it was reconsidered by the House of Commons in November, 1908, the opposition to this indefinite punishment became so intense that the Home Secretary met the House on this point and told them that " instead of proposing that the sentence should be during the King's pleasure, powers will be inserted giving authority to the Court to sentence to preventive detention for a maximum term of ten years and a minimum of five."[2]

Having met this objection, Mr. Gladstone soon found himself

---

[1] *Ibid.*, Vol. 190, Col. 469.   [2] *Ibid.*, Vol. 198, Col. 110.

pressed by another forceful line of criticism from those who preferred that preventive detention should be a single-track or dual-track punishment at the discretion of the trial Judge. Here the Government proved recalcitrant, the Home Secretary, after outlining the scheme for creating a new preventive detention prison at Camp Hill, on the Isle of Wight, stating that:

> " If the amendment were adopted and a judge used the power of sending a man straight to preventive detention, the effect would be that instead of adapting Camp Hill to this special purpose . . . the discipline there would have to be levelled up to that of ordinary prisons. . . . This matter has been most carefully considered, and it is quite impossible for me to give way. If we are forced to give way on this point of a period of preliminary punishment, I am bound to say that it would be necessary to withdraw this part of the Bill."[1]

This intransigent attitude of the Government carried the day, and preventive detention remained until 1949 a dual-track system.[2]

The debates in the House of Lords followed similar lines to those in the Commons, the most significant speech being an attack by Earl Russell on the dual-track system in which he alleged that society is not justified in inflicting two such pains on a prisoner; one or the other, but not both.[3]

Before proceeding to a consideration of any of the detailed provisions of the Act, it is necessary to advert to the Government's conception in 1908 of the type of criminal with which the Act would deal. The ideas on this point are to be found in two statements made by the Home Secretary, Mr. Gladstone, and they are reproduced here in full primarily because of their strange contrast to the criminals who, as will be seen, were in fact sentenced to preventive detention. First :

> " For 60 per cent. the present system was sufficiently deterrent, but for the professional class it was inadequate. There was a distinction well known to criminologists between habituals and professionals. Habituals were men who dropped into crime from their surroundings or physical disability, or mental deficiency, rather than from any active intention to plunder their fellow-creatures or from being criminals for the sake of crime. The professionals were the men with an object, sound in mind—so far as a criminal

---

[1] *Ibid.*, Vol. 198, Col. 132.
[2] " Dual-track system ", though not an accurate or descriptive phrase for this conception, has been accepted in the literature, and I have used it throughout this book. An alternative, " two stage system ", tends to be confused with the normal " stage system " adopted in many countries for all penal sentences.
[3] *Ibid.*, Vol. 198, Col. 690.

could be sound in mind—and in body, competent, often highly skilled, and who deliberately, with their eyes open, preferred a life of crime and knew all the tricks and turns and manœuvres necessary for that life. It was with that class that the Bill would deal."[1]

Secondly, Mr. Gladstone gave the House some idea of the number of such " professional " criminals who were liable to find themselves sentenced to preventive detention, saying:

" In this Bill we propose to deal with a class which might number as many as 5,000, and it is proposed to build an extra prison which would accommodate something like 500. The whole of that prison would be required for the class of person we desire to deal with . . . the dangerous professional criminal."[2]

On December 21st, 1908, the Prevention of Crime Act, 1908, received the Royal Assent; on August 1st, 1909, it came into operation.

In Appendix A to this study the full text of Part II of the Act is reproduced, and no purpose would be served by summarising it here for the sake of the logically complete development of this analysis. Instead, we will now consider only the type of criminal that was, on the face of the Act, liable to the new punishment it introduced—preventive detention of from five to ten years.

All the conditions precedent to the imposition of preventive detention were to be found in Section 10 of the Act, and were the following:

(*a*) Conviction on indictment of a " crime " ; and the expression " crime " is to be given the same meaning as in the Prevention of Crimes Act, 1871, namely :

" any felony or the offence of uttering false or counterfeit coin, or of possessing counterfeit gold or silver coin, or the offence of obtaining goods or money by false pretences, or the offence of conspiracy to defraud, or any misdemeanour under the fifty-eighth section of the Larceny Act, 1861."

(*b*) An admission by the accused criminal, or a finding by the jury, that he is an " habitual criminal ", provided that only in two circumstances shall a prisoner be found to be an " habitual criminal ", namely :

(i) that since attaining the age of 16 years he has at least three times previously to the conviction of the crime charged in the said indictment been convicted of a " crime " . . . and that he is leading persistently a dishonest or criminal life ; or

(ii) that he has on such a previous conviction been found to be a habitual criminal and sentenced to preventive detention.

[1] *Ibid.*, Vol. 190, Col. 499.   [2] *Ibid.*, Vol. 198, Cols. 118 and 132.

(c) A charge in the indictment that the offender is an habitual criminal ; provided that this charge cannot be inserted in the indictment :

    (i) without the consent of the Director of Public Prosecutions ; and

    (ii) unless not less than seven days' notice has been given to the proper officer of the court by which the offender is to be tried, and to the offender, that it is intended to insert such a charge.

Further, the notice to the offender must specify " the previous convictions and the other grounds upon which it is intended to found the charge."

(d) A sentence of penal servitude for the last offence or offences he has committed.[1]

(e) The court must be of opinion that " by reason of his criminal habits and mode of life it is expedient for the protection of the public that the offender should be kept in detention for a lengthened period of years."

If *all* the above conditions be satisfied then the court may also sentence the prisoner to a term of preventive detention.

These conditions precedent constituted, in the opinion of the legislature in 1908, sufficient defence against official arbitrariness. What was not considered was whether they emasculated the whole plan of the Act—the plan of segregating those whom the Home Secretary termed " dangerous professional criminals."

2. THE JUDICIAL INTERPRETATION OF PARTS OF THE ACT

In discussing the judicial interpretation of this Act, particular attention will be given to the effect of judicial decisions on the type of criminal punished.

Notwithstanding the Criminal Appeal Act, 1907, Section 11 of the Act allowed one sentenced to preventive detention to appeal against that sentence without the leave of the Court of Criminal Appeal. That Court interpreted Section 11 as giving a right of appeal only when the prisoner had been sentenced to preventive detention and not merely convicted of being a habitual criminal; but in the latter case an appeal could be allowed at the discretion of the Court of Criminal Appeal.[2] It also declared that though this right was confined to an appeal against the sentence of preventive detention, the court would, as a matter of practice, give leave to appeal against the primary sentence of penal servitude whenever there was an appeal as of right against the secondary sentence of preventive detention.[3] Consequently, the judicial interpretation of

---

[1] Penal servitude was by definition for a period of at least three years.
[2] Martin, 7 Cr. App. R. 196 ; Bennet, 9 Cr. App. R. 225 ; Beard, 20 Cr. App. R., 155.
[3] Smith and Weston, 3 Cr. App. R. 40.

the Act became almost exclusively the responsibility of the Court of Criminal Appeal.

It would be superfluous to review all the issues that arose over these forty years concerning the interpretation of the terms of the Act. Here we will advert only to certain selected points of particular criminological significance, or of particular significance to the draftsmanship of criminal legislation.

These points are:

(a) The notice to the offender of the intention to charge him as an habitual offender required by Section 10 (4) (b) of the Act;

(b) The interpretation of the phrase, " is leading persistently a dishonest or criminal life ";

(c) Penal servitude as a condition precedent to Preventive Detention;

(d) The effect of a previous conviction as an habitual criminal.

(a) The Statutory Notice to the Offender

The work of the Court of Criminal Appeal in interpretating procedural matters connected with this Act was intensified by the failure of the legislature to provide the machinery of proof in the body of the Act, or, as is often done, to provide for rules to be made for this purpose. The outcome was that the procedure to be followed for indictments laid under the Act was outlined in a particular case, Turner's Case[1] (which came before the Court of Criminal Appeal in 1909, just over three months after the Act had been put into force), and was restated in 1922 in the case of Harris and Others.[2]

Section 10 (4) (b) of the Act provided that a charge of being an habitual criminal should not be inserted in the indictment:

" unless not less than seven days' notice has been given . . . to the offender that it is intended to insert such a charge " ;

and further required that such notice should

" specify the previous convictions and the other grounds upon which it is intended to found the charge."

The contents of this notice to the offender of the intention to charge him with being an habitual criminal was a central issue in the judicial application of the Act.

[1] 3 Cr. App. R. 103.   [2] 16 Cr. App. R. 94.

The first problem that arose was the meaning of the phrase, " not less than seven days' notice", and in Turner's Case this phrase was held to mean " seven clear days' notice ".[1] Further, it was held that the due service of the notice would be presumed by the Court unless evidence to the contrary was advanced,[2] and that any objection to such notice because it was not served seven clear days before the offender was charged, or for any other technical reason, should be taken at the trial (so that, if necessary, the trial could be postponed).[3]

Given, then, a correctly served notice free from technical faults, let us consider what were its necessary contents; in other words, what interpretation did the courts place on the legislative requirement that the notice should specify " the previous convictions and the other grounds upon which it is intended to found the charge " ?

The phrase, " the previous convictions ", need not delay us, for it raises questions only of the mode of proof of the three previous convictions necessary to a conviction as an habitual criminal —questions with no criminological overtones. On the other hand, the " other grounds " which must be specified gave rise to one of the most troublesome difficulties in the application of this Act. In practice, these " other grounds " had to be those allegations on which the prosecution sought to establish the fact that the offender was " leading persistently a dishonest or criminal life ", which was an essential element in the proof of habitual criminality. The point basic to an understanding of what had to be alleged as " other grounds " was made by the Court of Criminal Appeal in Turner's Case:[4]

> " what has to be stated is the ground upon which it is intended to found the charge ; and the court is of opinion that that must be given in a real and substantial form, that he must be told the grounds, and that it is not sufficient to say : We propose to prove that you have been persistently leading a dishonest life, or that you have been persistently leading a criminal life."

and later:

> " The grounds must be stated, only they must be stated in a general way as grounds, not as evidence : that you are a habitual associate of thieves ; that you are doing no work and have no visible means by which you are earning an honest livelihood " . . . and so on.

[1] See also Dean 18 Cr. App. R. 21. The trial can be postponed to save the notice from being out of time. Lawrence (1914) 78 J.P. Jo. 196 ; and Conduit 11 Cr. App. R. 38.
[2] Taylor, 16 Cr. App. R. 4.   [3] Smith and Weston, 3 Cr. App. R. 90.
[4] 3 Cr. App. R. at pp. 159 and 160.

The whole purport of this allegation of " other grounds " was thus to enable the criminal charged with being an " habitual " to prepare himself for the type of evidence which was to be adduced against him to prove that he was leading persistently a dishonest or criminal life.[1] It did not preclude the admission (under Section 10 (5) of the Act) of evidence as to his character and repute as relevant to this question; nor did it require the prosecution to state the evidence on which the other grounds alleged were based—thus in Summer's Case, as an " other ground " it was alleged that Summers had consorted with thieves, and it was held not to be obligatory to state in the statutory notice their names, or the times, or the places of such association. However, with the above exceptions, the " other grounds " alleged circumscribed the evidence which could be adduced to prove the persistent dishonesty or criminality of the offender's life.

The prosecution was thus frequently placed in a dilemma—it had to allege sufficient " other grounds " in the statutory notice to support the charge of being an habitual criminal; it had to prove those grounds; and yet it could adduce no evidence not logically implicit in those allegations. In Appendix B, nine " other grounds " commonly included in the notice to the offender appear, and illustrate the type of evidence on which most habitual criminals were, during the last forty years, committed to preventive detention.

One of the problems constituting this dilemma was stated in the leading case of Harris and Others:[2]

> " Counsel for the prosecution should especially be careful to observe the grounds alleged in the notice of the Director of Public Prosecutions, and to see that his witnesses do not run on and give evidence of facts not set out in such notice. A general question to a police officer, ' What do you know about the prisoner ? ' may let in evidence of facts not so set out, and lead to the quashing of the conviction."

Nothing was clearer than that on the issue of whether the prisoner had been leading an honest life, no evidence was admissible of

---

[1] In Waller's Case (3 Cr. App. R. 213) the prosecution did not propose to adduce anything in evidence on the charge that Waller was an habitual criminal except his three " previous convictions ", relying on their duration and frequency to prove that Waller was leading persistently a criminal life. They therefore alleged no " other grounds " whatsoever in the statutory notice to Waller ; and it was held that in these circumstances such a notice was a valid one, and was sufficient to support a conviction as an habitual criminal.

[2] 16 Cr. App. R. at p. 98.

periods[1] or of facts which had not been set out in the statutory notice to the prisoner.[2]

Let us briefly consider the type of difficulties that often arose from the failure to include the allegation " that you are an associate of thieves and persons of bad character,"[3] and remember that the prosecution could only include this allegation in the statutory notice when at least seven clear days before the trial there was evidence to support it—evidence capable of convincing a jury (and a bench) frequently predisposed against the sentence of preventive detention.

In Fawcett's Case,[4] the statutory notice to Fawcett stated that he was going to be charged as an habitual criminal on the two following grounds:

1. his three previous convictions for " crimes " ; and
2. " that between the (date) . . . and the (date) . . . you were given various opportunities of earning an honest living ; nevertheless, you returned to your dishonest and criminal life."

A detective-inspector who knew Fawcett personally chanced to be in court when this charge was being heard and gave evidence to the effect that he had on some thirty or forty occasions seen Fawcett associating with several dangerous criminals, and acting in concert with them. Fawcett was convicted as an habitual criminal and sought leave to appeal against his conviction.[5] Channel J. granted his application and stated that

" prisoners are entitled to know what evidence is to be given in order that they may have an opportunity of putting in an answer. It is doubtful whether appellant has had that opportunity."

Before the Court of Criminal Appeal, the Crown made the point that they knew of Fawcett's association with convicted thieves only after the statutory notice had been given, and contended that the notice actually served had put him on his guard concerning the relevant period—that should suffice. The line between fair indication of the type of allegation to be met, and evidence of that allegation, is not an easy one to draw; but in this case it was held that the

---

[1] Thus, in Wood's Case (12 Cr. App. R. 29), it was held that though evidence of the accused's mode of life after the commission of the crime on which he had been primarily convicted was admissible, the statutory notice to him of such evidence must be as specific as possible.
[2] Moran, 5 Cr. App. R. 219 ; Westwood, 8 Cr. App. R. 273 ; Tyreman, 19 Cr. App. R. 4.
[3] See Appendix B.   [4] 5 Cr. App. R. 91 and 115.
[5] Not only against his sentence for which no leave to appeal was required.

statutory notice did not cover the case which was in fact made against the prisoner, and his conviction as an habitual criminal was quashed.[1]

The decision in Fawcett's Case is typical of a whole series of cases in which evidence of criminal associations was tendered at the trial though not alleged in the statutory notice. The facts in Fawcett's Case were almost identical with those in the cases of Moran, Maxfield, Nielson, Stockdale, Westfall, Baxter, Yarwood, and several others.[2]

Similar problems arose concerning the allegation, in the statutory notice, that warrants had been issued for the offender's arrest in connection with offences with which he had not been charged; or that he had been involved in other offences with which he had not been charged.[3] Here too there arose the conflict between the necessity to prove whatever was alleged in the notice, and the danger of evidence being given at the trial which went to allegations that had not been included in the statutory notice. However, the greatest difficulties flowed from the problem of including in or excluding from the statement of criminal associations the statutory notice.

There was a certain unreality in the problems thus created under the Act. All those charged with being habitual criminals must have spent considerable periods in prison to qualify for that charge. When the average man has thus been thrown frequently and for protracted periods into the company of prisoners, he will inevitably form associations with them, particularly when his natural gregariousness is unsatisfied owing to the tendency of his civilian associates to reject

[1] Though its application in this context gives rise to considerable difficulty, the proviso to Section 4 (1) of the Criminal Appeal Act, 1907, is applicable to convictions of being an habitual criminal and to sentences of preventive detention. For discussions and applications of this proviso to habitual criminals see the following cases : Marshall, 5 Cr. App. R. 25 ; Jones, 5 Cr. App. R. 29 ; Fowler, 8 Cr. App. R. 240 ; Webber, 8 Cr. App. R. 59 ; Westwood, 8 Cr. App. R. 273 ; Wilson and Marshall, 8 Cr. App. R. 20 ; Heron, 9 Cr. App. R. 29 ; Stockdale, 11 Cr. App. R. 108 ; Harris and Others, 16 Cr. App. R. 89 ; Dinsdale, 19 Cr. App. R. 123 ; Herbert, 23 Cr. App. R. 123 ; Murray, 23 Cr. App. R. 166 ; Whelan, 24 Cr. App. R. 189 ; Beadall, 24 Cr. App. R. 39. The proviso to section 4 (1) of the Criminal Appeal Act reads : " Provided that the court may, notwithstanding that they are of opinion that the point raised in the appeal might be decided in favour of the appellant, dismiss the appeal if they consider that no substantial miscarriage of justice has actually occurred."

[2] All cases here cited appear in the Criminal Appeal Reports as follows : Moran, Vol. 5, p. 219 ; Maxfield, Vol. 7, p. 230 ; Westfall, Vol. 15, p. 57 ; Nielson, Vol. 9, p. 218 ; Stockdale, Vol. 11, p. 108 ; Baxter, Vol. 18, p. 127 ; Yarwood, Vol. 21, p. 25.

[3] See for example : Marchall, 5 Cr. App. R. 25 ; Westwood, 8 Cr. App. R. 273 ; Heron, 9 Cr. App. R. 29 ; Russell, 12 Cr. App. R. 271 ; Westfall, 15 Cr. App. R. 57 ; and Beadall, 24 Cr. App. R. 39.

him.[1] It was too much to expect him to cut himself loose from such associates immediately on his discharge from prison, and some contact with them did not argue his intention persistently to lead a dishonest or criminal life; though such association did make it harder for him to reshape his mode of living. As an element in habitual criminality it was, therefore, grossly exaggerated, and attracted judicial attention out of proportion to its criminological significance. Basically the fault lay in the draftsmanship of Section 10 of the Act—certainly the interest of the offender had to be protected so that preventive detention was not indiscriminately applied; but protection springing from procedural complications is far from desirable.

(b) The interpretation of " is leading persistently a dishonest or criminal life "

This question of the criminal's mode of life was one of fact to be found by the jury on evidence. Accordingly, consideration must be given to the onus of proof, to some of the duties of the judge summing up for the jury's consideration; and to the type of evidence frequently advanced.

Of course, though the jury found a criminal to be an "habitual", there still resided in the court an independent discretion whether it should impose preventive detention—a discretion which it was to exercise on its opinion of whether preventive detention was " expedient for the protection of the public."[2]

The point of departure is Turner's Case, in which it was clearly established that the onus of proving that the prisoner has been leading persistently a dishonest or criminal life lay upon the Crown, and that the prisoner was never to be required to disprove that charge.[3] Further, Turner's Case laid it down that, as the verb in the Act was in the present tense, the Crown had to prove the dishonest or criminal character of the prisoner's life at the time when he committed the

---

[1] Even if they should not reject him, his contacts with the outside world are so few as to make him think they have no more use for him.

[2] See, for example, Paul, 18 Cr. App. R. 128.

[3] See also Stewart, 4 Cr. App. R. 175 ; Young, 9 Cr. App. R. 185 ; Driscoll, 18 Cr. App. R. 184. Thus, in Young's Case, where the deputy-chairman of the Bench at Quarter Sessions directed the jury to consider whether Young had made up his mind to reform, the Court of Criminal Appeal quashed Young's conviction as an habitual criminal : similarly in Jones, 15 Cr. App. R. 20. Nor did the prisoner's adduction of evidence of his having led an honest life shift this onus of proof. Later we will consider whether it was shifted by a previous conviction as an habitual criminal.

offence(s) for which he was primarily convicted.[1]   In Young's
Case,[2] it was suggested that the relevant time down to which proof
must be brought was the date of the prisoner's arrest (not the date
of commission of the last offence); but this seems inaccurate for if
evidence of the prisoner's activities subsequent to the commission of
his last offence could be advanced, the Crown should have been
obliged to give specific notice to the prisoner of its intention to do so.[3]

This insistence on the onus of proof remaining with the Crown,
and that this proof be brought down at least to the date of commission of the offender's last offence, was most salutary; for it is in
this type of case that the court must go to great lengths to safeguard
the prisoner : he had been tried and convicted on a serious charge
by the same jury and the same judge who then heard the charge
against him of being an habitual criminal, and who were immediately
informed of his criminal record; they would almost certainly be
predisposed against him. As a further counter to this predisposition
the Judge in summing-up was required to state, clearly and emphatically, to the jury any evidence which tended to show that the
prisoner had been striving to lead an honest life (such as any honest
employment he had undertaken, or any attempt he had made to
find work) in the period immediately preceding arrest,[4] or at any
time since his last discharge from prison.[5]

The question that was put to the jury was, then, a question of
fact; but it was a question in which the directions given to the jury
by the Judge had to restate for their consideration all the favourable
aspects of the prisoner's life. The jury was not expected to exercise
a criminological discretion, and the summing-up must not have
confused the issue by dealing with the policy of the system of
preventive detention.[6]

What period in the prisoner's life could the jury consider in
deciding on his persistent dishonesty or criminality ? We have seen
that the jury had to consider the prisoner's life at the time of the
commission of his last offence, and during the interval since his last

[1] See also Keane and Watson, 8 Cr. App. R. 12 ; Baggott, 4 Cr. App. R. 67.
[2] 9 Cr. App. R. 185.   [3] Wood, 12 Cr. App. R. 29.
[4] Sullivan, 9 Cr. App. R. 201. Even where the prisoner had done honest work during
a period in which he was avoiding arrest, this factor had to be put to the jury in his
favour : Brown, 9 Cr. App. R. 161.
[5] Mitchell, 7 Cr. App. R. 281 ; Hammersley, 14 Cr. App. R. 118 ; Harris and Others,
16 Cr. App. R. at p. 99 ; Weale, 20 Cr. App. R. 153 ; R. v. Jones (1939), 1 All. E.R. 181 ;
Wells, 5 Cr. App. R. 33. Similarly in Millichamp's Case (21 Cr. App. R.) it was held
that the jury's attention must be drawn to any protracted periods without conviction.
[6] Powell, 16 Cr. App. R. 23.

release from prison; our inquiry here is whether the jury was allowed to consider his mode of life before his last committal to prison. The following dictum in Turner's Case[1] gives the answer:

> "In these cases it very often may be extremely important to prove that he is now, at the present time, doing precisely the same thing that he used to do . . . and consequently we cannot say as a general proposition that evidence of something of his way of life prior to his last conviction is inadmissible. If you had only got that it would not prove the issue, that is quite clear, but it may be a step towards proving the issue."

Such evidence of the prisoner's earlier life was frequently admitted; and provided the prisoner had notice of the intention to introduce it against him, no objection could be taken.[2]

Now let us advert to the evidence that was required to support this allegation of the prisoner's persistently dishonest or criminal life.

The combination of the three statutorily required previous convictions for "crimes", and the brief interval between his last discharge from prison and the subsequent commission of an offence, could suffice to prove that he was an habitual criminal. This was well stated in Harris and Others:[3]

> "Upon this question of a man's leading persistently a dishonest or criminal life, where there has been a considerable lapse of time between a man's last conviction and the commission of the offence which forms the subject of the primary indictment at the trial, notice containing particulars must have been given and proved of the facts upon which the prosecution rely for saying that the offender is leading such a life. If, on the other hand, the time between a man's discharge from prison and the commission of the next offence is a very short one, it may be open to the jury to find that he is leading persistently a dishonest or criminal life by reason of the mere fact that he has again committed an offence so soon after his discharge from a previous one, provided the notice has stated this ground. This is a question of fact."

Thus six days, three weeks, and six and a half weeks were all held to be intervals sufficiently brief to prove, in themselves, the offender's persistent criminality.[4] On the other hand, when the interval was "substantial", something more than the statutory convictions and the statement of this interval was required.[5]

[1] 3 Cr. App. R., at p. 161.   [2] See also Wilson and Marshall, 8 Cr. App. R. 20.
[3] 16 Cr. App. R., at pp. 98-9.
[4] Foster, 3 Cr. App. R. 173 (six days) ; Sweeney, 4 Cr. App. R. 70 (three weeks) ; Condon, 4 Cr. App. R. 109 (six and a half weeks).
[5] Three months—Baggott, 4 Cr. App. R. 67 ; five months—Wilson, 12 Cr. App. R. 95 ; five and a half months—Mitchell, 7 Cr. App. R. 285 ; nine months—Kelly, 3 Cr. App. R. 248 ; and Heard, 9 Cr. App. R. 80.

Though something more than the three statutory convictions for " crimes " was necessary to establish habitual criminality, this added element could come from qualities inherent in those three previous convictions when considered in relation to the last offence committed. Three such convictions and a later offence forming no pattern of " professional " criminality would not produce this added element;[1] but it could be produced if the last offence for which the prisoner was convicted followed his previous discharge from prison at no great interval, and if it was the same type of offence as those for which he had been previously convicted[2] (that is, if it illustrated the " professional " quality of the prisoner's offences; for example, regular coining offences); or if the offences committed showed deliberate and systematic preparation, and were repeated at an early opportunity after release from prison.[3]

But in fact the type of evidence that could be adduced to establish that the prisoner was " leading persistently a dishonest or criminal life " was virtually limitless, provided it was implicit in the statutory notice to the offender of the intention to charge him as an habitual criminal. Frequently, as we have seen, his association with other criminals was adduced as evidence on this point;[4] frequently the number and type of offences (other than those forming the three previous convictions) for which he had been convicted,[5] or which he had requested should be taken into consideration when he was sentenced, or for which warrants for his arrest were outstanding,[6] were advanced to prove his persistent dishonest or criminal life.[7]

Other evidence that was advanced against the prisoner charged

---

[1] Baggott, 4 Cr. App. R. 67.
[2] Waller, 3 Cr. App. R. 213 ; Yates, 5 Cr. App. R. 222 ; Williams, 8 Cr. App. R. 49.
[3] Everitt, 6 Cr. App. R. 267.
[4] In Hammersley, 14 Cr. App. R. 11, and in the Scotch Sessions case of Stirling v. H.M. Advocate (1911) S.C. (J.) 84, such evidence was held insufficient in itself to establish this persistently dishonest life.
[5] Brummitt and Mathews, 4 Cr. App. R. 192 ; Westwood, 8 Cr. App. R. 273 ; Heard, 7 Cr. App. R. 80.
[6] Macdonald, 12 Cr. App. R. 127.
[7] In Beadall's Case (24 Cr. App. R. 39) the Crown alleged in the statutory notice to Beadall that he had committed a crime for which he had neither been convicted nor admitted his guilt. Hewart, L.C.J. (together with Avory and Hawke, JJ.) held that this was permissible, and stated that " in our view there is no objection to the prosecution proving then and there the commission of crimes with which the accused has not been charged." With all respect, it is submitted that in such a case the Crown is inevitably placed under a lesser burden of proof than it would be were it required formally to prove the commission of such crimes by an offender facing the jury in a less compromising position than when charged with being an habitual criminal ; and that this was an undesirable exacerbation of such an offender's already judicially difficult position.

with being an habitual criminal was his failure to report to the police,[1] or that he was a fugitive from justice;[2] or his failure or refusal to give an account of himself when requested by the police to do so.[3] The latter was never in itself sufficient evidence, together with the three statutory previous convictions, to establish that the prisoner was " leading persistently a dishonest or criminal life "; but it was important as tending to lessen, to a considerable degree, the weight of the onus of proof placed on the Crown. On arrest, the prisoner was asked by the police to give an account of himself—if he did so he knew that his story would be carefully checked and that if substantial errors or omissions were found in it they would tell heavily against him; if he refused to commit himself he knew that this also would tell heavily against him before any jury. However, this was a dilemma in which the offender's mode of life had placed him, and the practice of the police in so questioning him when arrested, and in making one of the alternative allegations set out in paragraph (j) of Appendix B seems wholly legitimate, and certainly infinitely preferable to the American equivalent practice—the " third degree ".

Finally, in considering the evidence that was frequently advanced to prove the prisoner's persistently dishonest life, let us advert to one type of evidence the importance of which was variously estimated in pronouncements by the courts, in statements by the Director of Public Prosecutions, and in expletives by habitual criminals themselves—the prisoner's employment record subsequent to his last discharge from prison.

First, the judicial opinion. It was clear that whether the prisoner had done any honest work during his period of freedom between discharge and arrest was a most important issue;[4] and if he had, the Judge, when summing-up, had to draw the attention of the jury to the merits of such an endeavour.[5] Similarly, the jury's attention had to be drawn to any attempts by the prisoner to obtain employment.[6]

Nothing was more firmly established judicially than that a period of honest work since the prisoner's last discharge from prison

---

[1] Mitchell, 7 Cr. App. R. 283.   [2] Brown, 9 Cr. App. R. 161.
[3] Webber, 8 Cr. App. R. 59 ; Wilson, 12 Cr. App. R. 95 ; White and Shelton, 20 Cr. App. R. 61. See also Appendix B, para. (j.).
[4] Hammersley, 14 Cr. App. R. 118 ; Driscoll, 18 Cr. App. R. 184 ; Winn, 19 Cr. App. R. 1.
[5] Wells, 5 Cr. App. R. 33 ; Winn, 19 Cr. App. R. 1 ; Harry, 21 Cr. App. R. 21 ; Counter, 23 Cr. App. R. 22.
[6] R. v. Jones (1939), 1 All. E.R. 181.

did not of itself constitute any bar to the finding that he was " leading persistently a dishonest or criminal life "; though it was an important factor tending to negative habitual criminality and had to be considered by the court. In Jenning's Case[1] this was affirmed for the first time, it being held that " if a man occupies a day or two of his time in doing work, that does not prevent him from being an habitual criminal." Gradually it became established that a period of honest employment—even a substantial period, or even employment throughout a brief interval of liberty[2]—did not prevent the jury from finding, as a fact, that the prisoner was living a " persistently " dishonest life.[3]

In Hayden's Case,[4] the Court of Criminal Appeal rationalized the fact that honest employment, even if engaged in for a substantial period, did not negative " persistent " criminality on the ground that such work may be a " cloak " for criminal activities. However, this rationalization did not find much favour, and in Hamblin's Case[5] (as yet unreported) the same Court held that " the mere fact that a man is doing some honest work is not to excuse him, upon the allegation that he is persistently leading a dishonest life, if at the same time, whether using the honest work as a cloak or not, he has in fact committed acts of dishonesty." Thus, honest employment was just one of the important factors that the jury had to consider in assessing habitual criminality, but it was not conclusive on this issue.

Secondly, let us consider the opinion held by habitual criminals themselves, and other criminals, of the importance of work to that issue. In Williams's Case, Channel J. said :[6] " The mere fact that he has done some work is not a sufficient defence to this charge, although an impression to this effect has got about among the criminal classes." In calling it an impression Mr. Justice Channel

---

[1] 4 Cr. App. R. 120.   [2] Bennett, 9 Cr. App. R. 225 ; Smith, 8 Cr. App. R. 150.
[3] Martin, 5 Cr. App. R. 31 ; Wells, loc. cit. ; Hayden, 6 Cr. App. R. 214 ; Martin, 7 Cr. App. R. 227 ; Heard, 7 Cr. App. R. 80 ; Keane and Watson, 8 Cr. App. R. 12 ; Williams, 8 Cr. App. R. 49 ; Hammersley, loc. sit. ; Driscoll, loc. cit. ; Winn, loc. sit. ; Hayes, 19 Cr. App. R. 157 ; Lavender, 20 Cr. App. R. 10 ; Harry, loc. cit. ; Counter, loc. cit.
[4] 6 Cr. App. R. 213. An analogy is frequently drawn between " habitual drunkenness " and " habitual criminality ", it being pointed out that just as the habitual drunkard has his sober moments and yet remains legally an " habitual drunkard ", so the habitual criminal need not permanently deny himself the pleasures of honest employment. See also Baggott's Case, 4 Cr. App. R. 167 for a judicial explanation of the importance of honest employment on the issue of habitual criminality.
[5] Heard in the Court of Criminal Appeal on October 15th, 1948.
[6] 8 Cr. App. R. at p. 50.

underestimated the force of this belief among criminals and habitual criminals—it was an article of faith. Like many other articles of faith it was not susceptible to logical controversion; and those who were sentenced to preventive detention despite having been employed for a period between their discharge and subsequent arrest regarded their sentence as just another glaring example of judicial incompetence and prejudice.

Thirdly, there is the opinion of the Department of the Director of Public Prosecutions:

> "The most troublesome matter, however, was to establish that the accused was ' persistently ' leading a dishonest or criminal life. The practical effect of this requirement, as interpreted, was that it was extremely difficult to obtain a conviction if the accused had been in employment for even two or three months after his release from a previous sentence. The ' old hands ' were well aware of this and, although they frequently used the employment as a cloak for criminal activities, this fact was not easy to establish. This difficulty was particularly marked in the war years when, apart from the ease with which employment could be obtained, prisoners were directed into employment or the Army on their release from prison."

How, then, are we to reconcile these three apparently conflicting views ? Their reconciliation is to be found in the day-to-day operation of Part II of the Act. The cases we have cited as establishing that honest employment was no bar to conviction as an habitual criminal were the exceptions—exceptions where other criminal tendencies and habits of the prisoner were so marked that they counterbalanced his period of honest employment. In the majority of cases, such employment was sufficient to protect the prisoner from conviction as an habitual criminal provided his defence was conducted with even moderate skill;[1] for it was not difficult to advance an argument, emotionally attractive to the jury, that the prisoner's employment did represent a sincere and desperate attempt to throw off the heritage of his past, to turn over a new leaf, to go straight; and many other hackneyed but intriguing clichés could be used to belabour the hearts of a jury already sceptical of the " double punishment " of preventive detention. Thus, though as a question of law the Court of Criminal Appeal placed the fact of the prisoner's employment in its correct perspective as one of the important but not conclusive elements in the issue of habitual criminality, the Courts of first instance hearing this charge with the assistance of a

---

[1] And it was held to be desirable that a prisoner charged as an habitual criminal should be defended by counsel : Andrews, 27 Cr. App. R. 12.

jury found that, as a matter of practice, whether the prisoner had or had not worked honestly was a vital and normally decisive point. Juries would hesitate long before convicting as an habitual criminal a prisoner who had worked honestly for any appreciable time. Practical considerations were cumulative because as juries tended to acquit such prisoners, so the Director of Public Prosecutions tended to refuse his consent to their prosecution as habitual criminals, and in turn the police tended not to forward such cases for the consideration of the Director of Public Prosecutions with a view to such prosecution. The upshot was that, although legally inaccurate, the expletives of criminals on this point held at least as much truth as the pronouncements of the Court of Criminal Appeal.

(c) Penal Servitude as a condition precedent to Preventive Detention

When the provisions of the Act were being considered in the House of Commons by Standing Committee C, Lord Robert Cecil proposed that after the words " penal servitude ", in Section 10 (1) of the Act, the words " or imprisonment " should be added. His proposal was not accepted, the Government refusing to budge from a dual-track system—a dual-track system involving at least a three-year term of penal servitude before preventive detention could commence. Any greater flexibility than this they would not allow. When the same section was being considered at the Committee Stage in the House of Lords, Lord Kinnaird and Earl Russell moved an amendment to the same effect as Lord Robert Cecil's proposal. Speaking for the Government, Earl Beauchamp rejected this amendment, saying:[1]

> " The Government are anxious to begin, at any rate, by providing that the period of detention should be confined to really hardened criminals, and they could not have a better definition of a hardened criminal than that he had been sentenced by a judge to penal servitude."

Let us now try to discover, from a consideration of decided cases, with what success this requirement did in fact exclude all but " hardened criminals " from preventive detention, and the effect it had on the type of criminals so sentenced.

It was well established that, as a condition precedent to preventive detention, the court had to take such a view of the substantive crime for which the prisoner had been convicted as to think it

---

[1] *Parliamentary Debates*, 4th Series, House of Lords, Vol. 198, Col. 1536.

proper to pass a sentence of penal servitude. Penal servitude[1] could
never be inflicted merely to found the jurisdiction of the court to
impose preventive detention; it had to be warranted by the substantive crime committed.[2] However, in evaluating the substantive
crime for this purpose, the court would take into consideration, in
addition to the details of that crime, the prisoner's previous convictions, his mode of life, and generally all that information which had
been given on the issue of whether he was an habitual criminal;
because the sentence for the substantive crime was not imposed
until after the jury had returned its verdict on the issue of habitual
criminality.[3] Thus, though in theory the punishment for the substantive offence could not be increased to found jurisdiction to
inflict preventive detention, the whole sentence imposed (penal
servitude and preventive detention) would almost inevitably be a
single decision in the mind of the judge—indeed, in Smith's Case,[4]
it was held that in fixing the term of penal servitude, the term of
preventive detention to be imposed must be considered. Nevertheless, the sentence of penal servitude had to be supportable otherwise
than as a condition precedent to the sentence of preventive detention.

Some surprisingly petty offences were held by the Court of
Criminal Appeal to be sufficient to found a sentence of penal servitude as a condition precedent to the infliction of preventive detention
—the larceny of a watch,[5] of a tobacco box,[6] of two shirts which had
been hanging outside a shop throughout the night (by a man of
sixty-five years of age),[7] all sufficed. Similarly, the Court of Criminal
Appeal upheld Turnbull's sentence of penal servitude and preventive
detention, in view of his previous record, notwithstanding the fact
(which unfortunately does not appear in the report) that the property
stolen was a £1 Treasury Note.[8] Minor offences also sufficed in the

---

[1] As has been mentioned, penal servitude was always for a period of at least three
years.
[2] Sweeney, 4 Cr. App. R. 70 ; Jones, 6 Cr. App. R. 1 ; Bell, 10 Cr. App. R. 262 ;
Vincent, 15 Cr. App. R. 19 ; Myers, 16 Cr. App. R. 116 ; Clarke, 17 Cr. App. R. 91 ;
Paul, 18 Cr. App. R. 128 ; Turnbull, 19 Cr. App. R. 155 ; Thomas (and Williams),
20 Cr. App. R. 172 ; and Harry, 21 Cr. App. R. 21.
[3] Turner, 3 Cr. App. R. 103 ; Coney, 17 Cr. App. R. 128.
[4] 3 Cr. App. R. 90. See also Taylor and Coney, 5 Cr. App. R. 168, in which it was
held that in the case of young men where there may be hope of reform the period of
preventive detention should begin as soon as possible. Therefore the sentence of penal
servitude was reduced from five to three years.
[5] Howard, 4 Cr. App. R. 62.
[6] Bell, *The Times* newspaper, November 19th, 1933 (not elsewhere reported).
[7] Jones, 6 Cr. App. R. 142.
[8] 19 Cr. App. R. 155 : information regarding property stolen kindly given by the
Director of Public Prosecutions.

case of men with only three previous convictions, and those not for serious offences—Sweeney, with a criminal record of a larceny, a vagrancy offence, and one assault, was convicted of the larceny of eleven shillings' worth of goods and sentenced to three years' penal servitude and five years' preventive detention;[1] Baggott, who had been previously convicted of stealing some flour, of stealing fowls, and of stealing some brass, was convicted of the larceny of a piece of mutton from a butcher's shop, and sentenced to three years' penal servitude and five years' preventive detention.[2]

The requirement of a term of penal servitude as a condition precedent to preventive detention did not, therefore, fulfil the hopes of those who insisted upon it, and was one of the less desirable provisions of the Act.[3] For many years the successive Judges of the Court of Criminal Appeal agreed in condemning it.

(d) The effect of a previous conviction as an habitual criminal

The first point to note in this context arises directly from the terms of Section 10 (2) (b). That section reads:

" (2) A person shall not be found to be a habitual criminal unless the jury finds on evidence :

(a) . . .

(b) that he has on such a previous conviction [of " crime "] been found to be an habitual criminal *and* sentenced to preventive detention."

The conjunction " and " means, therefore, that a prisoner previously convicted by a jury of being an habitual criminal, but in whose favour the judge had exercised his discretion (or did not regard the substantive offence as meriting penal servitude) and had not imposed preventive detention, did not fall under this provision of the Act.

However, let us now consider those who were both convicted as habitual criminals and sentenced to preventive detention, who were subsequently discharged from prison, committed a " crime ", and were then charged again with being habitual criminals.[4] Was a jury,

---

[1] 4 Cr. App. R. 70.

[2] 4 Cr. App. R. 67 : admittedly his conviction as an habitual criminal was quashed, but not on the grounds of severity of sentence.

[3] Shortly we will consider the substantive crimes pursuant to which prisoners were sentenced to preventive detention over the entire forty-year period.

[4] A previous conviction as an habitual criminal and sentence of preventive detention which was quashed on appeal was not admissible as evidence on a subsequent charge that the prisoner was an habitual criminal : Crowley, 9 Cr. App. R. 198, 201 ; Tyreman, 19 Cr. App. R. 4.

before whom the previous conviction was proved, bound to convict such a prisoner as an habitual criminal ? In other words, was their task limited to establishing the prisoner's identity ?

Until 1924 these questions would have had to be answered in the affirmative, the cases of Davis,[1] Stanley,[2] Vincent,[3] Wilcock,[4] Clarke,[5] and the Scotch case of McDonald v. H.M. Advocate,[6] being quite definite, and clearly limiting the jury's function as we have suggested. However, because a prisoner had previously been sentenced to preventive detention, that did not mean that he had subsequently to be sentenced to preventive detention were he charged with being an habitual criminal—true, the jury were bound to convict him as an habitual criminal; but a discretion still resided in the Court as to whether preventive detention was " expedient for the protection of the public "; and in several cases the courts did not reimpose preventive detention in such circumstances.[7] The finding of habitual criminality thus created an inalienable status,[8] but a status which did not necessarily involve that the particular sentence which had created it—preventive detention—should be inflicted subsequent to a conviction for a " crime " for which penal servitude was imposed.

In 1924, in Norman's Case,[9] the above line of judicial interpretation of Section 10 (2) (b) of the Act was reversed. This case was heard before thirteen Judges of the Court of Criminal Appeal. Travers Humphreys appeared for the Crown and defended the reasoning in the cases we have cited above. The Court divided nine to four, the majority holding that in every case it is a question of fact for the jury whether the prisoner is still an habitual criminal; that this question was not decided by the existence of a previous sentence of preventive detention; and that the prisoner was entitled to call evidence to prove that at the material time he was not an habitual criminal.[10] Mr. Justice Avory read a strong dissenting judgment in which, though he deplored the rigidity of Section 10 (2) (b), he contended that there could be no avoidance by judicial

---

[1] (1917) 13 Cr. App. R. 10 : Previously so decided in the unreported case of Collins heard by the Court of Criminal Appeal in September 1916.
[2] 14 Cr. App. R. 141.   [3] 15 Cr. App. R.19   [4] 16 Cr. App. R. 103.
[5] 17 Cr. App. R 91.   [6] (1917) S.C. (J.) 17.
[7] See for example Stanley 14 Cr. App. R. 41.
[8] On the question of the finding of habitual criminality creating a "status", see Hunter's Case, 15 Cr. App. R. 69.
[9] (1924) 18 Cr. App. R. 81.
[10] This did not mean that the onus of proof of habitual criminality was shifted from the Crown.

interpretation of the continuance of its harsh application, and that
the evil could only be remedied by the legislature.

New hope came into the lives of preventive detainees. Immediately after the judgment in Norman's Case had been given, fifty-six
prisoners sentenced to preventive detention petitioned the Secretary
of State for the exercise of His Majesty's mercy, each alleging that
his case fell within the decision in Norman's Case and that his
sentence of detention ought therefore to be remitted. The Secretary
of State referred these petitions to the Court of Criminal Appeal.[1]
The Court considered all these cases in private and advised that the
term of preventive detention should be remitted in seven of
them.[2]

The decision in Norman's Case was not disturbed,[3] and it had
always to be established that the prisoner was an habitual criminal
at the time when he committed his last offence. This decision did,
however, give rise to one unexpected difficulty—several prisoners,
not having comprehended the ratio decidendi of Norman's Case,
and regarding their status as habitual criminals as permanent, when
asked to plead to the charge of being habitual criminals pleaded
" guilty " under the mistaken supposition that they were merely
thus admitting a previous sentence of preventive detention. So many
did this that it became necessary for the Court of Criminal Appeal
to insist that before such a plea was accepted, its meaning should
have been carefully explained to the prisoner.[4] So much for the
myth of the skilful criminal carefully perusing his Criminal Appeal
Reports for loopholes in the law!

3. The Function of the Director of Public Prosecutions under the Act

The proviso to Section 10 (4) of the Act reads:

" Provided that a charge of being an habitual criminal shall not be
inserted in an indictment :

(a) without the consent of the Director of Public Prosecutions. . . ."

---

[1] Under Section 19 (b) of the Criminal Appeal Act, 1907.

[2] The principle upon which the court acted was to advise remission in every case in
which it was not clear that the petitioner must inevitably have been found to be an
habitual criminal under the law laid down in Norman's Case.

[3] Followed in Scotland in the case of McDonald v. H.M. Advocate (1929) S.C. (J.) 76.

[4] See Wilcock, 16 Cr. App. R. 103 ; Donovan, 19 Cr. App. R. 2 ; and Wallace,
21 Cr. App. R. 70.

In giving or withholding his consent the Director of Public Prosecutions would address himself to every aspect of the case, but certain principles became established. The procedure followed when the police forwarded a case to the department of the Director of Public Prosecutions, seeking consent to the prisoner's indictment as an habitual criminal, was:

(a) Consent was not usually given unless the accused was over the age of thirty years. There was no rule of law that prisoners under that age could not be sentenced to preventive detention,[1] but only in exceptional cases would the Director allow such a prisoner's prosecution as an habitual criminal.

(b) Consent was not usually given unless the accused had previously served a term of penal servitude.

(c) The police report, which accompanied the application, was then perused to see whether the substantive offence for which the prisoner was charged fell within the definition in the Act of a "crime". A mistake in this respect in the report was very rare. Consideration was then given to the question whether the substantive offence was likely to carry a sentence of penal servitude, and on this question the relationship between the accused's previous record and his last offence was important.

(d) The three statutory convictions which it was proposed to prove as part of the formal evidence were then checked to ensure that they fell within the definition of "crime" (though in the case of a man previously sentenced to preventive detention this was not necessary, as only this previous sentence needed to be proved instead of the three statutory convictions).

(e) The information in the report recounting the accused's activities in the interval since his last release was then considered. If he admitted other offences committed in this interval consent was usually given. Equally, consent was usually given in a case where this interval was quite short, for example, two or three weeks. The more difficult cases were those in which this interval extended to a period of

---

[1] Taylor, aged 24, Coney, aged 26 : 5 Cr. App. R. 168 ; Saunders, aged 26 : 7 Cr. App. R. 271 ; Merrall, aged 28 : 18 Cr. App. R. 102 ; Bayley, aged 29 (not reported —heard in the Court of Criminal Appeal on March 8th, 1926) ; Loftus, aged 26 (not reported—Central Criminal Court, October 19th, 1948).

months and the accused had sought employment, whether genuinely or in order to try and avoid conviction as an habitual criminal. This job-hunting was often only a cloak for further criminal activities, but it was not easy to prove this fact by concrete evidence.

(f) There were cases where the prisoner had made some real effort to obtain honest employment, but had found his past record an insuperable obstacle. These were the most difficult cases, and if the period between discharge and arrest was substantial, the Director of Public Prosecutions was unlikely to give his consent.

(g) Where the accused had obtained honest employment and retained it for a period, but relapsed into crime when he could have continued that employment, then consent to his prosecution as an habitual criminal was usually given.[1]

Though that was the thought-process followed in the department of the Director of Public Prosecutions when the police applied to charge a man with being an habitual criminal, it gives no clue to the many facets of each case which had to be considered. It does stress, however, the great importance attached to the question of the criminal's employment since his last discharge and supports the argument we developed on this point.[2]

The table on page 61 reveals better than any words the actual effect of proviso (a) to Section 10 (4) of the Act. It shows, for each of the years 1931 to 1948, the number of cases submitted by the police to the Director of Public Prosecutions for his consent to a charge of habitual criminality, the number of cases in which consent was refused, the number in which consent was given, the number not then sentenced to preventive detention, and the number so sentenced.

From these figures it would appear that the Director of Public Prosecutions had a useful selective effect on the operation of the Act, and certainly saved the courts from wasting much time on assured acquittals. The withdrawal of this function from the Director of Public Prosecutions by the Criminal Justice Act, 1948, may well prove to be a retrograde step.

---

[1] In such cases ground (e) in Appendix B was usually alleged.
[2] See pp. 51-4.

Year	Applications	Consent Refused	Consent Given	Not Sentenced to Preventive Detention	Sentenced to Preventive Detention
1931	61	16	45	21	24
1932	64	11	53	17	36
1933	47	14	33	9	24
1934	55	24	31	6	25
1935	65	21	44	12	32
1936	44	11	33	16	17
1937	49	19	30	15	15
1938	33	7	26	9	17
1939	25	12	13	4	9
1940	21	6	15	4	11
1941	15	6	9	2	7
1942	16	3	13	6	7
1943	25	6	19	3	16
1944	17	3	14	3	11
1945	17	8	9	5	4
1946	39	15	24	7	17
1947	22	7	15	3	12
1948	16	5	11	Nil	11
TOTAL	631	194	437	142	295
Average per year	35·67	10·77	24·28	7·89	16·39

4. THE DETAILS OF PREVENTIVE DETAINEES SENTENCED PURSUANT TO THE ACT

The following table is a statistical reflection of the lingering death of Part II of the Prevention of Crime Act, 1908. For each year of the Act's operation there appears:[1]

> in column I, the number of sentences of preventive detention imposed by the courts in England and Wales;[2]
>
> in column II, the number of men so sentenced;
>
> in column III, the number of those men who actually began preventive detention. This number differs from that in column II owing to the absence of

[1] The information appearing in columns I and II was extracted from the annual reports of the Commissioners of Prisons and the Directors of Convict Prisons (hence the gap in the years 1946-8 for which years Table X in Appendix 8 was not published) ; while the information in columns III and IV was gathered from records in the possession of the Prison Commissioners kindly made available for this study.

[2] Similar figures for Scotland appear on p. 78 of the Report of the Departmental Committee on Persistent Offenders, 1932, Cmd. 4090.

(a) those whose sentences or convictions were quashed by the Court of Criminal Appeal;

(b) those who died, committed suicide, or were certified insane during their term of penal servitude; and

(c) those whose sentences of preventive detention were remitted by the Secretary of State whilst they were serving their term of penal servitude.

in column IV, the average age at the time of sentence of those men who actually began terms of preventive detention.

	Number sentenced to Prev. Detent.		Men who actually began Preventive Detention			Number sentenced to Prev. Detent.		Men who actually began Preventive Detention	
Year	Total	Males	Number	Average Age when Sentenced	Year	Total	Males	Number	Average Age when Sentenced
	I	II	III	IV		I	II	III	IV
1909*	46	45	42	44·5	1929	29	29	26	46·6
1910	178	177	162	38	1930	37	37	33	43·9
1911	57	55	53	40·2	1931	20	20	15	48·5
1912	89	88	82	41·1	1932	39	37	34	48·8
1913	67	64	57	41·8	1933	21	19	18	42·9
1914	43	42	39	42·9	1934	22	21	18	46·9
1915	11	11	11	46·6	1935	31	28	26	51·3
1916	21	21	21	42·3	1936	21	20	20	48·3
1917	22	20	19	46·8	1937	13	13	13	45·5
1918	20	20	20	47·2	1938	17	17	12	52·6
1919	20	19	19	42·4	1939	9	9	7	55·7
1920	44	41	36	44·8	1940	9	8	3	43
1921	61	58	54	45·5	1941	7	6	5	50·8
1922	35	33	30	44·2	1942	11	10	5	45·2
1923	27	27	24	49·7	1943	13	11	9	45
1924	38	38	36	44·4	1944	8	8	4	46·7
1925	27	27	24	49·5	1945	3	3	2	42
1926	23	22	22	44·2	1946	not		15	53·1
1927	41	39	33	47·4	1947	published		13	45·5
1928	31	31	27	45·7	1948			6	45
					Total			1,095	

*August to December only.

Thus, from the introduction of the Act to the end of the year 1948, 1,095 male prisoners began sentences of preventive detention; an average of over twenty-seven per year. Should further proof be required that this represented an insignificant proportion of the habitual criminals who could properly be so declared, reference should be made to p. 27 of the Introduction.

Considering those who were sentenced to preventive detention over this period (column 1 of the above table), let us discuss:

(a) the length of the term of preventive detention imposed on them;

(b) the substantive " crime " for which they were sentenced to penal servitude as a condition precedent to their preventive detention; and

(c) the number of their previous convictions.

(a) The term of preventive detention imposed

This information appears in Appendix B, Table X, of the annual reports of the Prison Commissioners, and has been published for the years 1928 to 1945 (inclusive). From the records kindly made available to me by the Prison Commissioners, similar information for the years 1909 (last five months) to 1927 (inclusive), and 1945 to 1948 (inclusive), was deduced. However, the data in these records relates to those who actually began their sentences of preventive detention (column III in the above table). The following table is a synthesis of the official reports and the unpublished records.

In respect of 1,159 prisoners sentenced to preventive detention, sentence of detention for:[1]

5 years was imposed on 950 prisoners				
5½ „	„	„	„	2 „
6 „	„	„	„	52 „
7 „	„	„	„	106 „
8 „	„	„	„	17 „
10 „	„	„	„	32 „

I have been unable to discover any principle or principles upon which the term of preventive detention to be imposed was determined ; but it is strange that not even one prisoner was committed to preventive detention for nine years.

Five years' preventive detention was, therefore, the norm, accounting for nearly 82 per cent. of all such sentences.

[1] These figures do not take account of alterations to sentences made by the Court of Criminal Appeal—usually that court did not vary the term imposed when it allowed the sentence to stand ; occasionally it decreased the term ; and very exceptionally it increased the period of preventive detention originally inflicted (in 1946, one sentence of three years' penal servitude and five years' preventive detention was increased to three years' penal servitude and seven years' preventive detention).

(b) The substantive " crime " last committed

As we have seen, the substantive crime (as defined in the Act) committed by the potential habitual criminal had to be of such a nature as to merit a sentence of at least three years' penal servitude before preventive detention could be imposed. Between the years 1928 and 1945 (inclusive), the Prison Commissioners published in their annual reports[1] the details of the most serious of the prisoner's crimes for which he was sentenced to penal servitude before his sentence of detention was inflicted; and they did this by reference to the classification of offences adopted in the annual volumes of criminal statistics. The following table is an amalgamation of the information they published. Only male habitual criminals are considered, and the most serious of the last offences of the 325 who were sentenced during the period of eighteen years (1928-1945) can be classified as follows:

Criminal Statistics Ref. No.	Type of Offence	Number Convicted
5	Wounding	3
27	Sacrilege	2
28	Burglary	48
29	Housebreaking	77
30	Shopbreaking	44
32	Entering with intent to commit a felony	10
33	Possession of housebreaking tools, etc.	12
34	Robbery	2
36	Extortion by threat	1
38	Larceny of horses and cattle	5
39	Larceny from the person	5
40	Larceny in house	10
41	Larceny by a servant	1
44 to 49	Simple and minor larcenies	66
50	Obtaining by false pretences	18
51	Frauds by agents, etc.	2
54	Receiving stolen goods	6
56	Arson	1
58 & 59	Forgery and uttering	7
60	Coining	1
61	Uttering counterfeit coin	4
		325

[1] Appendix 8, Table X.

Thus, only seven of these 325 habitual criminals were sentenced to preventive detention pursuant to a crime involving violence, the threat of violence, or danger to the person; the remainder having been indicted for offences against property, many of which were of a relatively minor nature. Certainly, judging from their last offence, many of these 325 prisoners can in no wise be regarded as " dangerous " habitual criminals.

In a memorandum by the Secretary of State, prefixed to a draft of rules prescribing conditions to be applied in preventive detention, which was laid before Parliament in 1911,[1] the following statement appears:

> " Only the great need of society to be secured from professional or dangerous criminals can justify the prolongation of the ordinary sentences of penal servitude by the addition of such preventive detention."

And later:

> " The point of most importance, and also of most difficulty, is to restrict the selection to cases where the last offence is in itself substantial and serious. . . . The general test should be—is the nature of the crime such as to indicate that the offender is not merely a nuisance but a serious danger to society ? "

It is clear that a considerable number of the 325 crimes listed above cannot be regarded as fulfilling the conditions of this test.

Earlier in our discussion of the Act it was shown that the Act was intended to strike at the " dangerous professional " type of criminal, and the Home Secretary's test, if applied, would have fulfilled this intention. Unfortunately, in actual practice, the Act not infrequently impinged on criminals who can only be regarded as the habitual petty delinquent type, more of a nuisance than a danger to society, helpless rather than determined criminals.

(c) The number of previous convictions

In Part II of this book we shall analyse in some detail the records of thirty-two preventive detainees; but in the meantime, to conclude our statistical presentation of the information relating to a larger number of them, let us consider the previous convictions

---

[1] To be found in Appendix 4 to the Report of the Departmental Committee on Persistent Offenders, 1932, Cmd. 4090.

of those 325 detainees whose substantive offences we tabulated above.[1]

None of these habitual criminals had only the three statutorily required previous convictions. Their previous convictions were:

			Prisoners
Four to ten previous convictions	..	.. ..	76
Eleven to twenty previous convictions	..	..	186
More than twenty previous convictions	..	..	63
			325

Only seven of our 325 detainees had not been sentenced to penal servitude at least once before their conviction as habitual criminals. Assuredly none of them was a stranger either to the criminal courts or to the prisons.

5. THE FUNCTION OF ADVISORY COMMITTEES UNDER THE ACT

Section 14, sub-sections 4 and 5, of the Act provided for the appointment of committees to advise the prison authorities on matters connected with preventive detainees.[2] Rule 184 of the Statutory Rules and Orders for the government of prisons[3] provided that:

"The Advisory Committee appointed under Section 14 (4) of the Prevention of Crime Act, 1908, shall meet at the prison at least once a quarter, and as occasion arises shall make such individual reports on prisoners as will assist the Commissioners in advising the Secretary of State in regard to the discharge of such prisoners on licence."

Though there were other duties for these Advisory Committees, their most important function was to advise the Prison Commissioners when the preventive detainee should be conditionally discharged; and it is to this function that we shall now address ourselves.

The members of these Advisory Committees were the same type of people who become members of prison visiting committees or boards of visitors; and indeed when preventive detainees were held in the same prison as other prisoners the Advisory Committee was usually composed of exactly the same people as made up the visiting

---

[1] This information is also extracted from Appendix 8, Table X, of the annual reports of the Commissioners of Prisons and Directors of Convict Prisons for the years 1928 to 1945.

[2] See Appendix A.   [3] S.R. & O., 1937, No. 809.

committee or board of visitors. The purpose of such bodies was to bring to penal administration the clear common sense of the intelligent layman. It was customary for the Governor of the prison not to be present at the deliberations of the Advisory Committee,[1] so that the preventive detainee could see in that committee the just guardian of his hopes of discharge—a guardian largely independent of local official interference.

On the shoulders of the Advisory Committee was placed a tremendously heavy task; they had to decide the likelihood of the detainee's relapse to criminal activities, and on this decision to evaluate the competing claims of society to security and of the detainee to his freedom. In making this decision they were guided by the following data:

  (*a*) the detainee's criminal record as shown in the list of his previous convictions and sentences;

  (*b*) the records of any previous terms of penal servitude he served (but not previous periods of imprisonment);[2]

  (*c*) a précis prepared by the police of the information at their disposal; but concentrating mainly on the last offence he committed and its background;

  (*d*) the record of the detainee's activities and behaviour during his current term of penal servitude and preventive detention;

  (*e*) the medical record of the detainee, with the medical officer's comments;

  (*f*) the chaplain's estimation of the prisoner;

  (*g*) the governor's estimation of the prisoner;

  (*h*) their own opinion of the detainee gathered from regular interviews at which he was brought before them (cleaned and on his very best behaviour).

The fact is that this information was insufficient for the prognostic purposes to which it was applied, and provided little insight into the character of the offender, and therefore into the likelihood of his

---

[1] By contrast, at Parkhurst Prison where the detainees were held, the Governor was present and took part in the deliberations of the visiting committee or board of visitors.

[2] Such penal servitude records (" convict records ") are destroyed when a sentence of penal servitude was followed by a ten-year interval or more before the next penal servitude sentence. Previous Borstal records, when available, are the most valuable of all such records, and give some picture of the detainee's background. The Borstal record will be at the advisory committee's disposal only if the prisoner's first period of penal servitude followed his Borstal detention (if any) within ten years, and if not more than ten years intervened between penal servitude and preventive detention, or one penal servitude and another. Even in these circumstances it is not always available.

reform. Criminal and police records concentrate, by their very nature, on one aspect of the prisoner's life; and estimations of an individual's character made while he is in prison are notoriously unreliable—the " good " prisoner is either institutionalized or cunning, and he is not necessarily, or even probably, the " good " citizen. In the excursus to Part I the above bald contention concerning the inadequacy of the data at the Advisory Committee's disposal will be supported, and a remedy suggested. In the meantime this deficiency need not be stressed, since it is supported to a large extent by the actual practice of the Advisory Committees over the past forty years.

Between August 1909, when the Act came into force, and December 1st, 1948, when the relevant records were consulted,[1] 370 prisoners were discharged as " P. D. Expirees "—that is to say, having served their full term of preventive detention.[2] Over the same period, 892 prisoners were discharged on licence (" P. D. Licensees ").[3]

The " expirees " are made up of those who were returned to preventive detention, their licences having been revoked, and those who were obviously incorrigible criminals and intractable prisoners. With each succeeding year their numbers tended to diminish, and a large proportion of preventive detainees were discharged on licence before the end of their sentence.

Now let us consider the 892 licensees and observe how the Advisory Committee's discretion as to when a detainee should be conditionally discharged was gradually abandoned in favour of a rigid system—a rule-of-thumb and predictable date of discharge which relieved the committee of the heavy burden of making this decision in any but exceptional cases. From 1912 to 1914 inclusive, fifteen detainees were conditionally discharged—one after four months' detention; seven after between one year two months and

---

[1] The information which follows was made available by the very great courtesy of the Prison Commissioners, and comes from a perusal of their records of " P.D. Expirees " and " P.D. Licensees ". The list of P.D. Expirees shows : Serial number, convict number, name, sentence, place and date of conviction, date penal servitude determined, date of release, remarks. The list of P.D. Licensees shows all that shown for Expirees plus licence number, date licensed, date preventive detention expired.

[2] This does not mean 370 individuals because several individuals have been discharged as " P.D. Expirees " on two or even three occasions.

[3] Again, not 892 individuals for the same reason. Further it must be noted that pursuant to one sentence of preventive detention a prisoner could be both a " P.D. Licensee " and a " P.D. Expiree "—discharged on licence, licence revoked, and then kept the full term (or even let out on another licence).

one year seven months' detention; and seven after between two years one month and two years eight months' detention. Of these fifteen, ten had their licences revoked and were returned to preventive detention, one died a month after release, one was sentenced to preventive detention four years later, and three were successful in so far as they have not since been in penal servitude or preventive detention.[1] Such a large proportion failing on licence tended to make Advisory Committees more wary of early discharge; and though no fixed system of releasing detainees developed, between the years 1915 and 1920 inclusive, discharge was usually granted in the six months after the detainee had served half his term of detention. From 1921 to 1931, the beginning of a rigid system of release is perceptible, and detainees were normally conditionally discharged a few months after serving three-quarters of their sentence of preventive detention. There were, of course, exceptions to these norms; but they were either those whose detention was protracted as punishment for their offences in prison, or curtailed because of the immediate availability of employment and the particular likelihood of success. From 1932 to 1948, virtually all discretion on this question was abandoned by the Advisory Committees, detainees being until 1940 released after serving three-quarters of their sentence of detention, and thereafter after serving two-thirds of it. As these fractions represent the practice of remission of sentences of all convict prisoners (not only detainees), preventive detention had become in fact a rigid, exactly-predetermined sentence. Over the years 1932 to 1948, 371 detainees were released on licence, of whom 340 were released at the termination of the normal period (three-quarters of the sentence until 1940, two-thirds thereafter) and only thirty-one were detained longer because of their bad behaviour as prisoners, or released earlier because of their particular promise.

Thus the Advisory Committees ceased to operate effectively as a licence advising body in the majority of cases. This was, admittedly, the result of administrative policy, but it was a policy having its roots in the difficulty of prognosticating success on licence (much less thereafter). It is submitted that with more adequate information concerning the offender, and with more adequate means of testing the likelihood of his success on licence, the Advisory Committees could have preserved their function of deciding on the date of release

[1] Whether they were subsequently imprisoned is not shown.

of each detainee in relation to his individual qualities. To this question we shall return in the excursus to this Part.

6. The Conditions in Preventive Detention

From 1909 to 1930 preventive detainees were held in a special institution at Camp Hill, near Parkhurst Prison. In 1931, Camp Hill became a Borstal Institution and the detainees were moved to a separate wing of Lewes Prison. In April 1933, Portsmouth Prison, which had been closed since October 1931, was opened as a Preventive Detention Establishment, leaving Lewes as a local prison only. Then, in 1939, on the outbreak of war, Portsmouth was evacuated and the detainees were moved to a separate " hall " in Parkhurst Prison. Camp Hill and Portsmouth had been reserved exclusively for preventive detainees; in Lewes and Parkhurst such detainees were held with other prisoners, but as far as possible segregated from them.

It is natural that over these forty years the preventive detention régime should have changed with experience of this type of prisoner and with changes from one prison to another and from one governor to another.[1] To try to depict these changing circumstances over this period would be of no great value, especially as some excellent descriptions of the conditions in preventive detention are available,[2] and I will therefore concentrate on the treatment accorded the thirty-two detainees held in Parkhurst Prison during the three weeks I spent there in November 1948.

As a background to this discussion, reference should be made to Appendix C, in which those of the Statutory Rules for the government of prisons which were particularly relevant to preventive detainees are reproduced.

---

[1] For example, the availability of extra-mural work at Camp Hill, and of gardens at Lewes and Portsmouth was of great significance.

[2] See for example for preventive detention conditions in :

1913 : 9 Cr. App. R. 201 where an excellent resumé by the Lord Chief Justice of such conditions is to be found.

1924 : The *South Australian Government Gazette*, 1925, Paper No. 72, for a lengthy description of Camp Hill.

1931 : *Report of the Departmental Committee on Persistent Offenders*, 1932, Cmd. 4090, Chapter XIII.

1937 : Sir Leo Page's valuable book, *Crime and the Community*, p. 205, *et seq*.

1939 : An article by Commander F. A. P. Foster, ex-Governor of Portsmouth Preventive Detention Prison, appearing on p. 236 of the *Howard Journal*, Vol. V, No. 4. It was, perhaps, under Commander Foster at Portsmouth Prison that the system inaugurated in 1909 reached its penological zenith.

The preventive detention régime in force in November 1948 is only comprehensible when it is contrasted with the treatment accorded other convicts then in Parkhurst Prison. The detainees were the aristocracy of the prison community[1]—an aristocracy of finance and privilege living in an only slightly controlled capitalist system whose basic means of exchange and measure of value is tobacco (actual money beyond a few pence being contraband).

The fundamental principle of their governance was expressed in Rule 177[2] which required that the conditions of preventive detention should be in no way less favourable than the conditions of penal servitude.

Upon entering preventive detention, the habitual criminal moves from the " hall " in Parkhurst Prison in which he has served at least the last few months of his term of penal servitude, to "C Hall", is immediately given a credit of one shilling, and enters the " first stage " of preventive detention. He will pass through three stages during his detention—the first and second each lasting one year and the third until his discharge. Though these stages are strictly relevant only to his earning capacity, they help to mark off the period of detention for him, and they bring an appreciable improvement in his standard of living. There is also the Penal Grade, which constitutes an extra punishment imposable on preventive detainees because of, and to suit, their ameliorated penal conditions.

The extent of the detainee's economically favourable position in relation to the rest of the community in which he lives will be explained in detail, but as a preamble the secondary differences between the penal life of the ordinary convict and of the preventive detainee must be considered.

One change that the prisoner will perceive as he moves to C Hall will be an improvement in the regard in which he is held by other prisoners. His prison status has risen tremendously, and he is treated with a mixture of sympathy and awe—sympathy because, in the average prisoner's rigid criminological conservatism, the detainee is wronged by society and is suffering a " double " and unjust punishment for his crime; and awe because of his membership of a privileged and wealthy aristocracy. He will also be well

---

[1] As a " penal " community—not as a " criminal " community.
[2] See Appendix C.

received by the other preventive detainees who are delighted to welcome a new member as a butt of conversation and as an event in their tedious existence.

Let us stay with our habitual criminal transferred to C Hall and notice the other changes in his penal régime. His clothing will be replaced by more and better garments in which it will be practicable —which was hardly the case previously—to keep himself neat, presentable and comfortable. He will be segregated, as far as is possible, from other convicts who are not detainees (later we shall consider what contact he has with them). His cell will be unlocked at 7 a.m. until 8.15 p.m., and when he is not at labour he will be able to wander in and out of his cell and associate with the other detainees as he desires—previously association was for him a rare and great privilege, and the long hours locked in his cell a bitter burden. He will be allowed to decorate his cell, and he will be inspired by the lengths to which some of his fellow detainees have proceeded to conceal the fact that they inhabit a prison cell by covering its walls with the portraits of desirable females, painting frescoes, making loose covers for the existing furniture and building extra furniture, putting cushions on chairs, obtaining radio sets and building them into the other furniture, and generally exercising their leisurely wits on baroque interior decoration.

Our detainee will be delighted, after his long term of penal servitude, by the other rooms for his use, and particularly by one rather large room equipped for billiards, table tennis, and many other types of indoor games, as well as having benches and a stove. Here, if he is so minded, he can play snooker from 8 a.m. until his day's labour begins, and thereafter during any breaks in his working day.

Should he desire to increase his reading, he will find that he is still entitled to the weekly allocation of books he formerly received from the general prison library, with the addition of the unrestricted use of the preventive detainees' own library. More weekly and daily papers are available, and he may have up to four periodicals sent in to him weekly from outside the prison. One Sunday newspaper and one local weekly may also be purchased.

Generally the situation regarding private property is vastly improved, for though even in penal servitude he could, with per-mission, have books sent to him provided that after a reasonable period he handed them on to the prison library to become that library's property, he will now receive such permission more readily and in respect of articles other than books. Further, he will be allowed to keep such private property in his cell and it will be respected by the prison authorities (subject to certain powers of examination and search) and certainly by the other detainees.[1]

He can write to, and be visited by, his relatives and friends much more frequently, and is entitled to write[2] one letter each week, and to be visited once each week.[3] More letters may be permitted by special permission of the Governor.

One particular attraction to our detainee will be the fact that if he can persuade someone outside the prison to send him a battery radio set[4] he will be allowed to keep it in his cell, and to purchase batteries and other equipment to maintain it.

He will eat his meals in company with the other detainees —which is a great improvement on his previous solitary dining— and can supplement his diet in several ways. There are gas rings on which the detainees can cook food or brew tea, the raw materials for the exercise of their culinary skill being given to them in lieu of part of their ration entitlement, or purchased out of their earnings, or grown by them within the prison.[5]

Though preventive detainees are supposedly segregated from other convicts, there are many opportunities for contact between them—at labour, at divine service, and at other times during the week; but owing to one facility peculiar to Parkhurst Prison and available to all the prisoners, for three and a half hours each week unrestricted intercourse between detainees and other convicts takes place. This special facility at Parkhurst is called " the compound ". The compound is a piece of land about the size of the average " soccer " pitch surrounded by a space in which to walk and observe the play, and with two or three smaller fields devoted to basket-ball, baseball and any other sports of the moment. Here on Saturday and Sunday afternoons, weather permitting, the entire prison

---

[1] I am informed that the preventive detainees have a very high regard for one another's property—but then among a privileged class this is to be expected.

[2] Each letter " in " can only be in answer to a letter " out " written by the prisoner.

[3] Though the rather remote situation of Parkhurst Prison (on the Isle of Wight) lessens the advantage of this privilege.

[4] And often the chaplain or some other prison official will help him in this respect. Of course, if he has extra-mural credits he can purchase such a radio himself.

[5] Or stolen from the prison gardens.

population of Parkhurst (except those being punished for prison offences, and those in hospital) disport themselves for one-and-three-quarter hours—football or cricket matches between the various " halls " are played, bets made, and personal contacts renewed.[1] The large number of prisoners in the compound is supervised by a handful of prison officers (usually about twelve) who act only as a token force. The compound functions by consent of the prisoners and with their active co-operation, and there is never any difficulty in controlling the prisoners while they are there—all feuds are temporarily laid aside, all hatchets buried. It is a privilege to which the prisoners are greatly attached and they take great care that the misconduct of any one or any group of them shall not prejudice its availability. As well as making Parkhurst an easier prison to administer, and giving some outlet for the prisoners' gregarious instincts, the compound provides an admirable setting for the preventive detainees to act their acknowledged roles as prison aristocrats, to chat with their acquaintances and friends, and to exercise the advantages resulting from their favourable economic situation.

Let us now advert to the detainees' work, their remuneration, and their expenditure. These can best be illustrated by considering one particular week—that ending November 16th, 1948. During that week, of the thirty-two detainees, fourteen were employed on tagmaking (two pieces of tin joined by a coloured thread and used on Government files), and one on bookbinding—for both of which occupations they were on piece rates and could earn a maximum of one shilling and sixpence per week. The others were employed as cleaners (flat rate of pay: 1s. per week), on " works " (flat rate: 1s. 1½d.), on " miscellaneous tasks " (1s.), and in the gardens[2] (9d.). The period spent at labour each week varied, with these occupations, from twenty to twenty-four hours—an unfortunately brief working week.[3] Other odd tasks, such as barbering, were given to some of these men and extra remuneration paid. Details of their income during the week under review are as follows:[4]

[1] Being an Australian, it was here that I witnessed my first " soccer " match—between two teams of decrepit aged prisoners playing to provide comic relief.
[2] Desirable for its own sake, and because of opportunities of supplementing dietary and therefore income.
[3] This insufficient period of labour must be attributed, here as elsewhere, largely to a shortage of prison staff, in turn attributable to their inadequate remuneration.
[4] The penny deducted from their weekly incomes for the Common Fund goes to the purchase of newspapers and sundry other communal comforts.

Ref. No.	Stage	Occupation	Earnings		Stage Allowance		Gross Total		Common Fund Deduction	Nett Credit	
			s.	d.	s.	d.	s.	d.	d.	s.	d.
1	2	Tagmaking ..	1	6	1	8	3	2	1	3	1
2	1	,,	1	6	1	3	2	9	1	2	8
3	3	,,	1	6	2	0	3	6	1	3	5
4	3	,,	1	6	2	0	3	6	1	3	5
5	3	,,	1	6	2	0	3	6	1	3	5
6	3	,,	1	6	2	0	3	6	1	3	5
7	3	,,	1	6	2	0	3	6	1	3	5
8	2	,,	1	6	1	8	3	2	1	3	1
9	2	,,	1	6	1	8	3	2	1	3	1
10	1	,,	1	6	1	3	2	9	1	2	8
11	1	,,	1	6	1	3	2	9	1	2	8
12	1	,,	1	6	1	3	2	9	1	2	8
13	1	,,	1	6	1	3	2	9	1	2	8
14	2	Bookbinding ..	1	6	1	8	3	2	1	3	1
15	3	Cleaners	1	0	2	0	3	0	1	2	11
16	3	,,	1	3	2	0	3	3	1	3	2
17	3	,,	1	0	2	0	3	0	1	2	11
18	2	,,	1	0	1	8	2	8	1	2	7
19	2	,,	1	1½	1	8	2	9½	1	2	8½
20	1	,,	1	0	1	3	2	3	1	2	2
21	3	Works	1	1½	2	0	3	1½	1	3	0½
22	2	,,	1	1½	1	8	2	9½	1	2	8½
23	2	,,	1	0	1	8	2	8	1	2	7
24	3	Gardens		9	2	0	2	9	1	2	8
25	2	,,		9	1	8	2	5	1	2	4
26	2	,,		9	1	8	2	5	1	2	4
27	2	Miscellaneous	1	0	1	8	2	8	1	2	7
28	1	,,	1	1½	1	3	2	4½	1	2	3½
29	1	,,	1	3	1	3	2	6	1	2	5
30	1	,,	1	1½	1	3	2	4½	1	2	3½
31	1	Old age	1	1½	1	3	2	4½	1	2	3¼
32	3	In hospital				9		9	1		8

During that same week their accounts were debited as follows:

Ref. No.[1]	Articles Purchased	Amount Spent
		s. d.
1	Tobacco and cigarette papers	2 10¾
2	„ „ „ „	2 8¾
3	„ „ chocolates	4 4½
4	„ „ cigarette papers	2 0½
5	Tobacco	3 5
6	„ and cigarette papers	2 0½
7	Tobacco	2 6¾
8	Tobacco and cigarette papers	1 10½
9	„ „ „ „	3 0¾
10	Chocolates and toffee bar..	1 8½
11	Tobacco	2 0½
12	Tobacco and vinegar	1 10½
13	Nil	—
14	Tobacco, cigarette papers, one tea chest[2]	6 10½
15	Tobacco and cigarette papers	2 11
16	„ „ „ „ and matches	3 8¾
17	Tobacco	2 6¾
18	„ and cigarette papers	2 0½
19	„ „ „ „	1 10¾
20	„ „ „ „	1 11½
21	„ „ „ „	1 10½
22	Tobacco	2 7¼
23	„	2 7
24	„	3 5
25	„ cigarette papers, toffee bar	2 4¾
26	Nil	—
27	Tobacco and cigarette papers	1 10½
28	„ chocolates	2 4½
29	Nil	—
30	Tobacco and cigarette papers	2 7
31	„ „ a bottle of red dye[3]	.2 2½
32	Tin of plum jam	1 4

[1] These numbers refer to the prisoners in the previous table.
[2] The tea chest costs 1s. 6d. and is used to build furniture for the cell.
[3] Also for purposes of interior decoration.

Four prisoners, in addition to the above, spent on their radio sets:

Ref. No.	Articles or Service	Amount Spent
		s. d.
3	Accumulator charging	9
14	„ „	9
7	Acid and accumulator charging	1 9
19	Battery and grid bias	16 7

Preventive detainees were, in short, given many more privileges and were in a sounder financial position than other convicts (whose total income averaged 10d. per week), and they were subjected to as little official interference as possible.

But lest it be thought that they wallowed in luxury and comfort like the *Punch* burglar, it must be stressed that their lot was boring, wearisome and hopeless; living in a small group, knowing each other all too well, with too little work to occupy their attention or teach them diligence, and no training to develop any latent skills they might possess, and with few intellectual resources, the dull and burdensome weeks passed like months, and a life of fantasy absorbed more and more of their attention.[1] This will become clearer when we analyse, in Part II of this work, the qualities and histories of these thirty-two detainees. The Persistent Offenders Committee accurately epitomised preventive detention as follows:[2]

> " The great defect of the preventive detention system is that, while the life of a preventive detention prisoner is more comfortable and less irksome than the life of a penal servitude man, it is an empty life. There is little to stimulate interest or mental activity."

6. General Evaluation of the Act

Though preventive detention is not intended to be a reformative technique, it would be interesting to know the later convictions of those who have been so sentenced. Unfortunately this information is not available.[3]

---

[1] One great disadvantage of Parkhurst Prison was that there were very few official prison visitors. This was particularly unfortunate since prisoners were there detained for protracted periods.

[2] *Report of the Departmental Committee on Persistent Offenders*, 1932, Cmd. 4090, p. 57.

[3] What information that has been kept about their later convictions is presented hereafter. It does not tell us all their later convictions, but only those involving punishment by a protracted period of imprisonment.

Nevertheless, in the records held by the Prison Commissioners in which " P.D. Expirees " and " P.D. Licensees " are registered, and which we considered above, a note is made in the " remarks " columns when the discharged detainee is later sentenced to penal servitude; or when he dies shortly after release; or—in the case of a licensee—when his licence is revoked. This information is not very satisfactory as it does not tell us whether the discharged prisoner was or was not later convicted of a crime and sentenced to imprisonment, or to any punishment other than penal servitude. However, keeping that fact in mind, it is worth recording that:

(a) of the 370 preventive detainees discharged on the expiration of their sentences, 6 died or were certified insane within six months of their discharge; 218 were later sentenced to penal servitude; and 146 were not later so sentenced. Thus, defining " success " extremely generously as the absence of subsequent committal to penal servitude, this was achieved in 40 per cent. of the expirees.

(b) Of the 891[1] preventive detainees discharged on licence, 10 died[2] or were certified insane within six months of their discharge; 584 were later sentenced to penal servitude or had their licences revoked; and 297 were neither so sentenced nor returned to preventive detention. Thus, defining " success " generously as non-revocation of licence and no later sentence of penal servitude, there was just under 34 per cent. " success " amongst the licensees.[3]

In 1928, the Prison Commissioners published a report[4] on the first twenty years of the Act's operation, including information concerning later convictions of the preventive detainees discharged during the years 1920 to 1926 (inclusive). At the end of 1928, it was found that of the 81 men who had been licensed or discharged absolutely over this period of seven years, 8 had died or were in asylums for the insane, and only 7 had not reverted to crime. Not

---

[1] Here, as in (a), an individual can appear twice or even more frequently. See p. 68.
[2] Here are not included those preventive detainees discharged during the war years 1914-18, 1939-45, and who were killed in action. One of them, before his death in 1916, received the M.M. and the D.C.M.
[3] Unfortunately, when a licence is revoked, a subsequent sentence of penal servitude is not always recorded, thus preventing what would have been an interesting comparison between the " success " of expirees and of licensees on the basis on which we defined " success " in (a) above.
[4] Report of the Commissioners of Prisons and the Directors of Convict Prisons for the year 1928.

counting the former there was, therefore, a " success " of only 9·2 per cent.

It would seem that between 80 per cent. and 90 per cent. of all preventive detainees have reverted to crime on their discharge; but it must always be remembered that the object of preventive detention is not reformation. Were we able to state statistically the effect of the Act on serious crimes committed by recidivists, we could judge accurately its success or failure. This being impossible, let us proceed to a brief evaluation of the Act, drawing together the arguments we have already advanced.

The chief advantage of the Act was that it gave the prison authorities experience in administering preventive detention, and has served as an introduction to a new, more efficient system of treatment for habitual criminals. No comments will be made on the preventive régime introduced in 1909 and its later modifications. The penal authorities have benefited from their experience with this type of punishment, and as they had so few detainees to deal with at any one time they could hardly develop a system of detention completely adapted to its purpose.

Another advantage of the Act must also be admitted—by prolonging the incarceration of the criminals who were sentenced to preventive detention it must have prevented several thousand housebreakings and innumerable larcenies.[1]

Its disadvantages have been mentioned above, and it will suffice if we now summarise them. Before doing so, one practical difficulty that hindered the efficient operation of the Act, and which we have not so far mentioned, must be explained. One of the reasons why the police submitted relatively so few cases to the Director of Public Prosecutions with a view to their prosecution as habitual criminals was the short period of time available to them in which to conduct the rather elaborate enquiries necessary for a conviction under the Act. Full details had to be obtained concerning the accused's mode of living since his release from prison—often a matter of considerable difficulty if he had been moving about the country. It was also necessary to arrange for police representatives to be available to give strict proof of the three statutorily required previous convictions, and the consent of the Director of Public Prosecutions to the charge

---

[1] Whether this prevention was bought at too high a cost, and whether preventive detention also prevented the reformation of some who were subjected to it, are imponderables.

had to be obtained. All this had to be done in time to enable seven clear days' notice to be given to the accused that it was intended to insert a charge of being an habitual criminal in the indictment; and this notice had to contain accurate particulars of the previous convictions and other grounds which were to be relied upon to prove his habitual criminality. Since 1908 the average time between arrest and trial has shortened considerably, and this, combined with the shortage of police man-power, meant that fewer cases could be presented to the Director of Public Prosecutions for his consent.

Now to summarise the other disadvantages we have noted:

(1) The Act sought to protect the individual's rights by means of procedural complications—always a capricious protection.

(2) The Act was aimed at the " professional " and " dangerous " criminal—it tended to press largely upon the persistent minor offender, the habitual nuisance. The requirement of penal servitude as a condition precedent to preventive detention did not prevent this.

(3) The Act reached an insignificant proportion of the criminals who should have been declared habituals and sentenced to preventive detention.

(4) There is a widespread belief that one of the reasons why the Act was not more extensively applied was because it introduced a dual-track system of punishment, and especially because it required a term of penal servitude as a precursor to preventive detention. Whether or not a dual-track system more logically conforms to our ethical theory of punishment, it was certainly a tactical error to insist on it in 1908.

CHAPTER THREE

APPLIED COMPARATIVE LAW

1. TECHNIQUE

" COMPARATIVE Law ", Professor Gutteridge affirms, " denotes a method of study and research and not a distinct branch or department of the law."[1] Unfortunately, it is a method regarded with some considerable scepticism in this country where the contention of many is that English qualities of character, and social and political conditions, are so different from those of other peoples, and other countries, as to render the experience of the latter of little practical value. In the recent debates on capital punishment in the Houses of Parliament this contention was frequently made and widely accepted. Amongst other delusions implicit in this erroneous idea is a misconception of the purpose of studies in comparative law.

Nor has the comparative method found more than verbal acceptance among the majority of English jurists who continue to pay lip-service to it as a fine jurisprudential method, while themselves rarely adopting it.

There is a generally recognised division between " Descriptive Comparative Law ", on the one hand, and " Comparative Legislation " or " Applied Comparative Law " on the other,[2] the former being concerned mainly to catalogue and describe the various rules of law of two or more legal systems without seeking to apply this knowledge, the two latter involving a use of the comparative method " with a definite aim in view, other than that of obtaining information as to foreign law."[3] It would appear that this division is warranted as an organisational notion, the collection of information on various legal systems being logically divisible from the use

[1] *Comparative Law*, p. 1. Cambridge University Press, 1946.
[2] Professor Julius Stone in his excellent introduction to *The Province and Function of Law*, which he justifiably calls *The Province of Jurisprudence Redetermined*, uses the term " Comparative Jurisprudence ". Legal definitions being semantically confused and uncertain it is a matter of taste whether one adopts the term " Comparative Law " or " Comparative Jurisprudence ", though historically there is more justification for the former, the latter involving too many overtones as to the place of such a study in juristic endeavour.
[3] *Comparative Law*, p. 9.

made of that information ; but for our purposes it is not important, for there does not exist a comprehensive and modern collection of the details of habitual criminal legislation and its effects in various countries, and it is necessary to collate such information with the particular purpose we have in view—to understand habitual criminal legislation and its operation. Because the " law in action " is as important to this research as the " law in books ", the term " Comparative Legislation ", stressing as it does the formal character of the rules of law, is here rejected, and the analysis undertaken is termed a study in " Applied Comparative Law ".

" The success or failure of a particular policy in dealing with crime has its lessons, not only for the country which has made the experiment, but for all countries which have the like problem to solve. The diffusion of knowledge of the steps which are being taken in other countries to combat crime is, consequently, a matter of urgency and importance."[1] This is particularly true of that branch of criminal law dealing with the habitual criminal. Whatever theories of punishment a penal system adopts, wherever it draws the line between morality and crime, it will inevitably be faced with a similar problem, both in practice and law, in the person of the habitual criminal. Whether the prisoner has expiated his crime, whether retributive vengeance has been satisfied, whether he has been used as a means of deterring others and has himself been threatened with a repetition of the suffering he has undergone, or whether he has been subjected to the full force of reformative measures—whatever justification or purposes are adduced for his previous punishments will be of little consequence to the problem he poses if it is practically certain that he will revert to crime upon his discharge. Though we are concerned with a problem whose fundamentals have escaped from the bounds set by most societies to their reactions to crime, it is interesting to observe the relationship in each country between the entire penal system and this small section of it. Though there is not a complete escape from the *volksgeist*, which to Savigny lessened the usefulness of studies in comparative law, this problem as it faces every legal system presents sufficient similarity to make it an admirable subject for research on a comparative plane.[2]

[1] *Ibid*, p. 30.
[2] " In criminal law the many differences of terminology and historical development have not been able to obscure the similarity of social and legal problems which face the different systems." W. Friedmann, *Legal Theory*, p. 286.

Particular attention will be devoted in this work to the habitual criminal law of Australia, Canada, New Zealand, and South Africa, for two reasons: first, because of the close resemblance that exists between the institutions and conditions in those countries and those in England; and secondly, because very little descriptive comparative research has been done on the habitual criminal law of those countries. So as to preserve a perspective between these systems and those we shall consider thereafter, a similar comparative technique will be adopted throughout.[1] Before treating the law of any country, let us consider that technique.

The habitual criminal law and practice of each legal system or group of legal systems will be analysed by means of the following questionnaire:

1. *To whom do such laws apply ?*

Here we discuss the various concatenations of the ten qualities which we mentioned in developing our nominal definition of the habitual criminal (see pp. 5-6). These qualities can be divided into those that are objective and those that are subjective—into the criminal record of the offender, and his personal characteristics. Most legal systems include both objective and subjective factors in their definitions of those who shall be subject to their habitual criminal laws, though this is not, as we shall see, universally true.

Where it is necessary to an understanding of the habitual criminal law we will also refer to legislation dealing explicitly with recidivists.

2. *Who controls their application ?*

We shall here consider those variations of the normal procedure followed by each legal system in prosecuting habitual criminals. For example, for this country we would deal, *inter alia*, with the function of the Director of Public Prosecutions in relation to

---

[1] The habitual criminal laws of the United States of America are not treated in this work. In conception and execution they are of a different character from the European preventive detention legislation. As Professor Brown says : " In the United States the two terms "—recidivist and habitual criminal—" are virtually synonymous . . . and only in a few instances are the recidivist laws of the United States related to the preventive detention Acts or Measures of safety of European countries "—pp. 14 and 16 of *The Treatment of the Recidivist in the United States*, a pamphlet published in the English Studies in Criminal Science Series.

the Prevention of Crime Act, 1908, the special form of indictment required, notice to the accused, and similar procedural matters.

Also under this heading we shall inquire whether the application of preventive detention is mandatory on the judge before whom the habitual criminal appears; or whether a discretion is reserved to him; or alternatively whether, though there is a discretion, it is exercised by a special tribunal and not by the judge trying the last offence for which the habitual criminal stands convicted.

3. *Do such laws envisage aggravation of punishment, or special measures ? If the latter, do the special measures follow, or take the place of, the punishment for the last offence ?*

The issue in the first question needs no further elaboration, having been treated in the Introduction. The second question, however, is one of great importance to an understanding of each country's habitual criminal law, and is perhaps the point of closest contact between the ethical basis of each penal system and its particular provisions for this type of criminal; it is usually phrased as the alternative between the " single-track " or " dual-track " system. Thus, in this country, we have recently changed from the dual-track system of the Prevention of Crimes Act, 1908, in which preventive detention followed penal servitude, to the single-track system, in which preventive detention replaces the punishment for the particular offence for which the habitual criminal was last convicted.

4. *What is the form of sentence imposed ?*

Here there is only a limited number of courses open to the legislature introducing habitual criminal legislation. It may empower the trial judge to specify the term of preventive detention to be served, subject to the power of the penal authorities to release the offender conditionally before the expiration of that term. Alternatively, the sentence the judge imposes may be indeterminate or it may be indefinite. If it is indefinite, it may provide a minimum term to be served before release is possible or a maximum term beyond which the offender cannot be detained, or both. Finally, it may be fixed in relation to some other variable such as the last offence committed, though this is rare.

5. *If a special measure is applied, what is the degree of differentiation between it and other long-term imprisonment ?*

Here we shall advert to the conditions prescribed for preventive detention in each country, and discuss them in relation to the conditions under which other long-term sentences are served. Frequently the legislative provisions throw little light on this (for example, the Prevention of Crime Act, 1908), and we shall inquire as far as possible into the actual penal conditions obtaining for preventive detention.

6. *Who is responsible for the release of habitual criminals, and on what basis are decisions to release them made ?*

7. *What are the conditions under which the habitual criminal is discharged, and what is the juridical status of one so discharged ?*

8. *To what extent are such habitual criminal laws applied ?*

Each country adopts its own particular, and frequently peculiar methods of presenting criminal statistics, and exact comparison between one country and another is rarely possible. For this reason we shall not be able to relate the number of habitual criminals in each country over a stated period to the statistics of recidivism (as here defined) in that country, though this would be the best method of evaluating the extent to which that country applies its habitual criminal legislation. Nor is there any other useful concept to which the habitual criminal statistics of each country can be related and which is not itself variously interpreted in different countries. Accepting, therefore, the absence of exact quantitative comparative data on this point, we shall consider for each country such published statistical information as is most likely to assist us to a reliable qualitative, rather than quantitative, answer to this question.

It is hoped, by the use of this technique, to obtain a clear perception of the multifarious habitual criminal laws; to appreciate the relationships between them; and to appraise their relative merits and demerits. In short, to weigh, measure, collate and compare many different methods of dealing with a similar problem.

2. AUSTRALIA

France, by introducing *relégation* in her law of May 27th, 1885, became the first country to apply legislation adapted specifically to habitual criminals; Norway followed with clause 65 of her criminal code of 1902. Later we will consider both these provisions. The next legal system into which such laws were incorporated was that of New South Wales, where, on September 20th, 1905, the " Habitual Criminals Act "[1] received the Royal Assent. Though this New South Wales legislation had precursors, it can be regarded as the prototype of much European habitual criminal legislation, since it implemented an original scheme for dealing with habitual criminals which served as a model for many other legal systems.

The other Australian States followed the lead given by New South Wales, and Royal Assent was given to such legislation—for Tasmania, Victoria, South Australia in 1907; for Western Australia in 1913; and for Queensland in 1914.

Australia, with a federal system of government and a relatively homogeneous population, is a natural laboratory for criminological research. Though the Commonwealth Parliament, since its establishment in 1901, has exercised certain powers of protecting its legislation by penal sanctions, " the great bulk of the criminal law is a matter for the States."[2] Three States—Queensland, Western Australia, and Tasmania—have adopted criminal codes; while in New South Wales, Victoria and South Australia the common law, as modified by English Statutes passed prior to 1828 and by local Statutes since that date, is still in force. There is appreciable variation between the criminal laws of the various States, and this variation extends to habitual criminal legislation.

It is to be regretted that, for purposes of criminological research, insufficient attention has been given to the excellent opportunities afforded by the six States of Australia with their varying legislative provisions and administrative practices, their homogeneous populations and their similar ecological patterns.

Let us now consider the habitual criminal legislation of each of the States of Australia in order of population, making use of the questionnaire outlined above.

---

[1] Act No. 15 of 1905.
[2] *An Introduction to the Criminal Law in Australia,* by Barry, Paton and Sawer (Macmillan, 1948).

NEW SOUTH WALES

The Crimes Act, 1900, Section 443, provides that:

" In every case where, on the conviction of a person of an offence punishable under this Act, it is made to appear to the judge that the offender has been previously convicted of, and sentenced for an indictable offence, under this or any former Act, such judge may sentence him to a term of punishment, in addition to that prescribed for the offence of which he then stands convicted.

" Such additional punishment shall be :

(1) Where the offence of which he stands convicted is a felony—
    (a) if he has been once previously so convicted and sentenced—penal servitude for ten years, or not less than two years ;
    (b) if he has been twice or oftener previously so convicted and sentenced—penal servitude for fourteen years, or not less than three years.

(2) Where the offence of which he then stands convicted is misdemeanour—imprisonment for eighteen months, or not less than six months."

Thus, as from 1900, New South Wales had a statutory system of aggravation of punishment for recidivists, the imposition of such aggravated punishment being to a certain extent mandatory.

The Habitual Criminals Act, 1905,[1] as amended by the Crimes Amendment Act, 1924,[2] is the Statute by which New South Wales provides for the detention and control of habitual criminals; and references hereunder are to the sections of that Act so amended.

1. *To whom do such laws apply ?*

A schedule to the Habitual Criminals Act, 1905, divides crimes for purposes of that Act into five classes, as follows :

Classes I & II Certain offences causing danger to life or threatening or causing bodily harm.
Class III   Certain sexual offences.
Class IV   Certain offences connected with procuring abortion.
Class V   A long list of offences against property and property rights.

These classifications are defined by reference to sections of the Crimes Act, 1900, and their effect is to include the more serious crimes within each of the above classes—broadly speaking, those offences clearly involving moral turpitude.

[1] Act No. 15 of 1905.   [2] Act No. 10 of 1924.

Making use of this classification, the Act provides[1] that if an offender is convicted of an offence included in any one of the above five classes and if his offence is included in Classes I, II, III or IV and he

> " has been previously so convicted on at least two occasions of an offence within any of such classes ; or has been previously so convicted on one occasion of an offence within any of the said classes and on two occasions of an offence within class V "

or if he is convicted of an offence included in Class V and has previously been convicted

> " on at least three occasions of an offence within the same class and on one occasion of an offence within any other such class "

then,

> " the judge before whom such person is so convicted may in his discretion declare as part of the sentence of such person that he is an habitual criminal."

It is interesting to note that no number of offences against property or property rights are sufficient by themselves and without a serious offence against the person to qualify a person under this Act as an habitual criminal. In this respect the New South Wales legislation is exceptional; and had such a rule been adopted in England in 1908, though even fewer criminals would have been sentenced to preventive detention, these would not have included the many relatively harmless persistent criminals whose offences presented little danger to society.

Thus, of the ten factors suggested in the Introduction as possibly governing the definition of a criminal as "habitual", the New South Wales Act makes use of only three—the number and types of crimes committed, and the extent of danger to the public presented by such crimes. It lays down an entirely objective test, but one which is necessarily modified to suit the subjective characteristics of the particular offender by the permissive nature of the power given the courts.

The width of application of the Habitual Criminals Act, 1905, is shown in Section 3 (4) which provides that previous convictions will be counted for purposes of this Act

> " whether such previous convictions took place within or without New South Wales and either before or after the commencement of this Act."

[1] Section 3.

2. Who controls their application ?

As appears above, it is not mandatory upon the court to declare an offender an habitual criminal even if he qualifies as such. The trial judge " may in his discretion declare as part of the sentence of such a person that he is an habitual criminal."[1]

No special procedure or form of indictment is necessary under this Act.

Until the amending Act of 1924, offenders could be sentenced as habitual criminals only pursuant to conviction on indictment; but by that Act the system was extended to criminals who are convicted summarily. In such cases the discretion rests with the stipendiary or police magistrate, who may direct that an application be forwarded to a Judge of the Supreme Court or of a Court of Quarter Sessions to have the prisoner declared an habitual criminal. However, before a magistrate can make this application, the criminal before him must have been " previously convicted either on indictment or summarily on more than three occasions for an offence comprised in any of the classes in the Schedule "[2] and the last offence for which he was convicted must be of a type falling within a narrower group than those circumscribed by the five classes in the schedule. There is the further discretion residing in the Judge whether to comply with such a request of a stipendiary or police magistrate; but compliance has tended to become virtually an administrative action on the Judge's part.

3. Do such laws envisage aggravation of punishment or special measures ? If the latter, do the special measures follow or take the place of the punishment for the last offence ?

The Habitual Criminals Act, 1907, unlike the recidivist provisions in Section 443 of the Crimes Act, 1900, provides special measures to deal with habitual criminals. It introduced a " dual-track " system, Section 5, ordering that

> " Every habitual criminal shall, at the expiration of his sentence, be detained during His Majesty's pleasure and subject to the regulations, in some place of confinement set apart by the Governor, by proclamation in the *Gazette*, for that purpose."

[1] *Ibid.*   [2] *Ibid.*

4. What is the form of sentence imposed ?

In theory an indeterminate sentence is imposed, but in practice there is a fixed minimum term to be served. After serving the definite sentence for the offence for which he was last convicted, the habitual criminal is detained in a special institution, where he passes through three grades which we shall consider hereafter. At any time the Comptroller-General of Prisons may advise the Minister of Justice that an habitual criminal should be released, but generally the initiative is allowed to come from the detainee himself who may not petition for his release until he is in the senior grade. A minimum period of four years and eight months must be spent in the lower grades before he can reach the most senior grade.

In practice, therefore, it is an indefinite sentence, but in that the Comptroller-General of Prisons has power to allow the habitual criminal to present his application for release before the term of four years and eight months has expired, we must recognise that a potentially indeterminate sentence is in New South Wales imposed on the habitual criminal.

5. If a special measure is applied, what is the degree of differentiation between it and other long-term imprisonment ?

The Act provides merely for the confinement of habitual criminals apart from other prisoners, and that " every person confined as an habitual criminal shall . . . be required to work at some trade or avocation and shall be offered facilities for selling or otherwise disposing of the products of his labour ",[1] of which proceeds some part, to be fixed by regulation, is to be paid to him. However, the regulations that have been made to implement the Act are comprehensive, and being the forerunners of similar measures in other States of Australia, and indeed in other countries, they merit detailed consideration. The " regulations to be observed in places of confinement proclaimed under the Habitual Criminals Act, 1905," were promulgated in the *New South Wales Government Gazette* on July 2nd, 1913.[2] Since then there have been only minor amendments to these regulations, which will be mentioned where apposite, the main analysis being focussed on the 1913 regulations.

Regulations 2 and 3 provide for a Consultative Committee whose duties are confined to habitual criminals. This committee

---

[1] Section 6.   [2] Number 106.

consists of the visiting justice, the visiting surgeon, visiting chaplains, the governor of the prison, and any other person appointed by the Comptroller-General of Prisons. Quarterly meetings are held, and such extra meetings as may be found necessary. The visiting justice presides, minutes are kept, and, if it is a regular quarterly meeting, each habitual criminal is brought before the committee and interviewed. The committee also considers all promotions or reductions in grade, punishments awarded, marks earned, requests entered in the request book, and all other necessary details of the treatment accorded detainees.

The visiting justice, visiting surgeon, and visiting chaplains have duties in relation to habitual criminals apart from their work on the Consultative Committee. These duties are defined by regulations 4 to 8. The visiting justice has similar powers of hearing and determining charges against detainees to those he has for other prisoners in New South Wales, but for the former it is his duty also, on each obligatory weekly visit to their place of detention, to consult with the various officers concerned respecting their industry, conduct and progress. Further, he must interview all detainees on such occasions and carefully investigate any complaints made to him. Similarly, the visiting surgeon and visiting chaplains are required to give particular attention to habitual criminals.

Thus the Consultative Committee is an informed and interested authority competent to give careful attention to each habitual criminal in the indefinite stage of his imprisonment, and it is far from being a mere rubber-stamp for the use of the governor of the prison.

Regulation 9 provides that

" The prisoners [used throughout these regulations to refer specifically to habitual criminals] will be dealt with under a progressive stage system by which they will practically determine their own treatment as regards the enjoyment of privileges or the reverse. They will be classified into four grades—the lower, the intermediate, the higher, and the special. The lower will be divided into two sub-grades—the penal and the ordinary. Prisoners in the intermediate, the higher and the special grades will be competent to earn various privileges for which those in the lower grade will not be eligible. Every prisoner will have a separate cell in which he will sleep, have his meals, and keep his belongings."

Upon completing the definite portion of his sentence, the habitual criminal is placed in the intermediate grade. " From this he can rise to the higher grade by industry and good conduct, and can fall to either division of the lower grade, as the result of idleness or any offence against good order."[1] The industry and good conduct necessary for an elevation in grade are measured by a " marks system ". Each prisoner is tasked according to his ability and is able to earn a maximum of seven marks per week. In case of illness, industry marks may be allowed as if they had been earned. Also, for good conduct, a prisoner may earn a further maximum of seven marks per week. He thus has a marks potential of 14 per week. Al' arks are awarded by the governor of the prison after he has conferred with the officers immediately controlling the prisoner; and such awards are submitted to the visiting justices for his confirmation, and finally approved by the Consultative Committee.

A detainee is not eligible for promotion from the intermediate to the high grade until he has earned 1,400 marks (minimum of 100 weeks), nor from the higher grade to the special grade until he has earned 2,000 marks in the higher grade (a further 142 weeks at least). Before being eligible for promotion in grade he must also have earned full marks for a continuous period of nine months immediately preceding his promotion. Eligibility for promotion does not, as of right, ensure such promotion; but as a rule such a combination of time, industry and good conduct will be so rewarded.

For those who, having been released on licence, are recommitted whilst on licence, the marks system recommences; and again they start in the intermediate grade. This time, however, they have to earn only 730 marks to proceed to the higher grade and a further 1,460 marks for the special grade. There are also various other minor qualifications concerning their promotion.

Before considering the privileges allotted to the members of these various grades, let us deal with the earnings scheme which is common to them all, and which has been working successfully since 1905. Perhaps it is here that the New South Wales legislature took the boldest step, genuinely trying to give such prisoners an opportunity to earn some money with which to assist their relatives, ameliorate their prison conditions, and help themselves on discharge. Another object of such employment is clearly perceptible in the terms of regulation 20:

[1] Regulation 10.

" Every prisoner will be required to perform some fixed task daily, suited to his capacity and physical condition. The work should be of a productive, reformative and educational character, and, whenever practicable and not inconsistent with disciplinary requirements, the prisoner should be employed at the trade at which he is most proficient, and which will do the most to fit him for honest self-support when at liberty."

The products of such industry are sold through a Government agency and the habitual criminal is credited with " not less than one-half the net proceeds arising from the sale or disposal of the products of his labour."[1] Wherever possible the detainee is employed at such occupations as will give scope to his ability, but where, as is often the case, the detainee has not been trained in any branch of skilled labour, facilities are offered him, whilst serving the definite term of his sentence, to gain facility in some remunerative employment such as brush-making, boot-making, carpentering or tailoring. This is perhaps one of the few sound arguments for a dual-track system.

The Comptroller-General is empowered to remunerate as he thinks fit those who, for physical or other sufficient reason, cannot be employed in manufacture. They are to be put to whatever work they are suited, such as gardening or domestic employment; and the regulations direct the Comptroller-General to give " a liberal interpretation . . . to the matter of [their] earnings."

Credits remaining in the habitual criminal's account on his discharge are to be paid to him[2] through the managing secretary of the Prisoners' Aid Association " either in a lump sum or by such instalments as the Minister of Justice directs", but whilst he is in prison such moneys may be remitted to reputable relatives, provided a credit balance of at least £5 is maintained. This money is also subject to fines, for prison offences, imposed by the visiting justice; and part of it can be spent on " indulgences " to be consumed in prison. As these indulgences vary from grade to grade, let us now return to a consideration of the amenities in the intermediate, higher and special grades.

Upon completing his fixed sentence, the habitual criminal passes into the intermediate grade: his diet improves; his dress is more comfortable and presentable; he is allowed three fiction books per

---

[1] Regulation 21 as amended by regulations promulgated in the *Gazette* on October 11th, 1929.
[2] Regulation 22 A, 1929, promulgation.

week and as many educational books as are desired and approved; he may send and receive letters more frequently and these may be in plain envelopes; he may receive visits of double the former duration at monthly intervals; he may keep his cell lights on for half an hour after the usual time; and he may spend on an approved list of indulgences up to one-half of the net sum credited to his account during the preceding week. While in this grade, the habitual criminal will associate with other detainees during his working hours; but there is no associated recreation and meals are taken in his cell.

Having earned his 1,400 marks the detainee passes into the higher grade: his dress is further improved; he is allowed one extra fiction book per week; letters in and out are permitted more frequently; he may receive visits of thrice the ordinary duration still at monthly intervals; he may keep his cell lights on for one hour after the usual time; and he may spend up to two-thirds of the net sum credited to his account during the previous week on a list of indulgences which include a wider range of commodities than was available to him when he was in the intermediate grade.

Finally, having earned 2,000 marks in the higher grade, he passes into the special grade. Here he retains all the privileges of the higher grade but is even more presentably clothed; . is allowed to associate for recreation outside working hours; may receive visits at any time during working hours from reputable persons; and permission to write and receive letters is accorded him on request. In the special grade release becomes a probability.

All the above privileges are dependent on good behaviour and steady work, and all can be temporarily denied to the detainee if he be sentenced by the visiting justice to a period in either sub-grade of the lower grade. The conditions to be imposed in this lower grade are prescribed in detail in the 1913 regulations, but they need not concern us here.

Few of the above privileges are accorded to other long-term prisoners, the earnings scheme available to whom is much narrower. Indeed, other prisoners are paid a " gratuity " which bears no relation to their industry, being akin in many respects to the earnings scheme at present in force in English prisons. Particularly in this respect, there is in New South Wales a marked differentiation between the conditions under which habitual criminals are detained and those under which other criminals are imprisoned.

6. *Who is responsible for the release of habitual criminals, and on what basis are decisions to release them made ?*

Section 7 :

" If the Governor determines that an habitual criminal is sufficiently reformed, or for other good cause, he may grant to him a written licence to be at large, subject to such conditions endorsed on the licence as the Governor shall prescribe."

The Governor-General of New South Wales is thus nominally responsible for releasing the habitual criminal. He acts on the advice of the Minister of Justice, who in turn is guided by the report of the Consultative Committee on the habitual criminal in question—a report which is forwarded to the Minister of Justice together with the comments of the Comptroller-General of Prisons.

The initiative comes from the habitual criminal himself. When in the special grade, that is to say after a minimum period of four years and eight months after the conclusion of the definite sentence imposed on him, he is entitled to submit his case to the Minister of Justice with a view to his release on licence. The application then passes through the channels outlined above. Unless there are special reasons twelve months must elapse before a prisoner's case can again be submitted to the Minister. Though the initiative in this matter normally lies with the habitual criminal, he will, if he is wise, be guided by the advice of the Consultative Committee as to the appropriate time to apply for release. However, though it is not frequently done, a prisoner can be released on licence without his having applied for it, and further, " under special circumstances, such as for exceptionally meritorious conduct, for health, and for other good reasons, the Comptroller-General may allow a prisoner to place his case before the Minister at any time ",[1] and thus he may be released before he reaches the special grade.

Regulation 37 makes one important point about these application papers:

" Papers in such cases should state if definite employment can be found for the prisoner, and every facility should be offered to an eligible prisoner to communicate on this subject with the Prisoners' Aid Association, or any kindred organisations or reputable persons likely to find a situation for him. Prison officers are enjoined to render all possible assistance in this respect, as unless suitable employment is obtained for a prisoner prior to discharge there is little hope of his being able to lead a reformed life."

[1] Regulation 35, 1913, promulgation.

The Consultative Committee will advise the Comptroller-General of Prisons concerning the prisoner's release on the basis of all information it has been able to build up on him; but very important factors will be the availability of employment, the amount of money accumulated to tide him over the immediate post-discharge period, and the likelihood of his leading a reasonably settled existence.

The Comptroller-General also has personal experience on which to judge the merits of each application, and to evaluate the Committee's report, for by regulation 41 he is enjoined to see each habitual criminal when visiting the gaol, and this at intervals not exceeding six months. Every January the Comptroller-General forwards a report on each case to the Minister of Justice, giving particulars of conduct, health, prospect of reform and other necessary details. Thus the Minister also has prior cognisance of the case of every applicant for release.

7. *What are the conditions under which the habitual criminal is discharged, and what is the juridical status of one so discharged ?*

Under Section 7, as we have seen, the Governor-General can attach any conditions to the licence on which the habitual criminal is released. The same section provides further that

> " Every offender so released while he remains within New South Wales shall, once at least in every three months during the period fixed by licence or when no period is so fixed during the period of two years next after such release, report his address and occupation to the principal officer of police at the place in which he was convicted, or at such other place as the Inspector-General of Police may appoint. Such report may be made either by the offender personally, or by letter signed by him, and posted to the principal officer of police at that place."

In 1929 new regulations were promulgated[1] governing the disposal of the money accumulated by the habitual criminal during his sentence. These regulations provided that on release on licence the amount to his credit was to be paid to him through the managing secretary of the Prisoners' Aid Association " either in a lump sum or by such instalments as the Minister of Justice directs." It is the normal practice to use such credits to encourage the habitual criminal in his rehabilitation; and there is also provision for the Prisoners' Aid Association to charge against such moneys, expenditure on

[1] October 11th, 1929.

behalf of the dischargee for clothing or outfit required to take up employment.

If, during the period specified in the licence, or if no period is specified during two years, the discharged offender fails to comply with a condition of the licence or fails to report his address and occupation, or if there are reasonable grounds for believing that he is getting his livelihood by dishonest means, or if he is convicted of an offence for which imprisonment exceeding three months may be imposed, then a judge or magistrate may, in addition to punishing for the offence in question, order his recommittal to the place where he was imprisoned as an habitual criminal.[1]

If the licence is revoked, or if the offender is reconvicted before its expiration, the balance of moneys standing to his credit with the Prisoners' Aid Association is paid to the Comptroller-General of Prisons, placed to his credit in prison, and added to his future earnings.

Section 9 :

> " If during the period so specified none of the events aforesaid happens, the offender shall cease to be an habitual criminal."

It is worth remarking that the effect of " while he remains within New South Wales " in Section 7 was to encourage discharged habitual criminals to try their fortunes in other States of the Commonwealth where—certainly for two years—their life would be less restricted. This, in turn, encouraged the other States to introduce habitual criminal legislation.

8. To what extent are such habitual criminal laws applied ?

The estimated population of New South Wales in 1946 slightly exceeded 2,942,000. The number of prisoners under sentence in gaol at any one time in that State usually varies around 1,500.

Bearing in mind its population, the habitual criminal legislation of New South Wales has been quite extensively enforced; and though no complete figures are available for the period since 1905, the following table showing the numbers detained as habitual criminals at the end of eleven years from 1934 to 1944, and the numbers sentenced during these years as habitual criminals, demonstrates that this legislation has not been neglected.

[1] Section 8.

Year Ended June 30th	HABITUAL CRIMINALS THEN DETAINED				SENTENCED DURING YEAR
	In Definite Stage	In Indefinite Stage	In Asylums	Total	
1934	39	49	—	88	23
1935	52	36	2	90	35
1936	43	53	8	104	12
1937	23	68	8	99	15
1938	41	66	7	114	52
1939	40	84	8	132	29
1940	21	85	8	114	18
1941	25	84	8	117	11
1942	31	53	9	93	21
1943	29	36	9	74	16
1944	25	45	5	75	22
Total					254

(Information taken from *Annual Social Statistics*, New South Wales)

Unfortunately no statistical information is available as to the later conduct of discharged habitual criminals, and the only light on this question is to be found in the Official Year Book for Australia of 1929, where it is affirmed that in New South Wales " while old associations and habits have in some cases proved too strong for the released ' habituals', many of them have done well, and generally there is hope of reformation in the average prisoner other than the sexual offender."[1]

VICTORIA

In July 1908, " The Indeterminate Sentences Act " came into force in the State of Victoria. The relevant provisions are now to be found in the Crimes Act, 1928, which consolidated the Victorian law relating to crimes and criminal offenders; and section citations hereunder refer to that Act. Sections 514 to 543 govern the application of indeterminate sentences in Victoria.

Section 514 provides that:

" (1) When any person apparently of the age of seventeen years or upwards is convicted of any indictable offence and has been previously convicted on at least two occasions of any indictable offence or offences the judge of the Supreme Court or the chairman of the Court of General Sessions before whom such person is convicted may declare that he is an

[1] No. 22, p. 470.

habitual criminal and direct as part of his sentence that on the expiration of the term of imprisonment then imposed upon him he be detained during the Governor's pleasure in a reformatory prison. (2) Before passing any such sentence the judge or chairman may if he thinks fit hear evidence to enable him to determine whether or not any person so convicted should be declared an habitual criminal."[1]

It is worth noting that " the provisions with regard to previous convictions apply whether such previous convictions took place in Victoria . . . or elsewhere than in Victoria for any like offences and whether before or after the commencement of this Act."[2]

Were this the whole of the Victorian legislation on indeterminate sentences there would be no difficulty in interpreting it and rightly evaluating the place of habitual criminal legislation in the Victorian legal system. However, Victorian indeterminate sentence legislation goes far beyond habitual criminals, and Section 515 provides that

" (1) Where any person apparently of the age of seventeen years or upwards is convicted of any indictable offence (whether such person has been previously convicted of any offence or not) the judge of the Supreme Court or the chairman of the Court of General Sessions before which such person is convicted may if he thinks fit, having regard to the antecedents, character, associates, age, health or mental condition of the person convicted, the nature of the offence, or any special circumstances of the case—

(a) direct as part of his sentence that on the expiration of the term of imprisonment then imposed upon him he be detained during the Governor's pleasure in a reformatory prison ; or

(b) without imposing any term of imprisonment upon him sentence him to be forthwith committed to a reformatory prison and to be there detained during the Governor's pleasure.

(2) Before passing any such sentence the judge or chairman may if he thinks fit hear evidence to enable him to determine whether such person should or should not be so detained."

Section 516 extends the power in Section 515, in certain cases, to courts of petty sessions.

Thus, in Victoria the indeterminate sentence is of such wide application that it is impossible to distinguish with any formal clarity those provisions relating specifically to habitual criminals. Therefore, before concentrating on the treatment of habitual criminals, let us try to gain some idea of the general functioning of the indeterminate sentence in Victoria and of the number who have been subject to it.

[1] The words " of any indictable offence " appearing twice in that section of the Act have been held not to include convictions for indictable offences which were tried summarily." *R.* v. *Ward*, 1918, V.L.R. 418.
[2] S. 517 and *R.* v. *McKeown*, 1923, V.L.R. 577.

The administration of indeterminate sentences is the responsibility of the Indeterminate Sentences Board, consisting of three men appointed by the Governor in Council. By Section 531 of the Crimes Act, the Board is given wide powers regarding the classification of prisoners' sentences to reformatories, the determination of their promotion or demotion in grade and release on parole, the recommendation of their release on probation;[1] and other advisory and administrative duties concerning reformatory prisons and their inmates. The Board is required to report annually on its work for the preceding year, and these annual reports constitute the only published information on the functioning of the indeterminate sentence in Victoria. In making recommendations of release the Board is " to have regard to the safety of the public or of any individual or class of persons and the welfare of the person whom it is proposed to release."[2] The Board has power to release on *parole* offenders under its control; and while on parole the offender is technically still a prisoner liable to be returned to one of the reformatories administered by the Board should he fail to comply with the conditions of his parole. Parole is usually for a period of six months, but may be extended. The Chief Secretary, on the advice of the Board, has power to release offenders on *probation*: " probation " differs from " parole " in that it is either for the unexpired portion of the sentence—when applied to one transferred from a gaol to a reformatory under powers given to the Indeterminate Sentences Board—or for the fixed term of two years—when applied to all other prisoners. Additional formalities are required before a man released on probation can be returned to prison.

Between July 1908 and July 1947 there were 5,552 " receptions " (5,499 males and 53 females) into the care of the Indeterminate Sentence Board. This number represented 3,769 individuals (3,726 males and 43 females). All other receptions into prisons during that period in Victoria were of prisoners into " gaols " and not into " reformatory prisons " under the control of the Board. The Board has five reformatory prisons under its control, and some clue to the subsequent criminal careers of the 5,358 male " receptions " who had been discharged from these institutions before July 1947, is given in the following tables:

---

[1] " Probation " in this context refers, as we shall see, to a different type of system from that operating in England under the same name.
[2] S. 531 (5) (*d*).

Reformatory	Reconvicted or Returned	Not again Convicted (including those on Parole or Probation)
	%	%
Pentridge :		
Male	51·18	48·82
Female	32·69	67·31
Beechworth	43·59	56·41
Castlemaine	40·05	59·95
French Island	33·96	66·04
Geelong	48·31	51·69
	41·27	58·73

Of the 4,869 released on parole or probation from these institutions, the reconviction figures are as follows :

Reformatory	Released Parole or Probation	Probation Satisfactorily Concluded	Reconvicted or Returned to Prison	Still on Parole or Probation	Deaths During Parole or Probation
Pentridge					
Male	762	313	390	50	9
Female	52	33	17	2	—
Beechworth	546	254	238	53	1
Castlemaine	2,622	1,390	1,050	170	12
French Island	798	451	271	73	3
Geelong	89	43	43	—	3
	4,869	2,484	2,009	348	28

These figures are sufficiently striking to lead anyone interested in indeterminate sentence legislation to a consideration of the Annual Reports of the Victorian Indeterminate Sentences Board,[1] and to Sections 515 to 543 of the Crimes Act, 1928. Here they are presented as an introduction to the application of our questionnaire to Victorian

[1] In London these reports are available at Victoria House, Strand. It is from the 1947 report that the above statistical information is taken. On p. 6 of the 1947 report there is a clerical error which has been corrected in the preparation of the last table here presented—there the number shown as having successfully concluded their probationary period on release from " Beechworth " is " 234 ". If this figure be " 234 ", the columns add incorrectly, and reference to the previous reports shows that before 1947 the number 234 had been exceeded, and that it should now read " 254 ".

habitual criminal legislation, so that that legislation may be seen in its proper penological perspective.

1. To whom do such laws apply ?

To this question, Section 514, which is copied above, gives a complete answer. The only qualifications are that the criminal is of the age of seventeen years or upwards (and the Court may, without evidence, and on their own conclusions, fix the prisoner's age, it being for him to show that he is under age: Rex v. Benson *ex parte* Tubby[1]), that he is convicted on indictment of an indictable offence, and that he has at least twice previously been so convicted.

2. Who controls their application ?

The power to declare an offender an habitual criminal is discretionary. No special procedure is necessary; but, as we have seen, the Court may hear whatever evidence it desires on this point.

3. Do such laws envisage aggravation of punishment or special measures ? If the latter, do the special measures follow or take the place of the punishment for the last offence ?

A special measure is applied. The system is a " dual-track " one; the committal to a reformatory, and therefore into the care of the Indeterminate Sentences Board, following the expiration of the term of imprisonment imposed for the last offence.

4. What is the form of sentence imposed ?

The form is indefinite: it is subject to the minimum term imposed for the last offence, but to no maximum, the detention in the reformatory prison being " during the Governor's pleasure ".

5. If a special measure is applied, what is the degree of differentiation between it and other long-term imprisonment ?

Habitual criminals, and other male prisoners under the control of the Indeterminate Sentences Board, who are regarded as unsuitable for any of the other four reformatory prisons, are detained in Beechworth Reformatory. The daily average population of this

[1] 8 V.L.R. (L.) 2.

reformatory for the last four years (ending June 30th) for which
figures are available is as follows:

1944	..	..	..	48·0
1945	..	..	..	41·11
1946	..	..	..	41·84
1947	..	..	..	43·07

On June 30th, 1946, there were fifteen habitual criminals in
Beechworth Reformatory: on June 30th, 1947, seventeen. Thus
habitual criminals formed only a minority of the population of this
reformatory, and no differentiation was made between the conditions
to which they were subject and those of the rest of the men in Beechworth Reformatory. Nor is this reformatory differentiated from the
other prisons except by virtue of its geographical position, the
industry followed, and the type of prisoner it contains.

Beechworth Reformatory is a solid granite prison situated in
timber country, and, for Australia, it is a very old building. The
main industry followed is the cutting and sale of firewood ; and on
the ground thus cleared a pine plantation is cultivated. It is hoped
that in years to come this reafforestation project will prove financially
sound, although the revenue in 1946 and 1947 was only £750 and
£683 respectively. No effort is made to train the men at Beechworth,
all vocational training being carried out in the other reformatory
prisons. The official outlook on this institution was stated in the
Report and Statistical Tables for the year 1945—" for the real
habitual (whether so declared or not) who has been engaged in crime
for many years and has no sincere desire to reform, Beechworth
Reformatory Prison is adequate as it stands."

Though nominally a maximum-security prison, the type of work
followed at Beechworth facilitates an attempt at escape. In the year
ending June 30th, 1946, four men absconded, and in the next year
six. All but one of these ten men were recaptured, sentenced to a
definite term of imprisonment, and then returned to Beechworth
Reformatory Prison.

*6 and 7. Who is responsible for the release of habitual criminals, and on what
basis are decisions to release them made ? What are the conditions
under which the habitual criminal is discharged, and what is the
juridical status of one so discharged ?*

The Indeterminate Sentences Board

" by order in writing signed by any two members thereof may permit any person detained in a reformatory prison . . . who has not been released on probation to leave the prison temporarily in order to test the reform of such person. (2) Such leave shall be for the term and subject to the conditions specified in the order. (3) Any person so permitted to leave a reformatory prison temporarily—

(a) shall be deemed to continue in the legal custody of the superintendent . . . of the prison ; and
(b) may at any time during such leave or after the expiration thereof (if he has not returned to the reformatory prison) on an order in writing of the Board signed by any two members thereof be arrested without warrant by any warder of the prison or any member of the police force and by him returned to the prison."[1]

This parole is normally for a period of six months and is used before the Board advises the offender's release on probation.

Probation is granted, on the advice of the Indeterminate Sentences Board, by the Chief Secretary, who directs

" the release of such person on probation subject to such conditions as to the residence and employment of such person and his regularly reporting the same and as to his leading a sober and industrious life as are recommended by the Indeterminate Sentences Board and specified in the Order . . . for a period of two years."[2]

The Firearms Act, 1928, Section 31, introduces a prohibition on the use, possession, etc., of a firearm by one so released on probation. Section 527:

" Every person so released while he remains in Victoria shall unless otherwise prescribed once at least in every three months during the said period of probation personally report his address and occupation at the office of the member of the police force in charge of the police station at the place in which he was convicted or at such other place as may be prescribed provided that in the case of any person so released the Indeterminate Sentences Board may require as a condition of his probation that in lieu of his making any such report as aforesaid he shall in such manner and at such times as the Board directs report personally or by letter his address and occupation to such member of the police force or to such person or body of persons as the Board directs."

In the event of it appearing to a justice, by information on oath, that a probationer has failed to report his address and occupation as above required, or that he has been associating with reputed criminals, or that he has broken any condition of his probation, a warrant will be issued empowering the arrest of that probationer

[1] Section 529.   [2] Section 526.

and ordering that he be brought before a court of petty sessions, which court has power to order his recommittal to a reformatory prison. Similarly, if a probationer is convicted of any indictable offence or of any offence punishable on summary conviction for which imprisonment for a period exceeding three months may be imposed, the court so convicting him may order that he be returned to a reformatory prison after he has served the term of imprisonment then imposed on him.[1]

Section 528 (4):

> " If during the period of probation none of the events aforesaid happens the person so released shall be deemed to have suffered in full the imprisonment and detention . . . to which he was sentenced."

There is no general practice governing decisions as to release. The Board are directed by Section 526 to advise release when the habitual criminal " has sufficiently reformed " or when there is " some other good and sufficient reason for his release ". With such small numbers, and having at their disposal the excellent technique of parole, the Board can individualise its treatment of habitual criminals in this respect. The members of the Board usually visit Beechworth Reformatory Prison about six times every year and they thus gain detailed knowledge of each habitual criminal. Care is taken to discover as much as possible about him and his background, but the Board is not assisted with sufficient psychological and psychiatric advice.

Parole, as distinct from probation, is a very helpful means of discovering each offender's potentialities for reform, and is one of the most interesting features of Victoria's indeterminate sentences system—a feature that could well be copied in many countries.

The use of " while he remains in Victoria " in Section 527 (quoted above) is akin to the New South Wales Statute, and illustrates the endeavour of these States to persuade their habitual criminals to emigrate; the disadvantage being that they tend to exchange, rather than lose, their habitual criminals.

8. To what extent are such habitual criminal laws applied ?

The estimated population of Victoria in 1946 slightly exceeded 2,045,000. On December 31st, 1946, there were, in that State, 927 male convicted persons in confinement.

[1] Section 528.

As we have noted, between July 1908 and July 1947, there were 3,726 males committed to reformatory prisons. Of these, *307* had been declared habitual criminals.

Of those 307 habitual criminals, 17 were, on July 1st, 1947, in Beechworth Reformatory Prison, 4 were in gaol serving definite sentences before being transferred to Beechworth Reformatory, 2 absconders were still at large, and 16 other prisoners were on parole or probation. Thus a total of 39 were then under or about to come under the control of the Indeterminate Sentences Board.

Of the remaining *268*

> 149 had been reconvicted.
> 3 had been deported.
> 6 died in gaols and reformatory prisons.
> 5 died on parole or probation.
> ——
> 163
> ——

There remain *105* who did not again enter Victorian prisons after their release from Beechworth. What happened to these 105 criminals is not known; but certainly they avoided conviction for a criminal offence in Victoria, and to that extent the Victorian habitual criminal legislation does seem to have been effective. It is not known how many of them continued their anti-social activities in other States of the Commonwealth or in other countries.

From the above figures it will be seen that an average of 7·9 criminals per year were declared " habituals " in the years between 1908 and 1947. To illustrate the significance of this figure—the daily average of males imprisoned in Victoria during those years varied from 574 in 1919, to 1,428 in 1932, the average for the nineteen years from 1928 to 1946 being 971.

QUEENSLAND

The law relating to habitual criminals in Queensland is to be found in " The Criminal Code, 1899," as amended by " The Criminal Law Amendment Act " of 1914 and of 1945. Queensland was the last of the Australian States to adopt habitual criminal legislation, and we shall see to what extent she profited from the experience gained by other States, especially New South Wales. Section references are to the Criminal Code as amended in 1914 and 1945, unless otherwise specified.

1. To whom do such laws apply ?

Section 659A, subsections 1 to 4, defines the following as habitual criminals:

(1) those convicted on indictment of certain offences against morality who have been previously so convicted on indictment on at least *two* occasions for similar offences ;

(2) those convicted on indictment of any one of certain offences relating to the coin, of endangering life or health, of stealing or some like offences, of serious injuries to property, or of forging or some similar offences, and who have on *three* previous occasions been convicted on indictment of *three* previous offences falling within the above widely defined group ;

(3) those twice previously convicted on indictment of offences falling within the group referred to in (2) and who are convicted summarily of an offence punishable by imprisonment for not less than three months and who have been convicted summarily on two previous occasions at least of offences punishable by imprisonment for not less than three months ;

(4) those convicted of an offence under " The Vagrants Acts " 1851 to 1863 who have been previously convicted on at least *four* occasions of any offence mentioned in those Acts ;

(5) those convicted summarily of an aggravated assault (Section 344) of a sexual nature, on a child under the age of fourteen years, who have *twice* previously been convicted of such assaults ;[1]

(6) notwithstanding that the wilful exposure of the person in a public place is an offence under " The Vagrants Acts " referred to in (4) above, any offender so convicted who has *twice* previously been convicted of this offence may be declared an habitual criminal.

Convictions in other jurisdictions if for " similar offences under similar laws " are to be treated as previous convictions within the above provisions, and to this end regulations were made in 1915 by the Governor in Council facilitating the proof of previous convictions of offences committed in Queensland and elsewhere.

It is not easy to summarise all the above definitions, but it is clear that the net is flung wide. Habitual criminals are defined exclusively by reference to their previous convictions and the offence for which they stand convicted; the requisite number of previous convictions varying inversely with the moral turpitude of the offences as roughly estimated by their division into certain offences tried summarily, others tried on indictment and falling within a fairly extensive list, and others tried either summarily or on indictment but involving offences of a sexual nature. In other words, the test

---

[1] Regarding sexual offences on children in Queensland see the note beginning on p. 114 dealing with Part IV of the Criminal Law Amendment Act, 1945.

is a rather complex objective one, and considerations of the characteristics of the particular offender, such as his age or mental condition, are not enjoined upon the trial judge.

The courts in Queensland have shown themselves extremely reluctant to apply this legislation, though approximately the same matters are to be considered in declaring a person an habitual criminal in Queensland as in the other States of Australia, for example, South Australia; and the South Australian case of R. v. Tregaskis[1] in which such matters are defined has been narrowly interpreted in Queensland—see R. v. Molloy,[2] R. v. Roberts[3] and R. v. Lauder,[4] in all of which cases declarations that an offender was an habitual criminal were set aside on criminologically doubtful grounds, which, however, indicated the restrictive interpretation of this legislation by the Queensland courts.

2. Who controls their application ?

The application of this legislation to particular criminals is controlled, in the case of those convicted on indictment, by the judge (or judges) of the Supreme Court before whom the case is heard. In every such trial, where the qualifications detailed above are met, " the judge may in his discretion declare as part of the sentence of such person that he is an habitual criminal."[5]

Where an offender is convicted summarily, that is to say by a court of petty sessions, and he qualifies as an habitual criminal, " the court of petty sessions before which the charge is heard, in addition to sentencing such person to any lawful term of imprisonment, may order that such person be brought before the Supreme Court or a judge thereof to be dealt with as an habitual criminal."[6] A discretion is thus also given to courts of petty sessions, though there is an exception to this as regards one convicted summarily of an aggravated assault of a sexual nature on a child under the age of fourteen years, and who has twice previously been convicted of such offences. In such a case the court of petty sessions is compelled to refer the offender to a judge of the Supreme Court.

Section 659 (5) provides that when an offender is referred to the Supreme Court by the court of petty sessions in accordance with the above provisions, the " judge thereof may declare such person to be an habitual criminal."

[1] 1937—S.A.S.R. 358.   [2] 1938—Q.W.N. 21.   [3] 1938—Q.W.N. 37.
[4] 1940—Q.W.N. 15.   [5] Section 659A.   [6] Section 659A.

No special form of indictment as an habitual criminal is necessary either for trials upon indictment or those heard summarily, and a discretion invariably resides in the judge empowered to declare an offender an habitual criminal whether to exercise this power or not. Further, in most convictions by courts of petty sessions where the offender qualifies for this treatment, there is also a discretion in the court hearing the case whether or not to refer this criminal to the Supreme Court.

3. *Do such laws envisage aggravation of punishment or special measures? If the latter, do the special measures follow or take the place of the punishment for the last offence?*

Special measures are envisaged and power is given to the Governor in Council to establish a reformatory prison for the detention of habitual criminals, and to make all regulations necessary to implement this legislation. That such a prison does not and has not existed in Queensland does not affect the fact that special measures were envisaged, even if they have not been carried out.

Section 659D (1) provides that:

"Every habitual criminal shall at the expiration of his sentence be detained during His Majesty's pleasure"

thus instituting a dual-track system of punishing habitual criminals.

4. *What is the form of sentence imposed?*

An indeterminate sentence with no legal minimum or maximum is imposed by the Criminal Code, though in practice this is modified by the regulations which have been made implementing this chapter of the Code, and which introduce almost invariable minimum terms.

The regulations at present in force and to which all references hereunder refer were published in the *Queensland Government Gazette* of July 26th, 1924. These regulations are so framed that in all but exceptional cases the prisoner cannot be released "for a period of two years after the completion of the definite portion of his sentence."[1]

When the regulations for the treatment of habitual criminals in the reformatory are discussed below, especially those governing

[1] Regulation 53.

the stage system, it will be clear that in fact the effective minimum period to be served, after the completion of the definite sentence, is usually nearer four and a half, than two years.

Thus, the sentence on habitual criminals in Queensland is similar to that in New South Wales—potentially indeterminate but in practice indefinite.

5. *If a special measure is applied, what is the degree of differentiation between it and other long-term imprisonment ?*

The control and management of any reformatory prison for habitual criminals; the good order, discipline, diet and health of the prisoners therein; and the classes of labour, hours of employment, wages and deductions from wages of such prisoners are all to be controlled by regulations made by the Governor in Council.

The only positive statutory direction concerning the conditions under which habitual criminals are to serve the indefinite part of their sentence is to be found in Section 659F, where it is provided that the habitual criminal shall be employed in labour and receive wages which " shall be applied wholly or in part, as directed by the Home Secretary, towards maintaining his wife and children (if any) during the period of his detention, and the balance (if any) standing to his credit on his discharge shall be paid over to him."

The degree of differentiation in force will become apparent when the number of prisoners treated as habitual criminals in Queensland is considered. However, the regulations do give explicit directions for the governance of habitual criminals at the indefinite stage of their imprisonment—directions which could lead to an appreciably different régime. These regulations are dealt with briefly here since they follow closely the New South Wales regulations of 1913,[1] on which they were modelled.

A visiting justice is to interview each prisoner at least once a month and report to the Comptroller-General of Prisons. Similarly, a visiting surgeon shall report at least once every three months to the Comptroller-General regarding the health of each prisoner and any other circumstances he thinks fit.

The regulations classify habitual criminals into four grades —namely, " Lower ", " Intermediate ", " Higher " and " Special "—

[1] Considered on p. 90 *et seq.*

and direct what privileges are to be accorded prisoners in each grade. These privileges in the form of visitors, library books, cell lights at night, letters, wages, and the amount of wages that may be spent on indulgences to supplement rations, are extended and improved as the prisoner passes from the Lower to the Special grade. Prisoners in all but the Lower grade may remit to their relatives who are of good character such portion of their earnings as the Comptroller-General permits; provided that, except in special circumstances, a credit balance of at least £5 is maintained.

The Comptroller-General may vary any of these privileges, extending or retracting them as he thinks fit.

The progress from grade to grade depends on " good conduct and industry . . . prompt and cheerful obedience . . . loyalty to the government of the reformatory prison, faithful and diligent performance of work . . . and generally the manifestation of such a spirit as is indicative of a desire to reform."[1] However, unless both the Comptroller-General of Prisons and the Minister agree, a prisoner must remain in the Lower grade for at least three months, in the Intermediate grade for at least two years, and in the Higher grade for a further two years before he has any chance of reaching the Special grade. Only in the Special grade is there any real likelihood of his obtaining his discharge.

More particular attention is to be paid to habitual criminals than is accorded other prisoners, and Regulation 54 directs that the Comptroller-General shall annually " forward to the Minister a report on each prisoner, giving particulars of conduct, health, prospect of reform, and any other proper information."

In New South Wales similar regulations have led to a régime appreciably different from that imposed on other long-term prisoners, and a similar differentiation could have been achieved in Queensland had any appreciable number of habitual criminals been sentenced, and had a special institution, or part thereof, been available to them. As neither of these contingencies were fulfilled, the lot of the habitual criminal has tended to be simply a normal protracted sentence, qualified only by the availability of an adequate earnings scheme.

In Queensland, habitual criminals are detained in Brisbane Prison, and rarely have there been as many as five such prisoners there at any one time; and this amongst a prison population varying from

[1] Regulation 9.

200 to just over 300. Any extensive differentiation of treatment is thus impracticable.

6. Who is responsible for the release of habitual criminals, and on what basis are decisions to release them made ?

In this respect the Queensland legislation incorporates an original and interesting idea. Section 659G (1) provides that the habitual criminal may apply to the Supreme Court or a judge thereof " for a recommendation that . . . having sufficiently reformed, or for other sufficient reason, (he) may be discharged." The Court or judge applied to " may thereupon make inquiry in such manner as is deemed fitting, and on being satisfied that such person has sufficiently reformed, or that there is some other sufficient reason to warrant his discharge, may recommend the Governor to discharge him accordingly." Thus direct judicial influence is reintro-duced at this later stage as a limitation on administrative power

The bare bones of Section 659G (1) are covered by Regulation 53:

" Every prisoner who desires to make application to the Supreme Court or a judge thereof under Section 659 G shall first give notice in writing to the Comptroller-General of Prisons. The Comptroller-General of Prisons shall, as soon as possible thereafter, make a report in writing—

(a) As to whether there are reasonable grounds for belief that the release of such prisoner will not be detrimental to the welfare of society ;

(b) As to such prisoner's records and character as established in the reformatory ;

(c) As to the nature and character of the crime or crimes committed ;

(d) As to such prisoner's previous record and environment and his probable surroundings if released ;

(e) As to such prisoner's powers of self-control and of his leading a useful and industrious life and abstaining from crime ;

(f) As to all other facts which the Comptroller-General of Prisons may be able to obtain bearing on the advisability of the release of such prisoner.

Such report shall be transmitted by the Comptroller-General of Prisons to the Registrar of the Supreme Court."

It will be recalled that the Comptroller-General has received information independently from the visiting justice, and the visiting surgeon, as well as from the governor of the prison. Also he will himself have interviewed the prisoner applying for release. From all this information he prepares his report which is in fact the vital and almost conclusive evidence upon which the prisoner's application will be decided.

7. What are the conditions under which the habitual criminal is discharged, and what is the juridical status of one so discharged ?

Section 659G (2) empowers the Governor, on the recommendation of the Supreme Court or a Judge thereof, to direct the prisoner's discharge, and further permits the Governor to " order that so long as such person remains in Queensland he shall report his address and occupation " to the police at specified intervals for a period named in the discharge order—a period which must not exceed two years. The moneys standing to his credit on his discharge " shall be deposited with such person as the Minister may appoint, and shall be paid to such prisoner after his discharge in such instalments as the Minister may direct."[1]

If, during the specified period, the person so discharged fails to report his address and occupation as required, or if there are reasonable grounds for believing that he is getting his livelihood by dishonest means, or if he is convicted of any but a trifling offence, then any court before which any of the above conditions are established " may direct him, in addition to any penalty . . . then imposed upon him, to be recommitted to a reformatory prison."[2]

Section 659H (2) : " If during the period so specified none of the events aforesaid happens, the person so discharged shall cease to be an habitual criminal."

These provisions for discharge do not follow the normal practice of allowing for extensive " conditions " to be written into the discharge order. They nevertheless give ample powers of recommittal to the courts. There is much to recommend this variation from the norm.

8. To what extent are such habitual criminal laws applied ?

The brief answer is: rarely.

The estimated population of Queensland in 1946 slightly exceeded 1,098,000. The daily average of male prisoners in all prisons during that year was 382·3.[3]

Habitual criminal legislation was introduced into Queensland in 1914. In 1922 the first habitual criminal declarations were made, two persons being so sentenced during that year. From 1922 to 1926, eighteen persons were declared habitual criminals. Throughout

---

[1] Regulation 20.   [2] Section 659H (L)
[3] 1947 Annual Report of .he Comptroller-General of Prisons.

the ensuing years this legislation has been but fitfully applied, so that in 1945 there was a daily average of five habitual criminals in Queensland prisons, and in 1946 the average was three. This handful of prisoners has been detained in the Brisbane prison; and there has been a " chicken and egg " argument between the penal authorities and the judiciary, the penal authorities refusing to apply special segregated treatment to the very few habitual criminals which are so declared, and the courts refusing to declare criminals to be habituals until such treatment is available. Thus, in the case of Healy v. The King (1942 St. R. Queensland 114), Douglas J., considering an appeal from a sentence involving a declaration that a man was an habitual criminal, reflected on the difficulty he felt in condoning such a sentence when there are no means of " putting such men in a separate gaol or keeping them apart. They are simply put with other criminals, and instead of being given a sentence of a fixed term of years, they are there as long as the Government decides to keep them." In the same case, Webb C.J., said: " As regards the sentence, I know that judges of this court differ as to whether prisoners should be declared habitual criminals in the circumstances which still exist, that is in the absence of proper provision for such prisoners."

SEXUAL OFFENDERS

Note on Part IV of " The Criminal Law Amendment Act, 1945."

Though not strictly germane to our terms of reference, I think it appropriate and interesting to refer to the above named Statute which provides, by Section 17, for the use of a probation system for certain sexual offenders, and then, by Section 18, inaugurates an indeterminate sentence for any person, convicted of " an offence of a sexual nature committed upon or in relation to a child under the age of seventeen years ", concerning whom two medical practitioners (one a psychiatrist) report that he is "incapable of exercising proper control over his sexual instincts." This is either a dual-track or single-track system at the discretion of the trial judge.

Further, where two such medical practitioners report to the Attorney-General that any person serving a sentence of imprisonment for an offence of a sexual nature, whether involving a child under the age of seventeen years or a person over that age, is:

(a) incapable of exercising proper control over his sexual instincts; and

(b) that such incapacity is susceptible of cure by continued treatment; and

(c) that for the purposes of such treatment it is desirable that such person be detained in an institution after the expiration of his sentence of imprisonment,

the Attorney-General may cause an application to be made to a judge of the Supreme Court for a declaration that the offender be detained during His Majesty's pleasure.

Whether proceeded against under the first or second of the above methods, the prisoner, or his legal representative, may cross-examine the medical practitioners in relation to their evidence, which they must give upon oath, and may himself call evidence in rebuttal of their report. The prisoner is, of course, entitled to legal aid.

The system appears to be a genuinely indeterminate one, and release is made to depend upon medical and psychiatric decisions. There are many provisions, including administrative safeguards to protect the interests of the offender, amplifying the above outline.

An examination of the working of this legislation when it has been enforced for a few years should prove most interesting and informative, not only for the relatively narrow but nevertheless important group of sexual crimes to which it applies, but also to a much wider class of offences.

SOUTH AUSTRALIA

Legislation concerning habitual criminals was first introduced into South Australia by the Habitual Criminals Amendment Act, 1907. In 1937, this Act was consolidated, several minor drafting amendments being made, and is now to be found in Sections 319 to 328 of the Criminal Law Consolidation Act, 1937. All section citations hereunder are to that Act, unless otherwise stated.

1. To whom do such laws apply ?

Section 319, subsection 3, lists eight classes of offences which, for our present purpose, we can divide into two groups, " A " and " B ". Group " A " comprises four classes of offences—wounding, poisoning, certain sexual offences, and crimes connected with abortion; group " B " comprises the more serious larcenies and allied offences, arson, forgery, and coining. Section 319, subsection 1, provides that any person convicted on indictment of an offence falling within either of the above two groups may be declared an habitual criminal if

1. his offence falls within group " A " and he has been previously convicted on at least *two* occasions of offences of the same *class* (for example if his present conviction is for a sexual offence and he has a record of two prior convictions for sexual offences): or

2. his offence falls within group " B " and he has been previously convicted on at least *three* occasions of offences within that *group* (but not necessarily within the same class, as is required for group " A ").

Thus, in cases of offences against property, a history of three previous convictions is necessary, whilst for certain offences against the person, two previous convictions suffice for a prisoner to be declared an habitual criminal. In the latter case a much greater degree of specialisation is necessary, the recidivism required being much more " specific ".

It will be seen that in South Australia the habitual criminal is defined in a purely objective way, considerations neither of age nor of character being enjoined upon the court by law; though in that the power to declare a man to be an habitual criminal is permissive and not mandatory, it is clear that such individual qualities of the offender as the judge cares to consider will weigh in his decision.[1]

Subsection 2 of Section 319 provides that conviction taking place in or out of South Australia, both before and after 1907, are to be regarded as " previous convictions " for purposes of this legislation.

2. *Who controls their application ?*

No special form of prosecution is necessary; but it will have been noticed in the answer to question one that only upon indictment can a man be declared an habitual criminal, and further, that his criminal record must include a number of convictions pursuant to trials upon indictment.

---

[1] The subjective qualities of the offender and objective circumstances of the offence which should be considered in deciding the question of habitual criminality were discussed in *R.* v. *Tregaskis*, 1937, S.A.S.R. 358.

Section 319, having listed the conditions of prior convictions as specified above, states that " the Judge before whom such person is so convicted, may, in his discretion, declare as part of the sentence of such person that he is an habitual criminal."

3. *Do such laws envisage aggravation of punishment or special measures ?*
    If the latter, do the special measures follow or take the place of the
    punishment for the last offence ?

Section 321:

> " Every habitual criminal shall, at the expiration of his sentence be detained during His Majesty's pleasure . . . in some place of confinement set apart. . . ."

Thus the answer in brief is: special measures and dual-track.

4. *What is the form of sentence imposed ?*

A genuinely indeterminate sentence follows the period of imprisonment for the last particular offence for which the habitual criminal was convicted. Neither by statute nor in the regulations which implement the statutory law on this subject is either a minimum or a maximum term specified. Investigating the actual practice with this in mind, it is startling to discover that from 1909 to 1939 the average term of imprisonment served by habitual criminals at the determinate stage of their sentence was 5·2 years (standard deviation of 3·54 years within a range of from six months to fifteen years), and that the average time spent in the indeterminate stage of the sentence was 1·17 years (further information to calculate the dispersion from this average is not available).[1] In the Report of the Comptroller of Prisons for the year 1936, it was stated that " in order to increase the deterrent effect of the provisions relating to habitual criminals, it has been considered advisable to retain them for a longer period in the indeterminate " stage of their punishment. However, the war and consequent readiness to release such men, followed by a post-war disinclination to make use of this legislation has prevented this intention from revealing itself as yet in the statistics; indeed, at the end of 1946, there was only one habitual criminal in confinement in the indeterminate stage of his punishment, and he was in a hospital for criminal mental defectives at Parkside.

[1] Information extracted from the annual reports of the Comptroller of Prisons.

5. *If a special measure is applied, what is the degree of differentiation between it and other long-term imprisonment ?*

Section 322 insists on the provision of some trade or avocation for habitual criminals, and of facilities for selling or otherwise disposing of the products of their labours. Subsection 3 of that section further guarantees to the habitual criminal at least one-half of the net proceeds arising therefrom. Regulations brought into force on April 6th, 1911, and November 23rd, 1916, implement this section. Bootmaking and market gardening are the most usual occupations followed.

At the indeterminate stage of his punishment the habitual criminal has one other means of earning money. The 1911 regulations laid down a system of marks by which a full day's work with exemplary conduct earns eight marks, a fair day's work with good conduct seven marks, and an indifferent day's work or bad conduct six marks. On Sundays, holidays, or when in hospital, a well-behaved prisoner earns seven marks per day. These marks have the following values: six marks equal sixpence, seven marks ninepence, and eight marks one shilling. Half the value of marks earned per day is deducted for the prisoner's maintenance, the rest being credited to his account, and thus ideally the prisoner will be credited with sixpence each day except on days when he does not or cannot work, when he will receive fourpence-halfpenny. The disciplinary value of these provisions is clear, for not only does conduct control the number of marks earned, but fines can be imposed as punishments.

There is an extensive list of articles—called indulgences—which habitual criminals may purchase out of their earnings once their accounts exceed £5. However, only in exceptional circumstances are they allowed to spend in any one week more than one-half of the sum credited to their accounts during the preceding week. Thus a balance between their present comfort and future advantage is maintained.

The first twelve prisoners brought under this earnings scheme were each credited, after half their earnings had been deducted for their maintenance, with an average of just under £1 8s. 6d. per month. Since then the annual reports of the Comptroller of Prisons have shown that both the productivity and the value of prison labour have been steadily increasing; so it is certain that the above average does not over-estimate the detainee's present earning power in the indeterminate stage of his imprisonment as an habitual criminal.

With the consent of the Comptroller of Prisons, preventive detainees may remit, if they so desire, a portion of their earnings to relatives of reputable character; provided, except under special circumstances, a credit balance of £5 is maintained in their account.

A system of visiting justices, visiting surgeons and visiting chaplains was instituted by the 1911 regulations. Broadly speaking, their duty is to give more services and attention to individual habitual criminals than is provided for other prisoners. They also sit on a consultative committee whose function we will consider.

Male habitual criminals serve the indeterminate part of their sentence in a separate wing of the Yatala Labour Prison, and they have a separate recreation yard. There is, however, a limited amount of association during working hours with other inmates of the prison. Each habitual criminal has a separate cell (there is some dormitory accommodation in South Australian prisons) in which he sleeps and eats, and he is allowed special privileges in the form of extra books, more frequent and protracted visits by friends and relatives, lighting in his cell beyond the normal hours, extra letters, and so on. If his conduct merits it, these privileges are granted on a much more liberal scale than is allowed to prisoners serving fixed terms.

Thus there is a difference in degree between the treatment accorded to habitual criminals at the indeterminate stage of their detention and that given to other prisoners—the difference taking the form of a general amelioration of conditions, personal supervision of their cases by the members of a special committee, and, most significant of all, a comprehensive earning scheme which can benefit both the detainee and his relatives.

6. *Who is responsible for the release of habitual criminals, and on what basis are decisions to release them made ?*

Section 323 (1):

" If the Governor determines that an habitual criminal is sufficiently reformed, or for other good cause, he may, by his warrant, direct his release."

The Consultative Committee established by the 1911 Regulations advises the Comptroller of Prisons; he forwards their advice and his comments thereon to the Chief Secretary, on whose advice the Governor acts.

The Consultative Committee also has important functions

concerning the general welfare of the preventive detainees. The 1911 Regulations provide that

> " there shall, as to the prisoners detained in any particular place of confinement, be a consultative committee, consisting of a visiting justice, the gaoler, the visiting surgeon, and the visiting chaplain to whose denomination the prisoner belongs. The committee shall be required to consider carefully the case of each prisoner, to deal with any specific matter referred to it by the head of the department, and to advise the Comptroller of Prisons thereon. The visiting justice, or in his absence the gaoler, shall preside at each meeting of the committee. The gaoler shall arrange for holding regular quarterly meetings and such extra meetings as may be found necessary. . . . The case of every prisoner shall be brought singly before the committee at their regular meetings."

In practice, when their particular case is being discussed at these quarterly meetings, the preventive detainees are themselves interviewed, and their particular problems discussed with them. On this committee falls the burden of the decision as to when to release the habitual criminal.

There is, however, another procedure by which the preventive detainee can himself take the initiative in seeking release. The 1911 Regulations provide that

> " any prisoner [here and in the Act ' prisoner ' refers only to an habitual criminal] may petition for release during his detention on a form to be prescribed by the Comptroller of Prisons. The petition shall be referred to the court before which the prisoner was tried, and afterwards shall be forwarded, with the report of the court thereon, to His Excellency the Governor for his decision. . . . The gaoler, when forwarding a petition for release, shall state if definite employment can be found for the prisoner, and every facility shall be given to a suitable prisoner to communicate with the Prisoners' Aid Association or any kindred organisation or any reputable person likely to find employment for him. Prison officers are enjoined to render all possible assistance in this respect."

But even when this procedure is followed, the Consultative Committee is not by-passed, and the 1936 Report of the Comptroller of Prisons states quite definitely that a petition for release would not be granted by the Governor unless it is recommended by the Consultative Committee.

The numbers involved are so small, and the work of the Consultative Committee consequently so concentrated, that individual attention can be given to the problem of releasing habitual criminals from preventive detention. As a result no body of practice has been built up from which one can deduce which factors weigh with the committee; but certainly there is much emphasis on the availability of definite employment, and in the 1915 Report of the Comptroller of Prisons it is stated that

> " the practice has been for the Consultative Committee not to recommend a petition for release until an offer for employment has been received in writing. This is a necessary precaution before liberating an habitual criminal, but unfortunately there is nothing to compel an ex-prisoner to accept the employment offered."

Apart from the work of the Consultative Committee in building up information on each habitual criminal, the 1911 Regulations provide further guidance for the Chief Secretary by ordering the Comptroller of Prisons to report to the Chief Secretary on each prisoner, giving particulars of conduct, health, prospect of reform and any other details deemed necessary. Thus, when considering a petition for release, or the advice of the Consultative Committee that a prisoner should be released, the Chief Secretary has an appreciable amount of information at his disposal.

7. *What are the conditions under which the habitual criminal is discharged, and what is the juridical status of one so discharged ?*

Section 323 (2):

> " Every habitual criminal so released while he remains within South Australia shall, once at least in every three months during the period of two years next after such release, report his address and occupation to the Commissioner of Police."

Section 323 (3):

> " Such report may be made either by the habitual criminal personally, or by letter signed by him, and posted to the Commissioner of Police at Adelaide."

The use of the formula "while he remains in South Australia", similar to that appearing in the habitual criminal legislation of the other States of Australia, is again worth noting.

The released habitual criminal continues to be an " habitual criminal " within the meaning of the Act for two years after his release. If, during that time, and being in South Australia, he fails to report his address and occupation as required, or conceals his name and address when charged with any offence, or is convicted of any indictable offence, or of any offence punishable on summary conviction for which imprisonment for a period exceeding three months may be ordered (or of certain offences against the Police Act, 1916), then, after serving any sentence imposed upon him, he

will be recommitted as an habitual criminal to the special wing of
the Yatala Labour Prison. Failing any of the above contingencies,
at the end of two years from his release, " the offender shall cease to
be an habitual criminal."[1]

From 1911 to 1916 the preventive detainee received on release all
the moneys standing to his credit. The 1916 Regulations provided that

> " on the release of any prisoner such portion of the balance standing to his credit
> in the account as the Comptroller of Prisons deems necessary, shall be paid to
> such prisoner, and on the subsequent production of evidence to the satisfac-
> tion of the said Comptroller that the prisoner is of good behaviour and is earning
> an honest living, the said Comptroller may pay such offender at any time such
> further portion of the balance as he deems expedient and necessary ; and on
> such offender ceasing to be an habitual criminal within the meaning of the
> Act, any balance due to such offender shall be forthwith paid to him."

8. To what extent are such habitual criminal laws applied ?

The estimated population of South Australia in 1946 slightly
exceeded 641,000. On December 31st, 1946, there were in that State
260 male convicted persons in confinement.

Since the inception of habitual criminal legislation in South
Australia and up to the end of 1946 the following number of men
have been declared habitual criminals:

1909	..	..	..	4
1910	..	..	..	6
1911	..	..	..	2
1912	..	..	..	1
1913	..	..	..	2
1914	..	..	..	1
1915	..	..	..	1
1916	..	..	..	3
1917	..	..	..	1
1923	..	..	..	1
1925	..	..	..	1
1928	..	..	..	2
1929	..	..	..	1
1930	..	..	..	4
1933	..	..	..	2
1934	..	..	..	1
1937	..	..	..	2
1939	..	..	..	2
Total	..	..	..	37

[1] Section 325.

In the annual reports of the Comptroller of Prisons much is made of the extremely small number of habitual criminals who have been declared " habitual " a second time. For example, in the report for the year 1946, it is stated that since the habitual criminal provisions came into force, only two habitual criminals have been so reconvicted after release from Yatala Labour Prison. But this statement is misleading unless the words " while he remains in South Australia " are kept in mind. Information in support of this argument is available in the form of the later careers of the first nine habitual criminals whose earnings we considered above. This information is scattered throughout the yearly reports of the Comptroller of Prisons, and is to the following effect:

H.C. 1 : Aged 66 when discharged for medical reasons after only seven months in the indeterminate stage of his sentence. A charitable collection was made for him and his passage paid to England.

H.C. 2 : Returned to his own country—the United States of America.

H.C. 3 : Went to Tasmania and soon got into trouble there, receiving a sentence of 18 months for larceny. He is *not* one of the two failures.

H.C. 4 : Employment in New South Wales was obtained for him by the Prisoners' Aid Association, and he departed for that State.

H.C. 5 : Proceeded to Brisbane, Queensland.

H.C. 6 : Earned £29 0s. 2d. for himself, in the indeterminate stage of his imprisonment, of which he spent £6 16s. 4d. on indulgences, being given a lump sum of £22 3s. 10d. on discharge. Though offered employment he did not accept it, but instead spent the £22 riotously and then left South Australia.

H.C. 7 : Went to Melbourne, Victoria.

H.C. 8 : Left prison for Broken Hill, New South Wales. He failed to find employment there and returned to Adelaide, South Australia, and was assisted by the Prisoners' Aid Association to Melbourne, Victoria, where he had relatives.

H.C. 9 : Is one of the two failures. Having earned £19, and received £2 15s. on discharge, and definite employment having been found for him in Victoria, he was seen off on the Melbourne express and handed over to his would-be employer in the train at Adelaide. Despite their efforts to get him out of the State, he got off the train unexpectedly, returned to Adelaide, and was very soon there convicted on a charge of larceny, and again declared an habitual criminal.

Thus, the almost virginal records of habitual criminals discharged in South Australia is a reflection more of the efforts of the authorities in that State to persuade such people to live elsewhere, than of the reformation effected in the detainees' characters. Certainly, the citizens of South Australia are not again troubled by criminals whom they have once declared " habitual "; though they may be annoyed by the " ex-habituals " of other States of the Commonwealth.

WESTERN AUSTRALIA

The Western Australian Criminal Code of 1913 (Act No. 29 of 1913) provided for a dual-track system of punishing habitual criminals by which they were sent to preventive detention during the Governor's pleasure or for such period as the Court sentencing them thought desirable. Habitual criminals were defined objectively in terms of their prior offences, these offences being classified in a somewhat similar manner to that followed in the New South Wales habitual criminal legislation. Regulations were promulgated in the *Western Australian Government Gazette* on July 10th, 1914, implementing this legislation. These regulations inaugurated a preventive detention system modelled on the New South Wales pattern. Though this system was later abandoned in Western Australia, a brief survey of its leading characteristics will throw into great prominence the later developments in that State.

Under the 1914 regulations, habitual criminals were committed to Fremantle Gaol where, having served the fixed term of imprisonment imposed upon them, they became subject to preventive detention. At this stage they fell under the administrative control of a committee which met monthly and gave individual attention to the case of each preventive detainee. Regulation 5 of the 1914 regulations provided that

> " Persons subject to preventive detention shall, so far as the accommodation of the place of confinement permits, be treated as a separate class, and may have their cells lit up for an hour longer than is permitted in the case of prisoners under sentence, and may dine together if accommodation permits. They will also be allowed such recreation and games as the superintendent approves, and shall not be subject to separate treatment."

Preventive detainees were classified as follows:

(i)   Unskilled Labourers ;
(ii) Skilled Labourers ;
(iii) Artisans, Professional Men, Clerks.

Their remuneration varied according to this classification, unskilled labourers receiving eight shillings, skilled labourers ten shillings, and members of class (iii) twelve shillings per week, " provided that for those confinees who have no dependents, the rates of remuneration shall be one-half the above prescribed amounts."[1]

---

[1] Regulation 1, which also gave a fairly wide definition of " dependent ".

The regulations insisted that every preventive detainee be put to work at some trade or calling; and if on reception they had no particular skill at any avocation, they were to be put to tailoring, shoemaking, carpentry or smithing, commencing as labourers and having the opportunity of promotion to the second and then the third class as they became proficient. Those who through old age or infirmity were unfitted for work were to be classed as unskilled labourers, and paid only two shillings and sixpence per week. Regulation 4 is interesting, providing that

> " Any person subject to preventive detention may be required to teach other persons, subject to such detention, the particulai trade or calling in which he is proficient, and refusal to do so will be punishable by loss of marks or earnings."

In another respect preventive detention in Western Australia followed the methods of New South Wales. Privileges were related to membership of one of four grades, promotion from the first grade, through the second and third grades, to the fourth grade, depending on a marks system which took cognisance of behaviour and industriousness. However, in Western Australia, more privileges were given in the first grade, leaving only a few to be added in the succeeding grades, the threat of worse being regarded as a stronger incentive than the hope of better conditions.

This system was applied in Western Australia from 1914 to 1918; but during that time only ten criminals were subjected to it. The Comptroller General of Prisons, in his annual reports of 1917 and 1918 to the Minister of Justice,[1] pointed to the rarity of application of this legislation, advocated its abandonment, and suggested that Western Australia should model her indeterminate sentence legislation on that introduced in Victoria in 1908. Pursuant to his recommendations, Bills were brought before the Western Australian Parliament in 1917 and again in 1918, and on December 24th, 1918, the Criminal Code Amendment Act, 1918,[2] received the Royal Assent. It is this Act, as amended in one minor particular by the Criminal Code Amendment Act, 1945,[3] to which we will now address ourselves. Section references, unless otherwise specified, are to the Western Australian Criminal Code as amended by the above two Acts.

[1] Which were laid before the Western Australian Parliament and printed in the Government *Gazette*.
[2] Act No. 32 of 1918.   [3] Act No. 40 of 1945.

1. To whom do such laws apply ?

In Western Australia, following the Victorian model, the indeterminate sentence occupies an important place in the penal system, and applies to many classes of offenders besides habitual criminals.

Section 661 defines as an " habitual criminal " one " apparently of the age of eighteen years or upwards " who is " convicted of any indictable offence, not punishable by death, and has been previously so convicted on at least two occasions." The net is thus flung very wide, the test being primarily an objective one. Having convicted such a person for the offence charged, the Court may " declare that he is an habitual criminal, and direct that on the expiration of the term of imprisonment then imposed upon him, he be detained during the Governor's pleasure in a reformatory prison."

Section 664:

> " A person shall be deemed to have been previously convicted of an offence for the purposes of this chapter if so convicted anywhere or at any time whether heretofore or hereafter, and whether within or outside of Western Australia and such conviction shall, if such offence is of the same or substantially the same nature as any offence defined by the law of this State, be deemed for the purposes aforesaid a conviction for the offence so defined."

Parallel to those provisions, Section 662 empowers courts to order that any person " convicted of any indictable offence, not punishable by death (whether such person has been previously convicted of any indictable offence or not) shall be committed to a reformatory prison and detained there during the Governor's pleasure." This indeterminate sentence may be served forthwith or after serving a sentence of imprisonment for the offence of which the prisoner stands convicted. In deciding whether to apply this indeterminate sentence or not, the Court must have regard " to the antecedents, character, age, health or mental condition of the person convicted, the nature of the offence or any special circumstances of the case." This section is thus a foil to Section 661, providing a means by which similar treatment to that accorded to " habitual criminals " can be applied to those whose record does not permit them to be so classified in Western Australia; and enabling this decision to be taken with regard not only to the type of offence committed, but also to the personal qualities and particular characteristics of the prisoner. For such prisoners, the Court can decide whether a single-track or dual-track reformatory punishment would be more suitable.

Though Section 661 of the Western Australian Criminal Code is an " habitual offender " law within our definition of that phrase, it may be argued, with some force, that this is not true of Section 662 of that Code, the effect of which is to provide for reformatory training of indefinite duration for any person convicted of an indictable offence, and for whom the Court thinks this an appropriate punishment—all such offenders can hardly be regarded as " habituals " even within our wide definition of that term. This argument is strengthened by the fact that the Amending Act of 1945 deleted the words "apparently of the age of eighteen years or upwards " from Section 662, but left them unaltered in Section 661, such a deletion of the lower age limit from Section 662 being indicative of its wide application to the more dangerous youthful offender; again hardly "habituals". This juxtaposition of provisions dealing with habitual and youthful offenders is far from rare, as witness the English Prevention of Crime Act, 1908, but it is certainly unusual to find such a similarity of legislative provisions for such divergent types of offenders.

On the other hand, Sections 661 to 668 were inserted into the Criminal Code in place of provisions dealing exclusively with habitual criminals objectively defined, and it is therefore arguable that Section 662 is not likely to be entirely without relevance to such offenders. In truth, in any legal system where the indeterminate sentence is applied to an appreciable extent, the line between the treatment to be accorded habitual criminals and to certain other offenders tends to be blurred; and this is because, with the wide discretion given to the administrative authority, exact specification of the purpose behind particular indeterminate sentences is not necessary or desirable.

Those sentenced under Section 662, as well as those sentenced under Section 661, are sent to a reformatory prison; and the further specially relevant provisions of this Code, Sections 663 to 668, apply to them both. Certain it is that the application of these sections is such that those whom one can well regard as "habituals", whether they have been so declared or not, are caught by both Sections 661 and 662.

2. Who controls their application ?

Section 663 is explicit on this question:

> " Any question arising under this chapter as to whether any person is or is not an habitual criminal or has or has not been previously convicted, or should or should not be detained in a reformatory prison, shall be determined by the court on such evidence as the court may think fit to hear."

The declaration that a person who qualifies under Section 661 is an habitual criminal is left to the discretion of the trial judge, and no special form of indictment or other modification of normal procedure is necessary.

3. Do such laws envisage aggravation of punishment or special measures ? If the latter, do the special measures follow or take the place of the punishment for the last offence ?

Special measures are provided for the punishment of habitual criminals—special in the sense that mere aggravation of punishment is not intended; but not in the sense that such measures are exclusively confined to the treatment of habitual criminals.

For the habitual criminal as defined by Section 661, a dual-track system is applied. On the other hand, Section 662 leaves to the discretion of the Court the question of prior imprisonment. The adherence to the dual-track in Section 661, and the wide class of offenders covered by Section 662, mean that in practice " habituals " will have to serve a fixed term of imprisonment before graduating to the indeterminate stage.

4. What is the form of sentence imposed ?

A completely indeterminate form of sentence is imposed, the sentence directing that the habitual criminal " be detained during the Governor's pleasure in a reformatory prison."

5. If a special measure is applied, what is the degree of differentiation between it and other long-term imprisonment ?

Section 665, subsection 2, is the seed from which the conditions governing the organisation of reformatory prisons grow, but in itself it gives no details of these conditions. The Statute which directly controls the governance of gaols and reformatory prisons in Western Australia is the Prisons Act, 1903-1918. Sections 64A to 64N of that Act[1] contain explicit directions for the control of reformatory prisons; and these directions have in turn been amplified and put into operation by regulations made under the Prisons Act, 1903-1918, the actually operating regulations having been promulgated in the *Gazette* on August 14th, 1940. It is these statutory provisions and regulations which give the answer to this question.

[1] Inserted by Act No. 31 of 1918, Section 3.

Habitual criminals, as well as those sentenced pursuant to Section 662, are detained in a reformatory prison in which the conditions are appreciably different from those in Western Australian gaols. Fremantle Prison is the main reformatory prison, and a comparison between the treatment accorded prisoners there and in other gaols is, in terms of English penology, a comparison between the training prison at Maidstone in 1948 and any local prison in England in that year. In other words, there is a profound difference in the treatment of those serving their sentences in a reformatory prison, and those serving them elsewhere. This will become apparent when we examine the conditions in the former.

But both habituals, so declared, and those sentenced under Section 662, were consigned, as from 1919, to the " reformatory " part of Fremantle Prison; and between these two groups there is no appreciable differentiation of penal treatment. Further, Sections 64B, 64C and 64D of the Prisons Act, 1903-1918, give power to certain penal authorities to transfer from gaols to reformatory prisons, prisoners not sentenced to indeterminate sentences, but whom the Indeterminate Sentences Board, the Comptroller General of Prisons, the Minister, and the Governor agree should be imprisoned in a reformatory prison. Such transferees cannot be detained in the reformatory prison for a period longer than the residue of their sentence at the time of transfer.

Thus habitual criminals share the conditions of their imprisonment with many other types of prisoner, and therefore it can be stated that the special measures applied to them are not extensively differentiated from those applied to many other long-term prisoners. Indeed, the only difference is that, out of working hours, there is an endeavour to segregate " habituals " from other reformatory detainees, this segregation having, since 1919, been enforced, as far as possible, judging by the annual reports of the Comptroller General of Prisons. Even this segregation is more illusory than real, for in prison a segregation that is not enforced at all times is no segregation at all.

Since the Western Australian system of reformatory detention incorporates an interesting adaptation of ideas from several of the other States of Australia, with some original penological conceptions, let us consider the conditions under which all these detainees, including habitual criminals, serve their sentences in reformatory prisons.

Section 64E of the Prisons Act, 1903-1918, empowered the Governor to appoint an Indeterminate Sentences Board of three members, holding office for three years but eligible for reappointment. On this Board fell the general duty of supervising prisoners in reformatory prisons and in particular, Subsection 5:

" (a) to make careful enquiry as to whether any persons detained in any reformatory prison are sufficiently reformed to be released on probation or whether there are any good and sufficient reasons for the release on probation of any person so detained ;

(b) with the Comptroller-General to decide regarding transfers from gaols to reformatory prisons, and to report on the behaviour of such transferees ;

(c) to make recommendations to the Comptroller-General as to the release on probation of any person detained in a reformatory prison, or as to any such transfer, setting forth in each case the reasons for the recommendations ;[1]

(d) in making any recommendation as to such release, to have regard to the safety of the public or of any individual or class of persons and the welfare of the person whom it is proposed to release ;

(e) to report to the Minister on any prisoner or other matter, when required to do so, and to report generally as to its work each year."

Section 64F of the same Act provides that " every person detained in a reformatory prison shall, subject to the regulations, work at some trade or vocation or be employed in some labour " and then orders that the products of the prisoner's work shall be sold and that " of the net proceeds arising from the sale or disposal of the products of his work such portion as may be prescribed shall be credited to him, or such portion as may be prescribed of the wages earned by him according to the scale prescribed for the class of labour in which he is employed shall be credited to him." As in other States of the Commonwealth of Australia, part of this money may be applied to the maintenance of the prisoner's dependents, his account is accessible to him, and the money he accumulates is to be used to expedite his rehabilitation subsequent to his discharge, as well as for the purchase of " luxuries " during his confinement.

The regulations made under the Prisons Act, 1903-1918, and promulgated in 1940, amplify the above statutory provisions. They

---

[1] That reasons have to be given for such recommendations is a sound provision and has been adopted in England, in a different context, by Section 17, subsection 3, of the Criminal Justice Act, 1948, by which a Court of Quarter Sessions or a Court of Summary Jurisdiction, imposing a sentence of imprisonment on a person under the age of twenty-one years, is compelled to state the reasons for its opinion that no other method of dealing with him is appropriate.

require that the Indeterminate Sentences Board should visit each reformatory prison at least once every three months, and they prescribe its duties in detail. The Board is to be furnished by the Comptroller General with such records, reports and returns as it requires, and is further to have the guidance of advice from the Superintendent of Fremantle Prison, the chaplain and the medical officer.

Regulations 206 and 207 provide that all prisoners subject to reformatory treatment shall be graded as follows:

> 1st Grade : Those sentenced under Section 661, i.e. the habitual criminals so declared.
>
> 2nd Grade : Those sentenced under Section 662.
>
> 3rd Grade : Those prisoners undergoing sentences of imprisonment only, and wno were selected by the board as suitable for reformatory treatment—the transferees.

It is then ordered that " as far as practicable, and except when otherwise recommended by the Board, and approved by the Comptroller General, inmates of one grade shall be kept apart from inmates of any other grade." The remainder of these regulations, with few exceptions, apply to all three grades, equally. They are all to be dealt with " under a progressive stage system, by which they will practically determine their own treatment as regards enjoyment of privileges, or the reverse ", and all prisoners are to be classified into one of four classes—namely, primary, intermediate, high, or highest class. Members of the last three are eligible to earn various privileges denied to members of the primary class, which is in effect a disciplinary class.

On commencing reformative treatment, the detainee is placed in the intermediate class, from which he may rise by industry and good conduct measured by a marks system. Regulations 215 to 222 enumerate the privileges which may be accorded to such prisoners —better rations, weekly issue of 1 oz. of tobacco, right to purchase certain luxuries, facilities to improve their education, frequent changes of library books, lights in cells for longer period, monthly visits of twenty minutes' duration, to write and receive one letter per month, and better dress.

On promotion to the high class the detainee " shall be eligible to receive full privileges "[1] and these are very liberal. There is a sudden and very extensive improvement on the treatment given him during his membership of the intermediate class; for example, he

---

[1] Regulation 223.

may now change library books daily, and is given 1¾ ozs. of tobacco weekly. Indeed, on promotion to the highest class, the only change in conditions is in the insignia on his dress, and the greater likelihood of his release on probation.

Breaches of discipline are punished by order of the visiting justice, who has the same power as in relation to other prisoners. But since reformative detainees earn appreciable wages and have more privileges they are more susceptible to punishment by fine, and by deprivation of privileges; that is, by reduction to the primary class.

Regulations 236 to 239 give the Indeterminate Sentences Board power to control the industrial employment of the reformative detainee, and require every such prisoner to " be put to such work, or trade . . . as he is most suitable for, or proficient in, and which . . . will the most fit him for self-support when at liberty. Male inmates shall commence as labourers, and may be promoted . . . to be artisans as they become proficient." Those physically unfit for work are not eligible to earn wages, but on their release they will be credited with such sums as the Board (subject to the Minister's approval), after considering their particular cases, in its discretion recommends.

On the subject of wages, the 1940 regulations are very interesting:

" 240. The following shall be the scale of wages to inmates :

(a) Inmates in the intermediate class, not being artisans or clerks, shall receive the same scale of wages as prisoners who are not inmates of a reformatory prison, and when classed as artisans or clerks, such inmates shall receive double that scale. Provided that tradesmen or improvers, serving under sentence of imprisonment and transferred to a reformatory prison, may be allowed to continue to earn and receive such wages as were earned and received by them at the time when so transferred. Inmates in the intermediate class may spend one-half of the amount earned by them on the purchase of luxuries ; the balance shall be placed to their credit.

(b) For male inmates in the high and highest classes :

| Labourers .. | .. | .. | 4s. per week |
| Artisans and clerks | | .. | 6s. per week. |

Two shillings per week of the above amounts may be spent on the purchase of luxuries and the balance shall be placed to the credit of the inmate.

" 241. The board shall, from time to time, recommend what amounts (if any) shall be applied towards the maintenance of any inmate's wife and family (if any), or of any person dependent, or partially dependent, on him.

" 242. There shall be credited to each inmate such portion of wages earned by him as the board may from time to time recommend."

Though the above system constitutes a less generous scheme than is in operation in several other States of the Commonwealth, its organisation appears to be very fair and efficient.

The furniture of a reformative detainee's cell, his clothing, and his bedding are all superior to that which is allowed other prisoners. Also, every such detainee is provided with his own locker (and his own key!) in which to keep his belongings. To a prisoner this means a great deal.

Finally, the hours of association and recreation are very much more liberal than those permitted to other prisoners, and reformative detainees " will be provided with games, such as draughts, dominoes, chess and rope quoits and, when practicable, may, after tea, play games or read in the association room up to 8 p.m."[1]

6. Who is responsible for the release of habitual criminals, and on what basis are the decisions to release them made ?

The Governor of Western Australia is nominally responsible for their release. He acts on the advice of the Minister, who is advised by the Indeterminate Sentences Board and the Comptroller General of Prisons.

The initiative for release resides in the reformative detainee himself; though this does not, of course, detract from the over-riding power of the Governor, on the advice of the Minister, to release any prisoner at any time by the exercise of the Royal Prerogative of Mercy. Normally, however, the prisoner petitions for release on probation when the Indeterminate Sentences Board decides that he may do so, and the general practice is to allow this only when a reformative detainee has been a member of the highest class for six months.

Regulation 248 provides that " inmates when petitioning shall state if definite employment is available for them, and every facility should be afforded to an eligible inmate to communicate regarding employment with any organisation, or reputable person, likely to find employment for him." Though the availability of employment is regarded, as in other States of Australia, as of great significance in deciding on the release of a detainee, Section 64E of the Prisons Act, 1903-1918, directs the Board when considering such petitions with a view to reporting on them to the Minister (to whom they will forward the petition through the Comptroller General, together with

[1] Regulation 253.

their comments on it) " to have regard to the safety of the public or of any individual or class of persons, and the welfare of the person whom it is proposed to release." The priority here is important —first the community, then the offender.

Section 64H of the Prisons Act, 1903-1918, empowers the Indeterminate Sentences Board, by order in writing signed by any two of its members, and with the concurrence of the Comptroller General of Prisons, to permit any member of the highest class to leave the reformatory prison temporarily in order to test his reform and the likelihood of his rehabilitation. Such leave is for whatever term and under whatever conditions the Board specifies, and the detainee is deemed to continue in the legal custody of the superintendent of the reformatory prison, and may therefore at any time, on an order in writing signed by any two members of the Board, be arrested without warrant by any warder of the prison or any member of the police force. In copying this excellent Victorian idea of pre-probation temporary discharge, the Western Australian legislature gave to the Indeterminate Sentences Board one of its most effective means of assisting the prisoner while protecting the public.

7. *What are the conditions under which the habitual criminal is discharged, and what is the juridical status of one so discharged ?*

Section 666 (1):

"The Governor may at any time, subject to any provisions to be made under any law relating to prisons, and subject to any conditions which he may see fit to impose, direct the release on probation for two years of any person undergoing an indeterminate sentence . . . and such person shall be so released accordingly."

One condition frequently imposed is that the licensee shall place himself under the supervision of a society willing to take charge of his case, which will be required to report regularly on the licensee to the Comptroller General of Prisons.

Section 666 (3):

"Every person so released while he remains in Western Australia shall (except in so far as the Governor shall, in the case of a person placed under the supervision or authority of some society, otherwise order) be subject to police supervision."

If, during the two-year period of probation, the released prisoner is proved, at any court of petty sessions in Western Australia, to have failed to comply with any of the conditions of his release, or is proved to have been associating with reputed thieves or criminals, or is convicted of any offence punishable by a period of imprisonment exceeding one month, then he shall be recommitted to a reformatory prison during the Governor's pleasure. Such re-committal may be either directly or after imprisonment if it is a criminal offence by which the indeterminate sentence is revived.

On licence, and when temporarily released prior to such licensing, the detainee is controlled to a certain extent by the moneys standing to his credit which are handed over to the Minister, " who shall disburse it in such manner as the Board considers conducive to his welfare; but if during his period of probation he is sentenced to imprisonment he shall, if the Minister so directs, forfeit the said sum or so much thereof as is in the hands of the Minister (as the case may be), and the same shall be paid into Consolidated Revenue."[1]

If within two years the prisoner released on probation is not recommitted in Western Australia " then the indeterminate sentence shall be deemed to be annulled as from the end of such period."[2]

8. To what extent are such habitual criminal laws applied ?

The estimated population of Western Australia in 1946 slightly exceeded 498,000. The number of prisoners under sentence in gaols and prisons on June 30th, 1946, was 313.

Unfortunately, since 1929, the Western Australian statistics have failed to distinguish between habitual criminals and other prisoners subject to indeterminate sentences, and it is therefore impossible to answer our question with accuracy. However, during the period 1919 to 1929, thirty-two habitual criminals completed the finite portion of their sentences and were received into Fremantle Reformatory.[3]

From a consideration of the various other sources of information on Western Australia, it would seem that since 1929, the numbers so sentenced have, if anything, increased, and that from 1929 to 1932, nineteen more criminals were declared "habituals". In the year ending June 30th, 1945, six offenders were so declared, and a further six in 1946.

Considering its population and its low rate of crime, habitual

---

[1] Section 64 F, subsection 6, of the Prisons Act, 1903-18.
[2] Section 667, subsection 4.
[3] Figures gathered from the annual reports of the Comptroller-General of Prisons for the years 1919 to 1929. Since that of 1929 no reports have appeared in the *Western Australian Government Gazette*.

criminal legislation has assumed, in Western Australia, quite an important place in the penal system.

TASMANIA

We need not devote very much attention to the Tasmanian legislation and practice concerning habitual criminals. The course that has been followed is so very similar to that pursued in Western Australia that there is little to be gained by repeating the analysis we developed for that State.

From 1907 to 1921 the Habitual Criminals and Offenders Act, 1907, was in force in Tasmania. Under its provisions, which were akin to those of New South Wales and Queensland, 141 criminals were declared habitual and eventually released from confinement. In the Australian Year Book, Number 22, of 1929, it is claimed that of these 141 prisoners only four " defaulted " ; which probably only means that most of them left Tasmania shortly after their discharge. In 1924 the Indeterminate Sentences Act, 1921, came into force, and applied the Victorian approach to this problem. Thus, the Tasmanian legislature followed the course laid down in Western Australia and switched from the system adopted in New South Wales to that adopted in Victoria.

The Indeterminate Sentences Act, 1921, has since been amended by the Criminal Code Act, 1924, the Indeterminate Sentences Act, 1924, Statute Law Revision, and the Indeterminate Sentences Act, 1942. As in Western Australia, reformatory prisons are to receive those sentenced as habitual criminals, those committed either directly or after a finite sentence to an indeterminate term in a reformatory prison, and also those who are transferred from other gaols by authority of the Indeterminate Sentences Board and the Controller of Prisons. As in Victoria, indeterminate sentences may be imposed pursuant to conviction on indictment, and also by courts of petty sessions, who can order that certain persons shall be brought before a judge of the Supreme Court to be dealt with under the above legislation. The whole development in Tasmania and in Western Australia is indicative of the high regard in which the indeterminate sentence came to be held in Australia, as applied not only to habitual criminals but also to many other types of offenders.

None of this Tasmanian legislation includes any original conceptions which we need consider. His Majesty's Gaol, Hobart, is the only reformatory prison in Tasmania, and the regulations under which reformative detainees are imprisoned there were published in the *Tasmanian Government Gazette* on November 29th, 1923. The only point in which these regulations vary either from the Victorian or from the Western Australian practice is in the wages paid. Regulation 14 provides that the work which the detainee follows shall " as far as practicable be of a productive, reformative and educational character", and regulation 15 directs that " the scale of wages to be credited to such prisoners . . . shall be as follows:

Prisoners employed as skilled artisans	2s. per diem,
Prisoners employed on unskilled labour	1s. per diem.

The disposition of these wages is akin to the practice in Victoria.

No reports on the functioning of these Acts and the regulations made under them are available to the public, nor would the Premier's Office at Hobart divulge any such information. However, though no statistical information on the number of habitual criminals dealt with has been published, the Premier's Office did advise, for publication in this study, that from 1924 until August 1948, fifty-two offenders were sentenced as habitual criminals; that over the same period the daily average number of habitual criminals in Hobart Reformatory Prison was 4·2; and that the average duration of detention of individual habitual criminals at the indeterminate stage of their sentence was twenty-one months—a surprisingly short period.

Tasmania, which had an estimated population in 1946 slightly exceeding 253,000, and a very low rate of crime, has between 1907 and 1948 sentenced 193 persons as habitual criminals. Thus, in that State of the Commonwealth of Australia also, habitual criminal legislation has played a not inconsiderable part in the penal system.

3. CANADA

In Canada criminal law and penal practice are at present in a state of flux.

Widespread dissatisfaction among the public at the state of the prisons, and a plethora of riots in penitentiaries and provincial gaols led to the appointment in 1936 of a Royal Commission to investigate the penal system. The Commissioners who in 1938 finally reported[1] to the Minister of Justice were Mr. Justice Archambault,

[1] *Report of the Royal Commission to Investigate the Penal System of Canada.* King's Printer, Ottawa, 1938.

chairman, R. W. Craig, K.C., and J. C. McRuer, K.C. Their manifold recommendations were precisely formulated, and many were of a fundamental character. Unfortunately, the war and consequent staff shortages meant that those of their recommendations which involved new legislation or administrative reorganisation could not be introduced for some years.

In April 1946 General R. B. Gibson was appointed a Commissioner to consider, *inter alia*, the means of enforcing those recommendations of the 1938 Commissioners which were regarded as desirable, and had not till then been put into force. In February 1947 he presented his report.[1]

The study of both the above reports is a valuable and necessary background to any consideration of criminal and penal matters in Canada. They will be referred to hereunder as the Archambault Report and the Gibson Report respectively.

Until 1946 there were no sections of the Criminal Code applying specifically to habitual criminals. However, Sections 1051, 1052, 1053 and 1054, which were then in force, are of some relevance. Section 1051 provides that

" everyone who is convicted of any offence not punishable with death, shall be punished in the manner, if any, prescribed by the statute especially relating to such offence."

Section 1052 complements this by ordering that

" every person convicted of any indictable offence for which no punishment is specially provided, shall be liable to imprisonment for *five years*."

Sections 1053 and 1054 relate the above two sections to certain recidivists—and this includes habitual criminals—in the following terms:

Section 1053:

" Everyone who is convicted of an indictable offence not punishable with death committed after a previous conviction for an indictable offence is liable to imprisonment for *ten years*, unless some other punishment is directed by any statute for the particular offence. In such latter case the offender shall be liable to the punishment directed, and not to any other."

Section 1054:

" Everyone who is liable to imprisonment for life, or for any term of years, or other term, may be sentenced to imprisonment for any shorter term. . . ."

---

[1] *Report of General R. B. Gibson—A Commissioner Appointed under Order in Council, P.C. 1313, Regarding the Penitentiary System of Canada.* King's Printer, Ottawa, 1947.

Maximum penalties are set quite high in Canada. For example, the following offences carry a maximum sentence of fourteen years' imprisonment: larceny from a railway station, or from a dwelling house, or from the person of another; receiving stolen goods. Also most of the offences which are normally regarded as of greater social danger include in their statutory formulation a specified maximum term of imprisonment, and thus exclude the application of Section 1053 of the Criminal Code. In brief, prior to 1946 there was little aggravation of punishment specially provided for recidivists.

Before analysing the details of the Canadian habitual criminal legislation, introduced in 1946, it will be necessary to dispose of certain constitutional problems springing from Canada's federal structure. Section 91 of the British North America Act, 1867[1] states:

> "it is hereby declared that . . . the exclusive legislative authority of the Parliament of Canada extends to all matters coming within the classes of subjects next hereinafter enumerated, that is to say :
> 1. . . . .
> 27. The Criminal Law, except the Constitution of Courts of Criminal Jurisdiction, but including the Procedure in Criminal Matters.
> 28. The Establishment, Maintenance, and Management of Penitentiaries."

The legislatures of the Provinces were given power to make laws in relation to the establishment, maintenance and management of public and reformatory prisons in and for their Province. The scope of the Dominion power concerning penal matters, as distinct from the Provincial power, is therefore circumscribed by the word " Penitentiaries " in the British North America Act. The definition of this word has caused a certain amount of controversy, but its most recent formulation seems to be relatively secure from constitutional challenge. This is to be found in Section 46 of the Penitentiaries Act, 1939,[2] which provides that

> " everyone who is sentenced to imprisonment for life, or for a term of years, not less than two, shall be sentenced to imprisonment in the penitentiaries for the province in which the conviction takes place."

Thus, all those whose sentences of imprisonment are for terms of two years or more are imprisoned in "penitentiaries", which fall under the ægis of the Dominion Parliament at Ottawa. There is one exception to this rule: the Province of Ontario has an indeterminate sentence law by which prisoners can be sentenced to the provincial

---

[1] 30 and 31 Vict. c. 3.　　[2] Proclaimed September 1st, 1947.

gaol for a fixed term of anything up to two years less one day, and also to a subsequent indeterminate term which must not exceed two years less one day. The whole unrealistic division of penal powers between the Dominion and the Provincial authorities is sharply criticised and its abolition recommended in the Archambault Report.

The Archambault Report devotes entire chapters to " Recidivism " and to "Habitual Offenders ".[1] The basic assumption behind this report, constantly perceptible in the two chapters mentioned, is explicitly stated in the declaration that[2] " we believe we are on safe ground in stating that no system can be of any value if it does not contain, as its fundamental basis, the protection of society." One of the primary means to this end is, in the Commissioners' opinion, an efficient system of classification of prisoners and " the first step in the classification of the prison population is to segregate the incorrigible criminal in an institution specially designed for the treatment of this class of offender."[3] In the Gibson Report we see that this idea is under administrative consideration:[4]

" it is proposed to provide in Kingston Penitentiary in the East and in Manitoba Penitentiary in the West, for the detention of incorrigible and intractable prisoners whose conduct and anti-social attitude makes it desirable to separate them from the normal prison population in other institutions."

This primary segregation of incorrigibles is, of course, a very different matter from the special treatment of habitual criminals; but in Canada as elsewhere there appears to be a tendency to equate the penal treatment of both these groups, their essential difference being obscured by their inevitable overlapping.

On July 17th, 1946, " An Act to amend the Criminal Code "[5] received the Royal Assent. Part X (A) of that Act deals specifically and extensively with habitual criminals, Section 18 introducing into the Criminal Code Sections 575A to 575H. References hereunder are to those sections.

In considering these provisions, their tentative nature must be kept in mind. The last annual report of the Canadian Commissioner of Penitentiaries,[6] which treats the fiscal year ended March 31st,

---

[1] Also in Appendix III there appears a statistical study of recidivists in Canadian Penitentiaries who have over ten convictions.
[2] *Ibid.*, p. 8.   [3] Appendix III, p. 100.   [4] p. 10.
[5] Chapter 55 of the 1946 Statutes.
[6] King's Printer, Ottawa, 1949. See also the annual report of the Superintendent of Penitentiaries for the fiscal year ended March 31st, 1947. King's Printer, Ottawa, 1948.

1948, makes no mention of the application of the legislation which we shall consider; and it is quite possible that this legislation will never be applied, but that alternative measures will be introduced. As we shall see, this legislation is modelled closely on the English Prevention of Crime Act, 1908, which long before 1946 was regarded in England as a failure; and it appears that no great study went to the adaptation of the English Act to Canadian conditions.[1] It will not be necessary, therefore, to devote very much space to the analysis of this legislation.

1. To whom do such laws apply ?

Section 575c (1):

" A person shall not be found to be an habitual criminal unless the judge or jury as the case may be, finds on evidence,

(a) that since attaining the age of 18 years he has at least three times previously to the conviction of the crime charged in the indictment, been convicted of an indictable offence for which he was liable to at least five years' imprisonment, whether any such previous conviction was before or after the commencement of this part, and that he is leading persistently a criminal life ; or

(b) that he has on a previous conviction been found to be an habitual criminal and sentenced to preventive detention."

The dependence of this and other sections of the Canadian legislation on the English Prevention of Crime Act, 1908, is obvious.

A discretion is given the Court applying Section 575c, and this discretion is controlled by Section 575b, which provides that

" Where a person is convicted of an indictable offence . . . and subsequently the offender admits that he is or is found by a jury or a judge to be an habitual criminal, and the court passes a sentence upon the said offender, the court, if it is of opinion that, by reason of his criminal habits and mode of life, it is expedient for the protection of the public, may pass a further sentence ordering that he be detained in a prison for an indeterminate period and such detention is hereinafter referred to as preventive detention. . . ."

Thus, to be sentenced to preventive detention the criminal must, as well as having a criminal record involving three convictions of indictable offences punishable with at least five years' imprisonment (these convictions being on different occasions), be convicted of a further indictable offence at a time when he is (a) over eighteen

---

[1] Concerning this point and the violent opposition to this legislation which manifested itself in the Canadian House of Commons, see Vol. 86, No. 104, of the Canadian House of Commons Debates.

years of age; (*b*) leading persistently a criminal life; and (*c*) one whose criminal habits and mode of life require a special type of detention for the protection of the public.

2. Who controls their application ?

Section 575c:

" (2) In any indictment under this section it shall be sufficient, after charging the crime, to state that the offender is an habitual criminal.

(3) In the proceedings on the indictment the offender shall in the first instance be arraigned only on so much of that indictment as charges the crime, and if on arraignment he pleads guilty or is found guilty by the judge or jury, as the case may be, unless he thereafter pleads guilty to being an habitual criminal, the judge or jury shall be charged to inquire whether or not he is an habitual criminal and in that case it shall not be necessary to swear the jury again.

(4) A person shall not be tried on a charge of being an habitual criminal unless

(*a*) the Attorney-General of the province in which the accused is to be tried consents thereto ; and

(*b*) not less than seven days' notice has been given by the proper officer of the court by which the offender is to be tried and the notice to the offender shall specify the previous convictions and the other grounds upon which it is intended to found the charge."

Section 575E of the Code permits an offender sentenced to preventive detention to appeal against that sentence without leave of the appellate court.

In Chapter II we analysed the almost identical provisions of the English Act of 1908.

3. Do such laws envisage aggravation of punishment, or special measures ? If the latter, do the special measures follow, or take the place of, the punishment for the last offence ?

Section 575G:

" (1) The sentence of preventive detention shall take effect immediately on the conviction of a person on a charge that he is an habitual criminal.

(2) Persons undergoing preventive detention may be confined in a prison or part of a prison set apart for that purpose."

Elsewhere in the legislation we are considering, power is given for regulations to be made prescribing the conditions of preventive detention.

Thus, special measures are envisaged, and they are to be applied as a single-track system of dealing with habitual criminals.

4. What is the form of sentence imposed ?

Absolutely indeterminate.

5. If a special measure is applied, what is the degree of differentiation between it and other long-term imprisonment ?

The Archambault Report suggests[1] that

> " a special prison for habitual criminals should be erected remote from any other penal institution. In the erection of this prison it will be necessary to provide for safe custody by maximum security. Ample employment should also be provided. The attention of your Commissioners has been directed to the physical advantages, for the purposes of such an institution, of Grosse Isle, an island in the St. Lawrence river about 20 miles below the city of Quebec. This property was formerly used as a quarantine station by the Department of National Health. There are a number of buildings that could be altered for prison purposes. . . . The treatment to be accorded the prisoners in an institution for habitual offenders is a matter for careful study by the prison authorities. The purpose of the prison is neither punitive nor reformative but primarily segregation from society . . . if the punishment imposed in preventive detention is unduly rigorous, judges will refuse to commit habitual offenders for preventive detention and those who ought to be segregated from society will continue to be released from prison on the expiration of their sentences, so that the system will thus defeat its own purpose."

As yet,[2] no information is available concerning the implementation of these habitual criminal provisions; and, indeed, writing shortly before the passage of the legislation we are considering, General Gibson stated[3] that

> " With respect to the proposal that legislation be enacted to permit the permanent detention of habitual offenders, no institution is at present available for this purpose and it is considered that further study should be given to the results of such legislation in the United Kingdom and the United States and to the effect of the proposals for segregation in this report[4] before recommending that an institution for that purpose be established in Canada."

[1] Pp. 223-4.
[2] Information down to the end of March, 1948, is available in the annual report of the Commissioner of Penitentiaries.
[3] *Gibson Report,* p. 12.
[4] That is, the Kingston and Manitoba Penitentiaries for incorrigibles mentioned above.

Only time will provide an exact answer to this question of differentiation. In the meantime, one can legitimately doubt that the Canadian legislation has successfully exorcised the faults of the English Prevention of Crime Act, 1908, in adapting it to Canadian conditions. The two most important changes made are the duration of the punishment (indeterminate instead of a determined period between five and ten years) and the fact that Canadian preventive detention is a single-track system, while the English Act introduced a preventive detention sentence to be served after the fixed term of imprisonment imposed for the last offence.

6 and 7. Who is responsible for the release of habitual criminals, and on what basis are decisions to release them made ? What are the conditions under which the habitual criminal is discharged, and what is the juridical status of one so discharged ?

Section 575H of the Code provides that

> " The Minister of Justice shall, once at least in every three years during which a person is detained in custody under a sentence of preventive detention, review the conditions, history and circumstances of that person with a view to determining whether he should be placed out on licence, and if so, on what conditions."

No information, other than that contained in the above section of the Code, is yet available to provide an answer to these two questions. Presumably, habitual criminals would come under the provisions of the " Ticket of Leave Act "[1] which would subject them to the usual type of conditional release with regular reporting either to the police or to approved aftercare authorities. However, the conditions upon which habitual criminals would be released could hardly be circumscribed by that Act, and again we must await practical developments.[2]

4. NEW ZEALAND

The first statute to deal with habitual criminals in New Zealand was the Habitual Criminals and Offenders Act, of 1906. This legislation was consolidated into the " Crimes Act, 1908," which has since been amended on the subject of habitual criminals by three

---

[1] R.S., c. 150.
[2] Since the above was written, some interesting material on Canadian penology has been presented in the *Canadian Bar Review*, Vol. XXVII, No. 9, which is devoted entirely to " Penal Reform in Canada."

" Crimes Amendment " Acts, passed in 1910, 1917 and 1920 respectively. There are other statutes amending the Crimes Act 1908, which have had an indirect effect on the treatment of habitual criminals (e.g. Act No. 25 of 1945, which varied the appellate procedure in all criminal cases, including those involving a declaration that a man is an habitual criminal); but as these statutes have affected neither the purport nor the substance of the habitual criminal legislation in force, and do not apply specifically to habitual criminals, we shall not consider them in any detail. References hereunder are to the Crimes Act, 1908, as amended by the statutes of 1910, 1917 and 1920, unless otherwise stated.

Indeterminate or indefinite sentences are applicable in New Zealand to three groups or classifications of criminal—to those sentenced to reformative detention, to those declared habitual criminals, and to those declared habitual offenders. A brief discussion of the " reformative detention " sentence is a necessary background to an analysis of the habitual criminal and offender legislation.

Section 3 of the Crimes Amendment Act, 1910, provides that:

> " when any person is . . . convicted on indictment of any offence . . . punishable by imprisonment (or is committed for sentence to the Supreme Court by an inferior court) . . . the Supreme Court or a judge thereof before or to which or to whom such person is convicted or committed for sentence may, if the said court or judge thinks fit, having regard to the conduct, character, associations, or mental conditions of such person, the nature of the offence, or any special circumstances of the case—
>
> (a) Direct, as part of his sentence, that on the expiration of the term of imprisonment then imposed upon him he be detained in prison for reformative purposes for any period not exceeding ten years ; or
>
> (b) Without imposing any prior term of imprisonment upon him as aforesaid, sentence him to be forthwith committed to prison, to be there detained for reformative purposes for any period not exceeding ten years."

Section 4 of the Crimes Amendment Act, 1910, gives to magistrates power to sentence those convicted by them of any offence punishable by imprisonment for more than three months to reformative detention up to three years. The discretion given to magistrates is to be exercised on the same grounds as those specified in Section 3, and similarly magistrates have a choice between imposing reformative detention as a dual-track or a single-track system of punishment.

Thus, the particular characteristics of the offender are the major factors in leading judges and magistrates to impose this indefinite type of sentence, though, of course, among the more important indications of such characteristics are the crime for which the offender stands convicted and his criminal record. Courts may, and usually do, prescribe a maximum period for which a prisoner sentenced to reformative detention may be detained; and there are always the upper limits of ten years and three years circumscribing the powers of the Supreme Court and the Magistrates Courts respectively. The prisoner having been so sentenced, the discretion as to the actual time he will spend in prison, and as to when he will be released on probation and when discharged, passes to the Prisons Board—an authority whose function we will consider.

The annual report of the Prisons Board for the year 1946 reveals that

> " during the period from January, 1911, to December, 1946, 6,456 prisoners were sentenced to reformative detention under the provisions of the Crimes Amendment Act, 1910. The number of cases that have been recommended for release or discharge is 5,260. In 706 cases prisoners were required to serve the full sentence imposed by the court. Of the total number released after undergoing reformative detention, 25.18 per cent. have been returned to prison either for non-compliance with the conditions of the release or for committing further offences, leaving approximately 75 per cent. who have not been convicted of any further offence."

The above figures are thrown into even greater prominence when it is realised that normally there are approximately a thousand prisoners in New Zealand prisons at any one time and that this number represents somewhere between 6 and 7 per 10,000 of population. Nevertheless, the 75 per cent. success which is claimed in the above report (and that counting as failures all those whose licences to be at large had been revoked) is quite remarkable. But it is not the purpose of this study to investigate " reformative detention " in New Zealand, and an outline of that system is presented merely as a background to the habitual criminal legislation in force. The connection between reformative detention and the habitual criminal legislation will become clearer as we discuss the latter.

1. To whom do the habitual criminal laws apply ?

The Crimes Act, 1908, sections 29 and 30, defines those who may be declared " habitual criminals " or "habitual offenders". For clarity of exposition we shall divide certain offences there listed into two classes—class I comprising certain sexual offences and offences connected with abortion; class II comprising wounding, robbery, burglary, housebreaking, theft, false pretences, extortion, forgery and mischief.[1] Before he can be declared an " *habitual criminal* " a prisoner must be:

(1) convicted on indictment of an offence included in class I, and must be a person who " has been previously convicted on at least *two* occasions of any offence mentioned in such class I (whether of the same description of offence or not)"; or

(2) convicted on indictment of an offence included in class II, and must be a person who " has been previously convicted on at least *four* occasions of any offence mentioned in classes I or II (whether of the same description of offence or not)."

Before he can be declared an " *habitual offender* " a prisoner must be:[2]

(a) convicted summarily of any offence punishable by not less than three months' imprisonment, and must be a person who " has been previously convicted summarily on at least *six* occasions of any offence punishable by imprisonment for not less than three months," and who has also been convicted on indictment on at least two occasions of any offences falling within class I or on at least four occasions of any offences in classes I and II ; or

(b) convicted of any offences under Sections 49 to 52 inclusive of the Police Offences Act, 1908, and must be a person who " has been previously convicted on at least *six* occasions of any offence mentioned in such sections (whether of the same description of offence or not)." These sections of the Police Offences Act relate to certain vagrancy offences by " idle and disorderly persons " ; to persons armed by night with weapons or who carry a disguise or deleterious drug without lawful excuse ; to loiterers and trespassers by night ; to those guilty of escaping from prison ; to those dealt with as rogues and vagabonds who have previously been convicted as rogues and vagabonds or who violently resist arrest as rogues and vagabonds.

---

[1] For a more exact definition of these two classes see Section 29 (3) of the Crimes Act, 1908.

[2] It should be mentioned at this stage that the " habitual offender " provisions of this regulation are very rarely applied.

The above four types of criminal histories which may lead to a declaration that a prisoner is an habitual criminal or an habitual offender have been further clarified by their interpretation by the New Zealand courts; and previous convictions for the purpose of qualifying as an habitual have been much more widely interpreted than in most other countries.[1] The above sections apply to those who " have been previously convicted on at least (two, four, or six) occasions ". In 1910 these words were judicially considered for the first time in the case of R. v. Steele.[2] The facts in that case were not at issue, and were to the effect that Steele had on May 27th, 1907, pleaded guilty on four separate indictments for theft and false pretences. He was sentenced to four terms of eighteen months' imprisonment, the sentences to run concurrently. In December 1908 he pleaded guilty to nine separate charges, each being the subject of a separate information, and was sentenced to two years' imprisonment on each count, sentences to run concurrently, and in addition he was declared to be an habitual criminal within the meaning of Section 29 of the Crimes Act, 1908. On appeal from this declaration that he was an habitual criminal, he contended that he had not " previously been convicted on at least four occasions " of any offence mentioned in classes I or II as defined in Section 29, and that therefore the Court had had no power to declare him an habitual criminal. Steele conducted his own defence, basing his plea on the argument that the Legislature did not intend that a person convicted on several indictments at one sitting of the court should be declared an habitual criminal; and that " occasion " is an abstract term involving a series of instances, an indefinite period of time which must therefore be read in this context as including the conception of separate sittings of the court, and thus within the meaning of the section he had been convicted on only one previous occasion—that is, on May 27th, 1907. His appeal was refused, it being held that what took place on May 27th, 1907, constituted his conviction on " four previous occasions ". In the course of his judgment, Stout, C.J., said: " I do not think that the fact that he was called upon to plead guilty to those indictments on one day would alter what he did. They were separate events in his life. There were four separate indictments; they were different offences, and what he did were four

---

[1] Previous convictions for offences committed (and sentences imposed) before the passage of the Habitual Criminals and Offenders Act, 1906, count for purposes of this Act: Re Sparrow (1908), 28 N.Z.L.R. 143.
[2] (1910), 29 N.Z.L.R. 1039.

different things . . . four indictments, four pleadings, and four offences. Those form, in my opinion, four occasions, even though it all happened in one day."

In the later case of R. *v.* Ehrman,[1] the decision in R. *v.* Steele that each conviction of a prisoner is a separate occasion within the meaning of Section 29 of the Crimes Act, 1908, whether the several convictions are recorded on the same day or on different days, was upheld, and its application even further extended. Ehrman was, in September 1911 sentenced to imprisonment on four indictments of offences falling within class II of the offences mentioned in Section 29. When appearing in 1911 he had a record of one earlier conviction of an offence falling within class II this conviction having occurred in 1900. When sentencing him on the last indictment in 1911, the judge declared him to be an habitual criminal. The Court of Appeal rejected Ehrman's contention that his case was distinguishable from that of R. *v.* Steele, Stout, C.J., reaffirming that Section 29 " deals with convictions, not offences."

To a certain limited extent the above line of judicial interpretation of this section was reversed in the case of R. *v.* Trier.[2] Trier had a sufficient record to support the court's declaration that he was an habitual criminal if separate counts of an indictment referring to separate criminal transactions could be regarded as " previous occasions " within the meaning of Section 29 of the Crimes Act, 1908, even though his criminal record included convictions on only two previous indictments, four previous occasions being the qualification for his type of offence. His appeal against the declaration that he was an habitual criminal was upheld by the Court of Appeal, the Court dividing three to two. The essence of the view of the majority is contained in the statement of Edwards, J., that: " It appears to me to be plain that no person . . . who was present in the court and heard a prisoner tried and found guilty upon an indictment charging in four separate counts separate crimes, would afterwards think that any one correctly stated what he had himself witnessed or heard who asserted that upon four occasions he had seen and heard the prisoner tried . . . and convicted of crime. I agree, therefore . . . that the prisoner ought not to have been

---

[1] (1911) 31 N.Z.L.R. 136.
[2] He pleaded " guilty " to two indictments, one of which contained a total of five counts charging five offences in respect of four separate acts, the other containing four counts charging four offences in respect of two separate acts. Both the conviction and the two pleas of " guilty " were taken upon the same day. (1912), 32 N.Z.L.R. 136.

declared an habitual criminal." Stout, C.J., who dissented, argued that: " In Steele's case there were at least four separate indictments, four separate pleas, four separate offences, and the judgment in that case is not, therefore, conclusive of this case. It is not conclusive of this case solely on the ground that here, instead of having separate indictments for the separate four distinct offences, there were two indictments only. . . Can, then, each count and each plea to the indictment be treated as a separate occasion ? If it cannot, then it is a question of form overriding a matter of substance. I confess the matter is one of difficulty. If a wide meaning is given to the word ' occasion', then I am of the opinion that the case would come within the statute."

In the later case of R. v. Crago[1] it was established that each count in an indictment may be treated as a separate " occasion " for the purposes of Section 29, provided that the prisoner pleads separately to each count, and that each count is based on a separate transaction. The ultimate effect, then, of R. v. Trier and R. v. Crago is that a conviction on several counts of an indictment does not amount to several convictions on several occasions, unless the prisoner pleads separately to each count, and unless each count is a separate transaction and not an alternative way of stating the offence.

The case of The King v. Nesbitt in 1946[2] shows the scope that this line of interpretation has given to Section 29 of the Crimes Act, 1908. Here Nesbitt was charged on seven informations of separate offences, each based on a separate transaction, each being within class I in Section 29 (3) of the Crimes Act, 1908. He pleaded guilty to each information, each plea being attested by the magistrate, who signed one committal for sentence on all charges. When the prisoner appeared before the Supreme Court for sentence on these charges, he was sentenced to a term of imprisonment with hard labour on each charge, all sentences to be concurrent, and declared to be an habitual criminal. On appeal against sentence on the ground that the declaration that he was an habitual criminal was invalid, in that he had not been previously convicted on at least two occasions before being declared an habitual criminal, it was held by the Court of Appeal that there was a conviction in respect of each of seven charges of separate offences within class I, and, as there was necessarily a sequence of such convictions, there were seven separate occasions. Further, that as the head sentence was imposed in respect

---

[1] (1917), N.Z.L.R. 863.   [2] (1946), N.Z.L.R. 505.

of each charge, the declaration that the prisoner was an habitual criminal must be presumed to follow on the last of the seven sentences, and was accordingly a valid declaration.

Thus the objective requirements of Section 29 of the Crimes Act, 1908, are easily complied with, especially as the previous convictions requisite under that section need not necessarily be convictions on indictment, but may be convictions before a magistrate, provided they are convictions for the offences mentioned in classes I or II of that section.[1]

In New Zealand, therefore, though " habitual " is defined objectively, and though the consideration of any specific personal characteristics is not enjoined upon the court, not even a minimum age qualification being included, the objective definition is itself widely construed against the criminal. In this respect, the New Zealand practice can be contrasted sharply with that in other countries where there has been almost too much solicitude for the interests of the offender.

2. Who controls their application ?

When a person is convicted on indictment of an offence which, when considered with his criminal record, qualifies him to be declared an habitual criminal, " the Court may in its discretion declare as part of the sentence of such person that he is an habitual criminal."[2]

When a person is convicted by a court of summary jurisdiction of an offence which, when considered with his criminal record, qualifies him to be declared an habitual offender, " the Justice or Magistrate before whom the charge is heard, in addition to sentencing such person to any lawful term of imprisonment, may order that such person be brought before the Supreme Court or a Judge thereof to be dealt with as an habitual offender."[3] That having been done, " such Court or Judge may declare any such person to be an habitual offender, and may direct that on the expiration of his sentence he shall be detained in a reformatory prison under this Act."[4]

No special procedure, other than that indicated in the preceding paragraph, is required, and the power to declare a prisoner to be an habitual criminal or an habitual offender is discretionary, the ultimate decision resting in the hands of the Judges of the Supreme Court.

---

[1] *R.* v. *Lewis* (1910), 29 N.Z.L.R. 1208 ; and *R.* v. *Bagnall* (1907), 26 N.Z.L.R. 756.
[2] Section 29. [3] Section 29. [4] Section 30.

*3. Do such laws envisage aggravation of punishment or special measures ?
If the latter, do the special measures follow or take the place of the
punishment for the last offence ?*

This is not an easy question to answer for New Zealand. The
Statutes introducing and modifying this " habitual " legislation, and
setting up a " Prisons Board " with powers over people declared
habitual criminals and habitual offenders, also deal with reformative
detention, and give to the Prisons Board powers over reformative
detainees similar to those they have over habituals. Thus it would
appear that it was envisaged that these groups should have treatment
different from that accorded to the rest of the prison population. In
practice, the chief and almost the sole difference in the conditions of
their imprisonment is that both habituals and reformative detainees
are under indeterminate or indefinite sentence. Such a factor can
be regarded as in itself modifying penal conditions: certainly it
alters the prisoner's attitude towards his imprisonment. The
Comptroller-General of Prisons, in his report for the year 1945-1946,
illustrated the importance of this factor when he stated that " under
the present ameliorated prison conditions the loss of liberty is virtually the only punitive factor in imprisonment." Accepting this
statement for the time being, one can affirm that in New Zealnad
special measures are applied to habitual criminals, but that they
share these measures with those sentenced to reformative detention.

Section 29 of the Crimes Amendment Act, 1910, empowers the
Governor in Council from time to time " to make such regulations
as are deemed necessary for the effective administration of this
Act", and many have been promulgated. One published on
September 24th, 1925, in Vol. III of the *New Zealand Gazette*[1] is
worth consideration at this point, for it introduces a certain difference
in the penal treatment of habituals. These regulations give directions
for the treatment of all prisoners and provide, *inter alia*, that
" habitual criminals and habitual offenders shall be kept entirely
separate from other prisoners in the exercise yards and within the
prison. They shall, so far as possible, be kept apart from other
prisoners whilst at work." In practice, it is very difficult to segregate
them when they work in the same shops as other prisoners.

For the moment, putting aside the question of whether there are
special measures applied to habitual criminals in New Zealand, or

[1] P. 2623 *et seq.*

whether there exists merely a system of aggravation of punishment in which the lengthened and indeterminate duration of imprisonment is the only real difference, we can safely assert that the system is a dual-track one, this indeterminate part of the sentence following the sentence imposed for the offence last committed. This is obviously a deliberate policy, and not the unconscious carry-over from earlier penal ideas, since in the case of reformative detainees either single or dual-track systems are applicable at the discretion of the Court sentencing the offender.

4. *What is the form of sentence imposed?*

Absolutely indeterminate, being subject to neither maximum nor minimum limits. However, from the prisoner's point of view, there is a lower limit provided by the period of imprisonment imposed as a precursor to his sentence as an habitual criminal; but even this sentence may be remitted to a large extent by the Prisons Board.

5. *If a special measure is applied, what is the degree of differentiation between it and other long-term imprisonment?*

The answer to question three revealed that the most important division of penal treatment in New Zealand is between those sentenced to a fixed term of imprisonment and those imprisoned under indefinite or indeterminate sentences, and that therein lies the only significant difference in the conditions under which habituals are imprisoned. The annual reports of the Comptroller-General of Prisons, of the Prisons Board, and the Social Statistics which are published regularly all indicate that the conditions of imprisonment are not materially different for habitual criminals or habitual offenders. Indeed, many of the regulations explicitly order that habituals shall be " subject to the regulations laid down for hard-labour prisoners " as regards their occupations, and that " they shall receive the scale of rations laid down for hard-labour prisoners."[1] For habituals as well as for other prisoners a fairly extensive earning scheme is in force, and all prisoners may be permitted to make payments out of those earnings to their dependants; and when released on probation or discharged they receive the moneys standing to their credit, either in a lump sum or in instalments, at the discretion of the Minister of Justice.

[1] 1925 Regulations.

To prove this lack of differentiation of treatment, let us consider the distribution of the habitual criminals and habitual offenders throughout the prisons in New Zealand. In 1941 and 1942, habituals were imprisoned only in the undermentioned institutions. The table hereunder[1] shows their proportion to the daily average of all prisoners in each of these prisons:

	1941			1942		
	Daily Average		Percent-age of Habit-uals	Daily Average		Percent-age of Habit-uals
	Total	Habit-uals		Total	Habit-uals	
Auckland	206	11	5·34	226	9	3·98
Hautu (Takaanu) ..	35	1	2·86	35	1	2·86
Waikune (Erua) ..	47	2	4·25	54	1	1·85
Wanganui	17	2	11·77	19	3	15·79
New Plymouth ..	48	1	2·08	—	—	—
Paparua (Templeton)	98	3	3·06	—	—	—
Wellington	—	—	—	95	1	1·05

Similarly, at the end of the year 1945, their distribution was as follows:[2]

	All Prisoners	Habituals	Percentage of Habituals
Auckland	247	7	2·83
Napier	20	1	5·00
New Plymouth ..	40	1	2·50
Waikeria (Refty) ..	83	1	1·20
Wanganui	19	4	21·05
Wellington	110	1	·91

Accordingly, only in Wanganui Prison do habituals constitute any appreciable part of the total population of the prison. Since they are scattered throughout the prisons in this way it is quite clear that special treatment cannot be applied to them as a group, nor indeed is any attempt made to do so. Even in the annual reports of the Governor of Wanganui Prison, no special mention is made of this group of offenders.

[1] Information taken from the *Reports on Justice Statistics, 1941* and *1942.*
[2] *Report of Social Statistics, 1943-5*, p. 23.

If more proof were necessary, reference could be made to the regulations which control prison conditions in New Zealand, and which give the details of the treatment accorded all prisoners.[1] All apply equally to habituals and other prisoners, and the only regulation of particular interest to habitual criminals is that which has been quoted above, and which orders their segregation whenever possible from the rest of the prison population. Considering their disposition throughout the New Zealand penal system, such an order, when followed, can work only to their great discomfort.

6. *Who is responsible for the release of habitual criminals, and on what basis are the decisions to release them made ?*

The Crime Amendment Act, 1910, provided by Section 9 (1) that " for the purposes of this Act there shall be constituted a Board to be called the Prisons Board ",[2] and then proceeded to define its powers and functions. This Board is, in fact, responsible for the release of habitual criminals, habitual offenders, and reformative detainees. In all instances the release is formally in the name of the Governor-General of the Dominion.[3]

Section 12 (H) of the same Act requires the Prisons Board to report annually to the Minister of Justice on its year's work, and it is these reports rather than the bare bones of the Statute that clarify the function of the Prisons Board in the penal system of New Zealand.

---

[1] *Gazette, 1925*, Vol. III, p. 2623 ; *Gazette, 1920*, Vol. III, p. 3161 ; *Gazette, 1932*, Vol. II, p. 1894 ; *Gazette, 1936*, Vol. II, p. 969 ; *Statutory Regulations, 1936/37*, Serial No. 1937/175 ; *Statutory Regulations, 1940*, Serial Nos. 1940/129 and 1940/232 ; *Statutory Regulations, 1946*, Serial Nos. 1946/138 and 1946/100.

[2] *Year Book, 1946*, p. 157 : " *Prisons Board.*—For the purposes of the Crimes Amendment Act of 1910 there is constituted a prisons board, the members of which are appointed by the Governor-General in Council for a period of three years, and may be reappointed. As at present constituted the board consists of a judge of the Supreme Court, as president, and six other members.

It is the duty of the board to make inquiry from time to time as to whether there is reasonable cause for belief that any habitual criminal, habitual offender or other person under sentence of imprisonment or reformative detention is sufficiently reformed to be released on probation or discharged, or for granting discharge to any person who has been released on probation ; and to make recommendations as to the release or discharge of any habitual criminal, habitual offender, or other person under sentence of imprisonment or reformative detention, and as to the conditions which may be imposed on any such release or probation. The board is required to take into consideration, at least once a year, the case of every habitual criminal, habitual offender, or person under sentence of reformative detention."

[3] As a matter of practice the link with the judiciary is preserved by the board having as its president a judge of the Supreme Court.

The following information is given in the report of the Board for the year ended December 31st, 1945:

" It is the function of the Prisons Board . . . to make inquiry from time to time as to whether there is reasonable cause for belief that any habitual criminal or offender . . . is sufficiently reformed to be released on probation or discharged, or whether there are any other sufficient grounds for releasing or discharging such person, and in making any recommendation for release or discharge the board is to have regard to the safety of the public or of any individual or class of persons, and to the welfare of the person whom it is proposed so to discharge or release on probation. The regulations under the Crimes Amendment Act require that the board shall, as far as possible, give every prisoner eligible for consideration an opportunity of appearing before it and stating his case personally when the board visits each of the penal institutions once in each year. The secretary of the board is required to prepare and place before the board a full statement of the circumstances connected with each case brought up for consideration. In actual practice it is customary for departmental files to be produced, from which are summarised extracts from the depositions, the evidence, and the prisoner's history and record, which contains the family history, showing mental and criminal tendencies, career of crime, mode of life, conduct and industry whilst in detention, response to previous treatment (if any), magistrate's report, medical reports, police and probation reports, and reports and recommendations of institutional superintendents."

With such information before it, the Board is in a position to consider the petitions of the prisoners themselves, or any representations made on their behalf by relatives, friends, or social workers. Further, by an arrangement with the Mental Hospitals Department, in cases where it is considered necessary, the Board can obtain reports on the mental condition of prisoners appearing before it; but this is the exception and not the rule. The 1945 report adds that:

" the board regularly reviews cases, and frequently cases are considered several times before release or discharge is agreed upon, the aim in each case being the rehabilitation of the offender without undue risk to the community."

The prisoner has the right to petition the Board for his release, but not more frequently than once a year.

During the years 1944, 1945 and 1946 the Prisons Board dealt with a total of ninety-eight cases of habitual criminals and offenders seeking either release on probation or remission of their head sentences (which is statutorily a necessary preliminary to seeking release if still serving the fixed term of their sentence). This power of remitting part of the fixed term of imprisonment preceding the indeterminate part of their sentence is also given to the Prisons

Board. The Board dealt with these ninety-eight cases in the following way:

40 were recommended for release on probation.
7 were recommended for remission of head sentence.
47 were deferred for later consideration.
4 applications for release were refused.

7. *What are the conditions under which the habitual criminal is discharged, and what is the juridical status of one so discharged ?*

Sections 13 to 22 of the Crimes Amendment Act, 1910 (as amended by the Crimes Amendment Acts of 1917 and 1920), control the conditions of release of reformative detainees, habitual criminals and habitual offenders. These conditions follow the normal pattern of conditional release, and put no limits on the conditions which can be appended to the licence on which the prisoner is released, nor to the period for which the licence is to continue in operation. In practice, prisoners are usually released on licence, though a few are discharged absolutely. The former are still under control and their liberty is conditional upon their good behaviour and industry while at large. They are known as probationers and have to report at short intervals to the Probation Officer of the district in which they reside, who assists them to obtain employment, and generally helps in every way he can. Once a month the Probation Officer reports on each probationer under his care to the Chief Probation Officer, who reviews all reports, and admonishes or warns any probationer of whose conduct he is doubtful. If the probationer is convicted of a criminal offence, or if the conditions of his release are flagrantly broken (especially after he has been warned by the Chief Probation Officer), the Governor-General is recommended to cancel his licence; and he is then returned to prison until, in the opinion of the Prisons Board, he merits another chance on probation.

One peculiarity of conditional discharge in New Zealand is that by Section 15 of the Crimes Amendment Act, 1910, a breach of the probationary licence is itself an offence, punishable on summary conviction by a fine of twenty pounds or by imprisonment for three months.

If the probationer is not recommitted to prison, and if he satisfactorily complies with the conditions of his licence, then the Prisons Board may recommend to the Governor-General that the prisoner be discharged, and " the Governor may . . . direct the discharge of that person accordingly; and thereupon the declaration that he is an habitual criminal or habitual offender . . . shall cease to be in force."[1]

8. To what extent are such habitual criminal laws applied ?

The estimated population of New Zealand in 1946 slightly exceeded 1,784,000. On December 31st, 1946, there were in that Dominion 998 male convicted persons in confinement (Maoris included).

During the period January 1911 to December 1946, 737 habituals were released on licence on the recommendation of the Prisons Board. Of those released, 59·3 per cent. were returned to prison either for committing further offences or for non-compliance with the conditions of probation. No further offences are recorded against the remaining 40·7 per cent.

This is a remarkably high figure of success for this type of prisoner; but it is rendered less significant by excluding later convictions of members of the group who, though they were not later convicted in New Zealand, may have offended against the criminal law of some other country. In 1945 it was estimated that one half of those discharged habituals who had no further offences recorded against them in New Zealand had left the country. Nevertheless, it would appear that the habitual criminal legislation in New Zealand is more extensively applied than in most countries; is applied in a humane fashion ; and is a reasonably efficient instrument in protecting the community against habitual criminals.[2]

5. UNION OF SOUTH AFRICA

When the Cape of Good Hope was ceded to Great Britain in 1814, the Roman-Dutch criminal law was in force, and thus forms

---

[1] Section 20 of the Crimes Amendment Act, 1910, as amended by the Crimes Amendment Act, 1920, Section 10.

[2] After the above analysis of the New Zealand legislation was written an article by Lincoln Efford, President of the New Zealand Howard League for Penal Reform, appeared in the *Howard Journal*, Vol. VII, No. 4, p. 239. In this article the details of the New Zealand habitual criminal and offender legislation was presented, and a violent criticism of their operation made. However, the discussion of that legislation is to a certain extent vitiated by the failure to consider the reformative detention sentence which, it is submitted, is a necessary preliminary to an understanding of the " habitual " provisions. The interested reader is referred to Mr. Efford's article for a presentation of the New Zealand legislation primarily from the point of view of the habitual criminal himself and in a sense complementary to what appears above.

the basis of South African criminal law. Soon, however, the influence of English law came to be felt, owing mainly to the appointment of colonial judges trained in the English system and unacquainted with Roman-Dutch law. Certainly, when Holland adopted the Code Napoleon, South African colonial judges could not look to the parent country for any expansion or interpretation of criminal law concepts; and slowly the influence of English law became paramount. Now, as is stated in the standard textbook on South African criminal law:[1] " South African criminal law is much more akin to the law of England than to the Roman-Dutch law." Nor is its constitutional position complicated: the Imperial South Africa Act of 1909 abolished the legislatures of the four colonies and constituted a Parliament for the Union whose powers extended to the criminal law and penal administration of the Union. By the same Imperial Act, a Provincial Council was created for each Province of the Union with power to pass ordinances on matters within its jurisdiction, and, concerning such matters, to define crimes and provide for their punishment.

In October 1909, the Transvaal Criminal Law Amendment Act[2] came into force and empowered superior courts in the Transvaal to declare certain persons habitual criminals. By Act No. 9 of 1911 of the Union of South Africa, the provisions of the Transvaal Statute were extended throughout the entire Union. The Prisons Act, 1911,[3] continued this process, slightly modifying some of the relevant provisions of the Transvaal Act; and finally, those portions of Act No. 9 of 1911 remaining in force were re-enacted by Section 344 of the Criminal Procedure and Evidence Act, 1917.[4] The statutes now in force on this matter are, then, the following :

> Transvaal Act No. 38 of 1909
> Union Act No. 13 of 1911
> Union Act No. 31 of 1917

In the analysis of that legislation hereunder, particularly in relation to the conditions in South African prisons pursuant to it, much reliance has been placed on the *Report of the Penal and Prison Reform Commission, 1947*, which is a comprehensive survey and criticism of the penal system of the Union of South Africa. It is as fearless and incisive a document as the Canadian Archambault

---

[1] *South African Criminal Law and Procedure*, Gardiner and Lansdown, 3rd Edition, Vol. 1.
[2] Act No. 38 of 1909. [3] Act No. 13 of 1911. [4] Act No. 31 of 1917.

Report, and it is a pity that these two reports have not received more attention in this country. On the theoretical aspect of the problem of habitual criminality in a country having a racially mixed population, the South African Report is most interesting.

1. To whom do such laws apply ?

As the Transvaal Act of 1909 is the forerunner of South African legislation concerning habitual criminals, let us consider it first. Section 9, subsections 1 to 6, of that Act defined habitual criminals and provided for their punishment. The Union Act of 1911 repealed subsections 2 to 6 of that section, leaving in force only the following:

Section 9 (1) :

"Any person who, having been convicted on two or more separate occasions (either in this Colony or elsewhere, and whether before or after the coming into operation of this Act) of any such offence as is mentioned in the Schedule to this Act, shall, if he be thereafter convicted in this Colony of any of those offences, be liable to be declared by a judge presiding over any superior court before which he is then convicted an habitual criminal."

The schedule referred to is very similar to the schedule we will consider regarding the Union legislation, and includes those offences, not punishable with death, which the Transvaal legislature regarded as of appreciable social danger.

The repealed subsections 2 to 6 of Section 9, provided for the detention of habitual criminals for an indefinite period, their release on probation to be advised upon a board of visitors, and so on. These and other administrative directions in those subsections were incorporated into the later Union legislation and will be dealt with later.

Act No. 31 of 1917 is the Union statute at present in force; and it classifies certain offenders as habitual criminals in the following terms:

Section 344 (1):

"Any person who either in a territory which forms part of the Union or elsewhere :
(a) has been convicted, before or after the commencement of this Act, of an offence mentioned in the Third Schedule to this Act ; and
(b) has been thereafter convicted, before or after the commencement of this Act, of the same offence or another offence mentioned in the Third Schedule to this Act,
shall, if he be again convicted after such commencement of any of the offences mentioned in the said Schedule, before a superior court within the Union, be liable to be declared an habitual criminal by the judge presiding over that court."

⌐he third schedule lists the more serious offences against the person and against property.[1] Thus, throughout the Union of South Africa, a history of two or more convictions at different times of any crimes falling within an extensive list of more serious offences, and a further later conviction of such an offence before a superior court, renders the offender liable to be declared an habitual criminal. The test is entirely objective, considerations of neither age nor other subjective qualities of the prisoner being enjoined by law upon the presiding judge. But, as the judge has a discretion in the exercise of this power, personal characteristics of the prisoner other than his past criminal record will inevitably obtrude.

2. Who controls their application?

The decision whether a prisoner shall be declared an habitual criminal, once his criminal record qualifies him to be so declared, is entirely within the discretion of the judge presiding over the court where he is at last convicted.

In the Cape, Transvaal and Orange Free State it is not the practice for the prosecutor to apply for the prisoner to be declared an habitual criminal, the matter being left entirely to the initiative of the presiding judge. In Natal, on the other hand, the prosecutor normally does apply to the judge when it is desired that the prisoner be declared an habitual criminal; but it is not necessary to give the accused any notice of the prosecutor's intention.

[1] Third Schedule : Offences, a third or subsequent conviction whereof renders the offender liable to be declared an habitual criminal under Section 344 of Act. No. 31 of 1917 :

> Rape or any statutory offence of a sexual nature against a girl of or under a prescribed age.
> Robbery.
> Assault with intent to commit murder, rape or robbery, or to do grievous bodily harm, or indecent assault.
> Arson.
> Fraud.
> Forgery or uttering a forged document knowing it to be forged.
> Offences relating to the coinage.
> Breaking or entering any premises . . . with intent to commit an offence.
> Theft either at common law or as defined by any statute.
> Receiving stolen property well knowing the same to have been stolen.
> Extortion or threats by letter or otherwise with intent to extort.
> Offences described in any law for the suppression of brothels and the punishment of immorality.
> Offences against the laws for the prevention of illicit dealing in or possession of precious metals, precious stones, or of the supply of intoxicating liquor to natives or coloured persons.
> Any conspiracy, incitement or attempt to commit any of the above-mentioned offences.

Thus, only in Natal is there any slight variation from the normal procedure when it is sought to have a criminal declared an habitual.

*3. Do such laws envisage aggravation of punishment or special measures ?
      If the latter, do the special measures follow or take the place of the
      punishment for the last offence ?*

Once more the first question proves difficult to answer with any assurance. The form of sentence on habitual criminals differs from the norm, being completely indeterminate ; but there would appear to be no other significant differentiation between the sentence imposed on an habitual criminal and that on other long-term prisoners. In many ways the position is akin to that in New Zealand, which we have already considered: in both countries the authorities concerned with the release of habitual criminals—the boards of visitors—must consider the remission of the sentences of those prisoners serving sentences of over two years' imprisonment. So if we decide, as in the case of New Zealand, that the indeterminate quality of the sentence suffices to make it a " special measure ", then special measures are applied to habitual criminals in South Africa.

The second of the above two questions can be answered definitely. In the Cape, Transvaal and Orange Free State the sentence as an habitual criminal takes effect immediately and is not preceded by a term of imprisonment for the last offence committed. In Natal the position is different: in the case of Gandy *v.* R.[1] the appellant had been sentenced to three years' imprisonment with hard labour and declared an habitual criminal. Gandy appealed against this form of sentence. It was held that such a form of sentence was within the competence of the Court. Therefore, in Natal the habitual criminal sentence can take effect after a term of imprisonment for the last offence of which the criminal has been convicted. Gandy's case technically applies to the entire Union and therefore it is within the competence of a court in any Province to impose such a dual-track sentence. In practice, this is never done in any Province except Natal, and there only very rarely.

This dual-track, single-track, choice is always indicative of the general approach of the legal system in question not only to the punishment of habitual criminals but to punishment in general. On this point a statement in Gardiner and Lansdown's book[2] is not

---

[1] 1914, N.P.D. 333.
[2] *South African Criminal Law and Procedure*, 3rd Edition, Vol. I, p. 420.

without interest—discussing Gandy's case they conclude, "it is difficult to see what purpose can be served by an order in the form approved of by the Natal Court", and generally they find the dual-track system incomprehensible; which shows how profoundly penological ideas vary, for though many have doubted the wisdom of such a sentence as was imposed in Gandy's case, few have failed to see its origin in one of the motive forces of criminal law—called variously, vengeance, retribution, or the expiation of sin.

4. What is the form of sentence imposed ?

Indeterminate. Except in Natal, where very occasionally the declaration of habitual criminality includes a definite term of imprisonment, there is no minimum term whatsoever imposed, and in none of the Provinces is a maximum term ever specified.

In practice the habitual criminal knows that with exemplary conduct whilst in detention, he will be conditionally released on probation after 6½ to 7 years' imprisonment; but since the period of probation is normally five years, his total period of treatment as an habitual criminal, both institutionally and non-institutionally, is quite substantial.

5. If a special measure is applied, what is the degree of differentiation between it and other long-term imprisonment ?

Habitual criminals in the Union of South Africa are imprisoned in the following institutions:

those of European origin in Pretoria Central Prison,
those of non-European origin in either Cinderella Prison or
Barberton Prison.

All three institutions are in the Transvaal.

Barberton Prison is devoted exclusively to habitual criminals and during 1946 there was a daily average of 402·6 prisoners detained there. At Cinderella Prison, which also caters for non-European prisoners, habituals and other criminals are imprisoned, and at the close of 1946 there were 1,712 offenders in custody, of whom 766 had been declared habitual criminals.[1]

Pretoria Central Prison, where the European habitual criminals are detained, can accommodate 684 males. On March 4th, 1946, there were 385 male prisoners held in custody there; these being

[1] *Annual Report of the Director of Prisons for the Year 1946.*

habitual criminals, and recidivists with sentences of over two years.[1] Since during the thirty-five years from 1910, when the habitual criminal legislation came into force, until the end of 1946, there had been only 288 males of European origin declared habitual criminals, it is clear that the proportion of habituals to other prisoners in Pretoria Central Prison at any one time cannot have been very high.

Unless institutions for habitual criminals are set apart from other prisons, or unless there is a segregation of habitual criminals within the institution in which they are detained with other prisoners, any extensive differentiation of treatment is not practicable. Neither in Pretoria Central Prison, nor in Cinderella Prison is such segregation attempted; and indeed in the annual reports on these prisons no distinction is drawn between the treatment accorded habituals and other prisoners. But Barberton Prison is specifically for the custody of native and coloured habitual criminals, and conditions there must be investigated to see if an appreciably differentiated special form of treatment is applied. As is indicated in the annual reports on Barberton Prison,[2] this prison caters for those native and coloured habitual criminals who have previously served a sentence as habitual criminals and have been re-committed during the ensuing probationary period, or have again been declared habitual criminals after having previously been finally discharged. In 1929 the board of visitors briefly described the work done at that prison in the following way : " There, for the most part, the convicts work in the open air—on the prison farm ; in the sisal and cotton plantations ; the ropewalk ; the quarry ; while there are such under-cover occupations as basket and mat-making, and so on."[3] At the end of 1946 this pattern of labour had not changed and prisoners were still employed principally in the sisal industry, on the farm, in quarrying, and in the services of the prison. Nothing, in fact, serves to differentiate this prison from other prisons for the custody of non-European prisoners, except the period for which its inmates are held in custody.

For all prisoners, habituals and others alike, the working day is ten hours.

There is a fourfold classification of prisoners within institutions, ranging from the penal class through the probation and good conduct classes to the star class. With each elevation in class, the privileges

[1] *Report of the Penal and Prison Reform Commission, 1947*, p. 176.
[2] For example, 1945 *Report of the Director of Prisons*, p. 15.
[3] *Annual Report of the Director of Prisons for the Year 1929*, p. 7.

accorded to the prisoner increase. Habituals take their place in this system, though membership of the most privileged group, the star class, is denied them.

In brief then, there is no differentiation between the conditions under which habitual criminals are detained and the conditions under which other long-term prisoners are held in custody, unless it be that the treatment accorded to habitual criminals is more disagreeable.

It is difficult to consider conditions in South African prisons, particularly for natives and non-Europeans, without intense repugnance. A perusal of the Report of the Royal Commission, 1947, will explain this feeling. Since we have just analysed the practice in New Zealand, where there is also an admixture of races, this distress at the severity of treatment accorded natives and non-European prisoners in South African prisons is reinforced.

6. Who is responsible for the release of habitual criminals, and on what basis are decisions to release them made ?

Section 47 of Union Act No. 13 of 1911 penetrates to the kernel of this question:

Section 47:

" (1) " A person . . . declared an habitual criminal . . . shall not be released until a board of visitors appointed under the next succeeding section has reported that there is a reasonable probability that the habitual criminal will in future abstain from crime and lead a useful and industrious life, or that he is no longer capable of engaging in crime, or that for any other reason it is desirable to release him.

(2) The superintendent, assistant superintendent, or gaoler shall furnish to the board of visitors at least once in every year all books and documents registering the history, conduct and industry of the habitual criminals under his charge, and such further supplemental reports in writing as he may think fit or as may be required by the board.

(3) Upon receiving from the Minister the report, in relation to any habitual criminal, of the board appointed under the next succeeding section, the Governor-General may order the release on probation of the habitual criminal for such period and on such conditions as he may determine or may order his unconditional release."

Section 48 of that Act provides for the appointment of such boards of visitors for each Province and imposes duties upon them also in regard to all prisoners serving a sentence of over two years' imprisonment.

Boards of visitors are required to report at least annually to the Minister on every habitual criminal and on every person whose sentence exceeds two years' imprisonment, and for this purpose it is their practice to grant each habitual criminal a personal interview once a year.

Three boards of visitors have been appointed—one for the Cape Province excluding Griqualand West; one for the Transvaal; and one for Natal, Orange Free State and Griqualand West. Each board usually consists of three or four persons who for the most part are retired civil servants with magisterial or penal experience. Occasionally a medical officer or clergyman or lawyer with penological knowledge is a member. Boards are normally appointed for a term of three years.

It will be noted from the disposition of the three prisons in which habitual offenders are detained that the board of visitors for the Transvaal is the only board concerned with any appreciable number of habitual criminals. In the year 1946 that board reported on 112 European habitual criminals, of whom it recommended the release of 20, and on 1,724 native and coloured habitual criminals, of whom it recommended the release of 182. In every case its recommendations were accepted and acted upon. During the year 1945, the Transvaal board, which consisted of three members, considered a total of 3,876 cases (habitual criminals and those serving sentences of over two years' imprisonment)—far from a light case load.[1]

As appears from Section 47 of the 1911 Act, the decision to release the habitual criminal is to be taken on the grounds of his reform or when " for any other reason it is desirable to release him." When making its decision the board has before it the report of the prison superintendent of the institution in which the habitual criminal has been detained, and inevitably this report becomes the vital factor in their deliberations. With such a case load as that with which they are burdened, it is not surprising that their discretion has hardened into a system; and in fact, with good conduct, an habitual criminal can rely on conditional discharge about seven years after he has been so declared.

Some comments of the Commissioners of the Penal and Prison Reform Commission, 1947,[2] concerning the failure of boards of

---

[1] Information extracted from the 1945 and 1946 *Reports of the Director of Prisons.*
[2] Pp. 62-3.

visitors to exercise the discretion given to them, and similar matters, are worth reproducing here:

> " release should not take place until there is a real hope of a normal life in the community. . . . Whatever the methods employed, whether punitive as in the past or more positively rehabilitative which may be visualised in the future, there will always be some failures. There will always remain those anti-social persons who will not respond to any efforts. . . . It is probable that this residue will live out a great portion of the remainder of their lives in this preventive custody and, having regard to the necessary limitations of a confined existence, it is desirable to make the conditions as constructive as possible to allow the fullest life reasonable in such a situation."

7. *What are the conditions under which the habitual criminal is discharged, and what is the juridical status of one so discharged ?*

Union Act No. 31 of 1917, Section 380, is the vital statutory provision in this regard.

Section 380:

> " (1) Any offender declared an habitual criminal . . . and released upon probation may be ordered as a condition of his release to reside and labour during the whole or any part of such period of probation at any farm colony, work colony, refuge or rescue home established or approved by the Governor-General.
>
> (2) If any such offender fail to observe any conditions of such release on probation, he may be arrested and recommitted to any convict prison or gaol by warrant under the hand of the Minister and shall be detained in a convict prison or gaol as if he had not been so released. . . .
>
> (4) In the case of any such release on probation there may be included a condition that the person released shall not reside in or visit the Union or any defined portion thereof for a specified time :
>
> provided that, if the person released be a natural-born British subject or has been naturalised in any part of His Majesty's Dominions, there shall not be included a condition that he be banished or absent himself from the Union."

It will be recalled that Act No. 13 of 1911 gave the Governor-General power to " order the release on probation of the habitual criminal for such period and on such conditions as he may determine." This power is, then, virtually unlimited. The practice is as follows: the conditionally discharged habitual criminal is placed under the supervision of a probation officer in a locality where it is considered he has most chance of making good, and to which he is transported on discharge. He must report at prescribed intervals, not less than once a fortnight, to the probation officer, confine himself to prescribed geographical boundaries, and generally conform to all the conditions upon which he has been discharged on probation. The concomitant functions of probation officers involve their watching over the probationer and acting "as his best friend", helping him to observe the conditions of his probation, visiting him at least once a month, investigating any breach of conditions, reporting to the Minister of Justice any serious breach of conditions, reporting periodically to the Minister of Justice on each probationer, and "where practicable and advisable receiving wages from employers on behalf of prisoners placed in their care, where such has been consented to in writing by the latter, and administering the same for the benefit of such person and his family."[1]

These admirable functions are to a certain extent vitiated by the pressure of work on an inadequately staffed probation service whose duties, far from being confined to aftercare work, are predominantly connected with juvenile delinquency and other work in courts of summary jurisdiction.[2] In the general sphere of aftercare, the work of the probation officers is assisted by the South African Prisoners Aid Association, whose services, though voluntary, are apparently quite efficient ; but who do not specifically concern themselves with habitual criminals.

The period of probation imposed as a condition of discharge has also hardened into a system. The practice with European and non-European prisoners has followed a slightly different course, and is as follows:

European habitual criminals—usual period of probation

1910-13	..	..	..	2 years
1913-16	..	..	..	4 years
After 1916	..	..	..	5 years

Native and coloured habitual criminals—usual period of probation

| 1910-14 | .. | .. | .. | 2 years |
| After 1914 | .. | .. | .. | 5 years |

Union Act No. 31 of 1917, Section 380 (3) provides that " if any offender so released on probation completes the period thereof without breaking any condition of the release, he shall no longer be deemed an habitual criminal. . . ."

[1] Regulation 5.
[2] On this subject reference should be made to the *Report of the Penal and Prison Reform Commission, 1947.*

8. To what extent are such habitual criminal laws applied ?

A census of the Union of South Africa as at May 7th, 1946, revealed that the total population was then 11,391,949, comprising 2,372,690 Europeans, 285,260 Indians, and 8,733,999 natives and other coloured peoples.

The male prison population on December 31st, 1946, was:

European	..	..	..	917
Indian	..	..	..	344
Native and coloured			..	19,123
Total	..	..	..	20,384[1]

During 1944, 1945 and 1946 the following number of men were declared habitual criminals:

	Europeans	Indians	Natives and Other Coloured	Total
1944 ..	3	—	119	122
1945 ..	2	—	92	94
1946 ..	5	—	208	213

As we have seen, habitual criminal legislation was introduced into the Transvaal in 1910. From the inception of this legislation until the end of 1946, 4,146 males have been declared habitual criminals, of whom 288 were Europeans, 43 were Indians, and 3,815 were native and coloured men.

Of the 288 European males declared habitual criminals, 248 had been released on probation before the end of 1946, 95 of whom failed on probation. Of these 95 who were returned to custody, 56 had been released a second time and 11 a third time. Nine men who successfully completed their periods of probation were again declared habitual criminals.

Of the 43 male Indians declared habitual criminals, 20 had been released on probation, 11 were returned to custody during their probationary period, and 6 had been released a second time. None has again been declared an habitual criminal.

In relation to native and coloured males, the figures are—of the 3,815 declared habitual criminals, 2,436 had been released on probation, 1,106 were returned to custody during their probationary

[1] Information extracted from the *Annual Report of the Director of Prisons for the Year 1946*.

period, 503 had been released a second time, and 72 a third. Fifty who successfully completed their periods of probation were again declared habitual criminals.

Thus, as at December 31st, 1946, 58 per cent. of the European, 45 per cent. of the Indian, and 53 per cent. of the native and coloured male habitual criminals who had been released for the first time had not since their release returned to prison in the Union of South Africa. The total of immediate success for all three groups combined is 53 per cent. ; which at first sight and considering the human material involved, is very impressive. But to give any significance to this figure of 53 per cent. "success", we should know the number of discharged habitual criminals who had died or emigrated from the Union. This information is not available.

The operation of habitual criminal legislation in the Union of South Africa from 1910 to the end of 1946 is shown in the following table :[1]

	Euro-pean Males	Indian Males	Native and Coloured Males	Total Males
Number sentenced	288	43	3,815	4,146
Removed from class	1	—	11	12
Died	28	2	643	673
Escaped and still at large	—	—	31	31
To mental hospital and not returned ..	12	4	59	75
To leper institution	—	—	2	2
Released for :				
(a) Deportation	14	4	90	108
(b) Medical reasons	2	—	10	12
(c) Probation	246	20	2,426	2,692
Recommitted during probation	95	11	1,106	1,212
Released a second time for :				
(a) Deportation	—	4	2	6
(b) Medical reasons	—	—	4	4
(c) Probation	56	2	499	557
Recommitted during second probation ..	16	—	171	187
Released third time for :				
(c) Probation	11	—	72	83
Declared habitual criminals again after expiration of probation	9	—	50	59

[1] Taken from a table on page 2 of the *1946 Report of the Director of Prisons.*

6. Southern Rhodesia

By the Habitual Criminals Act, 1926, which came into operation in June 1927, the legislature of Southern Rhodesia first provided for the special treatment of habitual criminals. That Statute copied exactly the terms of the Union of South Africa legislation on habitual criminals, using the same definition of "habitual criminal", and providing the same conditions for their detention and eventual release on probation. The provisions of the Habitual Criminals Act, 1926, are now to be found in Chapter 28 of the Revised Edition 1939, of the Statute Law of Southern Rhodesia, "Criminal Procedure and Evidence Act ", Part IX, and in Chapter 18 of the same edition, entitled " The Prisons Act". Between these statutes and the Union Acts[1] there are not even drafting differences, and it would therefore be pointless again to analyse this legislation.

In Southern Rhodesia, as in the Union of South Africa, a Habitual Criminals Board was appointed.[2] It held its first meeting in June 1929, at Salisbury Gaol where, since 1927, all habitual criminals have been detained. Since 1929, this Board, consisting of the Assistant Chief Native Commissioner and two other members, has met annually at Salisbury Gaol to consider the individual cases of all habitual criminals. In these deliberations it has been assisted, since 1933, by the Director of Prisons, or the Assistant Director. The Habitual Criminals Board has tended to follow Union practice closely; and indeed, as stated policy, has copied the Union Board's practice as regards the usual period for which habitual criminals are detained. Thus, the Secretary of the Law Department reporting in 1932 on the work of the Habitual Criminals Board for the year 1932, wrote :

" The hardened recidivist, whom it has been found necessary to declare an habitual criminal, presents a problem of peculiar difficulty in prison administration. In the Union the indeterminate sentence is regarded as the equivalent of twelve years' imprisonment, and prisoners of this class whose conduct is satisfactory are usually recommended for release after imprisonment of from five to seven years. As none of the habitual criminals (in Southern Rhodesia) have served for more than five years, and the majority a considerably less period, it is hardly to be anticipated that a recommendation for their release could yet have been made by the board."

The period of post-release probation is as protracted as in the Union, the only difference being that since 1937 special representations have been made to the Native Commissioners in the areas to

---

[1] No. 13 of 1911, and No. 31 of 1917.　　　[2] Government Notice 660 of 1928.

which discharged native habitual criminals are confined by the conditions of their orders for release, requesting such Commissioners " to take a personal interest in the welfare of these probationers and to endeavour to arrange suitable employment for them. The result of this experiment has, up to the present, been very encouraging."[1]

Salisbury Prison, in which the habitual criminals are detained, also receives many other types of offenders. Judging from the annual reports of the Secretary of the Department of Justice, this establishment would appear to be an efficient and relatively humane institution. The daily average of all prisoners in Salisbury Prison during 1948 was 981·13, of whom approximately 145 were habitual criminals. As in the Union, no serious endeavour is made to differentiate the treatment accorded habitual criminals from that to which other long-term prisoners are subjected.

The following table shows the operation of habitual criminal legislation in Southern Rhodesia from its inception in 1927 until December 31st, 1946. It is prepared from information in the annual reports of the Secretary of the Department of Justice, and to facilitate comparison it is here presented in the same terms as were employed in the table concluding the analysis of the habitual criminal legislation and practice in the Union of South Africa.

	European Males	Native and Coloured Males	Total
Number sentenced	4	213	217
Died	—	6	6
Escaped and still at large	—	1	1
To mental hospital and not returned ..	—	5	5
To leper settlement	—	1	1
Released for :			
(a) Deportation	—	6	6
(b) Probation	4	83	87
Recommitted during probation period ..	2	28	30
Remaining in prison on Dec. 31st, 1946 ..	3	148	151
Declared habitual criminals again after expiration of probation	1	9	10

[1] *Report of the Secretary, Law Department*, for the year 1931.

These figures show that 56·99 per cent. of all habitual criminals who have been released on probation or deported, have not returned to prison in Southern Rhodesia. This proportion is akin to the figure of 53 per cent. reached for the Union of South Africa.

The population of Southern Rhodesia in 1946 was approximately 1,763,883, comprising :

82,382 Europeans
2,913 Indians, and
1,678,588 Natives and other coloured persons

On December 31st, 1946, 3,252 prisoners were in custody in the penal institutions of Southern Rhodesia ; but unfortunately it is not known how many of these were " adult male sentenced prisoners ".

Let us now endeavour to compare the extent to which habitual criminal legislation has been implemented in the Union of South Africa and in Southern Rhodesia, remembering that they have similar ecological patterns, identical habitual criminal legislation, and very similar administrative practice. The information given in answer to question eight regarding the Union of South Africa is comparable with the above figures provided that a correction is made for the difference of population and the period of functioning of the two legislative provisions.

Thus, in the Union, over thirty-seven years, *288* Europeans and *3,858* other persons have been declared habitual criminals ; this amongst a population in 1946 of 2,372,690 Europeans and 9,019,259 Indians, natives and other coloured peoples. The number of individuals so declared in Southern Rhodesia are 4 Europeans and 213 members of other ethnic groups. Correcting the Southern Rhodesian figures for purposes of comparison with the Union figures :

		Europeans	Natives and Coloured
for period of operation	.. ..	$4 \times \dfrac{37}{20}$	$213 \times \dfrac{37}{20}$
and for population ..	.. $4 \times \dfrac{37}{20} \times \dfrac{2,372,690}{82,382}$	$213 \times \dfrac{37}{20} \times \dfrac{9,019,259}{1,681,501}$	
equals	..	*213·1* and *2,113·6*	

Thus habitual criminal legislation has been applied proportionately less in Southern Rhodesia than in the Union of South Africa, despite the legislative and administrative similarity between the measures technically applicable in each country, and despite a very similar incidence of serious crime. In both countries such measures are much more readily applied to native criminals than to European offenders. The penal authorities in both countries express themselves well-satisfied with their habitual criminal legislation and its functioning in the penal system.

7. EUROPEAN HABITUAL CRIMINAL LEGISLATION

Whereas in our analysis of the habitual criminal legislation of certain legal systems within the British Commonwealth of Nations we have broken new ground in the field of Applied Comparative Law, the comparative investigation of certain European habitual criminal laws which follows is derived from, and dependent on, two distinct types of legal research. It is a synthesis of several existing comparative analyses of European habitual criminal legislation, together with various reports on the habitual criminal law prepared in certain European countries by lawyers who are frequently men holding official positions, and who occasionally suffer from a not entirely unexpected paralysis of the critical faculty.

It will be found that the comparisons here drawn, and the analysis here undertaken, is more comprehensive than that in any of the works on which it depends ; but it must be stressed that it is a synthesis of the works of others and not the result of original investigation. A bibliography appears at the end of this section.[1]

*   *   *   *   *

The idea that the aim of the punishment of habitual criminals is their segregation from society until the danger they present to the community is past was first clearly formulated in the early 1880's in Germany, by the Sociological School of Criminology, notably by Franz von Liszt in the Marburger Programme of 1882. It is, however, to the Swiss Criminologist, Carl Stoos, that the definition of this idea in its modern form must be credited, for in his Draft Penal Code for Switzerland in 1893, he coined the term *mesure de sûreté* and provided for the indeterminate detention of habitual criminals in institutions specially adapted for the purpose, such detention to take the place of punishment for the last offence committed. After forty-four years of earnest deliberation, this plan, subject to a few relatively minor amendments, was introduced into the Swiss Assembly on December 21st, 1937, and became a part of the new Federal Criminal Code.

---

[1] See pp. 224-227.

It can be argued that the French law of May 27th, 1885, which provided the special punishment of *relégation* for certain recidivists, is a law of this type anterior to the draft code prepared by C. Stoos. However, as we shall see, the method of dealing with habitual criminals adopted in France in 1885 was so different from the various methods adopted by the other legislatures in Europe that it is best to regard it as a law of an entirely different character. The distinction is between a *mesure de sûreté*, as sought by all the other countries, and a *peine complémentaire coloniale perpétuelle* as embodied in the French law of 1885. This distinction will become clearer as we proceed.

The first country actually to introduce a *mesure de sûreté* for habitual criminals was Norway. By Clause 65 of her law of May 22nd, 1902, Norway provided for the indefinite detention of habitual criminals. This law, for reasons which we shall consider, met active opposition in the Norwegian courts and between 1902 and 1924 only two persons were sentenced pursuant to its provisions.

The first legal system actually to implement a *mesure de sûreté* for habitual criminals was that of the Australian State of New South Wales, whose law of September 20th, 1905, we have already considered.

Between 1905 and 1937, most European countries introduced such measures into their penal systems. Before proceeding to an analysis of these various provisions by means of the same questionnaire as was applied to the Dominion habitual criminal laws, let us give special and separate attention to the French law of 1885 and its implementation ; to treat it together with the laws of other countries would be confusing.

FRANCE

In 1872 a committee was appointed in France to inquire into the penal system, and in particular to consider if transportation was a suitable measure to impose on recidivists, and if so, on what type of recidivist. Since 1854, transportation had been a punishment available for persons convicted of certain serious offences, and there was general satisfaction, in 1872, at the workings of this system. Thus, it was not surprising that the 1872 Committee advised the transportation of recidivists and that this recommendation was widely approved. Nevertheless, despite this general approbation, it was thirteen years before the French government acted on the Committee's advice, constitutional problems absorbing their attention in the intervening years. Between 1872 and 1882, there was a series of private members bills[1] seeking to extend transportation to various types of recidivists, and there was also much discussion in the technical journals and in the press. Thus the 1882 Bill, which eventually became law on May 27th, 1885, raised great interest and created much heat in its passage through the two Chambers. In particular it was criticised for its failure to allow the trial Judge to exercise any discretion as to the imposition of transportation.

The new type of transportation to be imposed on certain dangerous recidivists was to be called *relégation*, a term " *qui froisserait moins l'amour-propre des repris de justice.*"[2]

Let us now consider those who, in 1885 and thereafter, became subject to *relégation*. The applicability of *relégation* varies with the existence of certain sentences, and is thus a product of the legal state of recidivism.[3] In five sets of circumstances the imposition of *relégation* is mandatory upon the trial judge, that is if the convicted person qualified in any of the five following ways :

(1) Two sentences to " *peines criminelles* ".
" *Peines criminelles* " in this context is restricted to " *travaux forcés à temps* " or " *la réclusion* " (anglice, transportation for a period of years with forced labour, or solitary confinement for five to ten years).

(2) Three sentences, of which :
one must have been to a " *peine criminelle*", and the other two can be sentences of imprisonment for " *crimes* " (felonies) or sentences of imprisonment for more than three months for certain specified " *délits* " (misdemeanours).
By a decree of 1885, a sentence of imprisonment for " crime " can never be for a period of less than one year. The " *délits* " specified are those regarded as particularly dangerous to public order. There are ten of them, seven being established in 1885, and three added later.[4]

---

[1] Julien and others, Waldeck-Rousseau and others, Thomson, Fallieres.
[2] Leon Pignon : *De la Relégation des Recidivistes*, Thèse, Paris, 1886.
[3] Previous sentences terminated by a pardon count for this purpose, but not those terminated by an amnesty.
[4] See Donnedieu de Vabres : *Traité de Droit Criminel et de Législation Pénale Comparée*, 3rd Edition, p. 498, or Pinatel, *Précis de Science Pénitentiaire*, pp. 47-8.

(3) Four sentences to "*peines correctionelles*".

In this context "*peines correctionelles*" refers to such sentences as were mentioned in the preceding paragraphs, that is to say, sentences of imprisonment for "*crimes*" or imprisonment for more than three months for certain specified "*délits*".

(4) Seven sentences, divided into two groups :

    (a) two or three sentences of the types listed above, that is "*peines criminelles*" or "*peines correctionelles*", plus

    (b) four or five sentences, some of a specified minimum, for a long list of vagrancy offences.[1]

Strangely enough, the framers of the law of 1885 had such recidivist vagrant petty offenders particularly in mind ; not because the vagrancy offence was in itself so serious, but because it was argued that when repeated it portended the existence of a group of people forming a milieu of considerable danger to the community.

(5) One or two sentences for abortion.

(This category was added by the decree of July 29th, 1939.)

    (a) Two sentences, if they were inflicted pursuant to article 317 Section 1 of the Penal Code.

    (b) One sentence, if it was inflicted pursuant to article 317 Section 2 of the Penal Code.

This fifth category is an exception to the other four in that a person convicted only once of an offence under article 317 Section 2 of the Code may be sentenced to *relégation*, and need not be a recidivist when so sentenced. This is so despite the fact that the whole tenor of the law of 1855 was an attack on recidivism. The explanation is that Section 2 refers to the " habitual " commission of the offence of abortion and is aimed at the professional abortionist, whilst Section 1 omits the conception of habituality. Thus, this fifth category strikes at a recidivist whose two offences are specialised to this type of crime, and at a professional or habitual abortionist who has been fortunate enough to escape previous conviction. However, in attacking " special recidivism " and in being applicable to one who has not been previously convicted, this category is exceptional.

---

[1] Donnedieu de Vabres : *op. cit.*, p. 500 ; Pinatei : *op. cit.*, p. 48.

Arguing along the line that the whole purport of the law of 1885 was the segregation of the recidivist from society, certain courts have refused to pronounce *relégation* on one sentenced for the habitual commission of abortion ; for example, the Tribunal Correctionnel at Chartres on January 22nd, 1943. On the other hand, the Cour de Cassation has adhered to this law and has several times enforced it vigorously.

Later legislation has enabled the courts to impose *relégation* on many offenders not qualifying as above, but in every instance it has been left to the discretion of the trial judge to decide whether or not to inflict it on the particular offender before him. It is available for punishing a large number of crimes against morality, and is extensively used to eliminate *souteneurs* (pimps). The operation of this discretionary *relégation* is negligible as compared with its mandatory imposition in the five cases mentioned, and need not concern us here.[1]

There are a few more points to make before we advert to the operation of *relégation*. First, the above qualifications for *relégation* must be complied with during a period of ten years, not counting the time actually spent in prison. Secondly, the order in which the offences have been committed or the sentences imposed, is of no importance for purposes of *relégation*, but each of the offences for which the sentences were imposed must have been separated from the preceding offence by a definite sentence. Thirdly, sentences imposed for military and naval offences are not to be counted. Fourthly, *relégation* is neither applicable to youths under 21 years of age (though sentences on them count towards subsequent *relégation*), nor to men above the age of 60 years, nor, since a law of July 19th, 1907, to women. Finally, if the *relégué* is ill at the time of the expiration of his principal punishment, he is to be held in France until fit to travel.

All persons qualifying for *relégation* served the sentence imposed on them for their last offence, and were then transported to French Guiana or New Caledonia. This dual-track system was introduced because it was argued by all concerned in framing the bills considered in the Chambre des Députés between 1872 and 1885, that the *relégué* should live a free and full life in the distant colonies (hence not Algeria). He was to be limited only by the fact that he could not leave the colony to which he was transferred, much less

[1] See Donnedieu de Vabres : *op. cit.*, p. 310.

return to live in France. Having expiated his crime in the sentence imposed on him for his last offence, and especially as *relégation* could be ordered for a series of relatively minor vagrancy offences, it followed that the life permitted to the *relégué* in the colony should be free and untrammelled, and markedly more lenient than the régime imposed on the transported *forçats*. It was stated in the introductory memorandum to the Bill which became law in 1885, that the colony was to be *une nouvelle patrie* where the *relégué* could start a new life, " *à quels sentiments faire appel pour exciter leur courage, réveiller leur conscience, retrouver et faire des hommes.*"[1]

But, as a member of the Chambre des Députés said, such people know no trade " *si ce n'est le mode le plus parfait de fabrication des chaussons de lisière.*" And it was violently opposed by the Governor of Guiana and certain free colonists in New Caledonia who contended that to let such people wander about freely without means of sustenance, and with neither the ability nor the opportunity to work, would result in an intolerable increase of crime in the colonies. All this led to the introduction by the Senate of compulsory labour service for the majority of *relégués*. Thus, from being a purely segregative measure, *relégation* inevitably became punitive. Though this was realised even in 1885, and despite several forceful protests (notably by Desportes), the dual-track system of punishment first in France and then in the colony was quite indefensibly retained.

A decree of November 27th, 1885, under cloak of interpreting the Act, changed the entire shape of the system as originally intended, and created two distinct types of *relégation*, namely, " *relégation individuelle* " and " *relégation collective* ".

Relégation individuelle consisted merely in the obligation to reside in the colony and to submit oneself to a few special police controls, such as reporting at regular intervals. This régime was reserved for *relégués* with sufficient pecuniary resources to support themselves, or it could be given as a boon to *relégués collectifs* of specially good behaviour who were sufficiently skilled to support themselves in the colony. Their situation was very like that of those who were discharged from convict prisons in the colonies. It fulfilled the original idea of non-punitive segregation. However, very few *relégués* were so classified.

[1] *Bulletin*, VI, 1882, p. 777.

Relégation collective constituted the norm and was applied to all but a very few *relégués*. *Relégués collectifs* lived in prisons identical with colonial convict prisons, but they were kept separate from the convicts, and were compelled to work in association under the supervision of warders. Their life was very similar to that of the transported convicts and the differences between the two régimes are not worth recording. Both régimes approached the nadir of inhumanity ; indeed it would be difficult to describe them without laying oneself open to a charge of sensationalism. Some idea of the savagery emerges from the fact that, in 1905, the Inspector General of Prisons (Brunot) acknowledged that in the preceding eight years, 58 per cent. of the *relégués* committed to Guiana during that period had died, and this in spite of the decree excluding those in poor health and the administrative practice of transporting only the *robustes*. The onerous quality of *relégation collective* is further proved by the fact that in some years as many as 12 per cent. of the total population of *relégués* made serious attempts to escape.

When the *relégué* had served the principal punishment, a committee, appointed by the Minister of Justice, interviewed him and decided whether he should be classified as a *relégué individuel* or *relégué collectif*. Then, at a convenient time he would be shipped to one of the colonies—from 1885 to 1898 to New Caledonia, and from 1898 onwards to Guiana.

Only in two ways could *relégation* be interrupted or terminated. First, article 13 of the law of 1885 empowered the colonial authorities to permit *relégués* whose conduct had been exemplary to return to France for a period up to six months. Though occasionally there was a *relégué individuel* who could afford it, this was a privilege but rarely exercised since they had to pay their own fares. Secondly, as from the sixth year of *relégation*, the *relégué* could seek from the local court a definite dispensation from serving the remainder of his sentence; and this could be granted if justified by his good conduct, his financial security, and by the services he had rendered to the colony. As the *relégué* seldom contributed anything to colonial development, this termination of *relégation* was most exceptional. In effect then, *relégation* was for the term of the offender's natural life—not likely to be an unduly long term.

The following table gives some idea of the numbers annually declared *relégués*:

1887	..	.. 1,934	1910	..	.. 343
1888	..	.. 1,627	1911	..	.. 432
1890	..	.. 1,035	1912	..	.. 363
1895	..	.. 861	1913	..	.. 317
1900	..	.. 632			
1903	..	.. 500	1931	..	.. 233
1905	..	.. 605	1932	..	.. 370
1907	..	.. 511			
1909	..	.. 414	1940	..	.. 509

From 1885 to 1935 a total of just under 20,000 convicted persons were sentenced to *relégation*.

Before the war, with the wider recognition of the horror of its conditions and of its adverse effect on the colonies, informed opinion in France was becoming increasingly critical of the system of *relégation*. Despite being bound by the law of 1885, the judges went to great lengths to avoid awarding such sentences, using many subtle means to this end, the most obvious being a diminution of the severity of sentences generally imposed, especially for vagrancy, thus avoiding the *relégation* situation. As Donnedieu de Vabres says, " commes toutes les peines injustement sévères, la relégation contribue ainsi à l'énervement de la répression."[1]

Relégation is not, formally, a " *mesure de sûreté* ", it is a " *peine complémentaire coloniale perpétuelle* ", though in the nature of things its effect for France is that of a successful *mesure de sûreté*. The fundamental criticism of the system appears to be that it is posited on an irrebuttable legal presumption of incorrigibility, a presumption based on the existence of previous sentences of a certain gravity, and on that fact alone. Being a legal presumption, it binds the judge and prevents any individualization of punishment; with the result that palpably corrigible recidivists have frequently to be sentenced under a legal presumption of incorrigibility. Such sentences cause great tension in the minds of those bound to inflict them, and react adversely on French penology and criminology.

Röling concludes his analysis of the law of May 27th, 1885, by asserting that " it is a stain, not only on France, but on Western Europe."[2] Nevertheless, it is now very difficult for France to organise her penology without colonial *relégation*; for she has been in this connection an *enfant gâté*—as a noiseless and apparently bloodless

[1] Donnedieu de Vabres : *op. cit.*, p. 314.   [2] Röling—*cited infra*—p. 29.

way of destroying one's troublesome fellow citizens the system has no peer.

The draft of the Penal Code proposed in 1932 retained *relégation*, but by articles 744 *et seq.*, changed it into a genuine *mesure de sûreté*. A maximum term of fifteen years was to be served, the Court which ordered *relégation* having to decide, in each case, if such detention should be served in an industrial or agricultural institution in France, or in one of her overseas possessions. The judge was also to take account of the personal situation of the convicted person in deciding upon *relégation* and upon the institution the *relégué* was to inhabit.

Owing to the widespread dissatisfaction with transportation and *relégation*, a commission under the chairmanship of M. Paul Matter, then *procureur général* of the Cour de Cassation, was appointed to consider the suppression of transportation and *relégation*. This commission deliberated from October to December, 1936. Without waiting for its report, the Government, on December 29th, 1936, brought down a bill providing for:

(1) the cessation of transportation of those sentenced to *travaux forcés*, and

(2) the cessation of *relégation*, and its replacement by security imprisonment in France.

In principle, the security imprisonment in an institution in France was to be perpetual, but after five years there was the possibility of conditional release subject to an *interdiction de séjour* and to the supervision of an aftercare authority, this to be for a period of twenty years before the discharge became absolute. If during the twenty-year period, the detainee committed a serious crime, then, after punishment for that crime, he would be returned to detention, but on this occasion for a minimum period of fifteen years. This bill was not immediately accepted, but its provisions clearly inspired those who drew the law of July 6th, 1942. On June 17th, 1937, the Government, being sceptical of the value of the permanent security imprisonment which was to be substituted for *relégation*, decided to implement by decree that part of the Bill concerning the cessation of transportation as far as it pressed on those subsequently to be sentenced to " *travaux forcés* ". They also decided, despite the advice of M. Paul Matter's committee, to return to the system of *relégation* which had been interrupted between December 29th, 1936, and June 17th, 1937, by decision of the *conseil des ministres* who felt that *relégués* should not continue to be shipped away from France in the absence of a legislative decision on the Bill of December 29th, 1936.

In 1938, the exigencies of war compelled France to cease transporting prisoners to her colonies and to institute a new régime for *relégués* who were now to be held in the Maison Centrale at Riom. This régime was defined by a law of July 6th, 1942. As yet, France has not returned to the colonial system of *relégation*, and there seems some chance of her falling into line with general European practice regarding habitual criminals. However, as we have pointed out, she has been indulged by the availability of her colonies as dumping-grounds for many of her recidivists, and the abandonment of colonial *relégation* is by no means certain.

No country follows the lead given by France; no country has transported its habitual criminals as such. As the French system developed, and as its defects stood starkly revealed, the likelihood of such imitation diminished. It is for this reason that we have been compelled to treat it separately from other European habitual criminal legislation.

Let us now, by means of the questionnaire we have developed and applied earlier in this study, consider the habitual criminal legislation of a group of other European countries.

The laws we will canvass are the following:

Belgium :   Law of April 9th, 1930 (*dite de défense sociale à l'égard des anormaux et des délinquants d'habitude*).

Czechoslovakia :   Law of June 25th, 1929.

Denmark :   Penal Code of April 15th, 1930.

Finland :   Law of May 27th, 1932.

Germany :   Law of November 24th, 1933.

Holland :   Law of June 25th, 1929.

Hungary :   Law of January 31st, 1928 (Law X of 1928).

Italy :   Criminal Code of October 19th, 1930.

Latvia :   Criminal Code of 1933.

Norway :   Criminal Code of May 22nd, 1902 ; and Law of February 22nd, 1929.

Poland :   Penal Code of July 11th, 1932.

Spain :   Criminal Code of September 8th, 1928 ; and Law of August 4th, 1933.

Sweden :   Law of April 22nd, 1927 ; and Law of
                          June 16th, 1937.[1]
Switzerland :   Criminal Code of 1937.
Yugoslavia :   Criminal Code of January 27th, 1929.

1. To whom do such laws apply ?

It is possible to define the class of criminals to be subject to such legislative provisions in many different ways, and the various legislatures in Europe have certainly taken advantage of this possibility. Therefore, our best approach to this question is to analyse the two extreme and opposing types of definition, and having thus established our polarities, to fill in the intermediate definitions. These polarities are to be found in the 1885 law of France concerning *relégation*, already cited, and in the penal code of Fascist Italy.

As we saw above, the majority of criminals who were sentenced to *relégation* by the French courts were so sentenced because, and only because, of their penal records. Usually *relégation* did not depend on the type of crime committed, and in most cases the judge had no discretion whatsoever in deciding upon its imposition. It was the expression of an irrebuttable statutory presumption of incorrigibility, a presumption founded solely upon recidivity. Similarly, article 24 of the Belgian law of April 9th, 1930, compels the judge to order " *la mise à la disposition du Gouvernement* " (anglice, preventive detention) in certain serious cases of specific recidivism, again on the basis of an irrebuttable presumption of law.[2]

At the other pole lies article 108 of the Italian Penal Code of 1930, which empowered the court to declare certain persons to have a " *tendenza a delinquere* " and to apply special segregative measures to them even though they had never before been convicted of a crime or sentenced by a court. Here the judge's discretion is nearly as wide as it is restricted under the French law of 1885, but even so there are certain limits to it. Its limits arise from the fact that

---

[1] The Swedish law of July 1st, 1946, was not included in this analysis because of the paucity of information then available on its operation. There is now available, published in English (Stockholm, 1947), an excellent monograph by Professor Thorsten Sellin under the title *Recent Penal Legislation in Sweden*.

[2] The Norwegian legislation of 1902 having manifestly failed, it was desired, when introducing new provisions of this type in that country, to make them binding on the judges and their imposition mandatory. In a lecture to the influential Norwegian Criminalist Society, the well-known criminologist, Nissen, resisted such a suggestion and argued against following the French precedent. Largely owing to his efforts this idea was abandoned and the 1929 legislation was facultative.

article 108 applies solely to those individuals who are convicted of crimes against the person, which by the gravity of the injury or the danger caused to the person injured (by reference to article 133 (2)), and by the circumstances of the offence, disclose to the judge a special inclination to crime, " the cause of which is the particularly wicked nature of the convicted person." Article 108 does not, therefore, apply to an offence against property rights.

These, then, are our two extremes—an irrebuttable presumption founded on recidivism of a certain type, on the one hand; judicial discretion unfettered by the requirement of previous sentences or offences, on the other.

But no legal system adheres solely to either of these polarities. We saw that since 1885 the French legislature has empowered the courts to apply *relégation* in many new circumstances and has given the judge a discretion whether or not to impose it on the particular offender before him, while it has not extended the mandatory provision of the 1885 law very greatly. Also, we shall see that although article 24 of the Belgian law provides for the mandatory imposition of " *la mise à la disposition du Gouvernement* ", article 25 of the same law enables the judge to exercise his discretion in ordering it in a wide variety of circumstances.[1]

Thus the French and Belgian habitual criminal legislation vary from the polarity we have expressed in the light of their provisions. At the other extreme a similar variation is to be found. The Italian habitual criminal legislation is not completely circumscribed by article 108 of the 1930 Code, nor by the conception of the " delinquent by tendency". By articles 102 to 105 the judge is empowered to declare criminals to be " habituals " or " professionals " in a variety of circumstances. Article 102 does, in fact, approximate to the mandatory polarity of the French law, for it compels the judge to declare an habitual criminal one who, " after having been sentenced to imprisonment for terms together exceeding five years for three crimes of the same character (as defined very widely by article 101), within a period of ten years, receives a further sentence for a crime of the same character, within ten years subsequent to

---

[1] There is the further point that although " *la mise à la disposition du Gouvernement* " is pronounced, the penal administration need not order preventive detention but may, although it is not common, in the light of the offender's personal characteristics and the way in which he served the fixed term of imprisonment, subject him to some less profound measure such as protracted probation. He is, quite literally, placed at the administration's disposition.

the latest of the crimes aforesaid." Article 102 approximates to the absolute character of the French law and is not identical with it. This is so because in the interpretation " of the same character " in article 102 the Italian judge has to exercise a discretion in deciding upon the motive or motives actuating the offender. It is, of course, a discretion that goes to the applicability of the declaration that an offender is an habitual, which is a question of fact, and not to the judge's conception of the criminologic wisdom of such a sentence; but in fact the former will almost inevitably involve the latter.

Articles 103, 104 and 105 of the Italian Penal Code steer a middle course between articles 102 and 108. They blend the elements of previous offences, previous sentences, and judicial discretion in a fashion which we shall analyse when treating the habitual legislation of other countries which in no wise adhere to either of our polarities.

In the German legislation of 1933, and the Polish Code of 1932, a judicial discretion unfettered by the requirement of previous sentences is given. The German judge was empowered to declare an offender to be a " dangerous habitual criminal " if he had committed three malicious offences which created a general impression that he was such a dangerous person. This impression was supposedly to be gathered from the propensity towards crime as gauged by the professional character of the offences or their homogeneity. Thus, his discretion was circumscribed only by the requirements of previous offences of a certain type, and previous sentences were not a condition precedent to the declaration of habituality.

The Polish Code of 1932, by article 84, empowered the judge to order the detention, subject to no maximum term, of those offenders he regarded as professionals or habituals, and these terms were defined without reference to previous *sentences*, though implicit in their definitions were previous *offences*. The vital point was that the criminal committed the crimes professionally or as a habitual practice, and further that his freedom would menace public order. The notion of " professional " was based on objective standards, whilst the notion of " habit " was established upon the totality of the characteristics peculiar to the offender in question; but both involved previous offences.

Of course, the German and Polish Codes also provided for the special detention of other categories of habitual criminals, categories defined by reference to previous sentences and giving a discretion to the judge. Later we will consider these provisions.

Having disposed of these extreme definitions of the habitual criminal, we can now advert to the more usual types of definition, and treat in greater detail the more subtle variations between them.

These more subtle variations in the definitions of the " habitual " concept in various countries could only be described adequately in an exhaustive and separate analysis of each country's habitual criminal legislation, an analysis possibly akin to that we gave of the habitual criminal legislation in the member States of the British Commonwealth of Nations. For reasons adduced above such detailed consideration will not be given to the European legislation. Instead, we will concentrate on four elements in their definitions of those who are to be dealt with as habitual criminals. These four elements are :

> (a) the requirement of previous sentences,
>
> (b) the requirement of a certain gravity or certain motives in the offences committed—the homogeneity or specificity of these offences,
>
> (c) the period over which the offences or sentences may be spread, and
>
> (d) the personal characteristics of the offender which must be considered by the judge in the exercise of his discretion whether to apply measures designed to deal with habitual criminals.

In referring hereunder to the habitual criminal legislation of each country, we will not mention the date of its passage unless that is necessary to distinguish it from similar legislation in that country. In every case the legislation is that cited on pp. 183-184.

(a) *The requirement of previous sentences.*

Czechoslovakia and Sweden 1937 insist on at least two previous sentences of imprisonment as a condition precedent to the application of their habitual criminal legislation.

At least three previous sentences of imprisonment are required by Hungary, Poland and Yugoslavia; at least four by Sweden 1927.

The Belgian legislation requires at least two previous sentences of imprisonment to have been served unless there are at least three previous offences not necessarily followed by sentences of imprisonment.

Denmark, like Czechoslovakia, Norway, and Sweden 1937, requires that the criminal should have served at least two previous sentences of imprisonment, but it departs from the practice in those countries by reducing this requirement to one previous sentence if such sentence was pursuant to a serious sexual offence.

The previous sentences required by the Finnish law are either three sentences of imprisonment of which at least one had involved a term of at least one year, or, with or without interruption, one or more sentences of imprisonment involving a total period of ten or more years.

The Dutch requirements vary inversely with the period of imprisonment for the last offence, but in every case at least three previous sentences of imprisonment for a period of six months or more are required. If the sentence for the last offence is for a period of three or more years, then the previous sentences must have been together equal to or greater than a period of four years; if the sentence for the last offence is for a period of two or more years, then six or more years previous imprisonment is required; and if it is for a period of one year or more, then at least eight years previous imprisonment is a condition precedent to the application of provisions designed to deal with habitual criminals.

Articles 103 to 105 of the Italian Code must now be considered. The application of article 103 requires as a condition precedent the existence of two previous sentences (no type of punishment is specified), and the application of article 104 requires at least one previous sentence of imprisonment in respect of at least three offences. Article 105 cannot be applied unless the conditions of previous sentences required by either article 103 or article 104 are satisfied.

In Spain, the number of previous sentences required varies with the atrocity of the crimes committed; but recidivism, in the sense we use the word, is always necessary.

Norway 1929 and Switzerland have the most elastic provisions in this respect. An offender cannot be declared an habitual criminal unless he has previously been subject to " many " previous sentences, and the interpretation of " many " is left to the discretion of the court in the light of the particular offender before it.[1]

---

[1] The Norwegian law of 1902 achieved a similar result, the word " repeatedly " being used (i.e. one who has been repeatedly convicted of certain offences). In 1929 the word " many " was substituted.

Finally, under this sub-heading, we must consider the German law of 1933. As well as giving an almost unfettered discretion to the judge, this law laid down a supposedly mandatory application of a special sentence as an habitual for criminals who had been previously sentenced at least twice for " serious offences "—a very comprehensive list of crimes. This provision, for reasons which we will adduce below, did not, in fact, exclude judicial discretion in its application, and it is therefore considered together with the laws of other countries which steered a middle course between an absolute legal presumption which compelled the courts to declare certain persons habitual criminals, and an unfettered judicial discretion.

(b) *The requirement of a certain gravity or certain motives in the offences committed—the homogeneity or specificity of these offences.*

It need not be stressed that the requirement of previous sentences of imprisonment involves the previous commission of crimes of a certain gravity, and this was implicit in (a) above. But we are not concerned to discuss here the gravity of offences so implied. Here are presented only those explicit conditions precedent to the application of habitual criminal legislation which concern the gravity of past and present offences, and further, any requirement that all or some of the offences committed shall be of a similar character, estimated objectively by falling within various classificatory groups of crimes, or subjectively by the motive actuating the criminal.

Article 108 of the Italian Penal Code of 1930 was designed to combat a conception of a type of criminal advanced earlier, in Germany, by Aschaffenburg—the conception of the habitual criminal with an unblemished record. Carrying this idea to its ultimate conclusion, it is clear that, were our understanding of the springs of human conduct sufficient, we could classify a person as an habitual criminal even though he had never offended against the criminal law. To this length neither Aschaffenburg nor the supposedly " scientific " Italian Code would proceed. Every Statute dealing with habitual criminals requires, therefore, as a condition precedent to its operation, a certain gravity of the offence which last brought the offender before the court. This is so because all such legislation can be supported morally only on the basis of the overriding right of the community to protect itself against particularly dangerous criminals ; and until it can be proved that, for example, the larceny of a rubber doll by individuals of an exactly diagnosable psychological pattern is invariably followed by their attempted rape of a child, it is wise for the community to act empirically, and not to segregate a criminal for any lengthened period until he has given some palpable proof of his dangerousness.

The community must bear some risk, for the rights of the individual must also be respected. How, then, in the European habitual criminal legislation under consideration, is this requirement phrased ?

Generally, offences of a political nature, or motivated by political ideologies, are excluded from consideration, though this was not so in the German or Italian legislation in which the criminal law had admittedly racial and political purposes to fulfil.

Also, as a general rule, an individual pardon excludes the sentence in question from counting as a previous sentence, or previous conviction, in this context: this is not the case where a general amnesty has terminated the sentence, and in this circumstance only the punishment itself and not the existence of the conviction or the sentence is expunged for the purposes of habitual criminal legislation.

As has been pointed out, all habitual criminal legislation requires that the last offence(s) committed shall be of a certain gravity.[1] However, in some European legislation this requirement is implicit in the definition of the subjective qualities of the offender, whilst in other European legislation it is more definitely formulated.

Countries following the former practice are Czechoslovakia, Denmark, Hungary, Poland, Spain, Sweden 1927 and 1937, and Yugoslavia. The usual forms of this implied requirement are that the offence(s) must be of a type that allows one to conclude that the offender is a public danger (Yugoslavia), or that the likelihood of its repetition constitutes a danger to public order (Poland). Many means to this end are available ; for example, the Hungarian legislation applies only to a " hardened criminal " and the definition of this term includes the requirement that the last offence committed is a serious one.

The Swiss habitual criminal legislation incorporates the conception of gravity of offence in its subjective definition of the type of offender liable to its provisions, but it also requires that the last offence be punishable by imprisonment.

Belgium, Finland, Germany, Holland, Italy and Norway 1902

---

[1] The furthest departure from this rule is to be found in the French law of 1885 and its application to those habitually committing vagrancy offences.

and 1929, all explicitly define the requisite gravity of the last offence or offences committed, and we shall treat them seriatim.

Belgium requires for the mandatory operation of her habitual criminal laws that the last offence committed be a " *crime* " (felony) and also that it follow a previous sentence for a " *crime* ". Where her habitual criminal legislation operates at the discretion of the trial judge, the gravity of the final crime, as measured by the period of imprisonment imposed pursuant to it (for it must merit imprisonment) conditions the maximum duration of the preventive detention that can be imposed.

In Finland, the last offence must result in a sentence of at least three years' imprisonment before the habitual criminal provisions can apply.

The German legislation applied mandatorily only to those persons last convicted of a " serious " offence, and giving meaning to that term there was a very extensive list of offences. Where the German legislation was facultative, it applied only to those persons convicted of three " malicious " offences, and though there is no list exactly interpreting this term, a certain gravity of offence is involved in the very word "malicious", and in the later requirement that the offender must be a "dangerous habitual criminal".

The Dutch habitual criminal provision can be applied pursuant only to sentences of one year, two years, or three or more years imprisonment for the last offence(s) committed. The lesser the period of imprisonment last imposed, the greater must have been the total previous period of imprisonment before the offender can be declared an habitual criminal.[1]

The Italian definitions of those liable to be declared " habitual " or " professional " criminals, or " delinquents by tendency " all involve this conception of the gravity of the last offence. The judge is directed to take into account the gravity of the offences committed, and article 133, paragraph one, of the Code[2] is designed to aid him in so doing. A certain gavity of offence is thus

---

[1] The mechanism of this variation was explained on p. 188.
[2] " Article 133 : In the exercise of (his) discretional powers . . . the judge must take into account the gravity of the offence, as inferred from—
　(1) The nature, character, means, object, time, place and any other circumstances of the act ;
　(2) The gravity of the injury or of the danger caused to the person injured by the offence ;
　(3) The intensity of criminal intent or the degree of culpable negligence."

required equally where habituality is objectively presumed (articles 102-5) as where it is subjectively decided by the judge (article 108).

Norway's law of 1902 gave a list of thirty-four legislative provisions whose infringement was a condition precedent to the declaration that an offender was an habitual criminal. It thus exactly answered this question of the requisite gravity of the last offence. A law of 1925 added three more offences to this list, and the new habitual criminal legislation of 1929 added one more, bringing the total to thirty-eight offences.

As to the specificity or homogeneity of the crimes committed by an offender throughout his career. Where a discretion is given to the judge charged to decide whether an individual is to be treated as an habitual criminal, then the greater the homogeneity between the various offences committed by the person before him, the more likely he is to regard that person as meriting this special treatment. The more specific be his recidivism, the more manifest is his social dangerousness. This being so, all but three legislatures have regarded it as unnecessary to specify the degree of specialisation in crime for an offender to be declared an habitual criminal, such a decision being much better left to the judge *vis-à-vis* the particular offender before him. Therefore, we need consider only the provisions of the German, Italian, and Polish laws.

Germany: for the operation of the mandatory provisions of the German law of 1933, there must be a certain homogeneity between at least three offences, all of which must fall within a fairly extensive list of offences classed as " serious ".

Italy: articles 102 to 105 either explicitly or implicitly require as a condition precedent to their application that the last offences committed be " offences of the same character " as those for which the offender was previously sentenced. Article 101 defines this phrase as follows:

> " For the purpose of the penal law, not only offences which transgress the same provision of the law, but also those which, although contemplated in different provisions of the present Code, or in different laws nevertheless, owing to the nature of the facts which constitute them, or of the motives which determined them, present in concrete cases common fundamental features, are deemed to be offences of the same character."

Poland: In Poland three distinct groups can be sentenced to preventive detention (though or course one person could belong to all three). These are, triple recidivists, professional criminals and habitual criminals. The last two are defined subjectively, and the homogeneity of the offences they have committed will be one factor weighed by the judge, though it is nowhere specified. On the other hand, this legislation applies only to triple recidivists whose offences are inspired by the same motives or which fall into the same category of offences—this has been interpreted so that though a complete identity of type of crime is not required, a certain homogeneity between at least three offences is necessary.

(c) The period over which the offences or the sentences may be spread.

Where the conditions precedent to the imposition of preventive detention include previous sentences or offences and a subsequent conviction, it is not unusual to find a period statutorily established during which these conditions must be satisfied if the habitual criminal legislation is to be applied. Of the countries under consideration, this is the case in Belgium, Finland, Hungary, Italy, Poland, Sweden and Yugoslavia.

The Belgian law specifies such a period only in relation to those criminals who qualify (article 25) for preventive detention by virtue of at least three previous sentences of imprisonment for at least six months each. These three sentences must have occurred over a period not greater than fifteen years, and this period must also include the interval between the first of such sentences and the offender's present conviction.

Finland, Poland (concerning " triple recidivists "), and Yugoslavia measure a period from the absolute termination of the sentence imposed pursuant to the last of the " previous offences " to the commission of the " last offence ". If such period exceeds five years, then the conditions precedent for the application of the habitual criminal legislation have not been satisfied. In other words, after five years without conviction " previous sentences " are expunged from the criminal's record for this purpose, though reconviction, release and a further conviction within five years revives the earlier sentences as qualifications for preventive detention.

It will be recalled that the French law of 1885 laid down a period of ten years over which the conditions for *relégation* must be satisfied, and that, in computing this period, time spent actually in prison was to be excluded. Hungary and Sweden 1927 and 1937 follow the French legislation in this respect, with the difference that the period they establish is one of five years only.

Article 102 of the Italian Code varies from and yet combines, elements of all the above concepts. The three previous crimes must have been imposed within a period of ten years and the offence which now brings the criminal before the court must have been committed within ten years following the last of these three crimes. This does not argue a tender heart on the part of the Italian legislature in 1930, for article 107 of the Code stated for this and other purposes, that

> " the provisions relating to the declaration that a person is an habitual or professional offender shall also apply if one single sentence has been pronounced in respect of the various offences."

(d) *The personal characteristics of the offender which must be considered by the judge in the exercise of his discretion whether to impose preventive detention.*

Here the operative word is "must". None of the laws under consideration puts any limit on the factors to which the judge may turn his attention in deciding whether or not to impose preventive detention on the particular offender before him, but many of them insist that he shall come to an affirmative decision on stated questions before he exercises his discretion against the offender. In so far as the judge is here performing an individual legislative function— is deciding anew in each case before him between the conflicting claims of society and of individual liberty—it is not surprising that the legislature frequently limits this judicial discretion, or rather that it imposes its interpretation on the factors that should guide the judge in making this difficult decision.

Of course, this criminological discretion does not arise until the conditions precedent to the imposition of preventive detention, which we have already analysed, have been satisfied; nor does it arise when the habitual criminal legislation is mandatory and not facultative in operation (though in Germany there is an apparent exception to this). And further, we need not explore, in this context, those laws which give the judiciary no guidance in the task of deciding between the potentially conflicting interests of society and the criminal. We shall now consider the intervening category where though the judge is not bound by the legislature he is given some guidance by it.

In the debates in the Belgian Parliament during the passage of the law of April 1930, it was agreed that " *l'internement au-delà de l'expiration de la peine proprement dite ne peut trouver sa justification que dans les strictes nécessités de la défense sociale* ",[1] and this idea was embodied in article 25 of that law by the insistence that the trial judge consider the habitual criminal as "*présentant une tendance persistante à la délinquance.*" Article 26 then orders that :

> " Dans le cas où la mesure n'est pas prescrite par la loi, les procédures relatives aux infractions qui forment la base de la récidive sont jointes au dossier de la poursuite et les motifs de la décision y sont spécifiés."

This requirement that the judge specify his reasons for imposing preventive detention is most salutary, and should obviate any rule-of-thumb application of the law.

The Danish statute is unusual in this regard. The judge cannot subject the criminal to preventive detention without a certificate from a doctor—a certificate which must inform him as to the offender's mental and physical condition, his characteristic traits, and the qualities which in the doctor's opinion render him dangerous to society and not susceptible to reformation by ordinary punishments. The certificate must also declare, before preventive detention can be ordered, that the offender so differs from the normal individual that he should be subjected to special penal methods. Even when armed with such a certificate, the judge can order preventive detention only when he considers that the offender before him constitutes an appreciable danger to society and that he is either a " professional " or "habitual " criminal. These terms are defined respectively by reference to the conduct of crime as a means of livelihood, and to the psychological condition of the offender. The requirement of "habituality" is often satisfied by a combination of the information contained in the medical certificate and in the offender's criminal record.

The Finnish law of 1932 expressly requires the Minister of Justice to give the court all the information in his possession concerning an offender who is liable to be declared an habitual criminal. The judge, faced with a criminal who satisfies the conditions precedent for the application of this law, can order preventive detention " if the attendant circumstances lead him to regard the offender as dangerous to society or to some member or members of society."

Both the supposedly mandatory provisions of the German law, and those which give an almost unfettered discretion to the judge, incorporate the conception of the "dangerous habitual criminal". The existence of this conception in a formally mandatory part of this legislation returned to the judge much of the power of selection

[1] Session 1925-36, *Ch. Doc.*, No. 341, p. 1639.

which on the face of the law was denied to him. At first, the German Supreme Court interpreted this phrase very narrowly, insisting that it be satisfied objectively by a propensity towards crime, a propensity indicated by the professional pursuit of crime or the homogeneity of the type of offences committed, and further required that these qualities must be observable in the crimes actually committed, and not in the court's evaluation of the personality of the convicted person. However, as this law developed into an instrument of political and racial policy, this definition increasingly widened until relatively minor criminal traits sufficed for the prisoner to be declared a " dangerous habitual criminal ".

In Holland the terms " professional criminal " and " habitual criminal " do not appear in the law of 1929, but the law was intended to apply to such offenders, and those terms were used in the Royal Message accompanying the Bill when it was placed before the Dutch Parliament. When the conditions precedent for the application of the law are satisfied, the judge may order preventive detention if it appears to him necessary to prevent future crimes, and if he also regards it as justified in all the circumstances of the case.

The Hungarian legislature made use of the term " hardened criminal ". For an offender to be declared a " hardened criminal ", and subjected to preventive detention, it must be found that, as well as satisfying other statutory conditions, " he commits such crimes as a profession or habitual tendency ". Once this is established, the judge must consider the criminal's personal characteristics, his general mode of life and his particular mode of life when the crime was committed, the manner of its commission, and so on. In fact, he is directed to consider all the relevant circumstances.

Despite giving a virtually untrammelled discretion to the judge, the Italian statute provides, by article 133, a list of factors which he must take into consideration in exercising this discretion. He must advert to these factors, but he can, of course, also turn his attention to any other relevant (or even criminologically irrelevant) circumstances. On p. 191, para. 1 of article 133 appears ; para. 2 of that article reads:

> " The judge must likewise take into account the guilty party's capacity to delinquency, as inferred from—
> (1) The motives to commit delinquency and the character of the offender ;
> (2) The criminal and judicial antecedents and, in general, the conduct and life of the offender prior to the offence ;
> (3) The conduct contemporary with or subsequent to the offence ;
> (4) The individual, domestic and social conditions of the life of the offender."

Norway's law of 1902 was exceptional in so far as, when the offender had satisfied the conditions precedent to its application, the jury could be asked whether the offender was to be regarded as presenting very great danger to society, or to the life, health or well-being of any particular person or class of persons. This question the jury were to answer in the light of the nature of the *last* crime committed, the motive which underlay that crime, and the inclination which was revealed in it. Only if the jury found that the criminal was such a dangerous person could the judge impose preventive detention. He was not, however, under any obligation to do so. A discretion was thus superimposed upon a discretion, both judge and jury separately and successively adverting to the wisdom of segregating the offender from society ; for though in form the question of dangerousness left to the jury was one of fact, it inevitably involved a decision on their part as to the advisability of special punishment for the criminal before them.

The Norwegian legislation of 1929 greatly diminished the discretion given to the court with the expressed object of increasing the application of habitual criminal provisions. The conditions precedent having been satisfied, the judge was charged to consider the likelihood that the offender before him would again commit a crime of the type for which he was convicted. On this question he was bound to pronounce his conclusions, and if he concluded that there was an appreciable possibility of such crimes in the future, then he was statutorily compelled to order preventive detention.

In Poland, the offender having been shown to be a triple recidivist of a certain type, or a professional or habitual criminal as defined by the law of 1932, the judge must consider whether his freedom would threaten public order; on the basis of his conclusions he must either impose or not impose the special measures designed to deal with " incorrigible " criminals. There is thus considerable similarity between the Norwegian statute of 1929 and this Polish law.

The Spanish statute requires that the judge shall impose preventive detention only on those in whom he finds a persistent tendency to crime.

The Swedish laws of 1927 and 1937 ordered that special measures should be applied to those who satisfied the objective requirements of these laws, and for whom the normal punishments would probably be insufficient. In determining the likely sufficiency of the normal punishments, the judge is guided by the findings of a special commit-tee, the "Commission of Detention", one of whose functions is to guarantee that preventive detention shall not be ordered unless it is clearly necessary. Their finding that preventive detention should not be imposed closes the issue, but their advice that it should still leaves a discretion residing in the trial judge. Later, we will consider the composition and operation of this committee in greater detail.[1]

Switzerland combines the Spanish and Swedish guidance to the trial judge in so far as he is charged to declare offenders to be habitual criminals only when they have a persistent tendency to crime (" un penchant au crime ou délit ") and when normal treatment would probably be insufficient.

Finally, in Yugoslavia, the conditions precedent to the application of the law of 1929 having been satisfied, a person is to be sentenced to preventive detention " whose life and the crimes he has committed enable one to conclude that he constitutes a public danger " (article 51).

2. Who controls the application of the habitual criminal laws ?

In our treatment of question one, we have been compelled by the necessity for clarity of exposition to present much of the information that could as conveniently have been presented under this heading. Nothing is to be gained by repeating it here. We have considered whether the habitual criminal statutes are mandatory or facultative and we have noted where the judge is guided by a special committee and where he shares part of the discretion with a jury. Nor is there much to be gained from an investigation of the subtler procedural variations from the norm embedded in habitual criminal legislation, still less from an investigation, conducted by one trained in the Anglo-American accusatorial procedure, of European systems adhering to an inquisitorial procedure.[2] However, because of their particular interest, we must turn our attention to the practice in three countries, namely, Finland, Sweden and Poland.

The Finnish law of 1932 empowers the judge to declare, in

---

[1] See p. 200.
[2] It must be mentioned that the investigation of European habitual criminal laws has led me to be severely critical of the heritage of Dicey which has led many English lawyers to dismiss contemptuously the inquisitorial system in favour of the accusatorial method, affirming the latter's great protection of individual rights. There is much to be said in support of Continental criminal procedure, which unfortunately for us remains unsaid in the English language.

pronouncing judgment, that the offender before him *may* be ordered to be detained in a special institution for habitual criminals. Thus, the decision of the Finnish court is not final and does not *per se* lead to preventive detention. The actual detention *may* then be ordered by a " Penetentiary Tribunal " whose jurisdiction extends throughout Finland. However, every decision of a court of first instance that a criminal may be sentenced to preventive detention can be canvassed at the instigation of the criminal by the Court of Appeal. Armed with the permission of the court of first instance (confirmed if the prisoner requires it by the Court of Appeal) the Penitentiary Tribunal considers, at its leisure, the wisdom of detaining the prisoner beyond the fixed term imposed by the court. This finite sentence must be for a minimum period of three years, though the Penitentiary Tribunal has power to allow the finite sentence to be served, in part, in the special institution; but every potential detainee must serve at least two years in an ordinary institution. Before ordering the preventive detention, the Penitentiary Tribunal must consider the advice of the Governor of the institution where the person so sentenced is serving his finite sentence. The Penitentiary Tribunal need not decide as to preventive detention until the termination of the finite sentence imposed, that is to say, in no case need it decide for three years after the decision of the court, though it may do so at any time considered convenient. During this period it has ample opportunity to conduct a scientific and exhaustive investigation into the criminal whose detention it may order, and it is not pressed for time as is even the wisest court making the most careful use of remand facilities. The Penitentiary Tribunal is composed of the Director of Prison Administration, and three other members nominated by the President of the Republic and appointed for five years; amongst these three must be " a person familiar with the function of a judge ", and a psychiatrist. The procedure they follow is essentially that of a superior court, but there is no recourse from their decisions. The prisoner has full rights of audition before them, and may adduce evidence and have legal representation.

The Finnish idea of a Penitentiary Tribunal, operating as it does and composed as it is, constitutes one of the few valid arguments for a dual-track system of preventive detention, and is a remarkably interesting method of fusing the apparently competing claims of the ordinary courts and special treatment tribunals into a harmonious whole; claims that they should each have control over the sentence imposed. The rights of the individual are certainly well-protected from administrative caprice by the bulwark of the law, and yet there is scope for the scientific, leisurely and unemotional determination of sentence by an administrative body. In a recent book,[1] Dr. Mannheim forcibly argues that " in the field of criminal procedure, the question of a Treatment Tribunal will clearly be the central issue of any planning programme." It will be our loss if we do not profit by the experience of the Finnish Penitentiary Tribunal when devising such a programme—the compromise there adopted would surely satisfy the supporters of the Treatment Tribunal, and would hardly disturb those who rely on the courts as the citizen's most efficient defence against official arbitrariness.

Sweden, too, has established a special body with authority over the imposition of preventive detention. It is called a " Commission of Detention " and, unlike the Finnish Penitentiary Tribunal, functions before the sentence of the court is promulgated. All cases in which preventive detention is legally possible, that is to say, where the objective conditions precedent for its application are satisfied, must be submitted to a preliminary examination by the Commission of Detention. This body advises the court as to whether they consider preventive detention should be ordered, and without that recommendation the court cannot impose such a sentence. Their positive recommendation does not, however, close the matter, and the judge can still exercise an independent discretion, although in practice he invariably follows the Commission's recommendation. The Commission of Detention is composed of five members, being in 1938, two judges, one psychiatrist, the head of the prison administration, and one prominent citizen not possessed of special criminological or penological knowledge. Here too is a happy blend of penological wisdom and judicial consideration for the individual.

The Penitentiary Tribunal and the Commission of Detention also have functions in relation to the conditions under which preventive detention is served, and the release of detainees. Later we will consider these functions.

Regarding the Polish law, only a brief mention, and on a slightly different question, need be made here. The penal authorities may request a court to order the preventive detention of a person not previously so sentenced, who, during his sentence in prison, has

---

[1] *Criminal Justice and Social Reconstruction*, Dr. H. Mannheim, p. 263.

manifested such anti-social tendencies that his release would be a danger to the public. This request opens the consideration of the question whether he is a triple recidivist of the required type, or a habitual or professional criminal, which question will be decided on the same basis as if it had arisen during the trial which led to the prisoner's present sentence, except that the prosecution's case is strengthened by such a request by the prison authorities.

3. *Do such laws envisage aggravation of punishment or special measures ? If the latter, do the special measures follow or take the place of the punishment for the last offence ?*

It must be stressed that the answer to the first of these questions is based on matters of form, and cannot spring from a consideration of functioning reality. As we shall see, there is in practice frequently little enough difference between " aggravation of punishment " and " special measures ". Bearing this in mind, it can be stated roundly that all of the statutes we are analysing in this section of the work do " envisage " special measures for the treatment of habitual criminals, and that two of them, those of Germany and Italy, also statutorily provide for the aggravation of the punishment imposed for the last offence committed.

There is more substance in the second of the above two questions. Belgium, Czechoslovakia, Finland, Germany, Holland, Italy, Latvia, Poland, Spain and Yugoslavia adopt the dual-track system by which the special measures adapted to the treatment of habitual criminals are undergone after a fixed term of imprisonment imposed for the last offence committed.

The Norwegian law of 1902 introduced a single-track system, the law of 1929 altered it to a dual-track system. The Swedish legislation has followed exactly the opposite course ; in 1937 the single-track system replaced the dual-track system inaugurated in 1927.

Hungary and Switzerland adopt a single-track system.

Finally, Denmark, the home of social and political pragmatism, leaves the choice between the single- or dual-track system to the trial judge, a choice to be made anew for each successive offender. The tendency of the Danish judges is to prefer the immediate commencement of the special measure rather than to defer it until after a fixed term of imprisonment in an ordinary institution.

The single-track system is becoming more popular, and the countries which, more recently, have modified their habitual criminal legislation (Sweden 1937 and 1946, Switzerland 1938, and England 1948) have preferred that their special treatment of such prisoners should not be preceded by an ordinary sentence. The single-track system could well be called the " Swiss system", in that it was first formulated in the Swiss Draft Code of 1893, and since then has been retained in all subsequent projects for a Swiss Federal Code and in the Code itself. Thus, the ideas of Carl Stoos grow in force with the years.

The argument for the dual-track system rests on two grounds—the necessity for condign punishment, and the need to give the offender a " cooling off " period in the ordinary prison so that he shall not disrupt the smooth administration of the special institution. To my mind, neither of these contentions has as much force as the support of the dual-track system implicit in the Finnish law of 1932 in which the finite sentence imposed constitutes a period during which a special tribunal can decide whether it is necessary to subject the offender to the particular treatment designed for habitual criminals.

There are many arguments advanced in favour of the single-track system, but most of them have their roots in the concept that a prolonged detention, even under the mildest penal conditions, inflicts ample suffering on the offender even if it is considered necessary for him to purge his sin, to expiate the suffering he has engendered, in short, in the Hegelian sense, to restore the right. If a lesser degree of suffering is envisaged, then it is manifestly causing gratuitous suffering to insist that such a detention be preceded by the ordinary punishment suited to the last crime committed.

There is, of course, a profoundly different argument occasionally advanced for the single-track system: if it be impossible to differentiate, to any appreciable extent, the conditions of imprisonment and the conditions of preventive detention, it is entirely unreal to insist that one precede the other and to do so merely unnecessarily complicates a country's penal administration. Only in Hungary is this contention used to support the single-track system. Later we will consider, in some detail, the possibility of allowing preventive detainees substantially different conditions from those imposed on other prisoners; for it is a vital issue, not only to the question of whether preventive detention should follow or supersede imprisonment for the last offence, but to many other aspects of habitual criminal legislation.

One cannot, and should not, attempt to reach an absolute conclusion on the relative merits of either method of imposing preventive detention. It is a problem for each country, a problem to be considered in the light of the theory of punishment which is predominant when preventive detention is introduced, and it cannot profitably be discussed independently of the morality and purpose of punishment. It is, therefore, an inappropriate subject for further treatment on the comparative level until some agreement on the vexed question of the ethics of punishment is attained. So far, in the course of many meetings of the International Penal and Penitentiary Congress at which the problem of punishment has arisen in one form or another, the outcome is that there is no agreement whatsoever about it. But we are not seeking the unification of European criminal law, and in this as in other respects we can learn much from a knowledge of the practice in other countries.

4. *What is the form of sentence imposed ?*

In answering this question we will ignore the period of imprisonment served as a precursor to preventive detention in those countries where the dual-track system applies, and will consider only the form of the sentence of preventive detention itself.

In this context, the legal systems we are analysing fall into three broad groups—those adhering to : (*a*) the indeterminate sentence, (*b*) the indefinite sentence, and (*c*) sentences whose duration is predetermined by the judge.

First, the indeterminate sentence. Denmark and Germany, for widely different reasons, fixed neither the minimum nor maximum duration of preventive detention.

Secondly, the indefinite sentence. The Yugoslavian law introduced preventive detention for an indefinite period varying between three and ten years. Czechoslovakia, and Spain 1933, fixed both the minimum and maximum duration of preventive detention at not less that one year nor more than five years. Spain 1928, specified no minimum term, but fixed the maximum at five years. All the other countries adopting the indefinite sentence specified only the minimum term to be served and the sentence could be prolonged indefinitely. These minimum terms specified were as follows: Finland three years, Poland five years,[1] and Italy either two, three or four years varying with the article of the Code under which the

[1] In certain circumstances release can be granted in Poland after four and a half years.

offender was sentenced (for example, article 108—delinquent by tendency—minimum of four years).

The single-track system of preventive detention is in force in Hungary, Sweden and Switzerland. This has considerable bearing on the minimum term to be served because the court's conception of the minimum condign punishment must be respected. Therefore, in these countries, no maximum duration of preventive detention is fixed, but all provide for the judge to specify a minimum term that is to be served in each case, a term which cannot be less than a period statutorily determined. Thus, in Hungary and Switzerland, preventive detention must continue for three years or more, but when sentencing the offender to preventive detention, the judge can increase this minimum period if he so desires.

In Sweden, between 1927 and 1937, the dual-track system was operating and the minimum duration of preventive detention was two years (minimum: three years' imprisonment plus two years' preventive detention): in 1937, with the introduction of the single-track system, the judge was empowered to determine the minimum term of preventive detention to be served, but this period could in no case be less than five years.

Thirdly, the habitual criminal legislation of three countries—Belgium, Holland and Norway—provides that sentences of preventive detention shall be fixed exactly by the judge.[1] The Dutch legislation of 1929, and article 25 of the Belgian law of 1930, empowered the judge to fix the term of preventive detention to be served in each case, but provided that such a term could not be less than five, nor more than ten years; those sentenced under article 24 of the Belgian law could be detained for any period between ten and twenty years that the judge might determine. The Norwegian law of 1902 provided only a maximum period (fifteen years, or three times the punishment fixed by the judge for the offence last committed) beyond which the judge could not prolong the offender's detention. In 1929 this upper limit was abolished. In these three countries, Belgium, Holland and Norway (and similarly England 1908), the exact fixation in each case of the period of preventive detention to be served did not preclude, at the discretion of the penal authorities, conditional release before the termination of that period.

[1] Sentences under Part II of the Prevention of Crime Act, 1908, were similarly "determined".

When a detainee, during his period of probation following conditional release, commits a crime of a certain gravity, and as a result is eventually recommitted to preventive detention, the minimum period of preventive detention he must serve is often statutorily increased beyond the periods stated above. This is the practice in many of the legal systems we have been considering, but it has not been thought useful to list the many various means they have adopted of implementing this plan.

5. *If a special measure is applied, what is the degree of differentiation between it and other long-term imprisonment ?*

This is a complicated question, the theoretical and practical importance of which will be discussed at length pursuant to this comparative law study.[1]

It is clear that were one to present, for each country, the conditions in the preventive detention institutions and contrast them with the conditions obtaining in representative ordinary prisons (as would be necessary for a complete and accurate answer to this question), the whole study would be lost in minutiæ. And further, for reasons of national *amour-propre*, the information on this subject available to the foreign reader is particularly unreliable.

For the time being, therefore, we will turn our attention to two types of evidence bearing on this question : first, whether an entirely separate institution, or a separate part of an institution, is set aside in each country for preventive detainees; secondly, various conclusions on the subject of differentiation of treatment of habitual criminals to be found in the sources of our study in European comparative law. The first is particularly important because when preventive detainees are intermingled with other prisoners any differentiation of their treatment is practically impossible; and even when they are segregated in a part of a prison, administrative exigencies, and the desire for an economy of clerical and executive effort, render such differentiation extremely difficult. Only in entirely separate institutions can a régime suited to habitual criminals operate satisfactorily.

We will deal separately with each country for which such evidence is available.

[1] See pp. 234-243.

BELGIUM

An annex for male habitual criminals was opened at Merxplas in January 1932.[1] During the four years 1932 to 1935 it received a total of 181 such prisoners. Merxplas is an all-purpose prison in which many different classes of prisoners are incarcerated. Prisoners convicted of vagrancy offences, others sentenced to fixed terms of imprisonment for a great variety of crimes, and, since the war, a large number of persons being punished for collaborationist activities, are all gathered together in this mixed agricultural and industrial prison. Amongst them, but segregated as far as possible from other prisoners, are those criminals sentenced, pursuant to the law of 1930, to preventive detention. These habitual criminals are subjected to a progressive stage system (governed by a marks system), first entering the "*groupe d'observation*", then proceeding to the "*groupe d'épreuve*", and finally graduating to the "*groupe de confiance*". Their conditions of detention are progressively ameliorated, and as far as is possible in an institution in which other prisoners are held, their existence is made as comfortable as it can be in a maximum-security institution. The link between these ameliorated conditions and the dual-track system of preventive detention was elucidated in a speech in the Belgian Parliament by the Minister of Justice explaining the government's plan for this detention in which he said : "*Ces établissements doivent être des colonies de travail à régime ferme, mais sans rigueur inutile. Ils n'ont pas le caractère pénitentiaire, car les internés ont déjà purgé leur peine et payé leur dette à la vindicte publique.*"[2]

As the Belgian practice is very similar to that adopted in several other European countries, I have regarded it as useful to reproduce here some information concerning Merxplas as a preventive detention institution given by H. Bekaert, a senior official at the Ministry of Justice, who in 1936 surveyed the first four years during which Merxplas received such prisoners.[3]

" Il pourrait se caractériser par le formule de l'emprisonnement élargi. La situation rurale du pénitencier, son organisation intérieure et la disposition spéciale de ses locaux ont permis de graduer l'amendement et de créer, avant la libération, une atmosphère de semi-liberté propice au reclassement.

---

[1] Pursuant to a decree of December 15th, 1930.   [2] Session 1927-8, *Ch. Ann.*, p. 113.
[3] Hermann Bekaert : *L'application de la loi de Défense Sociale du 9 avril, 1930, aux recidivistes et délinquants d'habitude*, Louvain, 1936.

" Ils ont soumis au régime pénitentiaire mixte, c'est-à-dire l'isolement cellulaire la nuit et le travail en commun pendant la journée. La tâche imposée aux internés est en principe un travail d'atelier. Mais pour ceux qui sont parvenus au groupe de confiance, le règlement autorise le travail des champs. L'établissement dispose en effet d'une ferme parfaitement outillée et entourée de terres labourables. L'interné qui semble donner des signes suffisants d'amendement pourra bénéficier pour le travail du jour d'une certaine liberté. Il sera même autorisé à se rendre seul aux champs.

" L'isolement cellulaire auquel les internés se sont soumis la nuit se différencie lui aussi de l'emprisonnement répressif. Grâce à l'initiative de l'administration des prisons, la lucarne des cellules a fait place à une large fenêtre. L'interné trouve à sa disposition un écouteur radiophonique et des lectures. Il reçoit les visites du personnel et jouit de l'éclairage jusqu'à 22 heures du soir, s'il l'a mérité.

" Toute une série de menus détails rapprochent encore le récidiviste de cet état de semi-liberté qui devrait toujours précéder une libération : repas en commun, jeux et récréations, promenades, etc.

" L'internement semble à tel point s'etre dépouillé du caractère intimidant qu'au cours des années 1932 à 1935, il s'est trouvé des récidivistes proposés à la libération, qui ont préféré ne pas bénéficier de cette faveur !

" Pendant cette époque, le pénitencier a ouvert quatre-vingt douze fois ses portes à des internés libérés qui revenaient volontairement chercher l'hospitalité !

" Le vœu du législateur a donc été respecté : l'internement se limite aux strictes exigences de la défense sociale et l'expérience de la loi a été réalisée dans le domaine de la récidive avec le maximum d'effort et de garanties individuelles."

DENMARK

In Denmark an entirely separate institution is devoted to the detention of habitual criminals. There they are allowed ample opportunity for relaxation and personal development, and are subjected to as mild a penal discipline as the Danish authorities have been able to devise. Long experience with the indeterminate sentence, a criminologically enlightened administration, and, not least, the influence of Dr. G. K. Stürup and his work with psychopaths serving indeterminate sentences,[1] have combined to make preventive detention in Denmark a humane and efficient measure of social security.

[1] *Treatment of Criminal Psychopaths*, Dr. G. K. Stürup, and *On the Diagnosis of Psychopathy in Criminals*, Dr. J. F. Larsen, both in the *Report on the Eighth Congress of Scandinavian Psychiatrists*. See also *The Psychopath in Our Midst—A Danish Solution*, Dr. Stephen Taylor, the *Lancet*, January 1st, 1949.

In 1939, male habitual criminals, during the indefinite stage of their confinement, were detained in Finland in special parts of the central prison at Turku and in the auxiliary prison at Lyperto, the latter situated on an isolated island in the Gulf of Bosnia. The sections of these prisons to which they were confined were inspected regularly by the Penitentiary Tribunal (whose function in sentencing such prisoners we have considered), and this body reported to the Minister of Justice advising him on all matters connected with preventive detention.

The conditions of detention were as ameliorated as was compatible with the necessity to prevent their escape, and with their presence in institutions occupied by other prisoners. Detainees worked in association, the trades in order of preference being carpentry, shoemaking, tailoring and painting, and they received half the proceeds of their labour to spend on extra food, tobacco, and other comforts. The plan was that they should receive not half, but all of it; unfortunately the war intervened. As from 8 p.m. each evening they were confined in their cells, but until that time they associated with one another in special rooms for this purpose containing books, games, papers, magazines, and comfortable chairs. Their food and clothing was considerably better than that allowed other prisoners. Finally, two years after a detainee had commenced preventive detention, he might, with the permission of the Penitentiary Tribunal and subject to whatever conditions it thought fit, be given an annual holiday of anything up to two weeks each year. During this fortnight the detainee could visit approved friends or relations in Finland, live a normal life, and get a taste of complete freedom.

Writing in 1939, the Director General of the Finnish Prison Administration, A. P. Arvelo, described the conditions of preventive detention which we have briefly noted above; and notwithstanding the consideration shown in them for the prisoner, he dwelt on the difficulty of adequately differentiating such treatment from that accorded to other prisoners when they were confined in the same institutions, even though in different parts of them. He described the plan to establish an entirely separate institution for preventive detainees, in which the detainee would receive the full proceeds of his labour and where no difficulties would arise from the contiguity of other prisoners—thus perhaps might be realised the conception of a detention centre for habitual criminals with as few punitive elements as is humanly possible.

GERMANY, ITALY AND HUNGARY

None of these countries has seriously endeavoured to apply to habitual criminals any treatment different from that to which other prisoners are subjected.

Germany was quite open in aggravating the punishment for the last offence committed and in treating the subsequent preventive detention as an expiatory punishment.

In Italy, though supposedly agricultural colonies were established, the reactions of such an acute observer as Professor Ernest Delaquis[1] to these institutions make it clear that, as in Germany, preventive detention was, if anything, served under a more onerous régime than other long-term imprisonment.

The Hungarian practice was at least logical. There it was contended that preventive detention is inevitably so similar to ordinary imprisonment that no useful purpose could be served by establishing special institutions for habitual criminals. Therefore a single-track system was applied so that what was frankly a " punishment " should not be superimposed upon a previous " punishment ".

HOLLAND

The Dutch habitual criminal legislation provided that preventive detention was not to be served in the ordinary prisons but was to be undergone in institutions whose régime was akin to that already established in State workhouses (*Rijkswerkinrichtingen*) for beggars and vagrants. It is claimed that in such institutions there is a genuine endeavour to avoid any hardship that is not necessary for the protection of society or the exigencies of compulsory labour. There is much to be said for this equation of preventive detention to workhouse rather than to prison conditions.

NORWAY

From 1902 to 1929, on completing the fixed sentence imposed on him and passing into the preventive detention stage of his punishment, the habitual criminal in Norway remained exactly where he

---

[1] *Recueil*, Vol. XI, pp. 43-51.

was—this transformation in his estate could occur without his noticing it. There was, quite literally, no differentiation of treatment whatsoever.

Those who designed the new law in 1929 were thinking specifically of the reformatory at Opstad as a likely preventive detention prison. However, this institution was already filled in 1929 and the upshot was that the habitual criminals were divided between the prisons at Trondheim and Botsfengslet. No new institution was established, nor was a rigid segregation between preventive detainees and other prisoners statutorily required. The prisons at Trondheim and Botsfengslet were designed for ordinary prisoners and they stamped their repressive heritage on the conditions of preventive detention. Indeed, no genuine attempt was made to inaugurate milder conditions for preventive detainees. The new legislation was introduced without any investigation into the practice in other countries or any consideration of the régime to which the detainees should be subject. No supervisory committee was formed. No new institution was established. It is not surprising that no differentiation of treatment resulted. It is doubtful if it was ever really desired.

POLAND

Before the war there was a special establishment for habitual criminals at Koronowo in the Department of Pomerania. Here, though in general the treatment of the detainees was very like that of prisoners in other institutions, they enjoyed certain privileges not elsewhere available. These privileges, as in other countries, took the form of a more extensive earnings scheme, the right to purchase extra food and other comforts, a later "lights-out", permission to have in the cells private property sent in from outside the prison, ample recreation and association, more books, papers, tobacco, visits, letters and so on. The Polish system of preventive detention was, however, particularly interesting because of the endeavour made there to apply the rudiments of our gradually increasing understanding of group therapy. In combination with a progressive stage system much attention was paid to the problem of forming groups of detainees considered suitable for association with one another while isolating them from other groups. It was thus hoped to engender the most reformative group associations possible. Despite the apparently poor material at the disposal of the prison authorities, it was surprising what success was achieved by this careful selection of group associations—success not only in fitting the detainee for release but in avoiding dissension within the prison.

SWEDEN

Two special institutions existed in 1939 for preventive detainees —one at Karstad, the other at Norrköping. The Commission of Detention, which advises on the detention of those who have qualified as habitual criminals, also has functions connected with the supervision of these preventive detention establishments. As in Finland and Denmark, every endeavour is made to eliminate all possible punitive elements of the ordinary prison régime; and with considerable success.

YUGOSLAVIA

In Yugoslavia there was a clear distinction drawn between those institutions enforcing " punishments " and those applying " measures of security "; and the régime to be followed in each was to be suited to the different purposes involved in these two reactions to crime. Institutions applying measures of security were divided into three types:

(a) institutions for medical treatment of irresponsible and nearly irresponsible offenders,

(b) institutions for drunkards, and

(c) institutions for the detention of criminals who have undergone their punishment.

It was statutorily ordered that these institutions should be separated from prisons and separate from each other. Thus the habitual criminal, at the indefinite stage of his punishment, would normally be detained in the third of the above types of institution, though he might find himself in the first type. The régime imposed on the habitual criminal was different from that to which the ordinary prisoner was subjected, but it is doubtful whether in point of hardship there was much to choose between them.

SWITZERLAND

This question cannot be answered in relation to the Swiss penal system before 1962. On January 1st, 1942, the provisions of the Swiss Federal Criminal Code were put into force. By this Code the execution of preventive detention is a matter for the separate Cantons, though the sentence of preventive detention is passed pursuant to the Federal statute.   Though the execution of this measure is a separate problem for each of the Cantons, their rules for its execution must receive the approval of the Federal authorities, who have allowed the Cantons a period of twenty years in which to establish the necessary special institutions.[1]   In the meantime, preventive detainees are to be segregated as far as practicable from other prisoners, and their detention is to be as little punitive as possible. However, until separate institutions are established, there is a strong tendency for many of the distinctions of treatment between preventive detention and ordinary imprisonment to break down in practice, and it is to be hoped that these transitional defects will not harden into a permanent system.   The Federal authorities have clearly stated their conception of preventive detention:

> " Cet internement n'est pas une peine, la maison d'internement n'est pas un pénitencier. C'est un ' Arbeitskloster ', un ' home ', un asile. . . . Ne seront imposées à ces internés que les restrictions de liberté qui sont exigées par les buts de sécurité. . . ."[2]

To the preparation of their Federal Criminal Code the Swiss devoted much able and careful thought and were far from precipitate in arriving at its final form. Having, wisely enough, taken their time in legislating federally for habitual criminals, they have also allowed ample time for the gradual development of a wise execution of this law. It is to be hoped, and indeed can well be anticipated, that from this carefully and intelligently planned penal development will emerge a system of preventive detention suited alike to the needs of the community and of the detainee, and fulfilling the great expectations of its founder, Carl Stoos.

6. (a) Who is responsible for the release of habitual criminals ?

In order to safeguard the individual from official arbitrariness, some form of judicial supervision of an administrative decision is the norm. However, where the preventive detention legislation provides rigid minimum and maximum bounds for the duration of this measure, or where the sentence on an habitual criminal is for a determined period (as in Holland, Belgium, Norway and England), there is less need to introject judicial supervision of the release of such a prisoner at any later stage than the actual sentence.

[1] Federal Circular of November 14th, 1941, from the Department of Justice.
[2] *Recueil*, Vol. IX, p. 334.

The decision to release the habitual criminal from the preventive detention institution, and the conditions governing his release, are in several European countries (Belgium, Hungary, Italy, Poland, Spain and Yugoslavia) the responsibility of a judge—either the trial judge or the judge in whose venue the prisoner is detained. Usually the court's decision is a purely formal one taken only on the application of the detainee himself. Thus, in Belgium the detainee may apply to the court, at the end of every three years of his preventive detention, seeking an order that " *la mise à la disposition du Gouvernement* " be terminated, though even without such an application he may at any time be conditionally released from detention on the initiative of the penal authorities. In Hungary the initiative must come from the detainee in an application to the Minister of Justice who, on the advice of a special board he has appointed for that purpose, recommends to the court whether the detainee should be released, and advises the court on the conditions upon which it should allow such release. The judicial function is, therefore, largely formal.

Similarly, in Spain and Yugoslavia there is a special committee to advise the judge who orders the detainee's conditional discharge.

In Italy a " surveillance judge " is responsible for the detainee's release, and after the minimum term of preventive detention has been served (two, three or four years), the " surveillance judge " will either release the offender or determine when his release shall next be considered.

The Polish, like the Hungarian, legislation gives largely formal and supervisory powers to the judge who orders the detainee's release. At each preventive detention institution there is formed a " Committee of Assistance " composed of a judge, the Public Prosecutor, the Governor of the prison, and three prominent citizens appointed by the Minister of Justice. This committee advises the court on the detainee's release and on the conditions that should be imposed. The court can be approached for a formal order by the committee at any time after the five-year minimum period of detention has been served, but it must consider each detainee's release at least once every five years.[1]

---

[1] Article 84, Section 2 : " Confinement in such an institution shall last for such time as may appear necessary, in each case at least five years ; after the elapse of each period of five years the court shall decide whether it is necessary for the offender to remain in the institution for another five-year period."

In Germany, until 1941, the practice was similar to that followed in the above six countries in that until that date the release of a preventive detainee was the result of a judicial decision of the trial court. By a law of September 4th, 1941, this function was transferred to the Public Prosecutor General, thus facilitating the application of the habitual criminal legislation to criminologically illegitimate purposes.

In several other countries (Denmark, Finland, Holland, Norway, Sweden and Switzerland) the decision to release the preventive detainee is taken by administrative agencies. Denmark has established, for this purpose, a special board which must include one judge, one psychiatrist and one social worker. In Finland and Sweden the committees concerned with the habitual criminal's sentence to preventive detention (the Penitentiary Tribunal and the Commission of Detention, respectively[1]) also determine the date and conditions of the detainee's release. Likewise in Norway there is a special committee for this purpose, which also includes a judge as a member.[2] The Dutch legislation gives the power to release the habitual criminal to the Minister of Justice, acting on the advice of the Governor of the preventive detention institution (who reports annually to him, advising either the release of the detainee or stating his reasons for not so advising) and of the " Centra College voor de reclasseering", an aftercare or rehabilitative committee appointed by the Minister of Justice.

In this, as in other respects, the Swiss habitual criminal legislation is at present in a state of flux. The power to release the detainee is given by the Federal Code to " the competent authority". Being a formal and executive matter, the designation of " the competent authority " is the concern of the various Cantons, and no regular or settled practice has yet emerged. Whoever the Cantons may appoint as " the competent authority " will have to consult the officials of the special detention institution before ordering the habitual criminal's release and determining the conditions of such release.

All the above legal systems provide either statutorily or by administrative order for the regular consideration of the case of each and every habitual criminal with a view to his release. Once the

---

[1] For the composition of these two bodies see pp. 199 and 200.
[2] It will have been noticed that in these four countries, Denmark, Finland, Norway and Sweden, an element of direct judicial control is retained by the inclusion of a judge as a member of the body charged with the detainee's release.

minimum period for his detention has passed, the usual requirement is that his release shall be considered at least once every twelve months.

6. (b) On what basis are decisions to release them made ?

The basis upon which the above agencies decide on the detainee's release is frequently not statutorily specified, and even when the principles on which this decision is supposed to be taken are enshrined in a legislative formula, little enough guidance is given. Whatever phraseology is used, the question is one of evaluating the relative claims of the prisoner to his freedom and of society to its protection from dangerous criminals. Society must expect to bear a certain risk and it must stop short of denying human rights even to the habitual criminal. Were our knowledge of psychology an exact and complete science, and were we able to predict the activities of the previously dangerous offender, the task of deciding when to release the habitual criminal would not be difficult.[1] But as this is not so, a legislature can do no more than set up as efficient a body as possible to make this delicate decision, and to evaluate these conflicting social claims in a pragmatic approach to the problem posed by each offender. This has been done with the greatest wisdom in Finland, Denmark and Sweden where the judge, the psychiatrist, the prison administrator, the social worker and the intelligent layman meet to decide this issue, and represent in themselves those interests which must be equated by their decisions.

The basis of the decision is therefore undefined, even where it is articulated in a series of words which invariably has no semantic significance. The real problem is, then, rather the extent of information at the disposal of the discharging authority on which they can reach their difficult decision. To this question we will return at the conclusion of this comparative study. At present let us note two means available respectively in Finland and Poland, which assist the discharging authority in this regard.

In Finland, as we have mentioned, the Penitentiary Tribunal has power to allow the preventive detainee a fortnight's holiday away from the institution. Knowledge of the behaviour of the detainee over this period gives more guidance as to the likelihood of his rehabilitation into society than years of observation of his institutional behaviour.

---

[1] That such a time usually comes has been shown convincingly by the Gluecks in their studies of the relationship between criminality and " ageing ".

In Poland, though the conditional discharge from the preventive detention institution is formally the decision of the sentencing court, the Committee of Assistance (Judge, Public Prosecutor, Prison Governor and three laymen) which advises the court on this release has power, in its own right and on its own initiative, at any time after the detainee has served four and a half years in the indefinite stage of his sentence, to release him for a period of up to six months on whatever conditions it thinks fit. The satisfactory conduct of the detainee over this period gives the Committee of Assistance some reliable empirical evidence on which to advise the court to release him, and the conditions on which he should be discharged from the institution.

7. *What are the conditions under which the habitual criminal is discharged and what is the juridical status of one so discharged?*

The pattern of all European habitual criminal legislation is in this respect so uniform that a brief mention of its salient features will be sufficient for our purposes.

It is usually statutorily provided that the habitual criminal shall not be released except on condition that he be placed under the supervision of a named aftercare authority. This probationary supervision must be for a period of from one to five years in Finland, for any period up to three years in Hungary, for ten years in Sweden 1927, and for at least three years and up to ten years in Sweden 1937; but more frequently the period of supervised probation is left to be determined by the discharging authority in the circumstances of each case.

The agency which releases habitual criminals has absolute power to devise the conditions governing the offender's right to be at large, limited only by the above requirement of supervised aftercare and the duration of their authority. They can, as a condition of his discharge, require him to live in a certain district, to follow a certain trade or vocation, not to visit another district, not to enter public houses, not to associate with certain people, and in general, by the threat of depriving him of his liberty, they can endeavour to shield him from the grosser criminal temptations and inclinations. They will almost invariably require him to report regularly and frequently to an aftercare authority or to the police.

The conditions the discharging agency attach to his discharge will govern his activities until the termination of his sentence of preventive detention (in those countries where it is a determined sentence or where a maximum term is provided), or until his sentence is declared to be completed (as is possible in Belgium on the application of the habitual criminal), or for whatever period the discharging agency determines. Occasionally this period is statutorily determined; for example, a maximum of three years in Hungary and Switzerland, five years in Finland, and ten years in Sweden.

At the conclusion of the above period, if his discharge certificate has not been revoked or if he has not been recommitted to preventive detention, the habitual criminal's discharge from preventive detention ceases to be conditional and becomes absolute.

Every legislature has provided that a conviction for an offence of a certain gravity during the probationary period automatically revokes the offender's discharge certificate and that, either immediately, or after any penalty imposed for that offence, he will be recommitted to preventive detention. In such cases it is common to increase the minimum term of preventive detention that must now be served before conditional release again becomes possible. For example, in Hungary and Switzerland the minimum period of preventive detention to be served is increased from three to five years, and in Finland from three to ten years.

Revocation of the discharge certificate may also be ordered should the released habitual criminal infringe any of the conditions of his discharge. In Switzerland, however, in such circumstances formal warning by the aftercare authority, and subsequent continued failure to observe the conditions of his discharge, are conditions precedent to his reinternment. Recommittal for breach of a condition of discharge is usually decided upon and ordered by the agency responsible for the original discharge, though in Holland it can be ordered also by the chief of police in the area in which the dischargee resides, or by the senior local officer of the Ministry of Justice. There is rarely any procedural requirement for such recommittal, and it does not normally prejudice the subsequent availability of conditional discharge. However, in Finland such revocation precludes the habitual criminal from being conditionally discharged for a further period of one year, and in Yugoslavia he will be obliged to serve a total preventive detention (previous period included) of ten years, at which time he will be discharged absolutely.

One condition which could be attached to the discharge of a preventive detainee is of some interest. For people who have passed so many years in institutions, even those of a segregative and non-punitive character, some half-way-house between preventive detention and absolute freedom seems desirable. Ideally they should all be discharged to hostels which would shield them from some of the sudden temptations and tensions of liberty, and at the same time would gradually accustom them to the struggle to build a new life for themselves. There is ample means to implement this idea in the practically unlimited power to attach conditions to the original discharge of the habitual criminal.

8. *To what extent are habitual criminal laws applied ?*

A comparison of European criminal statistics raises problems of very great complexity: that of European habitual criminal statistics increases this complexity. There is no reliable and valid unit of comparison. What does it signify, for example, to affirm, as is the case, that the Swedish habitual criminal law of 1927 led to the preventive detention of approximately 150 offenders before it was replaced, in 1937, by a law which, it was hoped, would double the incidence of this punishment ? For Sweden this means something when it is correlated to the general pattern of crime in that country and to the objects of that habitual criminal legislation; but to endeavour to correlate this figure to, say, the habitual criminal statistics of Hitler's Germany, where a profoundly different pattern of crime and an entirely different approach to penology obtained, is an unrewarding occupation.

There is a general tendency to contend that habitual criminal legislation fails unless it is extensively applied. This is emphatically not the case. The preceding analysis surely demonstrates that preventive detention constitutes a delicate balance between two conflicting social claims, a balance that can be disturbed as seriously by the over-frequent as by the insufficient application of preventive detention. The equation of these opposing forces can only be judged in the light of each country's political and sociological ethos.

What really would be of great interest and importance, were it known, is the effect such habitual criminal legislation has had on the number of offences committed by certain types of recidivists who are potentially declarable, or have been declared, habitual criminals. If habitual criminal legislation led to a decrease of persistent crime it would have fulfilled its primary function of assisting in the protection of society. But this is not and, for the time being, cannot be known, for the following reason—it will be agreed that every cause of crime is a cause of recidivism and that every cause of recidivism is a cause of habitual criminality; successively some causative factors will have been added but, by definition, none will have been subtracted. We must then admit a multiplicity of factors causing (in this sense) habitual criminality. In non-static, that is, in all present societies, this multiplicity of causative factors changes, interacts, recombines and intermingles in such a fashion that the artificial isolation of one of them, necessary to any scientific analysis of it, is logically impossible. We might, therefore, segregate every individual we are prepared to declare an habitual criminal yet still find recidivist crime rapidly increasing. The macrocosm is no laboratory.[1]

We cannot, therefore, in the present state of our knowledge, quantitatively and comparatively evaluate the habitual criminal legislation of various countries, either intrinsically by the number of individuals affected, or extrinsically by its effect on persistent crime. So, when it is said that in Denmark, Finland and Sweden until 1939 preventive detention was never ordered in more than fifty cases per year[2] this fact casts no light on the habitual criminal legislation of those countries until it is considered for each country in connection with the terms, spirit and aims of that legislation.

Having thus destroyed much of the point of this question, let us turn our attention to certain habitual criminal statistics of Belgium, Finland, Germany, Italy, Norway, Poland and Yugoslavia—not for any comparative purposes but to assist us in the understanding of the legislation of each of those countries, the details of which we have already considered.

European statistics subsequent to 1939 are not informative and are not here presented; during the war years they reflected little more than the varying fortunes of war; and in the immediate post-war period, the treatment of collaborators.

BELGIUM

The law of 1930 was put into effect on January 1st, 1931. From

---

[1] It was for similar reasons that the suggested abolition of the death penalty in Britain in 1948 *as an experiment* was unreal. Desirable or not desirable, in itself an experimental abolition would not have added anything of significance to the evidence available in 1948. There are too many other factors involved. Neither an increase nor a decrease of murders would have settled the issue of the deterrent effect of capital punishment.

[2] There is one exception to this. In 1937, in Finland, fifty-one persons were sentenced to preventive detention.

that date until the end of 1935 the following number of prisoners, having served the fixed term imposed for the offence last committed, was subjected to *la mise à la disposition du Gouvernement*:

in 1931	.. ..	4
1932	.. ..	40
1933	.. ..	32
1934	.. ..	49
1935	.. ..	60

185=37 per year.

H. Bekaert[1] gives considerable information concerning the age, previous convictions, and subsequent conduct of these offenders, and we will make use of it for comparative purposes when considering similar information concerning English preventive detainees.

FINLAND

The Finnish law was promulgated on May 27th, 1932. The Penitentiary Tribunal subsequently ordered the following number of prisoners to be subjected to preventive detention :

in 1933	.. ..	2
1934	.. ..	18
1935	.. ..	32
1936	.. ..	33
1937	.. ..	51
1938	.. ..	43
1939 (6 months)		22

=32 per year

Fourteen other prisoners who, during that period, had been placed by the courts in the hands of the Penitentiary Tribunal, were not required to undergo preventive detention, but when they had concluded the fixed term imposed on them were conditionally discharged. Again, considerable information concerning these prisoners will be presented in Chapter VII.

Meanwhile, let us look at a statistical movement which A. P. Arvelo, the Director General of the Penal Administration, Helsinki, considered[2] to have been in part the effect of the Finnish habitual criminal legislation on the commission of serious crimes in Finland.[3]

Taking the index number " 100 " to represent the total number

---

[1] H. Bekaert : *L'application de la loi de Défense Sociale . . .*, Louvain, 1936.

[2] *Recueil*, Vol. XIII, Book 1, September 1947, p. 5.

[3] We must however bear in mind the criticism already advanced of such *post hoc propter hoc* arguments.

of individuals sentenced in 1932, the proportionate figures for the subsequent years are:

	Murder, Attempted Murder and Grievous Bodily Harm	Serious Assaults	Robbery and Aggravated Larceny
in 1932	100	100	100
1933	102	107	111
1934	65	86	79
1935	67	60	78
1936	57	61	60
1937	42	55	53

On a basis of these figures, Arvelo contends that :

" comme on le voit, ces chiffres forment un tableau très avantageux au point de vue de la diminution de la criminalité. En vertu de la loi de 1932, on a, en effet, pu éliminer du milieu social quantité de criminels incorrigibles qui indubitablement auraient commis des infractions graves s'ils avaient été libres, et, d'autre part, cette loi a constitué une menace sérieuse et préventive pour les sujets libres qui sont enclins à la criminalité."

Wisely, the author of the above quotation does not argue that this improving position is solely the result of habitual criminal legislation, but adduces other possible and probable causes for it. He does contend, reasonably enough, that part of this diminution in the incidence of serious crime can be attributed to the habitual criminal law of 1932.

GERMANY

From 1934 to 1938 the German habitual criminal law of November 24th, 1933, was applied to the following number of prisoners:

in 1934 ..	.. 3,935
1935 .	.. 1,318
1936 ..	.. 907
1937 ..	.. 692
1938 ..	.. 805
	7,657

A larger number was sentenced to preventive detention in 1934 and 1935 owing to the retroactive quality of the German legislation, and most of these 5,000 were prisoners who were already in prison serving fixed terms when this habitual criminal legislation was introduced.

In 1938 the Minister of Justice exhorted[1] the courts to make more frequent use of this legislation and suggested that they hesitate to release detainees unless confident that the danger they presented to society was past. Finally, in 1941, owing to dissatisfaction with the supposed clemency of the courts, the power of deciding when the detainee was to be released was taken from the judiciary and given to an official of the Ministry of Justice.[2] At the same time, and by the same instrument, the courts were empowered to inflict capital punishment on dangerous habitual criminals if the protection of the community or the requirement of a just punishment called for it.[3] To such lengths can paranoia proceed !

ITALY

The Italian courts, like those of Germany, made savage and extensive use of the comprehensive habitual criminal legislation at their disposal. In the first four years subsequent to its introduction, this legislation was applied as follows:

	1932	1933	1934	1935
Habitual criminals (arts. 102-4)	1,509	1,231	901	828
Professional criminals (art. 105)	122	65	71	54
Criminals by tendency (art. 108)	158	46	40	40
	1,789	1,342	1,012	922=5,065

Italian authorities ascribed to the Penal Code of 1930 the ensuing steady diminution in the number of offences—especially of more serious offences—committed, and they regarded the legislative provisions we have considered as of great influence.

NORWAY

From 1902 to 1929, clause 65 of the 1902 Penal Code was applied in only seven cases.

---

[1] The General Order of the Minister of Justice of March 3rd, 1938.
[2] Law of September 4th, 1941.
[3] The death penalty was not the rule. It was only to be inflicted in the gravest cases and at the discretion of the judge. One such grave case particularly named was that of *Rassenschande*—racial defilement. Such perversions of the judicial function are hard to comprehend.

The law of 1929, designed expressly to increase the number of declared habitual criminals was applied as follows:

in 1929 to 32 individuals (6 months only)
1930 „ 84 „
1931 „ 35 „
1932 „ 30 „
1933 „ 8 „
1934 „ 9 „

The opinion in Norway is that the sudden decline in the extent of its application in 1932 and 1933, and again in 1934 and 1935 and thereafter, was a direct result of judicial and popular realization of the fact that no special institutions were to be provided for preventive detainees, and that they were simply relegated to the ordinary prisons.

POLAND

In Poland, between January 15th, 1934, and March 1st, 1939, preventive detention was ordered in 1,706 cases. Each year it was applied to an increasing number, and there was general satisfaction with the operation of this legislation.

This figure is given as from 1934, because though the habitual criminal legislation was incorporated in the Penal Code of July 11th, 1932, the special institutions for " incorrigibles " were not functioning until January 1934.

YUGOSLAVIA

In Yugoslavia, pursuant to legislation put in force on January 13th, 1930, preventive detention was ordered for the following number of prisoners:

in 1930 32
1931 25
1932 35
1933 6
1934 12
1935 4
1936 13
1937 7
                    ─────
                     134

* * * * *

The above statistics are of relevance only when they are considered in relation to the legislation of each particular country, and alone give no indication of the "success" or "failure" of habitual criminal legislative measures. What is significant for that question is that, though very many countries have adopted habitual criminal legislation, and though some have changed and remodelled it in the light of experience, no country has ever completely abandoned the attempt to legislate specifically for this type of criminal. Now, and for many years to come, habitual criminal legislation is an essential and important element of a modern legal system.

GENERAL SOURCES

Röling, B. V. A. : *De Wetgeving Tegen de Zoogensamde Beroeps-en Gewoontemisdadigers* 1931. Nijhoff, The Hague.

Timasheff, N. S. : " The Treatment of Persistent Offenders outside of the United States "—*Journal of Criminal Law and Criminology (J.C.L. & C.)*, Vol. XXX, No. 4.

Grünhut, M. : *Penal Reform*, pp. 389-403. Oxford, 1948.

Radzinowicz, L. : " The Persistent Offender "—in *The Modern Approach to Criminal Law*. Cambridge, 1945.

Donnedieu de Vabres : *Traité de Droit Criminel et de Législation Pénale Comparée*— 3rd Edition—Recueil Sirey. Paris, 1947.

E. Ferri : " Les mesures de sécurité et les peines " : *R. I. de D. P.*, 1925, No. 2.

Q. Saldana : " Peines et mesures de sécurité " : *R. I. de D. P.*, 1927, No. 4.

SOURCES REGARDING PARTICULAR COUNTRIES

Belgium

O. Picard : *Délinquants anormaux et récidivistes*. Bruxelles, 1931.

H. Bekaert : *L'application de la loi de défense sociale du 9 avril 1930 aux récidivistes et délinquants d'habitude."* Louvain, 1936.

H. Bekaert : *Rapport sur le problème des délinquants d'habitude et de leur traitement, présenté en 1939. Recueil de documents en matière pénale et pénitentiaire* (hereinafter cited as *Recueil*), Vol. XIII, Book 1, September 1947.

C. Didion and M. Poll : " Arrêtés et circulaires concernant l'application de la loi du 9 avril 1930, de défense sociale à l'égard des anormaux et des délinquants d'habitude." *Recueil*, Vol. II, p. 144.

Denmark

A. Goll : " Rapport concernant les décrets promulgués en 1932 et 1933 à l'occasion de la mise en vigueur de nouveau Code pénal danois, le 1 er janvier 1933." *Recueil*, Vol. II, 1932-33, p. 391.

Brun, Nørvig, Smith and Stürup : *Danish Psychiatry*, 1948. Published by Det Schønbergske Forlag, Copenhagen, 1948.

FINLAND

A. P. Arvelo : " La loi du 27 mai 1932 sur les récidivistes dangereux." *Recueil*, Vol. II, 1932-33, p. 289.

A. P. Arvelo : " Rapport sur le problème des délinquants d'habitude et de leur traitement, présenté en 1939." *Recueil*, Vol. XIII, Book 1, p. 5. September 1947.

FRANCE

Many articles in the *Recueil* and in the *Revue de Droit Pénal et de Criminologie* were consulted. However, the following three text-books give considerable information concerning " relégation ", and also provide an extensive bibliography : Jean Pinatel : *Précis de Science Pénitentiare*. Recueil Sirey, 1945.

Fréjaville : *Manuel de Droit Criminal*. Librairie Générale de Droit et de Jurisprudence. Paris, 1946.

Donnedieu de Vabres : *Traité de Droit Criminal et de Législation Pénale Comparée*. Recueil Sirey, Paris, 1947.

Note particularly :

Revue de Science Criminelle, 1938, Vol. III, p. 318, Les règlements pénitentiaires "— A. Mosee.

Revue de Science Criminelle, 1939, Vol. IV, p. 119 : " Chronique Législative "— A Jouffret.

Essay by Magnol in *Etudes de science criminelle et de droit pénal comparé*, edited by Huguency et Donnedieu Vabres.

GERMANY

H. Mannheim : " The German Prevention of Crime Act—*J.C.L. & C.*, 26, p. 517.

M. Grünhut : *The Development of the German Penal System 1920-1932*. Cambridge Pamphlet Series.

Stolzenburg : " Rapport sur le problème des délinquants d'habitude et de leur traitement, présenté en 1939." *Recueil*, Vol. XIII, Book 1, p. 91. September 1947.

J. Schafheutle : " La loi du 24 novembre 1932 relative aux délinquants d'habitude dangeruex et aux mesures de sécurité et d'amendement." *Recueil*, Vol. III, p. 237.

Rietzsch and Löscher : " L'ordonnance générale du Ministre de la Justice du Reich, du 3 mars 1938, concernant les causes pénales contre les délinquants d'habitude dangereux." *Recueil*, Vol. VIII, p. 200.

Schmidt-Leichner : " La loi du 4 septembre 1941 portant modification du Code pénal du Reich." *Recueil*, Vol. X, p. 125.

Revue de Science Criminelle, 1937, Vol. II, p. 589—" Les mesures de sûreté en Allemagne," 1939, Vol. IV, p. 714—R. Beraud : " L'internement de sûreté en Allemagne."

HOLLAND

N. Muller (translated by S. Van der Aa) : " Loi du 25 juin 1929 contenant des dispositions relatives aux délinquants professionels et aux délinquants d'habitude." *Recueil*, Vol. I, 1931, p. 238.

HUNGARY

G. Racz : " Le développement de la législation pénale hongroise d'après-guerre."
Recueil, Vol. III, 1933-34, p. 315.

Report of D. Horvatth to the International Penal and Penitentiary Congress at
Berlin in 1935.

E. Hacker : " Rapport sur le problème des délinquants d'habitude et de leur
traitement, présenté en 1939." *Recueil*, Vol. XIII, Book 1, p. 40, September
1947.

ITALY

Penal Code of the Kingdom of Italy, 1930 (English translation). U.K. Stationery
Office.

A. Leone : " Rapport sur le problème des délinquants d'habitude et de leur
traitement, présenté en 1939." *Recueil*, Vol. XIII, Book 1, p. 62, September
1947.

J. Stone : " Theories of Law and Justice in Fascist Italy." *Modern Law Review*
(1937), p. 177.

POLAND

Lemkin and McDermott : *The Polish Penal Code of 1932.* Duke University Press,
North Carolina, 1939.

G. Sliwowski : " L'Ordonnance du Ministre de la Justice, du 15 janvier 1934,
relative à l'organisation des établissements pour criminels incorrigibles."
Recueil, Vol. V, p. 16.

T. Krychowski : " Rapport sur le problème des délinquants d'habitude et de
leur traitement, présenté en 1939." *Recueil*, Vol. XIII, Book 1, p. 54.
September 1947.

SWEDEN

K. Schlyter : " Rapport sur la loi du 18 Juin 1937 sur l'internement dans les
établissements de sûreté." *Recueil*, Vol. VII, p. 84.

SWITZERLAND

H. Pfander : *The Leading Principles of the Swiss Criminal Code.*" Cambridge Pamphlet
Series.

Friedlander and Goldberg : Translation of the Swiss Criminal Code—*J.C.L. & C.*,
Vol. XXX, No. 1, Supplement, 1939.

E. Delaquis : " Les peines, mesures de sûreté et autres mesures dans le Code
pénal suisse de 1937." *Recueil*, Vol. IX, p. 334.

E. Delaquis : " L'Exécution des peines et des mesures de sûreté en Suisse."
Recueil, Vol. XI, p. 43.

O. Wettstein : " Le traitement des délinquants incorrigibles en Suisse." *Recueil*,
Vol. XI, p. 123.

A. Kielholz : " Le dépistage et le traitement des délinquants anormaux et
récidivistes en Suisse." *Recueil*, Vol. XI, p. 254.

O. Wettstein : " Rapport sur la problème des délinquants d'habitude et de leur traitement, présenté en 1939." *Recueil,* Vol. XIII, Book 1, p. 111. September 1947.

YUGOSLAVIA

D. M. Soubotitch : " La nouvelle législation et pénitentiaire en Yugoslavie." *Recueil,* Vol. I, p. 103.

D. M. Soubotitch : " Les ordonnances pénales et pénitentiaires Yugoslaves complétant la nouvelle législation pénale et pénitentiaire." *Recueil,* Vol. II, p. 346.

A. V. Makletozov : " Rapport sur le problème des délinquants d'habitude et de leur traitement, présenté en 1939." *Recueil,* Vol. XIII, Book 1, p. 83. September 1947.

Since this analysis of European habitual criminal legislation was made, further information on penal practice in several of the above countries has been published in Vol. XIV, Books 3-4, of the *Recueil de Documents en Matière Pénale et Pénitentiaire,* November 1949.

CHAPTER FOUR

EXCURSUS IN COMPARATIVE LAW

IN the comparative law study and in the discussion of the English statute virtually every important problem connected with habitual criminal legislation was raised. Depending on the time and purpose of discussion, every one of these problems could be relevant; and it is hoped that we have analysed sufficient aspects of habitual criminal law for this study to be of general use in such discussions. However, it would be burdensome and of doubtful value to endeavour, by proceeding from analysis to synthesis, to project all such issues from the factual to the theoretically discursive plane, and we will concentrate on the following three points which are of immediate interest and importance:

1. A suggested aid to deciding when conditionally to discharge preventive detainees.

2. *Nulla poena sine lege* and differentiation of treatment of preventive detainees.

3. The XIIth International Penal and Penitentiary Congress.

1. *A suggested aid to deciding when conditionally to discharge preventive detainees*

" Society should utilise every scientific instrumentality for self-protection against destructive elements in its midst, with as little interference with the free life of its members as is consistent with such social self-protection."[1]

It is hard to devise a more succinct and complete definition of the socio-ethical principle lying behind the just punishment of habitual, as well as other criminals.

We have seen that many countries—some applying such a conception of punishment—segregate habitual criminals for protracted periods. Pursuing the idea in the above quotation it might be argued that the reconviction statistics of these discharged habitual criminals illustrate such a degree of continuing danger that to release them while they still have strength to endanger the community, or any members of it, is sentimental and misguided. But

---

[1] Sheldon Glueck, " Principles of a Rational Penal Code ", *Harvard Law Review*, Vol. XLI, 1927-8, p. 453.

we have stressed that the community must bear some risk, and this type of argument was faced in the Introduction[1] where for diverse reasons we rejected the completely logical application of measures of social protection against criminals. Happily, we need not now labour this point for, as a matter of practice, all those countries which provide for the segregation of habitual criminals also provide for their eventual release. And there is good reason for this. Sheldon and Eleanor Glueck in their valuable follow-up studies[2] established beyond all doubt the vital significance to reformation of the process of " ageing " (measured as biological development or maturation)—a process virtually independent of reformative techniques and therefore occurring amongst preventive detainees also.

Thus, there comes a time when preventive detainees should be released, and this is so even where the indefinite sentence with the fixed maximum term governs the duration of detention.[3] The task is to select the appropriate moment for release; to capture possibly the one occasion in the habitual criminal's period of detention when there is a chance of his leading a life the community will tolerate. This is always an " administrative " and not a " judicial " task, whoever does it; and it involves the reconciliation of the two conflicting claims of individual liberty and social security.[4]

As a positive guide to this moment, the success of the prisoner in conforming to the requirements of prison discipline is useless. As Commander Foster wrote:[5]

> " But it is very difficult to make up your mind when to let your man out. There are so many things that you ought not to take into consideration and so many intangible things that you should consider. For instance, you should not really consider whether a man has been a good or a bad prisoner ; that does not matter much."

[1] See p. 20 et seq.

[2] Five Hundred Criminal Careers ; One Thousand Juvenile Delinquents ; Five Hundred Delinquent Women ; Later Criminal Careers ; Juvenile Delinquents Grown Up ; Criminal Careers in Retrospect.

[3] Though clearly some detainees will be released at the expiration of their term though manifestly not yet fit for freedom.

[4] It is interesting to note in this context two propositions advanced in the Seventy-second Annual Report of the Prison Association of New York in 1916 (p. 72) :
" 1. That the prisoner ordinarily arrives at a period in his imprisonment when further incarceration will be of less service to him and to the State as a reformative measure than a like period passed in liberty under parole supervision.
  2. That in the determination of the proper time at which to admit the prisoner to parole an exhaustive and painstaking study will be made of the individual case, in order that both the right of society to be protected, and the right of the prisoner to rehabilitate himself, may be preserved."

[5] The Howard Journal, 1940, Vol. V, No. 4, p. 237.

The Persistent Offenders Committee went even further, contending that:[1]

> " By observing a man in the limited and artificial conditions of prison life, it is seldom possible to judge whether he is or is not likely to lead an honest life on release."

It is respectfully submitted that these statements go rather too far, and that were we prepared to apply even the psychological understanding we now have at our disposal a great deal more could be learnt about the prisoner while he is in custody. Nevertheless, the basic point is undeniable—obedience to prison discipline is, in itself, no indication of the likelihood of reform. It all too frequently proves only that the prisoner is well-adapted to the prison régime, and is completely institutionalized; it certainly does not indicate that he can adapt himself to life in an open society where responsibility for his own life will be forced on him.[2]

We found that in England an attempt to suit the period of detention to the qualities of each detainee failed, and was superseded by a rigid system from which variation was made only for the exceptional case; and we traced this failure largely to the lack of information available to the advisory committees. Many suggestions have been made by which this information might be rendered more adequate—more details of the prisoner's background, observation of the prisoner by some psychologically trained members of the prison staff, and so on ; and the Scandinavian countries have shown how much could be done along these lines. At present, however, I shall not discuss such means of increasing the releasing authority's understanding of the prisoner, but shall concentrate on one possible piece of empiric evidence which has been largely neglected in all countries. The germs of my suggestion will be found scattered throughout the comparative law study, but they have never been collected, modified, shaped and advanced as a developed plan.

Conditional discharge of preventive detainees is the rule, and it is a rule that I do not seek to challenge. However, when a detainee is handed his licence and placed under the supervision of an aftercare organisation there is a quality of finality about the procedure that marks another stage in his life, and indicates that the releasing authority has decided that there is some possibility of his not

---

[1] *Report of the Departmental Committee on Persistent Offenders*, 1932, Cmd. 4090, p. 58.
[2] Equally, the converse is false—a prisoner suddenly reacting against prison discipline might well be at the correct psychological stage for successful discharge.

subsequently relapsing into crime. They have come to this conclusion from their knowledge of his life before his committal to preventive detention and of his conduct during that sentence. The licence can be revoked if the discharged detainee fails to conform to its terms, and will be revoked if he commits a serious crime.

It is submitted that this procedure places too great a strain on the prisoner, who finds himself after years of institutional existence suddenly subjected to all the strains, stresses and temptations of freedom. It also entails too great a risk to society; for the reformation of the prisoner previously regarded as a dangerous habitual criminal has in no wise been tested.

What alternatives are there ? First, there is the provision of a half-way house between detention and freedom—a half-way house possibly in the form of hostels where selected discharged prisoners (and this suggestion applies equally to all long-term prisoners as well as to habitual criminals) would be compelled to reside, subject to a curfew, leaving daily to pursue the employment which had been found for them. Here they would live, paying for their board, until it was considered that they were fit to be freed from all direct supervision. There is a great deal to be said in favour of this plan, and one or two criticisms that could be made ; however, it is a second plan with which we are now concerned.

Were it possible for the prison authorities to allow the detainee to spend a brief period away from the prison, living and working with an approved employer prepared both to receive him and to keep in touch with the prison, it is suggested that some valid empirical evidence would be available on which to estimate the likelihood of the detainee's adaptation to society. Let me sketch this plan in more detail in relation to, say, Parkhurst Prison as a preventive detention centre, and then try to defend it as a useful and practically operable conception.

The first requisite is that the Advisory Committee (to adhere to Prevention of Crime Act, 1908, terminology) and the Governor of the prison should be on friendly terms with several farmers and other employers on the Isle of Wight who would be prepared to co-operate in the task of assisting detainees to a new life. This requirement is probably already fulfilled. Then, when the Advisory Committee and the Governor agree that the time is ripe to test a detainee (the availability of employment being one vital factor in this decision), one such employer would be approached and asked to employ this detainee on the following terms: to pay the prisoner his worth as a workman; to treat him as far as possible as an ordinary employee; to notify the prison immediately if the prisoner does not report at the correct time on any morning; and should the employer have the slightest trouble with the prisoner, or even the slightest suspicion of him, to telephone the prison, when the experiment would be abandoned immediately. The prisoner would live in a hostel or in any other accommodation he could find (or which was found for him), or alternatively he could live at the prison, paying for his accommodation in either case.

Such a prisoner, on leave from the prison, would remain in law in the custody of the Governor of the prison, and no formality whatsoever would be necessary to reintern him. The employer would keep in close touch with the prison. The prisoner would know that unless he succeeded over the period of leave given him—say, a month—there would be no chance whatsoever of his conditional discharge on licence for some time to come.

It may firstly be objected—such prisoners will immediately endeavour to escape. Presuming that this does occur frequently, what has been lost ? At all events the Advisory Committee and the Governor had concluded that the detainee might possibly be conditionally discharged, and all that has happened is that the prisoner has immediately declared his present incompetence to live in society. It will be easier to capture an escaping prisoner, especially one trying to escape from the Isle of Wight, than to arrest a conditionally discharged prisoner; and in the former case there are likely to be fewer crimes committed by the prisoner before his arrest, his reversion to crime being much sooner known to the authorities. But few would attempt to escape, seeing the opportunity of legitimate freedom within their grasp if only they can conform to society's demands for a few weeks.

This leads us to another possible objection—such prisoners will conform for the month, though not intending to abandon crime; they will behave well temporarily solely as a means to freedom. Giving due weight to this contention—which places too much emphasis on the cognitive factor in criminality—the same reply can be made as was made above. Also, if prisoners are so inflexibly and consciously wedded to criminality there is little we can do to prevent them, except to retain them permanently in segregative detention; and we have already decided that we cannot do this.

One fundamental objection might be raised—you will not find employers, even farmers, prepared to employ such prisoners when they are not under the direct supervision of prison officers.[1] Further, the employers you seek must have sufficient tact and understanding to co-operate with the prisoner, and with the Advisory Committee and the Governor. This objection cannot be met here ; it can only be disproved in practice. It is my firm belief that with the correct robust approach many such employers are to be found on the Isle of Wight, as elsewhere.

Now to the advantages. First, from the point of view of society. There is demonstrably less risk of the recurrence of crime. On conditional discharge or on my suggested month's leave from the prison there is an equal opportunity for crime—except that being under closer supervision there is probably less during the month's leave. It will be admitted that the recapture of a prisoner committing a crime on the Isle of Wight, and who is seen *daily* by someone in touch with the prison (otherwise the prisoner is trying to escape and will immediately be sought on that basis) is an easier matter than when the same prisoner is under less close supervision in a part of the country of his own choosing. Thus, month for month, there is, if anything, less danger to the community during the month's leave. Then, when the prisoner is conditionally discharged after serving his leave successfully, it will be known that he *can* live, at least for a month, without breaking the law, and there is therefore less danger to society. Inevitably, many will fail to maintain their record of the month ; but the chance of failure is less than in those who have not successfully met this month's test. Further, the individuals most likely to suffer by the loss of their property have elected to bear that risk in one case, and not in the other.

Secondly, from the point of view of the preventive detainee himself. There is here no doubt of the wisdom of the month's leave. A prisoner who satisfactorily concludes this period is strengthened in the knowledge of his ability to conform to society's demands should he so desire. A prisoner who cannot satisfy his employer for a month, or who steals or misbehaves flagrantly during this month, can feel no bitterness towards the Advisory Committee or the Governor who will not immediately recommend his conditional discharge. He will seek another chance, and this

---

[1] For, at present, farmers on the Isle of Wight are delighted to have selected prisoners working on their land. These prisoners are, of course, under supervision ; but such supervision is only a token force and could never prevent the prisoners' immediate escape, and indeed could hardly hinder them doing anything else they desired.

chance must be made available to him, after a due interval, with another employer.[1]

The vital point of this idea is—if a prisoner is not capable of satisfying a reasonable employer for one month, and of leading a normal life for the period, he is not ready for conditional discharge. If he cannot conform to society's demands for a month, how can he be expected to conform for a longer period ?[2]

* * * * *

Some months after advancing the above suggestion I visited several penal institutions in Sweden. Here I found, in those two prisons established under their new penal legislation—Hall and Häga (and was informed that the same applies elsewhere)—that many prisoners, especially those serving indeterminate sentences, are housed in a separate wing of the institution before it is intended to discharge them. They have the keys to their own cells, wear ordinary clothes, work somewhere in the neighbourhood for normal civilian wages, and use the prison as a hostel, paying for their enforced board and lodgings. The Governors of these institutions, and several others prominent in Swedish penology, expressed themselves as well satisfied with this experiment.

2. Nulla poena sine lege *and differentation of treatment of preventive detainees*

Nulla poena sine lege has come to be regarded as one of the fundamental and traditional principles of criminal law. Its antiquity has been variously estimated[3] and frequently exaggerated ; but the generality of its appeal to what are sometimes called " Western Values " is undoubted.

---

[1] Sometimes it will not be entirely the prisoner's fault that the employer requests his withdrawal. The prisoner's story must be considered in every case : the Governor will know its veracity. If there is some justification for the prisoner's actions he must soon be tested with another employer.

[2] This plan, like many others, depends for its success on the personality of the men operating it. It will need the guidance of a Governor with tact and understanding, and who is prepared to suit his methods to the individual detainee and the individual employer. Such a Governor—and I have met several such—will have no difficulty in gathering round him a body of co-operating and interested employers.

[3] See, for example : H. Mannheim, *Criminal Justice and Social Reconstruction*, pp. 207-8 ; Jerome Hall, *Principles of Criminal Law*, pp. 20-7 ; also H. Donnedieu de Vabres, *Traité de Droit Criminal et de Législation Pénale Comparée*, 3rd Edition, 1947, where on p. 899 its history is summarised as follows :

"Cette règle, étrangère au droit romain classique, affirmée par des jurisconsultes du moyen âge, qui cherchent à l'appuyer sur les sources du droit de Justinien, s'est effacée sous notre Ancien Régime, où les peines sont arbitraires. Elle est proclamée sous la Révolution, inscrite dans la Déclaration des droits de l'homme, puis dans la Constitution du 24 juin, 1793. Aujourd'hui, elle reçoit l'approbation de la quasi-unanimité des Ecoles."

Perhaps the earliest official statement of the principle of " nulla poena " in its modern form occured in August 1789, in the French Revolutionary Declaration of the Rights of Man, article eight of which read :

> " Nul ne peut être puni qu'en vertu d'une loi établie et promulguée antérieurement au délit et légalement appliquée."

This principle was reaffirmed in the French Constitution of 1791, and has remained a vital part of all subsequent French penal codes. Indeed, article 4 of the present Code Pénal provides that:

> " Nulle contravention, nul délit, nul crime, ne peuvent être punis de peines qui n'étatient pas prononcées par la loi avant qu'ils fussent commis."

This type of formulation of " nulla poena " is largely the result of the work of Feuerbach, who incorporated a similar phraseology into the Bavarian Code of 1813. In 1801, in his *Lehrbuch des peinlichen Rechts* (Par. 24), he had given the principle its modern and generally accepted shape, as follows:

> " Nulla poena sine lege, nulla poena sine crimine, nullum crimen sine poena legali."

This trinity of the principle of legality has come to be regarded as basic to a just system of criminal law; and, as habitual criminal legislation so frequently offends two of the concepts of this trinity, it is necessary that we examine the relationship between the principle and the legislation.

The two facets of " nulla poena " frequently controverted by habitual criminal legislation are (a) the objection to retroactive legislation, and (b) the insistence that the punishment be defined by law.

(a) Non-Retroactivity

An insistence that what was legal when done shall not later be held to have been illegal and subject to penal sanction antedates the conception of " nulla poena " by many centuries, and is deeply ingrained in our ideas of justice.[1]

---

[1] It has frequently received judicial support. See, for example: *Phillips* v. *Eyre* (1870), L.R., 6 Q.B. at p. 23 ; *R.* v. *Griffiths* (1891), 2 Q.B. at p. 148 ; and the Australian cases of *R.* v. *Kidman* (1915), 20 C.L.R. at pp. 432, 434-5 and 443, and *Millner* v. *Reith* (1942), 66 C.L.R. at p. 9. In 1916 the case of *Midland Railway* v. *Pye*, 10 C.B. (N.S.) at p. 191, Erle, C.J., summarised the emotional attraction of this principle, saying : " It manifestly shocks one's sense of justice that an act legal at the time of doing it should be made unlawful by some new enactment. Modern legislation has almost entirely removed that blemish from the law."

As we have seen, it is customary for habitual criminal legislation to be applied to criminals who, having suffered a certain number of punishments, or committed a certain number of offences, whether before or after the promulgation of the habitual criminal legislation, later commit a crime of a stated gravity. It is sufficient that the last crime committed (whose punishment is involved in the preventive detention or pronounced at the same time as it) should be posterior to the promulgation of the legislation; and that the earlier offences which qualified the criminal for preventive detention were committed before such promulgation is not relevant. A strict application of the principle of non-retroactivity would not allow of this practice.

(b) The insistence that punishment be legally defined

The conception " nulla poena " carries with it an insistence that the punishment to be imposed on the criminal shall be adequately defined by law. It therefore excludes any wide administrative discretion, or at least insists that such discretion shall be at all times clearly defined and delimited by the law.

In the comparative law study we encountered many instances of habitual criminal legislation not conforming to this requirement. Frequently, the special punishment for habitual criminals having been imposed by the court, the administrative discretion became virtually boundless. We noticed, too, that this was the case in many countries whose preventive detention régime was well adapted to its purpose—for example, Denmark and Finland.

Habitual criminal legislation is not the only type of legislation which tends to ignore the desiderata of " nulla poena ". Legislation against juvenile offenders and many statutes providing punishments for vagrancy offences likewise deviate from any rigid adherence to them. Nevertheless, it is submitted that where departures from this principle are made, some justification for this step must be advanced —for juveniles and vagrants this justification is invariably sought in the manifest advantages accruing to the offenders themselves; for habitual criminals it is sought in the advantages accruing to the community.

The argument defending the wisdom of a legislature enacting an habitual criminal statute which does not conform to the principle of " nulla poena " is that, in so doing, they are seeking to give wider scope to administrative action and less to judicial decision only in so far as this is necessary for the more effective and humane application of the community's resources to the problem of habitual criminality. The contrary argument is that in abandoning any of the cherished principles of the criminal law we must be sure that we are not undermining our traditionally high regard for the value of the individual and his rights; and that " no person is (to be) regarded as good enough or wise enough to dominate any normal human being or to dispose of his person or property arbitrarily."[1]

The line of cleavage is sometimes more clear cut than I have suggested, and occasionally the different approaches to criminology involved are defended with the fervour of religious conviction. Nevertheless, for our purposes, the schism is sufficiently apparent for one section of the problem to be detached for separate consideration.

If preventive detention is to be long-term imprisonment under another name, then, for the time being, the contention that habitual criminal legislation should conform to the principle of " nulla poena " is of great force. As many criminologists have denied the possibility of practically differentiating between preventive detention and long-term imprisonment it is important that we should examine this question.

At the XIth International Penal and Penitentiary Congress, held in Berlin in August 1935, one of the specific questions submitted for discussion was germane to our subject and read:

" How must the execution of penalties restrictive of liberty differ from the execution of measures of security involving deprivation of liberty ? "[2]

The commentary which accompanied this question when it was circulated before the congress excepted from consideration educational measures applied to adolescents, and medical therapeutic

---

[1] Jerome Hall, *Principles of Criminal Law*, p. 59. Professor Hall concludes his defence of the present sanctity of "nulla poena " by contending that (p. 60) : " In the light of the above discussion it is necessary to conclude that there should be a strong presumption in favour of the principle of legality within the sphere of criminal law. The burden of proof should be on those who claim superior knowledge and ability to attain better results by extra-legal methods." One can agree with this contention in so far as it deals with the *onus* of proof and yet be doubtful of the *burden* of proof he seeks to impose on those who desire to increase the role of what he calls extra-legal methods. To require proof beyond reasonable doubt and yet to deny the opportunity for the gradual development of progressive administrative penological techniques is sophistry, and is not the point of Professor Hall's argument in which only a " strong presumption " in favour of the rigid adherence to " nulla poena " is suggested. It is submitted that this onus of proof has frequently been accepted and a reasonable burden of proof satisfied—twenty years ago Professor Sheldon Glueck did so in theory in his " Principles of a Rational Penal Code ", *Harvard Law Review*, Vol. XLI, p. 453 ; many countries, especially in their punishment of juvenile offenders, have done so in practice. On this whole problem see H. Mannheim, *Criminal Justice and Social Reconstruction*, pp. 207-18.

[2] For the full discussion of this question see the *Proceedings of the Eleventh International Penal and Penitentiary Congress, 1935*, published by the Bureau of the I.P.P.C. at Berne, Switzerland, in 1937.

measures. Thus corrective education as in Borstal institutions, and
the confinement of the insane, of mental defectives, of alcoholics,
and of drug addicts all being excluded, the point at issue was
confined to the special treatment of habitual criminals.

Fifteen written reports treating this question were presented to the
secretariat of the congress, and handed to Count Gleispach (Germany)
on whom as "rapporteur général" fell the task of summarising and
synthetising them. Count Gleispach's task was complicated by the
diverse approaches to this question in the fifteen reports. He dealt with
those reports which advocated many differences between the penal
conditions in the two types of sentence, and contended that " it is
impossible to say how far the above-mentioned proposals would provide
us with a *fundamental* and *real* distinction between the application of
measures of security and the execution of penalties." He then adverted
to the views of those who could see no feasible administrative differentiation between such sentences, and concluded by proposing the
following resolutions and recommending their adoption:

" 1. The decisive difference between punishment and measures of security,
especially between punishments depriving the individual of liberty and
measures of security implying the loss of liberty, does not lie in the difference of application but in the diversity of the conceptions upon which
they are based.
2. The difference of principle will be manifested and marked by the differences of application, in so far as this may be possible without compromising the aim of the measures of security.
3. It is, therefore, advisable to apply the measures of security in special
establishments, separated from the prisons and penal establishments.
4. The treatment of persons so interned ought to be clearly distinct from that
of individuals condemned to severe sentences of imprisonment.
5. Otherwise differences might be made as regards the type of dress, the
amount of remuneration, the extent and choice of subjects of instruction,
and other similar matters."

Eight members had asked to speak on these resolutions, but
owing to interruptions caused by dissension on an earlier resolution
on a different subject, only four managed to be heard. In the end,
resolutions two, three, four and five were accepted unchanged, an
amendment being adopted to resolution one, which then read:

" 1. The decisive difference between punishment and measures of security,
especially between punishments depriving the individual of liberty and
measures of security implying the loss of liberty, consists in the diversity of
the conceptions upon which they are based."

Though the resolutions were far from completely according with it, the official commentary to the congress stated that:

> " On close study it is found difficult to make a definite and clear theoretical distinction. But it is still more difficult to establish in practice, that is to say, during the period of execution the proper characteristics for differentiating between the two forms of detention."

Thus, the impossibility of clearly differentiating between the conditions in preventive detention and those in other long-term imprisonment has considerable international support. It is also supported in two recent English criminological works. First, Dr. Radzinowicz contends[1] that because habitual criminal legislation " presupposes a basic difference between imprisonment and preventive detention, an institution for preventive detention ought to be so organised as to actually differ from the prison in which the delinquent has served his punishment. . . . However, because of the great affinity which exists between these two kinds of penal detention, all attempts to give effect to this assumption have so far failed." Secondly, Dr. Grünhut writes:[2]

> " in practice no essential difference can be maintained between the treatment of convicts and (preventive) detainees,"

and later:[3]

> " These suggestions rule out any substantial difference in the practical administration of legal punishments and measures of public security as long as both imply a long-term deprivation of liberty."

Let us be clear as to the scope of this argument. The motives for the infliction of the two punishments are admitted to be different;[4] and it is agreed that the types of men who will be subjected to them are distinct. What is contended is that because of the necessity for

---

[1] " The Persistent Offender," at p. 165 of *The Modern Approach to Criminal Law.*
[2] *Penal Reform*, p. 393.   [3] *Ibid.*, p. 397.
[4] These differences are concisely stated by Professor Donnedieu de Vabres on p. 400 of his *Traité de Droit Criminel et de Législation Pénale Comparée* as follows :

  " 1. La peine, étant la conséquence d'une violation de la loi morale, d'un mauvais usage de la liberté, a le caractère d'un châtiment. Elle fait souffrir. Elle inflige un mal au délinquant. La mesure de sûreté n'a pas de but afflictif.
  2. La peine, quant à ses modalités, quant à sa rigueur, est proportionée, essentiellement, à la gravité objective du délit. Elle regarde le passé. A l'égard des mesures de sûreté, l'infraction n'est considérée que comme un symptôme de l'état dangereux qui est le seul fondement, et qui règlera les modalités, de la réaction sociale. Elle est orientée vers l'avenir.
  3. A l'application de la peine une idée de flétrissure, ou, tout au moins de blâme, est attachée. Cette idée est étrangère à la mesure de sûreté qui tend uniquement à la protection sociale, réalisée, soit par le réforme, soit par l'élimination, définitive ou temporaire, par la ségrégation du délinquant."

the safe custody of the preventive detainees—and also, as is occasionally added, because of the desirability of a gradually improving régime for each detainee so as to " counteract the enervating effects of long confinement and to facilitate the maintenance of discipline "[1] —no " fundamental ", " real ", " actual ", " essential ", or " decisive " difference between the conditions in preventive detention and in imprisonment can be created.[2]

Considering the authority of those who advance the above argument, it is with considerable trepidation that I shall try to cast doubt on it. A criticism could be advanced on semantic lines—the difference between a " difference " and a " fundamental-real-actual-essential-decisive difference " being an elusive abstraction; but to make such a criticism would be to avoid the point. Can we adapt preventive detention to fulfil the aim with which it is imposed —segregation and not punishment—or must it inevitably be only a slightly ameliorated form of imprisonment ? That is the issue.

It is admitted that many advantages are given to preventive detainees which are not allowed to other prisoners—more remuneration, better food, better clothes, better accommodation, more association with one another, and all the other privileges which we considered on pages 70 to 77 and elsewhere in this work ; but it is suggested that these are only " minor " advantages. If by " minor " is meant that they are not sufficient to outweigh the fundamental fact of loss of liberty for a protracted period, one can but agree.[3] Similarly, it is undeniable that such ameliorations of

---

[1] Grünhut, *Penal Reform*, p. 397.

[2] Having analysed the German Prevention of Crime Act, 1933, Dr. Mannheim took a more hesitant view of the possibility of such differentiation, writing : " A decisive difference between the treatment of prisoners and that of preventive detention inmates, however, is very difficult in practice, since it may result either in too much severity for the first group or in an undesirable leniency for the second " (*Journal of Criminal Law and Criminology*, Vol. 26, p. 537). Later, in 1939, having considered the English Prevention of Crime Act, 1908, the same author wrote : " Though it may not have been easy, the English Prison Commissioners—as every visitor to Portsmouth Prison knows—have certainly succeeded in making their only preventive detention establishment more comfortable than a prison " (*The Dilemma of Penal Reform*, p. 72).

[3] " Take any bird, and put it in a cage,
And do all thine intent and thy courage
To foster it tenderly with meat and drink,
Of all dainties that thou canst bethink,
And keep it also cleanly as thou may ;
Although his cage of gold be never so gay,
Yet hath this bird, by twenty thousand-fold,
Leifer in a forest, that is rude and cold,
Go eatë worms and suchë wretchedness."
GEOFFREY CHAUCER (1340?-1400).

penal conditions regarded from the point of view of those with no
practical experience of prison life are but unimportant trifles;
whereas to the prisoner, and especially to the habitual criminal with
much experience of prison and prisons, they are the very breath of
life. That, then, is my first point—" minor " alleviations of the
normal prison routine are of vital significance to the prisoner
himself.

It is also sometimes argued that the preventive detention régime
is even less pleasant than that under which certain prisoners, for
whom there is much hope of reform, are held in minimum-security
institutions, living an untrammelled life in prison camps. This, too,
must be admitted; but it can be pointed out that in establishing
such camps the community is concentrating almost exclusively on
the reform of the prisoner and is hardly considering any deterrence
supposedly involved in the conditions of imprisonment, and therefore
any gratuitous suffering is weeded out from this type of punishment
for another reason. It is, therefore, natural that the régime in, for
example, the camp at Aldington, which operates as an adjunct to
Maidstone Prison, should allow a more natural and (to the average
man) more pleasant existence than any preventive detention régime
yet imposed, which for the time being insists on maximum-security
conditions as one facet of its primary aim of segregation. Neither
segregation nor reformation, *per se*, requires the infliction of any
suffering that can be avoided; but the avoidance is easier in the
latter than in the former. It must be remembered that the advantages in the penal régime springing from the likelihood of reformation
cannot reach preventive detainees who, by definition, are the
failures of the community's reformative techniques.[1] To the
preventive detainee, the contrast with his present detention is not
life in an open camp but existence in a convict prison.[2]

Another truth advanced as an argument against the possibility
of differentiation of treatment of detainees is that what is to-day
given to preventive detainees as a special amelioration of penal
conditions, to-morrow percolates throughout the penal system,[3] and

[1] Though, of course, reformation for them may come from within by a process of
" ageing ".
[2] Till now, owing to the modernity of the minimum-security institution technique,
none of the preventive detainees has had any experience of it.
[3] In this regard see Crowley's Case (9 Cr. App. R. 198 at 201) in which the then-
existing (1913) preventive detention régime was described, and its non-penal character
stressed—reading this description in 1949 is like reading a description of a rather harsh
form of recently operating penal servitude !

soon becomes a part of the ordinary prison régime. But this process would seem rather to accentuate the fact of the possible differences in conditions, for it will be many decades before our conception of punishment has rendered ordinary imprisonment as free from gratuitous suffering as it could be. If the preventive detainees are an experimental group of the penal reformer, then provided the experiments are in the line of alleviated conditions, this would not seem to detract from the adaptation of their régime solely to the exigencies of segregation. For example, were detainees to be employed for a normal working week (instead of the soul-destroying twenty-odd hours) on useful industrial effort[1] and paid a living wage, their cost to the community would be lessened, and no one would deny that this would constitute a " real difference " in their penal régime. If subsequently this is allowed to other prisoners—which is hardly likely to come for very many years (and may well not be a desirable reform for general application)—by that time many other changes in the preventive detention régime will surely have been made.[2] What if preventive detainees are only in the vanguard of new measures of penal administration—provided the prison authorities are doing their utmost to exorcise from the preventive detention régime all traces of suffering not necessarily involved in the fact of detention, then, for many decades, preventive detention will be something very different from ordinary long-term imprisonment.

One last point on this subject. Dr. Radzinowicz and Dr. Grünhut, in developing their arguments, both make much of the failure of other countries to differentiate between the two systems. Dr. Radzinowicz in a footnote[3] refers to the Austrian, German, Belgian and Italian experience; Dr. Grünhut to the German and Norwegian practice.[4] From our comparative law study it will be remembered that these countries were certainly not those where any degree of differentiation of treatment of preventive detainees was either sought or achieved, and it is submitted that it savours of " special pleading " to draw conclusions from their experience without citing that of other countries—say Denmark, Finland or Sweden—where such differentiation was genuinely sought and largely achieved. A like division of countries carried the day in the

---

[1] As, indeed, they are in some countries whose habitual criminal legislation we have analysed.

[2] For example, penal colonies with families living in them, and their members living a normal existence subject to their remaining within the area allocated to them.

[3] *Op. cit.*, p. 165, note 2.   [4] *Op. cit.*, p. 393, note.

deliberations of the Berlin Congress of 1935; representatives from countries where no practical penological distinction was drawn between imprisonment and preventive detention outnumbering the representatives from those countries where this distinction was drawn and implemented.

But all ratiocination apart—surely it is not beyond the wit of man to adapt preventive detention to the type or types of criminals who should be subject to it,[1] and to its single aim.of segregation.[2] If this be the case, then we need fear no infringement of the conception of "nulla poena", for preventive detention will not be a "poena". It will have none of the individual and selective quality of a "poena", but will express only the collective quality of an act of humane social defence. As Dr. Mannheim has affirmed:

> "The fate of civil liberty depends on the men who have to administer criminal justice much more than on . . . any legal formula."[3]

Given enlightened prison administration—which we are fortunate to have in England—the formal infringement of the traditional conception of *nulla poena sine lege* in our habitual criminal legislation need not disturb us.

3. *The XIIth International Penal and Penitentiary Congress*

One question on the agenda for the XIIth quinquennial International Penal and Penitentiary Congress which was to have been held in Rome in 1940 was:

> "What is an habitual or incorrigible offender? What practical experience has been gained of the systems at present in force? If these systems have not given satisfaction, what system would be more suitable for the treatment of these offenders?"

This congress was, of course, postponed; but by 1939 ten preliminary papers discussing the above question were in the hands of the secretariat of the International Penal and Penitentiary Commission. In September 1947 these papers were published as Book 1, Volume

---

[1] As the numbers of detainees increase, some classification of types of detainees will be necessary; and an adaptation of preventive detention to these diverse classifications may require the imposition of several different detentive régimes. It is likely that with the increasing application of our psychological knowledge more and more habitual criminals will be found to be psychological inferiors, and will require special treatment adapted to their inferiority.

[2] When I say "single" aim this does not exclude reformation as a by-product of time and the preventive detention régime—but reformation is not a significant aim of preventive detention.

[3] *Criminal Justice and Social Reconstruction*, p. 213.

XIII, of the *Recueil de Documents en Matière Pénale et Pénitentiaire*, which we have considered in our comparative law study.

The postponed XIIth Congress is to be held at The Hague in 1950, and one question on the revised agenda is : " The treatment and release of habitual criminals."

In its Berne session, August 1946, the Commission set up a subcommittee, under the chairmanship of Professor José Beleza dos Santos, of Portugal, to study this question, to proceed with an enquiry into the treatment of habitual criminals in various countries, and to prepare a report on this problem for presentation to the congress. In co-operation with the permanent office of the Commission, this subcommittee has laid the foundation for an informed and possibly fruitful discussion of preventive detention and the release of habitual criminals. Their survey of the practice in various countries is to be published in the next issue of the *Recueil*;[1] and, in the last issue,[2] an interim report was presented by Professor Beleza dos Santos on the subject of the deliberations of the subcommittee, and a preliminary indication was given of the approach they have made to this question, as well as a statement of several suggestions advanced by them.

The 1950 congress is likely to be of great significance to the immediate developments in penological theory and practice; and it will be of particular importance to those countries in which, as in England, there is a general desire to remodel the preventive detention régime but considerable doubt as to the details of this renovation. Such careful preparatory work having been done on this question of the treatment and release of habitual criminals, it is to be hoped and anticipated that some interesting and practically useful suggestions will emerge at The Hague.

[1] Vol. XIII, Book 5.   [2] Vol. XIII, Books 3/4, Berne, November 1948.

CHAPTER FIVE

THE CRIMINAL JUSTICE ACT, 1948

RARELY does the passage of a statute excite such widespread public interest as did that of the Criminal Justice Act, 1948. Unfortunately, however, the emotional attachment of the Press and the public to certain issues in the debates in 1938 and in 1948 tended to concentrate parliamentary attention on those issues to the detriment of many other sections of the Act of equal criminological importance—those issues were, in 1938, whipping and hanging; in 1948, hanging and whipping.

Many accounts are available of the background to and parliamentary treatment of Sir Samuel Hoare's Criminal Justice Bill in 1939, and the remodelled copy of it which was brought down in 1948,[1] and we can therefore address ourselves immediately to the provisions in the Act dealing with habitual criminals.

The genetic force behind section 21 of the Act (which gives the courts new powers in relation to certain recidivists) was the Report of the Persistent Offenders Committee published in 1932.[2] That committee—whose report we have in part considered—recommended that two new forms of sentence should be instituted; and these two sentences have found their way into the 1948 Act as " corrective training " and " preventive detention ". The committee had been appointed to enquire into:

" the existing methods of dealing with persistent offenders, including habitual offenders who are liable to sentences of preventive detention, and other classes of offenders who return to prison repeatedly. . . ."[3]

Thus, the scope of their deliberations and recommendations covered a much wider classification of offenders than habitual criminals as we have defined them. Further, when considering the incorrigible habitual offender one is inevitably forced to a consideration of the methods of punishment which, by failing to correct him, have given

[1] See, for example, two articles by H. Mannheim in *The Fortnightly* (August 1946 and January 1948). The 1948 Bill is discussed in my article in *Res Judicatae*, Vol. IV, No. 1. An excellent summary of the 1939 Bill appears in Vol. V, No. 3, of the *Howard Journal* (spring 1939). The best general introductions to the present Act are to be found in the first twelve pages of Morrisson and Hughes *The Criminal Justice Act, 1948*, and in a book of the same name by Rees and Graham (Butterworth & Co., London, 1949).

[2] Cmd. 4090.   [3] *Ibid.*, p. ii.

meaning to the concept of incorrigibility or habituality; for incorrigibility is a concept relative to our knowledge and techniques and will be modified according as more efficient means are found of preventing the offender from falling outside society's practicable means of reclamation. For that reason, and because their terms of reference plainly included the problem of the younger more trainable persistent offender, the committee recommended that:

" For the purpose of enabling the courts to deal more effectively with those persistent offenders who are likely to profit by a period of training . . . we recommend that a new form of sentence should be introduced and that courts should be given power as an *alternative* to their present powers of ordering imprisonment or penal servitude, to order, in suitable cases and subject to proper safeguards, detention for any period being not less than two nor more than four years with the object, not of imposing a specific penalty for a specific offence, but of subjecting the offender to such training, discipline, treatment or control as will be calculated to check his criminal propensities."[1]

After sixteen years, this recommendation was accepted by the legislature and appears as section 21, subsection 1, of the Act, which reads:

" Where a person who is not less than twenty-one years of age—
(a) is convicted on indictment of an offence punishable with imprisonment for a term of two years or more ; and
(b) has been convicted on at least two previous occasions since he attained the age of seventeen of offences punishable on indictment with such a sentence,
then, if the court is satisfied that it is expedient with a view to his reformation and the prevention of crime that he should receive training of a corrective character for a substantial time, followed by a period of supervision if released before the expiration of his sentence, the court may pass, in lieu of any other sentence, a sentence of corrective training for such term of not less than two nor more than four years as the court may determine."[2]

We shall not here further consider " corrective training ", as it is manifestly a sentence not applicable exclusively to habitual criminals as we have defined them.[3] The committee in making their recommendation for this type of sentence envisaged an adult Borstal —a form of punishment concentrating on reformative training and giving the prison authorities sufficient time to reshape so far as possible the criminals committed to their care. In the intervening sixteen years the Prison Commissioners have gained much experience with this type of offender in Maidstone and Wakefield prisons, and

---

[1] *Ibid.*, p. 16.
[2] It will be noted that there is no upper age-limit to those who can be sentenced to corrective training.
[3] It is unfortunate that two widely different penological measures should have been included in the one section of the Act.

it may well be that in the régime at Maidstone over the past few years the nucleus of the necessary conditions for corrective training can be seen. From the point of view of preventive detention, the most significant feature of corrective training is that, as the latter develops into a functioning system, courts will hesitate to commit a criminal to preventive detention unless he has previously been sentenced to corrective training. Thus, though not specified in the Act, a previous sentence of corrective training will gradually become, in practice, a condition precedent to the imposition of preventive detention.

Let us now concentrate on those parts of the Act dealing specifically with preventive detention. The recommendation of the Persistent Offenders Committee concerning habitual criminals was as follows:

" Where a person is convicted on indictment of a crime and since attaining the age of sixteen years he has at least three times previously been convicted of a crime, the court, if of opinion that the offender is of such criminal habits or mode of life that it is expedient for the protection of the public that he should be kept in detention for a lengthened period of years, may, in lieu of any other sentence, pass a sentence of detention for a term of not less than five years and not more than ten years."[1]

The statutory acceptance of this recommendation appears in section 21, subsection 2, which reads:

" Where a person who is not less than thirty years of age—
(a) is convicted on indictment of an offence punishable with imprisonment for a term of two years or more ; and
(b) has been convicted on indictment on at least three previous occasions since he attained the age of seventeen of offences punishable on indictment with such a sentence, and was on at least two of those occasions sentenced to Borstal training, imprisonment or corrective training ;
then, if the court is satisfied that it is expedient for the protection of the public that he should be detained in custody for a substantial time, followed by a period of supervision if released before the expiration of his sentence, the court may pass, in lieu of any other sentence, a sentence of preventive detention for such term of not less than five nor more than fourteen years as the court may determine."[2]

Thus the Act incorporates the committee's recommendation, modifications being in matters of detail only.

In the Parliamentary debates in 1938 and 1948 on the two Bills, little attention was given to preventive detention. On the floor of the two Houses only passing references to corrective training or

---

[1] *Op. cit.*, p. 20.
[2] It will be noted that in this subsection no mention is made, as in subsection 1, of the expediency of the sentence as regards the offender's reformation.

preventive detention were made; and at the Committee Stage in 1939, of the sixteen days occupied in discussing the individual sections of the Bill, only one hour and seven minutes was devoted to these new punishments.[1] In 1948, at the Committee Stage in the House of Commons, of the sixteen days allocated to the Bill, only one hour and forty minutes was spent considering the provision that became section 21. This cursory treatment of two profoundly important penological measures, though a compliment to the Persistent Offenders Committee, was of doubtful wisdom[2]—was it really so clear, for example, that a judicially predetermined sentence should be imposed on preventive detainees, and did the question of an indefinite sentence within fixed limits not warrant discussion ? But it is still too early for adequate criticism of this measure. All that it did was to give powers to the courts and to the Home Office (and through the Home Office, to the Prison Commissioners), and it is not possible to evaluate section 21 until some indication is given of what will be done with these powers.[3] To this point we will return —let us now lift the habitual criminal provisions from their setting in the Act and consider their formal application.

In the first place, the finding of habitual criminality is no longer necessary, and the jury is relieved of its function of deciding on this condition; nor is there any problem about the " status " resulting from such a finding since " Habitual Criminal " ceases to be a current term of art in English criminal law.

No special procedure,[4] apart from that followed for an indictable

---

[1] Most of this short time was occupied by an amendment in which the provision of a new sentence for habitual petty delinquents was discussed, and there was difficulty in maintaining a quorum of 20 members during the discussion of this part of the Bill.

[2] As Dr. Mannheim wrote : " Among the predominantly constructive clauses of the Bill none should be given a more careful second reading than those dealing with persistent offenders."—*The Fortnightly*, January 1948, p. 41.

[3] " This Bill . . . gives a very large blank cheque to the Home Office."—Mr. Benson, Member for Chesterfield, on the second reading debate. *Parliamentary Debates*, Vol. 444, No. 29, Col. 2292.

[4] The complications in the 1908 Act regarding the contents of the " notice" to the accused and to the court of the intention to charge the accused as an habitual criminal are swept away. Nevertheless section 23 of the 1948 Act requires that :
" 1. For the purpose of determining whether an offender is liable to be sentenced to corrective training or preventive detention . . . no account shall be taken of any previous conviction or sentence unless notice has been given to the offender and to the proper officer of the court at least three days before the trial that it is intended to prove the conviction or sentence ; and unless any such previous conviction or sentence is admitted by the offender the question shall be determined by the verdict of a jury.
2. For the purposes of this section evidence that a person has previously been sentenced to corrective training or preventive detention shall be evidence of the convictions and sentences which rendered him liable to that sentence."

offence, is necessary as a preliminary to a sentence of preventive detention. In addition to this obvious simplification, the 1948 Act introduced a further procedural change of particular relevance to habitual criminals. Many potential preventive detainees commit indictable offences of the type that can be heard summarily, and, before this Act, the procedure to be followed in such cases was provided by section 24 of the Criminal Justices Act of 1925, the relevant portions of which read:

> " 1. Where a person who is an adult is charged before a court of summary jurisdiction with an indictable offence, being one of the offences specified in the Second Schedule to this Act, the court, if it thinks it expedient so to do, having regard to any representation made in the presence of the accused by or on behalf of the prosecutor, *the character and antecedents of the accused*, the nature of the offence, the absence of circumstances which would render the offence one of a grave or serious character and all the other circumstances of the case (including the adequacy of the punishment which a court of summary jurisdiction has power to inflict), and if the accused . . . consents . . . may . . . deal summarily with the offence, and, if the accused pleads guilty to, or is found guilty of, the offence charged, may sentence him to be imprisoned for any term not exceeding six months or to a fine not exceeding £100 or to both such imprisonment and fine."

The difficulty frequently arose that some magistrates hesitated to inquire into the " character and antecedents of the accused " before hearing the evidence concerning the last offence charged in the fear that should they do this they might prejudice their impartiality in deciding the guilt of the accused. Accused persons usually prefer their cases to be heard by courts of summary jurisdiction (especially if they are in fear of the more onerous sentences which can be inflicted by courts of quarter sessions or assizes), and police superintendents also often desire that such cases should be disposed of quickly so that police witnesses can be freed for other urgent tasks. The upshot was that very many cases which were heard by courts of summary jurisdiction should have been sent to trial upon indictment; and many prisoners with substantial criminal records continued to be sentenced to the relatively short term of imprisonment to which the courts of summary jurisdiction were limited. A great deal of judicial criticism was directed against this practice, and in the recent case of Sampson,[1] the Lord Chief Justice adverted to this point, saying:

> " The Summary Jurisdiction Acts were never intended to deal with a prisoner with a record such as this. . . . I do hope that magistrates will remember that it is their duty to inquire into the prisoner's character and antecedents before they consent to deal with him summarily. They have to take into account what the police say, but they ought not to be bound solely by the view of the police superintendent, who may want to get rid of the case quickly instead of having it sent to the assizes. Magistrates ought to exercise judicial discretion before they decide, in the cases of prisoners with records, whether they will deal with them summarily or not. . . . I believe some benches of magistrates feel the difficulty about inquiring into the prisoner's record. If they would carefully read the judgments of my brother Humphreys, which were given in the well-known cases of Sheridan[2] and Grant[3] they would see that this court pointed out that the statute requires magistrates to inquire into the character and antecedents of an accused person. The judgments point out that if the character is good, or, at any rate, not bad, no harm will be done by the magistrates knowing that fact before they proceed to adjudicate. On the other hand, if they are informed that an accused person has an exceedingly bad character . . . again no harm is done, because their plain duty in such a case is to commit him for trial."

Though this judgment reaffirmed the undoubted duty of courts of summary jurisdiction, it did not, it is submitted, give sufficient weight to the genuine difficulties with which such courts were faced—those accused persons with manifestly " bad " criminal records, and those whose characters were "good", presented no difficulty; but those whose characters were, in Lord Goddard's words, " at any rate not bad " did trouble the average magistrate, conscious of his own limitations and striving to do justice. The legislature eased this strain on magistrates by relieving them of the duty of making a pre-trial inquiry into the accused's character and antecedents and by providing, in section 29 of the 1948 Act, a means whereby courts of summary jurisdiction, having convicted a prisoner of an indictable offence, and having then heard information as to his character and antecedents, may commit him in custody to quarter sessions for sentence.

Thus potential preventive detainees will no longer be able to escape such sentences by having the good fortune to persuade courts of summary jurisdiction to enter upon the hearing of the last offence with which they have been charged; for now preventive detention

---

[1] 32 Cr. App. R. 94.   [2] 26 Cr. App. R. 1.   [3] 26 Cr. App. R. 8.

can be imposed pursuant to an indictable offence heard, in the first instance, by a court of summary jurisdiction.

Let us now turn from procedural questions to matters of substance. As we have seen, by section 21, subsection 2, the conditions precedent to the imposition of a sentence of preventive detention—between five and fourteen years at the discretion of the court—are:

the prisoner must be

(a) not less than thirty years of age;
(b) convicted on indictment;[1]
(c) convicted of an offence punishable with imprisonment for two years or more;

and must have been

(d) thrice previously so convicted since attaining the age of seventeen years;
(e) sentenced, at least twice previously (pursuant to convictions in accordance with (d)), to Borstal training, imprisonment or corrective training;[2]

and

(f) the court must be satisfied that preventive detention is expedient for the protection of the public.

Such a sentence is in lieu of and not in addition to any other sentence the court could impose; in other words, the " dual-track " is replaced by the " single-track " system.[3]

Thus, many of the difficulties we discovered in the preventive detention system introduced in 1908 have been avoided—the procedural complications, the " dual-track " system of punishment, the requirement of a term of penal servitude, and the emotional resistance of the average juryman to this sentence. It is likely, therefore, that the courts will inflict preventive detention more frequently in the future.

---

[1] Subsection 6 reads :
" For the purposes of paragraph (b) of subsection 2 of this section, a person who has been convicted by a court of summary jurisdiction of an indictable offence and sentenced for that offence by a court of quarter sessions, or on appeal from such a court, to Borstal training, imprisonment or corrective training shall be treated as if he had been convicted of that offence on indictment."
Thus, the test is the sentence which could have been passed if the three or more previous convictions had been tried on indictment ; and the actual manner of their trial as distinct from conviction is not relevant.
[2] The Act abolished " penal servitude."   [3] But see Appendix F.

One very sound recommendation of the Persistent Offenders Committee is not enshrined in the Act:

> " Judges [should] warn offenders who are becoming eligible for a sentence of [preventive detention] that on the occasion of their next appearance before the courts they may find themselves being sentenced to detention for a lengthened period of years. Offenders so warned might be served on discharge with a suitable notice reminding them of the warning and the warning could be brought to the attention of the prosecution and of the court on the occasion of a subsequent charge. Some offenders might be induced by some such stern warning to pause before continuing further in their criminal career."[1]

The value of this suggestion is self-evident; and though, perhaps wisely, it was not incorporated in the Act, there is nothing to prevent the Prison Commissioners and the courts from making a practice of so warning potential preventive detainees. This is one of the few advantages of the proximity of corrective training and preventive detention in the construction of the Act. In hesitating between preventive detention and corrective training, and finally deciding on the imposition of the latter, the court is likely to inform the prisoner of this doubt and of what may well happen to him should he again appear in a criminal court.

There were, as we saw, many reasons why Part II of the Prevention of Crime Act, 1908, was so rarely invoked—one being the paucity of information at the disposal of the sentencing court. We noted the short time available for the police to collect their information concerning the accused, and the effect this had on the frequency of charges of habitual criminality. Nor was there any provision in the Act for the collection or presentation of more information about the prisoner than is normally at the court's disposal. Subsection 4 of section 21 of the 1948 Act remedies this by requiring that:

> " Before sentencing any offender to corrective training or preventive detention the court shall consider any report or representations which may be made to the court by or on behalf of the Prison Commissioners on the offender's physical and mental condition and his suitability for such a sentence."

And subsection 5 provides that:

> " A copy of any report or representations in writing made to the court by the Prison Commissioners for the purposes of the last foregoing subsection shall be given by the court to the offender or his counsel or solicitor."

The court will thus be advised by the people who have had experience of the criminal under prison conditions, and who can report

[1] *Op. cit.,* pp. 18-19.

how he reacted to previous sentences.[1] This type of information has for many years been given in relation to potential Borstal detainees, and has been of great assistance to the courts.[2]

Having statutorily segregated our preventive detainee for a fixed term between five and fourteen years, let us enquire what treatment the Act prescribes for him. Subsection 3 of section 21 is our point of departure:

> " A person sentenced to corrective training or preventive detention shall be detained in a prison for the term of his sentence subject to his release on licence in accordance with the provisions of the Third Schedule to the Act, and while so detained shall be treated in such manner as may be prescribed by rules made under Section 52 of this Act."

The Third Schedule to the Act provides for the conditional release of a detainee on licence after he has served " such portion of his sentence as may be determined in accordance with rules made under section 52 of this Act " (hereunder called the fixed portion), such licence to be on whatever terms the Prison Commissioners think expedient, and revocable by them.[3] However, power is given to the Secretary of State to require the Prison Commissioners to release a preventive detainee at any time during his sentence (not only after the fixed portion thereof has been served) and it is ordered that " the Prison Commissioners in exercising their functions under this Schedule shall act in accordance with any general or special directions of the Secretary of State." Thus, though it is clear that release is at present envisaged at the expiration of a fixed portion of the sentence imposed, there remains power in the Secretary of State to make preventive detention an indefinite sentence. What will, in fact, occur one can only surmise, since the Home Secretary has, as yet, given very few indications of his Department's intentions

---

[1] This statutory provision also is the result of a suggestion by the Persistent Offenders Committee on p. 17 of their report : " The court ought to know of any view the prison authorities have formed as a result of observation of the offender while in prison and of their experience in dealing with other cases."

[2] Though the court must consider any report or representation made to them by the Prison Commissioners, it is not compelled to accept their advice. See *R.* v. *Watkins and Others* (1910) 74 J.P. 382 ; but see *R.* v. *Tarbotton* (1942) 1 All E.R. 198.

[3] On May 2nd, 1949, the Home Secretary approved the establishment of a Central After-Care Association for England and Wales, in which the Borstal Association, the Aylesbury After-Care Association and the Central Association for the Aid of Discharged Convicts are to be merged. Under the provisions of the Criminal Justice Act, 1948, this new association will supervise, amongst others, released preventive detainees. The association is to be governed by a council of about twenty appointees of the Home Secretary. The chairman of the Prison Commission, L. W. Fox, will be the first chairman of the new association.

in this respect.   On the Second Reading of the Bill he did mention that:

> " A provision in the Third Schedule will enable release on licence to be given to persons sentenced to corrective training or preventive detention who, while serving their sentences, may prove themselves worthy of such leniency."[1]

and later in committee stated:

> " It is not to be thought that because a person receives a very heavy sentence of preventive detention . . . that will of necessity mean that he will have to complete the whole of his sentence if, in accordance with these rules and under the provisions of the Third Schedule, he shows that he is capable of reformation."[2]

Perhaps the recommendation of the Persistent Offenders Committee will be carried out: they suggested that as the avoidance of overt misconduct or demonstrable idleness gave no clue to the detainee's likely reaction to freedom, all detainees should be licensed after a fixed portion of their sentence had been served unless by such overt misconduct or idleness they had forfeited this right, and further that " any time after he has completed one-third of his sentence " the detainee should be released if the prison authorities " are satisfied that there is a reasonable probability that he will abstain from crime, that he is no longer capable of engaging in crime, or that for any other reason it is desirable to release him." They recommended that at least one-third of the sentence should always be served, on the ground that otherwise courts might hesitate to make use of the sentence of preventive detention in certain cases for fear of too much leniency on the part of the authorities administering that punishment.

At present, as a general rule, all prisoners are released after they have served two-thirds of their sentence unless they have misconducted themselves while in prison. The committee thus desired to continue this practice also for preventive detainees but considered that the judicial sentence should condition the terms of preventive detention actually served to a lesser extent than other sentences.[3]

The committee's suggestion that for the majority of detainees a fixed date for release should be provided springs largely from their doubt of the adequacy of the information at the disposal of the releasing authority—adequacy in relation to the prognostic task for

---

[1] *Parliamentary Debates*, Vol. 444, No. 28, Cols. 2151-2.
[2] *Parliamentary Debates*, Standing Committee A, Seventh Sitting, Col. 296.
[3] When they wrote most prisoners were normally released after serving three-quarters of their sentences. It has since been reduced to two-thirds.

which it is to be used. They also observed what had happened in this respect under the Prevention of Crime Act, 1908. To this problem we adverted when considering that Act, and in the Excursus to the Comparative Law Study. The whole trend of modern habitual criminal legislation is towards an indefinite period of preventive detention—to allow discretion because it is hoped to take advantage of any prospects of an individual's reform that might occur. The continued insistence on a judicially determined sentence and the restriction of administrative discretion is, it is submitted, unfortunate; and does not sufficiently protect the community. A failure to trust the prison administration does not argue a defence of the prisoner's rights or of the community's interests, both of which may just as likely be endangered by the exigencies of statutory requirements adapted to the lowest common denominator of habitual criminality. However, it remains within the power given to the Secretary of State by this Act to make preventive detention an indefinite sentence subject, for each prisoner, to a judicially fixed maximum term, and it is to be hoped that the courage will not be lacking to adapt this system of preventive detention to its particular purposes.[1]

Section 52 of the Act empowers the Secretary of State to make rules for the regulation and management of preventive detention prisons, and subsection 4 of that section provides that:

" Rules made under this section shall provide for the special treatment of the following persons whilst required to be detained in a prison, that is to say—
(a) any person serving a sentence of preventive detention."

The rules which have been promulgated appear in Appendix F.

On the Second Reading debate in the House of Lords, the Lord Chief Justice, speaking about corrective training and preventive detention, said :[2]

" I hope that before this Bill becomes law, if it does become law, we in the courts will have that which I think we are entitled to have—namely, full information as to what these novel methods of training are."

[1] The Prison Commissioners can still call on the board of visitors to the preventive detention prison for advice regarding the detainee's release, Section 53 of the Act allowing the Secretary of State to make rules for the constitution and function of such bodies, and subsection 4 of that section providing :
" Rules made as aforesaid may require the board of visitors appointed for any prison or Borstal institution to consider periodically the character, conduct and prospects of each of the persons sentenced to corrective training, preventive detention or Borstal training who is detained therein, and to report to the Prison Commissioners on the advisability of his release on licence or under supervision."
[2] *Parliamentary Debates, House of Lords*, Vol. 155, No. 67, Col. 495.

Here Lord Goddard raised a most important consideration—courts hesitate to impose a protracted sentence of whose conditions they are not fully conversant ; and on the other hand the Prison Commissioners cannot create an efficient régime until the type of sentence is imposed on an appreciable number of prisoners. Thus, in their 1945 annual report,[1] the Prison Commissioners considering the preventive detention provision in the 1938 Bill wrote:

" the main problem concerns the courts, and how they may be induced to use such statutory powers as may be available to them, and not the treatment of the offender while in prison.

It may however be remarked here that uncertainty on this subject is one of the factors that makes it difficult now to forecast future developments with any certainty. The difficulty is perhaps made most clear by stating that on the one hand there are now some thirty ' habitual criminals ' serving sentences of preventive detention, while on the other hand there are some 2,000 prisoners serving sentences of penal servitude or imprisonment who would qualify for this form of sentence under the formula of the 1938 Bill. If the courts use the powers it is proposed to give them to the full, evidently the make-up of the prison population and the allocation of accommodation will be radically changed."

The solution to this dilemma will have to work itself out under the stress of practical exigencies—it can hardly be planned.

Having observed the dissidence between the aims and achievements of the framers of Part II of the Prevention of Crime Act, 1908, and the great hopes placed in it, one would be rash to try to foretell the future developments in the new system of preventive detention. Basically, the success of this system depends on two factors—the régime that is devised for preventive detention, and the skill of the courts in selecting those criminals for whom preventive detention is an appropriate punishment.[2] Profiting from experience of the 1908 Act, we avoided, in 1948, many of the procedural, technical and emotional hindrances to the extensive application of preventive detention ; and it is therefore likely that more use will be made of this legislation. What will be done with the preventive detainees once they are sentenced will be as interest-

[1] *Report of the Commissioners of Prisons and Directors of Convict Prisons for the Year 1945*, pp. 64-5.
[2] Their task is complicated by the overwhelming necessity to fix the appropriate maximum duration of the detention in relation to the offender and not, as was often done under the Prevention of Crime Act, 1908 (see Hamilton's Case, 9 Cr. App. R. 89) in relation to the offence.

ing to observe as it is at present unpredictable. How will the Prison Commissioners cook their hares now that they have been caught ?

＊   ＊   ＊   ＊   ＊

This chapter remains as it was written before the publication of the Rules made under the Act for the governance of prisons, the relevant portions of which are reproduced in Appendix F.

It would be of little permanent value to criticise these rules, and their implementation, during what is an experimental and formative period in the development of a new preventive detention régime. However, one cannot avoid expressing surprise at the reintroduction of the " dual-track system " by administrative regulation after its hearty, formal, public and repeated denunciation during the operation of the 1908 Act.

When section 21 of the Act came into force the Secretary of State authorised the issue to all courts of the following memorandum on Preventive Detention :

" 1. Hitherto the indictment of ' habitual criminals ' under the Prevention of Crime Act, 1908, has been confined by the prosecution to cases of professional criminals with a long record of crime, who are a danger to society. The qualification for preventive detention under the Criminal Justice Act is much wider than the definition of ' habitual criminal ' in the Act of 1908, and it will be for the courts to decide in the case of any offender fulfilling the qualification by age and record presented by the section whether his prolonged segregation is expedient for the protection of society.

2. For many years past the numbers of offenders in preventive detention have been very small (they are now about 30), and the existing system is based on the assumption that the sentence is primarily custodial and has no positive aspects. When section 21 comes into force the situation will be different. It may be expected that much larger numbers will be sentenced to preventive detention, including a high proportion of the most difficult and dangerous prisoners in the country.

3. The new system of preventive detention has therefore to take account of three factors ; first, that the sentence is in its nature preventive rather than punitive ; second, that nevertheless for a majority of the prisoners so sentenced maximum security and strong disciplinary control will be essential ; and third, that both on general grounds and in the light of the recommendations of the Departmental Committee on Persistent Offenders as to the nature and purpose of preventive detention, it will be important to make the régime a positive rather than a negative one, and to do whatever is possible to send these men out both able and willing to live an honest life. There is the further, if transitory, condition that in the present acute shortage of prison accommodation it may be impossible for

some time to come to set aside suitable prisons solely for the confinement of prisoners sentenced to preventive detention. The régime will, therefore, have to be such as can be administered in the central prisons in which recidivist prisoners serving long sentences of imprisonment are also confined.

4. Careful consideration has been given to the type of régime to be set up in the light of all these considerations, and the conclusion that has been reached is that the system of preventive detention should be one of progress through a series of establishments of different types, each of which will serve a particular purpose, their total effect being to break up the monotony of a long sentence.

The first stage, which will not exceed two years and will usually be less, according to the nature of the individual and the length of his sentence, will be passed in his local prison. This period will serve two purposes ; the first will be that of observation : the prisoner will be carefully studied in the light of his history and record, and sufficient knowledge of his character will be gained to determine whether he is of the " anti-social " or " a-social " type, to decide to what extent reformative influences are likely to be effectual, what forms of training will be most useful, and so on. The second purpose will be to bring home to him that he is not by virtue of his sentence a member of a privileged class, but that he has received a long sentence because he has a bad record and has committed another serious offence : his progress will depend on his own behaviour and efforts. There is a third reason, in that so long as the present pressure on accommodation exists it may be necessary in any case to keep these men in local prisons until vacancies occur in the central prisons.

The second stage will be spent in one of the central prisons for long-sentence prisoners, of which at present there are two—Parkhurst and Dartmoor. Here the prisoner's treatment will approximate to that of the last stage of a long sentence of imprisonment, with certain additional privileges appropriate to the custodial nature of the sentence.

The third stage will begin not more than twelve months before the date at which it is provisionally decided to release the prisoner. This will be a stage of re-adaptation intended to fit him for release and will be subject to recommendation that the individual is suitable for it. It will include vocational training in a skilled trade, if the prisoner is fit for it, and will be spent in conditions as closely approximating to freedom as possible ; as soon as it becomes possible to do so provision will be made for this stage to be spent by those who are selected for it in a special establishment, more like a hostel than a prison.

5. Release from preventive detention will be on a conditional licence, normally after five-sixths of the sentence has been served. Those selected for the third stage will however be eligible for licence, on the recommendation of an Advisory Board, when they have served two-thirds of their sentence. Prisoners released from preventive detention will be under the control and supervision of the Central After-Care Association, which will do its best to establish and assist them."

In April, 1950, prompted by judicial enquiries and by an adjournment debate in the House of Commons on the motion of Mr. Maude, K.C., the Prison Commissioners drew the attention of all Judges, Recorders and chairmen of Quarter Sessions to the above memorandum and added the following information :

" Since all those who have subsequently received this sentence are still serving the first stage in local prisons, there is nothing to be added to the memorandum in the light of actual experience. It has however been provisionally decided that initially the second stage men shall be accommodated in a portion of Parkhurst prison, which is being prepared for the purpose, and the second stage women in a portion of Holloway. It may however become necessary to make other arrangements for women if their numbers exceed, as they well may, the facilities available at Holloway : and since the number of preventive detention sentences on men *already exceeds 300*, the arrangements for their accommodation and the effect on the central prison population generally may require further consideration in the course of 1950."

PART II

CHAPTER SIX

"I'LL EXAMPLE YOU WITH THIEVERY"
(Timon of Athens).

COMMON to the police, prison officers, public and prisoners themselves is a high regard for the probity and efficiency of the criminal courts. Few other institutions are held in such general esteem. Indeed, at the time of the recent capital punishment debates in Parliament there was considerable argument as to whether, within living memory, anyone convicted of murder had later been discovered to be innocent of that crime—true, it was urged that the hangman disposes of the courts' errors in capital cases as efficiently as does the undertaker of those of the medical profession ; but it is nevertheless a tribute to the efficiency of the criminal courts that such a discussion should arise. Were the decision as to the guilt or innocence of accused persons, as it is in capital cases, the only duty of the criminal courts he would be a churlish perfectionist who would criticise them ; and it is because the public tends to evaluate their work from this standpoint that approbation is so widespread. Criminologists, however, have for many years been stressing the other duty imposed on criminal courts—that of fixing the punishment appropriate for each offender ; and they have contended, with much force, that concerning these judicial reactions to crime and to criminals much more room for criticism exists.

It can be said without exaggeration that there is no sentencing policy common to English criminal courts, unless we can describe as a system an ill-defined and varying tariff assigning certain periods of imprisonment to certain offences, the whole modified by the offender's past criminal record and functioning within wide statutory limits.[1] Certainly, it lacks uniformity and equality of application, is entirely capricious, and can be shown to fit neither the crime nor the criminal. This I regard as so self-evident as to need no further elaboration here ; if any doubt it, let them try to discover any system in the 4,591 punishments inflicted on the criminals whose records we will later consider. Any list of previous convictions read out

---

[1] For an official pronouncement to this effect see the *Report of the Departmental Committee on Persistent Offenders*, pp. 9-11.

before sentences are imposed on prisoners appearing at, for example, the Central Criminal Court will equally suffice. To certain aspects of the problem of sentencing policy we shall return in chapter nine.

The Criminal Court, then, achieves greater success as a fact-finding and law-applying agency than as a sentence-inflicting body. Its excellence in the former function springs largely from its unemotional, painstaking and objective approach ; and, it is submitted, its relative failure in choosing appropriate punishments arises from its emotional, expeditious and subjective reaction to the established offence and the convicted criminal. Until the unemotional, painstaking and objective approach is extended from the proof of the crime to the analysis of the criminal there will be no rational, functioning sentencing policy.

Although the flow of our argument brings us back to the problem of Treatment Tribunals to which we referred above,[1] we shall not consider that subject beyond asserting that the criminal court as at present constituted (and equally any Treatment Tribunal that may be established) will need considerably more knowledge about the criminal than is available to it to-day if it is adequately to fulfil its sentencing function.

As a step in this direction, all that is known to the prison authorities about 302 criminals, and which is relevant to the question of their sentences, is here presented. This information is never less than that which was at the disposal of the court and in most cases considerably exceeds it. The underlying contention is that the lawyer's approach to the proof of crime can be applied to the " proof " of the criminal—that fact-finding can be carried a stage further.

Until we can see a cross-section of our criminals presented as a single comprehensible unit, and their faculties and qualities analysed in the light of all our available knowledge of them, it is unlikely that any sure scientific progress will be made towards the solution of the problem they propound. But this, though true, may give the impression that such is the aim of this Part. Not only is the target less ambitious, but even this more humble target is felt to be inaccessible until a follow-up study has been conducted into the later histories of these 302 criminals. Only in the light of their later histories, and by comparing them with similar information concerning many other types of prisoners, will

[1] See p. 22.

information emerge of *positive* significance to the development of an enlightened sentencing policy. In the meantime, certain *negative* conclusions can be reached, and a picture of the types of criminal whose records have been analysed should emerge—a picture useful, among other purposes, for the construction of tentative hypotheses for further research.

To the objection that the plea for individualization of punishment, for the exact adaptation of the sentence to the particular offender, renders worthless the consideration of criminals or prisoners *en masse*, no better answer can be given than in the words of Sheldon and Eleanor Glueck, who wrote :[1]

> " we must have not only individualisation, but individualisation based upon objectified experience rather than deceptive ' common sense ', and mere ' consideration of the individual case '. The points of difference, of uniqueness, in the individual case cannot be safely determined without a careful evaluation of that case in the light of the points of similarity in hundreds of other cases. This fact is vital and basic, and has almost uniformly been ignored by social workers, judges and probation officers."

Our present target is a more humble one than we at first proposed because only a limited group of criminals is considered. They are distinguished from the totality of criminals by :

(*a*) the fact that they were prisoners,
(*b*) their sex,
(*c*) their age,
(*d*) their last sentence,
(*e*) the locality in which they were last sentenced,
(*f*) the date on which they were last sentenced, and
(*g*) their previous criminal and penal records.

To put it as accurately as possible : I have analysed two groups (in chapters seven and eight respectively) :

1. Thirty-two preventive detainees, being *all* those male prisoners sentenced as habitual criminals and actually undergoing preventive detention during the week ending October 16th, 1948.

2. Two hundred and seventy male convicts,[2] who were over the age of thirty years when admitted to Wandsworth

---

[1] *Five Hundred Criminal Careers*, New York, 1930, p. 83.
[2] A " convict " was (before the 1948 Criminal Justice Act) one on whom was imposed a sentence of penal servitude. By statutory definition a sentence of penal servitude had to be for a term of three years or more.

Prison between July 1st, 1946, and September 30th, 1948, and who since attaining the age of seventeen years have been convicted of indictable offences punishable with imprisonment for two years or more on *six* or more previous occasions, and who have been committed to Borstal detention or imprisonment on *four* or more of such previous occasions— these I shall term " confirmed recidivists ".

The reason for choosing the qualifications of the first group is sufficiently obvious—these thirty-two detainees constituted at that time the total population of male preventive detainees in England and Wales. The qualifications of the second group were fixed in relation to section 21 subsection 2 of the Criminal Justice Act, 1948,[1] which we have considered—the qualifications, as regards previous convictions and sentences, for the 270 being exactly double those required for a sentence of preventive detention under the Act. The Act requires conviction on indictment on at least three previous occasions, since the prisoner attained the age of seventeen, of offences punishable with imprisonment for a term of two years or more ; the members of our group have at least six such previous convictions. The Act requires two previous sentences of Borstal training or imprisonment pursuant to such previous convictions ; the members of our group have at least four such previous sentences. Further, the Act requires that the last offence be an indictable offence punishable with imprisonment for a term of two years or more ; for their last offences the members of our group have all been punished with terms of penal servitude for three years or more. It is, therefore, no exaggeration to regard our 270 " confirmed recidivists " as potential preventive detainees under the new Act.

Perhaps the chief limitation to our 270 confirmed recidivists as being completely representative of those criminals who may find themselves subject to the new preventive detention is that they are all men whose last crimes were committed in the Greater London area ; for all recidivist convicts who are sentenced in this area are sent to Wandsworth Prison.[2] This is the almost invariable practice.

---

[1] See p. 247.

[2] This areal limitation to our " confirmed recidivists " does not detract from their interest—the extent to which confirmed recidivism is predominantly an urban phenomenon is an important but largely unresolved question ; nevertheless, that fact does not lessen the relevance of a study of urban confirmed recidivism or of the particular problem of confirmed recidivists convicted in London, for there are, in all conscience, enough of them to constitute a challenging and difficult group.

Later some of them may be sent to other convict prisons, and when this happened to members of our group their records were followed to such prisons—of those who do not serve their entire sentences in Wandsworth Prison, the majority are allocated either to Dartmoor or Parkhurst Prisons, and records and conditions at both these prisons were investigated. The number 270 was chosen only because it embraced *all* convicts who fitted the qualifications listed above, and who were admitted to Wandsworth Prison between July 1st, 1946, and September 30th, 1948—the records for which period were made available to me by the very great courtesy of the Prison Commissioners.

Records alone were consulted for most of the 270 confirmed recidivists, though some were interviewed when ambiguities in their records could not otherwise be resolved. All the thirty-two preventive detainees were interviewed as an adjunct, but not a very reliable or relied-on adjunct, to their records.

With the generous consent of the Prison Commissioners, and the active and interested co-operation of many members of the prison staffs, I passed an absorbing period of nearly six months collecting the information on which this Part of the book rests. One week was spent at Dartmoor, over three weeks at Parkhurst, and the remainder of the time at Wandsworth. The records of a few qualifying prisoners who, for various reasons, had been transferred from Wandsworth to prisons other than Dartmoor and Parkhurst (twelve in all) were sent by these prisons to the Head Office of the Prison Commission where they were made available to me. The kindly assistance of the prison officials was unfailing.

It is strange that one should feel the need to justify such an investigation as has been undertaken in this Part. That some knowledge of the individuals on whom our criminal law presses should not be confined to a few members of the police and prison authorities seems irrefutable ; equally that this information should be related to the function of the criminal law and the criminal courts. This, in brief, is what is aimed at in the ensuing two chapters for two groups of prisoners—in chapter seven, those who were preventive detainees ; in chapter eight, those who are likely to be preventive detainees.

As an introduction to this study of case records, we will now consider the histories of eight preventive detainees. These detainees were the *first eight whose records were seen* when I visited Parkhurst

Prison, and they have not any noticeable variations, as a group, from the thirty-two detainees who made up the total population of such prisoners, and who are considered later.[1]

These case histories are presented in full for the following reasons. First, the statistical analyses which make up the ensuing two chapters serve to break down each individual's traits, personal qualities and environmental circumstances, which are then classified severally with those of other members of the group. There is a tendency for such an analytic technique to mask the subjective and often intricate correlations of different circumstances, traits and qualities in the particular individual's career. Therefore, a few cases are now presented as single entities in order to emphasise the organic character of every criminal career ; a fact which tends to be over-looked when such careers are considered *en masse*. Secondly, being truly representative of the extent and quality of the information on which all the statistical analysis which follows is based (confirmed recidivists as well as preventive detainees), they will illustrate the possibilities and limitations of such information. They are merely individual presentations of the similar data which I collected for all 302 prisoners—just as they vary in quality, so the 302 vary in quality and for the same reasons. The reader will not, therefore, be misled as to the foundation on which the later analysis is based. Thirdly, these case histories are inherently interesting, and may cover the massed bare bones of our statistical study with the living flesh of human beings, and thus help us to obtain a humane understanding of the individual criminal, which is a prerequisite to progress in criminology.

ARTHUR

Aged 43, Arthur is serving a sentence of five years' penal servitude and the remanet (1,237 days) of a preventive detention sentence imposed in 1937. His last offence was that of burglary, and indeed since the age of eighteen he has specialised in burglary and housebreaking. Since 1927 he has been out of prison for short periods only and normally takes to crime within a few weeks of discharge from prison. In all he has been convicted on thirteen occasions of indictable offences, these convictions being in respect of seventy-three offences (including those " taken into consideration " before sentencing). He has also been convicted on four occasions of summary offences, sleeping out, etc.

He was born in a seaport city. He has two sisters and one brother all consider-ably older than himself. Neither his sisters nor his brother has a criminal record,

---

[1] Though, of course, these eight are in no way meant to be representative of the thirty-two : the extent to which they conform to the norm—if there is a norm—we will be able to judge after the thirty-two have been treated.

though all of them tell of an unhappy youth and an early departure from their parental home. His memories are of a very unhappy home life, his mother being extremely bad tempered and his father excessively strict with him. This is confirmed by the report of a social worker who visited the home and interviewed his mother in 1923. Material conditions were good, the home being a typical middle-class suburban one, but there were regular violent dissensions between his parents which frequently culminated in varying periods during which they lived apart. At such times Arthur was taken by his father to live with him in the home of his aunt. Both his parents were severe with him on account of his lazy habits and frequent truancy which they deeply resented.

When he was twelve years of age, his parents, feeling that they could not control him, sent him to a nearby boarding school. Here he progressed normally and was no trouble whatsoever. On leaving that school he went to live with his father and aunt, it being a period of temporary separation of his parents. Then it was that he committed his first recorded criminal offence, stealing money from his father, for the purpose, he says, of paying his fare to go and see his mother. Asked whether he had stolen before he went to the boarding school he replied, " I might have done."

As a result of this theft from his father, and his continued truancy which all his father's severity could not check, he was sent to an industrial school. Here he remained until the age of 16, neither absconding nor stealing. Then he returned home to his parents who were living together again and went to work as a carpenter. His employer held his work in high regard and stated that he showed considerable promise at this trade. After a few months he was discharged, apparently for continued absence from work (" truancy " in another form). There followed a violent quarrel with his parents, who contended that he was not looking for work and that if he did not soon obtain employment they would no longer tolerate his presence in their home. Immediately after this argument he stole £5 2s. 5d. from a drawer in his father's dressing-table and absconded. Two days later he was caught and returned home, a Petty Sessional Court binding him over for twelve months. He still did not obtain employment, though he had many opportunities of doing so, and the arguments with his parents increased in frequency and in violence. Several times he ran away from home, and on four occasions he stole money from his parents, once being convicted in the local Petty Sessional Court of stealing £1 2s. from his father and dismissed under the Probation of Offenders Act, 1907.

In March 1922, aged 17, he ran away from home, having once again stolen money from his parents, and on this occasion his father refused to have him at home any longer, and he was sent to a boys' home, where he remained for twelve months, apart from several brief periods in which he was an absconder from this home. On one occasion when he ran away from the home he managed to reach his parents' residence and steal 4s. 6½d. and some clothes therefrom. For this he was sent to prison for three months.

On discharge from prison, aged 18, he was sent back to the boys' home, but refused to stay and ran away. He went to the locality of his first boarding school, stole cash from two gas meters, and broke into a house and stole 7s. 9d. and a coat. These were the first offences he had committed against anyone but his parents.

All three offences took place within two days of leaving the home. He was arrested, convicted, and in October 1923 sentenced to three years' Borstal detention. At this time the medical officer of the Borstal to which he was sent reported :

> " This inmate is lazy, dishonest, restless, criminally inclined and quite out of control. He says that he could not get on well at the boys' home and thinks that the cause of his crimes. He has not profited by his time in schools and homes, and is sadly in need of discipline. His home life has been unhappy and he will need careful watching at first, but may after a while settle down and benefit by Borstal training. Mental age 13.5."

He spent 709 days under Borstal training before being licensed in September 1925. At Borstal he did very well and was said to be pleasant and reliable. He did not steal, and made no attempts to abscond. He returned home and took up employment which had been found for him by the Borstal Association as deck and galley boy on coastal vessels. In this employment he remained until April 1927, when he was discharged for his lazy and unsatisfactory conduct on his last voyage. He returned home, but took up no employment. The old arguments with his parents recommenced. In July of the same year, aged 22, he stole £6 from a person living with his parents, left home and entered upon his criminal career in earnest. Since then he has had no further contact with his parents whatsoever and they have completely disowned him. His later record can best be grasped when set out in tabular form :[1]

Date	Age	Offence(s)	Sentence	Days In	Out
July '27	22	Found on enclosed premises (4 T.I.C.)	1 day and Borstal licence revoked	139	110
April '28	23	Housebreaking and larceny 3 cases (10 T.I.C.)	12 months	320	52
April '29	24	Burglary and larceny, 2 cases (1 T.I.C.)	12 months	326	70
May '30	25	Burglary and larceny, 3 cases (18 T.I.C.)	3 years' P.S.	845	50

[1] Column 5—Days In—represents the number of days spent in prison subsequent to each sentence ; column 6—Days Out—the number of days of freedom between the ensuing discharge from prison and subsequent reconviction. In this, and later tables, several abbreviations have been used. They are :

T.I.C. :	Offences taken into consideration by the court when sentencing the prisoner.
P.S. :	Penal servitude.
P.D. :	Preventive detention.
L.F. :	Licence forfeited.
L.R. :	Licence revoked.
P. of C. Act :	Prevention of Crime Act, 1908.
R. & V. :	Rogue and Vagabond.
lcy. :	Larceny.
dghse., whse. :	Dwelling-house, warehouse.
bkg. :	Breaking (thus—whsebkg.).
conc. :	To be served concurrently.
consec. :	To be served consecutively.
A.P.C.F. :	After previous conviction for felony.

Date	Age	Offence(s)	Sentence	Days In	Days Out
Oct. '32	27	Housebreaking and larceny; attempted housebreaking; burglary and larceny (4 T.I.C.)	5 years' P.S. and licence forfeited	1,581	129
June '37	32	Burglary and larceny; housebreaking and larceny; possn. housebreaking implements by night; being an habitual criminal (13 T.I.C.)	3 years' P.S.; 6 years' P.D. and L.F.	1,974	106
Mar. '43	38	Burglary and larceny	5 years' P.S. and P.D. licence revoked (1,237 days)		

His manner of occupying the short time he spends out of prison is well illustrated by his last period of freedom. He was discharged on November 23rd, 1942, and, seven days later, employment was found for him as a labourer in a Merseyside shipyard. Here he remained, working well, until December 30th, 1942, when for no apparent reason he absented himself from work. Two days later he again resorted to crime and remained so engaged until his arrest and subsequent conviction. This is the pattern of all his periods of freedom, and, indeed, it is one which he has followed, with slight variations, since his schooldays.

He has committed more than the seventy-three offences for which he has been sentenced, rarely being prepared to have taken into consideration all those offences which the police know he has committed. The police have never thought it worth while to press such charges to trial after he has been sentenced for those offences for which he has been convicted.

Arthur has never married nor is there any record of any liaison with a woman.

He is possessed of a violent temper, and this has made him a difficult prisoner. Periodically he gets into trouble with the prison authorities and until recently showed no signs of settling down as a typical " old lag ", quiet and well behaved whilst in prison. For example, during this present sentence he has been punished for six offences—twice for being in possession of contraband, twice for making insolent and obscene remarks to prison officers, once for making an improper remark to an officer, and once for assaulting an officer. For this last offence he was kept in close confinement for fourteen days, given thirty-six days' dietary punishment (fifteen days' No. 1 diet, twenty-one days' No. 2 diet), lost stage privileges and remission, as well as being a non-earner for twenty-eight days and kept out of associated labour for twenty-one days. Despite this, within a few days of this punishment having concluded he was again punished for a prison offence. After that there followed fifteen months of good behaviour before he again misbehaved.

On March 2nd, 1939, the medical officer at Dartmoor Prison made the following report on Arthur :

" He is an asthmatic who has recently sustained a broken rib ; in these respects he makes good progress. He has, however, become very unstable emotionally and falls into fits of considerable depression in which he says he feels suicidal. He has come to the idea that other prisoners tell each other stories to his discredit and that they are generally inimicable to him. At one time he was a quarrelsome man and relieved tension in that way, but he is now much quieter, depression and apprehension having, to some extent, replaced former violence. I doubt that he would actually harm himself, but I regard his distress as genuine and needing observation."

Arthur is a pleasant and easy conversationalist. He is not unintelligent. It is as clear to him as it is to anyone reading the above history that there is no likelihood of any change in his mode of life. This he seems to accept without rancour.

ALFRED

Of many habitual criminals one might suspect that preventive detention is the only environment to which they have learnt to adapt themselves—of Alfred this is quite certain and as obvious to him as it is to the prison authorities.

Alfred was born in 1890. His father worked as a general farm labourer, hiring himself out to various farmers and leading a normal labourer's existence. Material conditions in the home conformed to the circumstances of the father's employment, and Alfred and his brother attended the local school until they could conveniently escape from it and take their place at their father's side as farm labourers. Alfred's mother died when he was 15 years of age—his father did not remarry.

Until September 1914 Alfred remained living with his father and working on various farms. In that month he enlisted in the army. He served overseas and was discharged in June 1919, his character being assessed as " fair ". His brother did not return from the war. Alfred re-enlisted the day after his discharge and served for a further twelve months, being then discharged as no longer fit for military service owing to the gradual deterioration of his hearing. He received a disability pension of 25s. per week for six months, 12s. per week for the next six months, and a final grant of £10 when his pension ceased.

Upon discharge from the army he resumed his former occupation as a farm labourer and lived with his father, but in 1922, following a difference between them (the details of which I could not discover) he left home. He continued to do casual farm work until 1926, wandering about the countryside and spending only a short time in each job. During this period his deafness became more and more pronounced, and his life more and more solitary and lonely. In October 1926, aged 35, he came under the notice of the police. The rest of his story is best related in the light of his criminal record.

Date	Age	Offence(s)	Sentence	Days In	Out
Oct. '26	35	Housebreaking and larceny	6 months		
Dec. '26	35	Larceny, cigarettes	1 month concurrently	152	205
Oct. '27	36	Housebreaking and larceny (2 cases) (50 T.I.C.)	3 years' P.S.	821	20
Feb. '30	39	Ex-convict failing to report	7 days	7	7
Feb. '30	39	Pauper refusing task	14 days	14	33

				Days	
Date	Age	Offence(s)	Sentence	In	Out
Apr. '30	39	Housebreaking with intent; housebreaking and larceny; larceny, A.P.C.F.	3 months and L.F.	298	28
Feb. '31	40	Ex - convict failing to notify change of address	1 month	26	120
July '31	40	Loitering with intent	14 days	13	68
Oct. '31	40	Larceny, pair of boots and food, from dwelling-house, A.P.C.F.	2 months	51	5
Dec. '31	40	Being reputed thief, frequenting	2 months	52	25
Feb. '32	41	Larceny, cycle ; wilful damage to shop window	3 months	74	53
June '32	41	Burglary and larceny; shop-breaking and larceny, A.P.C.F.	9 months	227	70
April '33	42	Reputed thief, frequenting	3 months	26	96
Aug. '33	42	Sleeping out	1 month	30	32
Oct. '33	42	Burglary, housebreaking and larceny, A.P.C.F.	18 months	461	23
Feb. '35	44	R. & V., lodging out	1 month	27	32
April '35	44	Loitering with intent	1 month	26	78
July '35	44	Housebreaking with intent (4 T.I.C.)	3 years' P.S.	851	77
Feb. '38	47	Burglary and larceny; house-breaking with intent (2 cases) (2 cases T.I.C.) ; being an habitual criminal	18 months and L.F.	565	402
Oct. '40	49	Housebreaking and larceny	4 years' P.S.	974	116
Oct. '43	52	Burglary with intent (3 cases) ; being an habitual criminal	3 years' P.S. and 5 years' P.D.		

Despite the length of this criminal record it tells a story of one who is a nuisance to society rather than a danger. He specializes in inchoate crimes and when he does summon the nerve to complete the larceny he takes goods of trifling value.

During the 205 days of freedom following his first prison sentence, the only substantial period until 1939, he travelled through his home county committing offences of housebreaking. He was charged with three such offences, to which he pleaded guilty and asked that fifty other cases of housebreaking should be taken into consideration when he was sentenced. Beyond pleading guilty and asking for these offences to be taken into consideration he said nothing at his trial, inhibited, it may well be, by his deafness as well as his rather poor intellect.

The method of housebreaking he adopts has not varied since 1926. He breaks into houses between 11 p.m. and 9 a.m. by forcing (or breaking and then opening) a ground-floor window in the rear of the building, usually the kitchen window, enters and steals any odd petty cash or readily saleable articles found lying about. Rarely does he collect in this way as much as 20s. worth of money or property. Usually, seeing nothing immediately, or thinking he hears some slight noise, he hurries away empty-handed.

Once, and only once, has he been in employment since 1926. In June 1943, when he was licensed, he was given £1 5s., shoes, overalls and socks by the representative of the Central Association for the Assistance of Discharged Convicts and referred to a Salvation Army hostel, where he was offered work, in return for which he would receive 5s. per week and his board. This offer he rejected. The Central Association representative then found him employment as a labourer, and between June 11th, 1943, and July 3rd, 1943, he worked for ten days, receiving a total of £5 9s. for his services. During this period, on June 6th, 1943, and June 16th, 1943, he visited the Central Association representative, and on each occasion was given the sum of 12s. 6d. On June 19th, 1943, he was found wandering by a police constable and taken to the Central Association representative, who gave him a further 10s. and another pair of shoes, for he had sold the first pair. He left the labouring job of his own accord, saying he was "fed up" with such work. On July 14th, 1943, he was arrested on three charges of burglary with intent to steal, and at the time of his arrest was in possession of exactly twopence. Not a hopeful period "out", and yet it is the most hopeful of them all, for in it he at least took up some employment. His longest period "out" was in 1939-40, during which time he resided at Salvation Army hostels and other charitable institutions, but he has since then forcibly and frequently reiterated his objections to such places and flatly refuses to repeat the experience.

But comprehension of Alfred will never come from a study of his criminal and employment records : it is to be found in his medical history. In 1926 his deafness was such as to inconvenience him seriously and to cut him off from normal human relations—he is now stone deaf. Add to this that he is prematurely senile, with an intellect approaching mental deficiency, has a right inguinal hernia and a pronounced cardiac insufficiency, and one begins to understand his life. The last medical report on him, made in June 1948, states that " his health is only fair. There is a myocardial degeneration, heart sounds are impure with a systolic bruit. He gets occasional syncopal attacks. He will require care and medical supervision for the rest of his life. He is very deaf. He is of a very restless disposition and most unlikely to stay more than a few days in any outside hospital. He is unfit for work." Another doctor reported on Alfred in similar terms in 1946, but added the comment that " He has been in hospital for long periods during his sentence, when he is very well behaved, grateful for any attention, and quite inoffensive. Unless somebody is willing to look after him, I think preventive detention is the place for him : he needs care and supervision and is quite unfit to earn his own living. He seems perfectly happy in prison, but would soon return to crime if discharged."

Briefly to conclude Alfred's history. He is a solitary man both in and out of prison. When approached he is polite but childlike. He has always lived a sober life. Certainly since 1926 he has known no woman, and one gains the impression that this is true of the earlier period of his life. Since 1930 all prison governors and chaplains who have had Alfred under their care have recognised the hopelessness of his case. He is, of course, a very well-behaved prisoner.

Being what he is, Alfred is suited to preventive detention. Is preventive detention suited to the " Alfreds ", or, for that matter, is prison ?

BARMY

This prisoner is a most charming and entertaining man. He is now 65 years of age, jovial and popular, a small, white-haired man with a round, cherubic face and twinkling eyes—a figure in the prison and very proud of it. He is serving a sentence of three years' penal servitude and five years' preventive detention. In the course of his criminal career he has been convicted of indictable offences on twenty-nine occasions, and of summary offences (drunk, drunk and disorderly) on five occasions. There have never been any other offences taken into consideration. Such is his criminal record that it is best to consider it before anything else.

Date	Age	Offence(s)	Sentence	Days In	Out
Mar. '28	44	Larceny, motor rug	Bound over		186
Oct. '28	44	,, ,, ,,	1 month	29	30
Nov. '28	45	,, ,, ,,	1 month	30	63
Mar. '29	45	,, ,, ,,	2 months	52	77
July '29	45	Receiving	9 months	230	5
Mar. '30	46	Larceny, suit-case and contents	6 weeks	40	7
April '30	46	P. of C. Act	4 months	107	9
Aug. '30	46	Larceny, suit-case and contents	6 months	154	8
Jan. '31	47	Larceny, A.P.C.F.	12 months	310	5
Dec. '31	48	Larceny, suit-case and contents	6 months	154	24
May '32	48	P. of C. Act	3 months	77	41
Sept. '32	48	Larceny from unattended car	6 months	156	13
Mar. '33	49	Larceny of motor rug	4 months	103	29
July '33	49	Stealing bicycle, stealing book	6 and 1 month consecutively	182	22
Feb. '34	50	R. & V. ; loitering with intent	3 months	76	1
April '34	50	R. & V. ; loitering with intent	14 days	14	17
May '34	50	Larceny, A.P.C.F.	3 years' P.S.	824	23
Sept. '36	52	Receiving, A.P.C.F.	12 months and L.F.	545	35
April '38	54	Larceny, A.P.C.F.	18 months	547	128
Mar. '40	56	Larceny, motor rug	3 months	79	32
June '40	56	Larceny, attaché-case, contents	6 months	122	18
Nov. '40	57	Larceny, suit-case and contents	6 months	124	13
Mar. '41	57	Larceny, bicycle	6 months	127	6
Aug. '41	57	R. & V. ; loitering with intent	3 months	61	51
Nov. '41	58	Larceny, bicycle	6 months	122	8
April '42	58	Larceny, 2 parcels and contents	6 months	131	9
Aug. '42	58	Larceny, suit-case and contents	4 months	87	24
Dec. '42	59	Larceny, bicycle	6 months	123	105
July '43	59	Burglary and larceny ; being an habitual criminal	3 years' P.S. 5 years' P.D.		

His last two sentences were imposed in the provinces, all the rest by various courts in the Greater London area. His five summary convictions for drunkenness all precede 1934. None of his offences relates to property of much value, and, of course, he never uses violence, being of mild and gentle disposition. Broadly speaking, he has specialized on two types of crime throughout his career, namely, larceny from unattended motor cars (displaying in this pursuit a penchant for motor rugs), and larceny of suit-cases, parcels or bicycles from railway stations. Until this last crime, which was almost his first serious venture, he liked to refer to himself by the name of a London railway station, and this title was indeed attached to him by many prisoners and railway policemen. The offence which was rewarded by his present sentence involved property of little value and was only exceptional in that for the first time Barmy did not work alone but enticed a young naval rating with no previous convictions to accompany him on this burglarious exploit. So much for his criminal record—now let us consider what is known of the man.

He was born in London. His father was a professional soldier. Nothing else is known of his childhood and youth except that he attended a military school in London until the age of 14 years, when he enlisted as a band boy, serving until February 1902, when, aged 18, he was discharged as a band corporal with an exemplary record. On his discharge he was immediately employed as a porter at an army clothing depot for a period of twenty-four years. During this time he married, made a home, and reared, in quite comfortable circumstances, two sons who have proved themselves good, stable and successful citizens. Both sons have married, and Barmy is inordinately proud of them and of his grandchildren. During this twenty-four years of steady employment Barmy had no financial worries, for his income was supplemented by the money his wife earned in the skilled trade she practised.

In 1926 Barmy was discharged from his employment, the explanation in the firm's records for his dismissal being " reduction of staff ". He failed to obtain a permanent position, and from 1926 to the end of 1929 his only employment was as a porter with various furniture firms in London for brief periods during their summer sales in each of these four years. During this period he left home, deserted his wife, and gradually drifted into crime. His only other job since that date was from December 1939 until March 1940, when he served as a private in the army, being discharged when the military authorities became aware of his criminal record. The police succinctly describe his means of livelihood as " stealing, begging, and carrying luggage in the street."

As can be seen from his criminal record above, since 1928 he has spent very little time out of prison. He has never returned to his home, though until quite recently Barmy and his wife maintained an amicable correspondence, and she would send him those things which prisoners are allowed to receive. His wife has not suffered financially and has managed to support herself and their home. When out of prison Barmy lives in common lodging houses.

The senior medical officer at Parkhurst reported on Barmy's health to the advisory committee in June 1948 as follows : " His general health is only fair. He suffers from raised blood pressure and is fit for light labour only. He is a hypomanic type and at times is mentally unstable. He was certified insane about ten years ago. He is not insane at present." This certification occurred in 1938 whilst Barmy was serving a term of eighteen months, and he was removed to a civilian hospital. On the expiration of his sentence he was discharged from this hospital as having recovered.

It is perhaps his hypomania that makes him so popular amongst both prisoners and staff. His frequent wild talkative outbursts are characterised by an extremely rapid association link-up, many of these associations being amusing and most of them obscene. In prison such attributes combined with a genial and kindly nature are much valued. His letters also portray this instability—for example, one letter he wrote in 1944 was carefully surrounded by crosses representing barbed wire, many of the words were " covered off " in remembrance of his military service, and though no thought runs through any paragraph there is a continuous flow from one sentence to the next, usually hinging on a particular word in the preceding sentence.

Barmy's cell is a show-place. The conditions under which preventive detention is served have been outlined in chapter two, and Barmy has taken full advantage of these amenities. Not a patch of the wall is visible between the innumerable " pin-up girls "; his bed, chair and table are covered with multifarious, highly coloured and garish materials, as are some other odd pieces of furniture he has managed to put together. His wireless is in a large ugly cabinet on which he has placed a stand supporting four small coloured bulbs of different hue which can be attached to a battery, so that in the evenings he can put out the cell light, connect his coloured illuminations, turn on his radio, and imagine himself where he will. The general effect is really quite startling.

Though never in serious trouble with the prison authorities, Barmy is not infrequently charged with and convicted of prison offences. These, however, are never of a serious nature. For example, during this term he has been charged with six prison offences, and dealt with as follows :

1943	Obscene and threatening language to an officer	Close confinement 2 days ; loss of stage privilege 7 days ; loss of remission 4 days
1943	Failing to complete cell task	Dismissed
1943	Insolence and disrespect to an officer	Cautioned
1945	Obscene and threatening language to an officer	Admonished
1946	Improper remark to an officer	Cautioned
1946	Fighting with another prisoner	Penal grade 7 days

The advisory committee decided to release Barmy after he had served two-thirds of the five years of preventive detention. He was released before the end of 1948. This is not a follow-up study, and I have not investigated the question, but there is little doubt that shortly thereafter Barmy offered to carry someone's bags near a railway station and quickly disappeared, or in some similar fashion managed to find his way back to his home—prison.

ANGUS

Angus, a Scot of good physique and prosperous appearance, is at present serving a term of three years' penal servitude and seven years' preventive detention imposed in 1944, when he was charged with and convicted of four cases of larceny from dwelling-houses and of being an habitual criminal. Before being sentenced for the four larceny offences he requested that thirty other cases of larceny from dwelling-houses should be taken into consideration when he was sentenced. Of these thirty-four offences the first was committed on the eighteenth day after his release from a previous term of imprisonment, which had involved his passing 626 days in prison. The last of these offences was committed on the ninety-eighth day after his release and he was arrested on the 104th. Thus his thirty-four offences were spread over a period of eighty days. The last offence during this period was committed in an almost identical manner to that practised in the other thirty-three offences and, indeed, in all his offences committed since the end of 1938—107 in all. The method was as follows: In answer to her advertisement, " furnished room to let ", appearing in the window of a shop, Angus called on the prosecutrix and informed her that he had been bombed out of his room at Euston during a recent air raid. He gave a false name, inspected the room, came to terms with her, and moved in the next day. The following morning the prosecutrix went to work at 8.15 a.m., leaving Angus in the house. On her return at 12.45 p.m. she found that property to the total value of £15 was missing from various bedrooms, and so was Angus. On each occasion the property he takes in this way is worth about £10. He never uses brutality.

Angus's criminal record is :

				Days	
Date	Age	Offence(s)	Sentence	In	Out
Sept. '25	21	Larceny, motor cycle ; larceny, sweater	1 month	28	77
Jan. '26	21	Larceny, motor cycle ; false pretences	6 weeks	37	372
Mar. '27	22	Housebreaking and larceny (4 cases) ; housebreaking with intent	18 months	495	50
Aug. '28	24	Larceny (9 cases) ; breach of licence	12 months and L.F.	327	18
Aug. '29	25	Larceny (10 cases)	20 months	376	620
May '32	27	Larceny (5 cases)	3 years and deported	358	298
Feb. '34	29	False pretences, suits	3 months	77	16
May '34	29	Fraud (3 cases)	6 months	156	141
Mar. '35	30	Fraud (8 cases) ; theft from lodgings (8 cases) ; theft by opening lock-fast place	9 months	232	439
Jan. '37	32	Theft (18 cases) ; fraud (2 cases) ; attempted fraud	18 months	463	340
Mar. '39	34	Larceny, money, etc., in dwelling-house (3 cases) (70 similar cases T.I.C.)	4 years' P.S.	979	119
Mar. '42	37	Larceny, purse and contents in dwelling-house ; fraudulent conversion A.P.C.F.	15 months and L.F.	626	178
June '44	40	Larceny from dwelling-house (4 cases) (30 T.I.C.) ; being an habitual criminal	3 years' P.S. ; 7 years' P.D.		

His first two sentences were imposed on him by English courts, the next four by courts in various States of Australia, the next four by courts in Scotland, and the last three by English courts. Whenever he has remained " out " for any appreciable time (apart from one occasion dealt with hereunder) he has been moving from one country to another or from one State to another.

Angus was born in 1904. Until the age of 21 years he managed to avoid arrest, not by any display of honesty but because he was shielded by the large and relatively prosperous family of which he was the youngest member. Before Angus left home his father had become a justice of the peace. His brothers and sisters were also most respectable people. Indeed, in Angus's eyes, they were all overwhelmingly virtuous and he became, and has cheerfully remained, the black sheep.

In 1925, when he had attained his majority, Angus left home and travelled to the South of England. He took up no employment but relied on petty larceny for a meagre living. He was soon in the hands of the police. For his first offence Angus was sentenced to imprisonment, and no other method of punishment has ever been applied to him. When discharged from prison towards the end of 1925 he still avoided employment. After his discharge from prison in 1926 his family paid his fare to Australia, hoping to give him a chance to start his life afresh. But Angus avoided the " back-country " as he had avoided work, preferring the cities of Brisbane and Sydney. Here he again endeavoured to support himself by criminal activities, but again without success. In 1933, after serving a term of three years' imprisonment, he was deported from Australia to Scotland.

Angus did not inform his family of his return. In December 1933, after a very short acquaintance, he married a girl in Scotland. He did not inform her of the less edifying details of his past career, but led her to believe that he was a successful engineer with large engineering interests in the Antipodes. Angus, being fascinated by this ability to deceive others which he had thus fortuitously discovered within himself, turned from larceny to false pretences and petty fraud. In February 1934 he was arrested for an offence arising from his business relationship with his tailor, a relationship based entirely on Angus's false pretences. At the ensuing trial his wife learnt of his earlier criminal record. Apart from two brief meetings, in 1934 and in 1936, she has not seen him since that trial.

And so the pattern of Angus's days continued " in " and " out " until his discharge from prison towards the end of 1935. Then he returned to his family, who obtained employment for him and did their best to lead him away from his criminal career. For a time they succeeded. Employment was found for him with an iron foundry, and as this is the only employment Angus has ever enjoyed, or as he put it " endured ", it is interesting to note his employer's opinion of him. He reported that Angus was employed for nearly eight months at a salary of £2 5s. 6d. per week, that he started as an engineer's labourer, and when this was terminated became a warehouse labourer, and that " he has no trade, but has a ready brain and an uncanny ability of impressing anyone he comes in contact with. . . . He was not industrious, though he was honest and sober in his dealings with us. He left our employment of his own accord. In the latter part of his employment he was continually asking for afternoons off, and when he was refused he cleared off and did not return."

Not two months after Angus left his only employment he was back in prison again, and has since then made no attempt whatsoever to be anything but a petty thief.

When out of prison he wanders from one place to another with the sole purpose of committing crime, but the crimes he commits are of such a nature that they provide him with temporary lodgings. His good presence and glib tongue facilitate the commission of his offences, and by leading a sober life and sedulously avoiding the company of any person whom he knows has been in prison he has no difficulty in persuading lady householders that he is the perfect lodger. However, when out of prison, his avoidance of ex-prisoners and the peregrinations necessitated by his mode of life involve him in much loneliness ; and as he is a genial and gregarious type of man it may be wondered whether preventive detention is perhaps conducive to his greatest contentment, though of course he will not consciously subscribe to this view.

Since 1936 Angus has had no further contact with his family and now declares himself, quite falsely, to have no next-of-kin.

In prison Angus is well behaved, and is popular with prisoners and warders. Since 1940 he has been charged with prison offences on only four occasions, and dealt with as follows :

Feb. '40	Refusing labour	2 days' close confinement ; 2 days' No. 1 diet, 224 stage marks, 42 remission marks
Sept. '41	Contraband	Admonished
Dec. '44	Failing to have his black-out curtain drawn at the proper time	Non-earner one week
May '48	Improper remark to an officer	7 days' penal grade

Considering the time he spends in prison this is really a very good record and is indicative of a remarkable adaptation to prison conditions.

Angus is in sound physical condition, fit for class 1 labour. He suffers occasionally from dyspepsia. The only medically significant fact in his life is an operation on his cervical glands, performed on him at the age of six years. Were more known about this operation and about his early family relationships we would be in a better position to understand Angus's career.

To conclude Angus's history, the opinions of his recent prison governors and chaplains are presented :

Chaplains

1. 1941 " Capable of succeeding in work outside if he applies himself consistently to such effort."
2. 1944 " He is a persistent thief, and seems to have no desire to be anything else."

Governors and Deputy-Governors

1. 1939 " Intelligent type and should have no difficulty in obtaining employment."
2. 1941 " A persistent thief who is not likely to alter."
3. 1944 " Unlikely to reform. Very evasive when questioned. A criminal who has no interest in honest work."

Angus is a nuisance rather than a danger to society. He is intelligent and healthy. The expense of keeping him in prison has far exceeded the value of the property he has stolen. It does not seem impossible to devise means by which society could benefit from the existence of such men as Angus, or at least not suffer from it.

ARNOLD

Arnold was born in a Midland city in 1911 to middle-aged working-class parents. He was their second and last child, the first, a girl, having been born more than ten years earlier. Until 1924 Arnold's home life was unexceptional, the family living happily enough in marginal circumstances, and Arnold attending a council school. In 1924, however, Arnold's father died, his sister married and left home, and his mother took him with her to a new home. His mother, being now in very poor circumstances, and not being over-fond of Arnold, sent him to a boys' home, and later shifted him to another boys' home. In 1926 Arnold's mother died, and in June of that year he was transferred to a training colony, where he remained until January 1930. Whilst at the colony he worked well and gained a reputation for honesty and reliability.

From the above history it may be surmised that Arnold was an unwanted baby, and that during his youth he did not receive a great amount of loving care. Certainly his later career would lead one to include him in that group so well-defined by Dr. John Bowlby in *Forty-Four Juvenile Thieves*, namely, the " affectionless character ".

At the age of 18 years he left the training colony and went to live with his sister. Here he found employment for about three months at an iron and steel works, being discharged owing to shortage of work. Upon losing this job he left his sister's home and tramped the country for a month, taking odd jobs where he could find them and eventually returning to the training colony in June 1930, arriving there in a poor physical condition. The colony took him in and cared for him, and in November of the same year found employment for him on a farm. In this employment he remained for only two weeks, leaving of his own accord and returning to his sister's home. Three days later he recommenced his wanderings, but this time he took with him £2 16s. belonging to his brother-in-law. He has not seen his sister since then. For nearly three months he avoided arrest for this crime. His later career is best related to his criminal record, which is :

Date	Age	Offence(s)	Sentence	In	Days Out
Mar. '31	19	Larceny of £2 16s. cash	Probation (condition of residence in a home)		72
May '31	19	Larceny, driving licence, etc., from motor van (2 T.I.C. and breach of recognisances)	3 years' Borstal	872	555
April '35	23	On enclosed premises for unlawful purpose	1 day's imprisonment	1	32

Date	Age	Offence(s)	Sentence	Days In	Out
May '35	23	Shopbreaking and larceny, torch, etc. (2 T.I.C.)	9 months	247	118
May '36	24	Shopbreaking and larceny, money, etc. ; larceny, £9, from dwelling-house (4 T.I.C.)	18 months	475	77
Nov. '37	26	Larceny, 2 packets cigarettes from dwelling-house (3 T.I.C.)	9 months	234	62
Sept. '38	26	Burglary with intent ; burglary and larceny, money (4 T.I.C.)	18 months	456	41
Jan. '40	28	Officebreaking and larceny, money, A.P.C.F. (6 T.I.C.)	4 years' P.S.	993	38
Nov. '42	31	Burglary with intent(2 T.I.C.)	2 years and L.F.	819	88
May '45	36	Burglary (2 T.I.C.) ; being an habitual criminal	3 years' P.S. ; 5 years' P.D.; plus 140 days' P.S. remanent		

His longest period of freedom followed his release from Borstal towards the end of 1933. During this period he joined the army, absented himself without leave, was sentenced to fifty-six days' detention for so doing, and then settled down reasonably enough. In March 1935 he was granted a month's leave, and during this month he returned to barracks and stole clothing from a comrade. He then failed to report at the expiration of his leave, but commenced the life from which he has not later varied when " out "—tramping the country and relying on the commission of petty larcenies for sustenance. In April 1935, when he appeared in court, an officer from his regiment attended and informed the justices that the army did not want him back.

Since 1935 Arnold has had no employment whatsoever. When " out " he leads a sober, wandering life, awaiting opportunities for minor larcenies, and sure of his return to prison. He is not popular in prison and has no companions or associates when out of prison. This does not mean that he is actively disliked, but rather that he is a completely negative and dull individual.

None of the offences he commits is of any gravity, and his last offence is typical : he asked a widow, eighty years of age, who was sitting in the garden of her small country property, for a drink of water. She took pity on this tattered figure, took him into her house and gave him coffee, cake and cigarettes, and then sent him on his way. Later that night he returned, broke into her house without disturbing her, and stole property to a total value of £8. This offence was committed twenty-seven days after his release from prison, and was chronologically the third of the offences for which he was sentenced.

In his statement to the police when last arrested he told them " how much better off he is in prison ".

In prison he is and always has been well behaved, though in January 1947 he did involve himself in two minor prison offences—using obscene language to an officer and refusing labour. For the former he lost his week-end privileges for one week-end, for the latter he was put on No. 2 diet and denied associated labour for ten days and lost stage and remission. However, such occurrences are the trivia of prison life and do not controvert the statement that Arnold is a well-behaved prisoner.

Arnold is marked fit for class 1 labour and is in good general health. Throughout his prison sentences he has never been received into the prison hospital.

The comments of the prison governors and chaplains will complete this picture of Arnold :

Chaplains

1940	" A more than usually hopeful case."
1945	" Might make good."
1945	" Easy-going type, not much worried by this or past convictions. Has hopes that preventive detention may do him good ! "

Governors and Deputy-Governors

1942	" He is content to drift along in his present style. A thorough crook."
1945	" Very little hope of his making good."

The exclamation mark after the comment of the chaplain in 1945 points to the real crux of the problem that Arnold presents to society. Is this the best we can do with such a person ? When sentencing him to four years' penal servitude in 1940 the Recorder of a Borough Quarter Sessions pointed out to Arnold that he was one of the cases where every effort had been made to keep him straight, and expressed the hope that " a sentence of four years' penal servitude would have the effect of stopping him from committing further crime." It has not. In the present state of our knowledge, and readiness to apply it, only the slow passage of years has any chance of enabling Arnold to support himself outside an institution without reverting to crime. In the meantime can we not lessen the expense of maintaining Arnold and at the same time give him a chance of doing more worthwhile and profitable labour than twenty hours per week tagmaking ? Under supervision he is still a steady, honest and reliable worker, and there is no need of a wall to contain him.

ALBERT

In November 1943 a Court of Quarter Sessions convicted this man on three charges of obtaining money by false pretences and sentenced him to five years' penal servitude to be followed by five years' preventive detention. He appealed against this sentence, and in March 1944 the Court of Criminal Appeal reduced his penal servitude sentence to one of three years, leaving the preventive detention sentence unaltered. At this time he was 47 years of age. As well as the above terms of imprisonment he has to serve the remanet of a preventive detention sentence imposed in 1936. Throughout his criminal career he has been convicted no eleven occasions of indictable offences. He has been sentenced for thirty-one offences in all, including those " taken into consideration ".

Let us first consider the details of his criminal record :

Date	Age	Offence(s)	Sentence	Days In	Days Out
Sept. '21	25	Stealing motor cycle by trick	6 months	172	56
May '22	25	Stealing bicycle	6 months ⎱ consec-	237	57
May '22	25	Stealing bicycle	3 months ⎰ utively		
Feb. '23	26	Obtaining credit by fraud ; stealing £3 from lodgings ; stealing clothes from dwelling-house (4 T.I.C.)	21 months	522	79
Oct. '24	28	False pretences, food ; false pretences, £2	3 years' P.S.	822	102
April '27	30	False pretences, food; false pretences, cash	3 years' P.S. and L.F.	1,086	82
July '30	34	Obtaining credit by fraud, 2 cases	12 months and L.F.	515	27
Jan. '32	35	Stealing police uniform from lodgings (2 T.I.C.)	3 months and L.F.	145	42
July '32	36	Shopbreaking and larceny (8 T.I.C.)	5 years' P.S.	1,391	176
Oct. '36	40	Receiving stolen property ; habitual criminal	3 years' P.S. ; 5 years' P.D. and L.F.	2,380	166
Oct. '43	47	Obtaining money by false pretences, 3 cases ; habitual criminal	5 years' P.S. ; 5 years' P.D. and L.F.		

The police suspect him of many other offences besides those shown above.

He was born in a small town in the South of England. Very little is known of his life before he came into contact with the police in 1921 at the age of 25. He is, and always has been, very secretive about his youth. Nor is anything known about his family background, apart from the fact that he has a sister who still assists him financially. It appears, however, from fragments of his conversation, that he attended a council school until the age of 14 years, and that he then worked as an errand boy and later as a labourer in a steel works. He enlisted in the army during the 1914-18 war, saw service in France, and was eventually discharged with a good record. Towards the end of his military service he married. Two children were born of this marriage. To this point his story, as he tells it, is quite clear and not at all unusual. Then he becomes very vague, talking rather wildly about his wife and their separation, which apparently shortly preceded his first offence in 1921. All the blame, not only for the broken marriage but also for his criminal career is, of course, cast on her.

The above brief outline of his life up to 1921 is in no wise corroborated, but merely constitutes the more consistent details of the various stories he told me. The details of his life since September 1921 are much clearer and more certain.

As will be seen from the above table he has spent only 787 days out of prison since September 1921. Even that is an exaggerated period, because it takes no account of any time spent in prison after arrest awaiting trial. He has never enjoyed six consecutive months out of prison in these twenty-seven years. He has been employed but once, and that only for a period of twenty-four days (in 1943).

For the rest of the time he has lived on the proceeds of crime and the charity of his sister. In 1923-24 he switched from larceny to false pretences, and when at liberty thereafter travelled the country posing as a man of means and importance, obtaining his food and lodgings by false pretences and imposing on credulous people whenever possible for small amounts of money. During his periods of liberty in 1932 and 1936, though continuing the above pose, he has gained his livelihood more by housebreaking than false pretences. He was last discharged from prison in April 1943, and employment was found for him as an engineer's labourer with a firm of constructional engineers at a weekly wage of £4 10s. per week. He remained in this employment for three and a half weeks, and then left without notice, immediately resuming his life of crime.

There is nothing unusual about his methods of committing crimes. The three offences for which he was last convicted involved three false cheques, two for £5 each, which he cashed with tradesmen, and one for £6, for which he obtained goods to the value of £2 2s. and £3 18s. in cash. All these transactions took place on the same day. Immediately after committing these three offences he left the district. As a convict on licence he should have notified his change of address. This, not surprisingly, he did not do.

As the time he spends in prison increases, so his behaviour therein improves. From being a very troublesome prisoner he has become a reasonably well-behaved one. At no stage, however, was he violent, and his prison offences have never been serious. During the present sentence of preventive detention he has twice been punished, once for disobedience and once for tampering with his cell in an unauthorised way.

During this present sentence he has assiduously studied a correspondence course on radio technology and has shown himself to be both capable and intelligent. Preventive detainees are allowed their own radios in their cells, and this prisoner has himself built a really excellent set. This is the one ray of hope in the inevitable prognosis of a continuing criminal career. He feels that there may be a chance of " going straight ". In this regard it will be appropriate to reproduce a report on Albert sent to the Prison Commissioners and thence to the Home Office. Such reports are prepared for every preventive-detention prisoner shortly before two-thirds of the preventive-detention sentence has been served, and it is one of the factors considered by the Home Secretary in deciding when the prisoner shall be licensed. When these reports leave the prison they include the comments of the governor, the medical officer, the chaplain and the advisory committee. The reports of these authorities on Albert were as follows :

Governor

" An emotional and unstable man with a degree of low cunning in his make-up. Fairly hardened in his ideas and outlook, but he is a satisfactory worker and is capable of making an effort on his release from prison."

Medical Officer

" He is in poor health and is a patient in hospital under treatment for thyrotoxicosis. He is emotionally unstable, but shows no sign of insanity or mental deficiency. He should be fit for light work on discharge."

Chaplain

" Somewhat neurotic, nevertheless a shrewd character, with a knowledge which he is ready to turn to his own advantage. In prison has studied all things connected with wireless in a thorough manner. It seems to me that the outstanding cause of all his past failures is outstanding vanity, and love of an easy life."

Advisory Committee

" During this, his second period of preventive detention, he has worked well and his spare time has been devoted to the study of wireless. He now appears to appreciate the uselessness of the kind of life that brings him to prison and hopes to apply his knowledge of wireless to earn an honest living in future. The committee recommend that he be released on licence in —— (the date when he has served two-thirds of his sentence)."

ARCHY

Archy is 59 years of age, 4 ft. 10 in. high and very slight. He is a sprightly and amusing fellow, popular with his fellow prisoners as well as with the prison officers.

Archy was born in a Midland town. His father owned a reasonably profitable business but occasionally found himself in prison for receiving stolen property. Nothing else is known of Archy's early environment. He attended a council school until 14 years of age, and then worked as an errand boy at a store for twelve months until he received his first prison sentence of fourteen days for two cases of larceny. He then hawked firewood, using a horse and cart which his father bought him, and this and begging constituted his form of livelihood until the 1914-18 war. In 1911, aged 19, he married. His criminal record until his enlistment in the army is as follows :

| | | | | | Days | |
Date	Age	Offence(s)	Sentence		In	Out
Dec. '05	15	Larceny (2 cases)	14 days		14	87
Mar. '06	16	Larceny, 131 lb. of worsted tabs	4 months		111	140
Dec. '06	16	Larceny, 11 gold rings	3 months		79	550
Aug. '08	18	Larceny, cake of tobacco	2 months		51	65
Dec. '08	18	Frequenting	3 months		76	1,347
Nov. '12	22	Begging—rogue and vagabond	2 months		58	2,481

As well as the above six sentences he was twice sentenced to imprisonment between 1908 and 1914 for begging, but the dates of these sentences and the terms imposed are not known.

He enlisted shortly after the outbreak of war in 1914 and saw service overseas, eventually being discharged with a " good " character in September 1919. By this time Archy and his wife had four children—three boys and one girl—and when his army pay and allowances stopped life became very difficult for them. Finally, in 1920, Archy deserted his family and since then has not contributed to their maintenance.

Archy's post-war history is closely related to his post-war criminal record, which is as follows :

Date	Age	Offence(s)	Sentence	Days In	Days Out
Oct. '19	29	Larceny, rolls of cloth (4 cases)	41 days		
Oct. '19	29	Larceny, cloth from shop (value £10 13s. 6d.)	4 months consecutively	123	241
Oct. '20	30	Shopbreaking and larceny, A.P.C.F. (value £15 8s. 1d.)	12 months	317	172
Mar. '22	32	P. of C. Act, on enclosed premises (3 cases)	9 months	227	80
Jan. '23	33	Larceny, diamond ring (value £45)	3 years' P.S.	837	124
Aug. '25	35	Convict failing to report	3 months	80	22
Dec. '25	35	Convict failing to report	6 months	152	59
July '26	36	Larceny, money and cheque from till, A.P.C.F. (22 T.I.C.)	3 years' P.S.	821	115
Jan. '29	39	Housebreaking and larceny (2 cases), A.P.C.F.	5 years' P.S. and L.F.	1,674	70
Nov. '33	43	Larceny, cashbox, etc., from office, A.P.C.F. (2 T.I.C.)	15 months and L.F.	693	13
Oct. '35	45	Larceny, cheque from hotel (5 T.I.C.)	6 months ; L.R.	245	36
July '36	46	Shopbreaking with intent, A.P.C.F. (8 T.I.C.)	12 months	324	31
July '37	47	False pretences	3 months	83	140
Feb. '38	48	Housebreaking and larceny (2 cases) ; housebreaking with intent (3 cases) ; being an habitual criminal (36 T.I.C.)	5 years' P.S. and 5 years' P.D. Sentence of P.D. quashed by C.C.A.	1,257	78
Oct. '41	51	Housebreaking and larceny (4 T.I.C.)	6 months and L.F.	514	311
Jan. '44	54	Larceny (2 cases) (34 T.I.C.) ; being an habitual criminal	5 years' P.S. and 5 years' P.D.		

During that time he has also twice been sentenced to terms of imprisonment for begging—dates of these sentences and the terms imposed are not known.

None of the above offences relates to property of any great value, and his biggest single " haul " was in 1923 when he managed to steal a diamond ring worth £45. He has never used any brutality in the commission of his offences.

The police description of his qualities is : "Moderate drinker. Confirmed criminal and steals at every opportunity. Seldom tries to get work. Associates with thieves."

All thirty-six of the offences for which he was last sentenced were larcenies from hotels or lodgings and were committed over a period of three and a half months in company with a young woman with whom he was living. She also had a long criminal record at this time. They would register under a false name at an hotel, or rent lodgings, and leave after a few days, taking with them property from their own room and from neighbouring rooms which could be entered without the necessity of breaking the lock. The total value of all property stolen in these thirty-six offences was about £800.

When " out " Archy usually stays at fairly good hotels, living with a woman, for he is, in his own phrase, " a great one with the ladies ", and spends the proceeds of his crimes as quickly as possible. His last period of freedom was the most industrious of his adult life. He was discharged from prison in March 1943. Five days after his discharge he obtained employment in a United States Army officers' club as a waiter, and this job he retained for a month before he was discharged when enlisted men were substituted for civilians. For this month he worked as a kitchen porter and lived with a woman also working at the club, and throughout this time he was honest and regarded as a reliable worker. He was then employed for ten days in an hotel as a waiter, and then three weeks in another hotel, also as a waiter. From both these jobs he was dismissed following dissension between Archy and the rest of the staff. He then obtained employment as a kitchen porter at a Y.M.C.A. institution, and this job he retained, giving satisfaction, until July 1943. He then met the woman with whom he committed the thirty-six larcenies, left his employment of his own accord, and resumed an active criminal career. When he was sentenced as an habitual criminal to preventive detention he was incensed, as he thought his employment protected him absolutely from this. He genuinely believes that he was " framed " and that the police and the judge combined to suppress his employment record. Actually it was very favourably presented. This blow has turned him finally against work. If it cannot protect you from preventive detention, what can it do ?

During other periods " out " he has rarely taken up employment, and has never retained it for more than a few days.

Archy has not the ability for anything but manual labour. He has had heart disease and kidney disease in the past, and his present mild heart disease and cardiac insufficiency, when combined with his diminutive stature, render him fit for class 2 labour only, and would seriously hinder him in any endeavour to earn his living by honest work, even were he so minded.

In prison he has a long record of minor offences, the intramural complement of his extramural activities. He is constantly involved in tobacco dealings, and not being very subtle is regularly discovered. Most of his prison offences relate to contraband, though until the " cell task " ceased to be a part of prison routine he was frequently in trouble for failing to complete it.

Finally the opinions of governors and chaplains on Archy :

Chaplains

1933   " A merry soul and quite unreliable."
1938   " Will return to prison."
1944   " Confirmed criminal."

Governors

1933   " Well behaved and cheery—will return again and again."
1938   " I doubt whether he will ever get on when at liberty."
1944   " An old hand who has few regrets and no scruples. He will always be a
         nuisance to society."

ALAN

Until the age of 22 years Alan did not come into contact with the police. As he professes amnesia about his early life I could discover nothing definite about his childhood and youth. Certainly when he first came before the courts in 1920, aged 22, he was scholastically well up to standard and of good intelligence. He had been reared by a couple in fairly comfortable surroundings in the East End of London, having been adopted by them at about the age of 5 years.

Upon leaving school at the age of 16 years he had been apprenticed to a barber and had applied himself industriously and to the general satisfaction of his master and his " parents ". He then joined the army and saw service in France, receiving gun-shot wounds in the back lumbar region (bilateral) in 1917, and being discharged from the army with an exemplary character in 1919. He returned to his profession and enjoyed steady employment with good prospects of eventually owning his own business. Early in 1920 he was engaged to be married. Then came the first break in his apparently satisfactory career.

In a jealous quarrel with his fiancée he became very violent and wounded her most grievously. For this offence he was sentenced to a term of three years' penal servitude. The governor and chaplain of the prison to which he was sent were in agreement in their reports on him, the former stating that there was " no reason why he should return. A very decent type. Not a criminal ", and the latter affirming that " this crime was the outcome of jealousy and he is not a criminal."

Now let us consider his criminal record in the light of the above :

				Days	
Date	Age	Offence(s)	Sentence	In	Out
July '20	22	Wounding	3 years' P.S.	826	317
Sept. '23	25	Larceny, two shillings from gas meter	Bound over	—	609
May '25	26	Larceny, cakes, etc., from billiard hall	Bound over	—	67
July '25	27	Sacrilege (2 cases) ; storebreaking and larceny, A.P.C.F.	3 years' P.S.	826	189
April '28	29	Sacrilege ; storebreaking and larceny ; pavilionbreaking and larceny, A.P.C.F.	18 months and L.F.	659	19
Mar. '30	31	Larceny, cigarettes from machine	6 months and L.F.	222	66
Dec. '30	32	Storebreaking and larceny (2 cases) ; possessing housebreaking implements ; schoolbreaking and larceny, A.P.C.F. (2 T.I.C.)	18 months ⎫ ⎬ ⎭	870	53
Feb. '31	32	Housebreaking and larceny (value £250) (5 T.I.C.)	3 years' P.S. concurrently		
June '33	35	Pavilionbreaking and larceny (2 cases), A.P.C.F. (3 T.I.C.)	4 years' P.S. and L.F.	1,296	159

Date	Age	Offence(s)	Sentence	Days In	Out
June '37	39	Possessing housebreaking implements ; larceny, tools from factory ; pavilionbreaking and larceny ; officebreaking and larceny, A.P.C.F. (5 T.I.C.)	18 months and L.F.	784	112
Dec. '39	41	Larceny, coin box and cash from telephone booth (3 cases) (5 T.I.C.) ; receiving	3 years' P.S.	821	118
July '42	44	Larceny, from telephone booth as above, A.P.C.F. ; possessing housebreaking implements by night	18 months and L.F.	539	144
May '44	46	Larceny, from telephone booth as above (3 cases) ; being an habitual criminal	3 years' P.S. ; 5 years' P.D.		

It will be seen that, including those offences " taken into consideration ", he has been sentenced in respect of fifty-seven offences, mostly of a fairly serious nature, and that since 1939 he has been specialising in stealing money from telephone coin-boxes. His method subsequent to his release in December 1943 was to remove the entire coin-box while another man, also with a criminal record, remained outside the booth keeping watch. When arrested Alan was with this other man and in their possession was found one coin-box recently stolen, and a quantity of tools with which they were endeavouring to cut a key to fit the lock of the cash containers in telephone booths, thus hoping to expedite and facilitate their future activities. In his statement to the police Alan admitted some sixty other such offences, but he declined to have them taken into consideration when he was sentenced. There is no doubt that he was responsible for them, and, in fact, he assisted the police in recovering several damaged coin-boxes he had stolen and then left in a bombed house.

Presumably, if there is such a person as a professional criminal, Alan must be so classified. Certainly he has not fulfilled the promise he showed to his first prison governor and chaplain, and it is interesting to note the opinions of governors and chaplains under whose control he subsequently found himself :

1925	Chaplain	" Rather hardened and calculating but there is some chance for him."
1929	Governor	" I think he means to make a real effort to go straight."
1931	Governor	" Now offers little prospect of refraining from crime."
	Chaplain	" A totally irresponsible fellow."
1936	Chaplain	" I believe he will make some effort and keep straight."
1939	Governor	" He has got used to the idea that there is not much hope for him and has ceased to concern himself about it."
	Chaplain	" I doubt if he will ever make good. Himself says—I'll probably be back."

1941	Chaplain	" A hardened criminal who boasts that he does quite well in prison."
1944	Governor	" Thoroughly institutionalised. Says he finds it easier to settle down in prison than outside."
	Chaplain	" Has no plans for the future—quite satisfied and resigned to die in prison."

When first released from prison in 1922 Alan did not return to his " parents ", but took up residence in a furnished room in London. Employment was found for him as a barber and at first he appeared to settle down well enough. Not long afterwards he married and went to live with his wife's parents. Two children were born of this marriage, but the marriage itself was far from a happy one, and early in 1924 he deserted his wife, child and baby, and has not since then lived with them. Nevertheless until 1942 Alan and his wife corresponded, and it appears that she has managed to rear their two children as best she could. Now he is out of touch with her and does not even know her whereabouts. There has been no separation order or divorce. Since leaving his wife he has resided either in prison or common lodging houses, and has enjoyed no extramural fixed abode.

For a few months after his discharge from prison in 1922 he worked as a hairdresser, then left this employment for some reason which I could not discover, and soon was convicted of stealing two shillings from a gas meter. He was bound over and again employment with a hairdresser was found for him. Again he appeared to be making good, married and became quite industrious. Then again he dropped this employment, took a job with another barber, then tried his hand at labouring, and so the unsettling process continued until crime became his avocation. From petty larceny he progressed to sacrilege and breaking into various buildings and stealing therein, and this continued until 1937. In 1930 he tried his hand at stealing from a machine, and as from 1939 he has applied the technique then practised, and the experience he early gained with gas meters, to telephone coin-boxes. In the periods after discharge from prison and before the recommencement of a criminal life he has had various jobs as a hairdresser and as a labourer, but with the passing years these have gradually become more transitory. For example, after his discharge in August 1939 he worked with a hairdresser for exactly two days, being paid £1 for his services. He left of his own accord, and took up no other employment. He invariably associates with criminals and lives exclusively on the proceeds of crime.

Alan is a very well-behaved prisoner indeed and gets on almost too well with the staff. (The chaplain's comment in 1941 is very relevant here.) During this term of imprisonment he has only once been before the governor on a charge and that was for fighting with another preventive detainee, for which offence he was cautioned. In 1940-1, however, his contraband dealings became rather too much for him and were discovered, and in a period of months he received three quite severe punishments which culminated in forty-nine days spent in solitary confinement. This brought him to an hysterical condition, and one evening he swallowed a fork, part of a knife and the handle of a spoon. All these objects were vomited or passed rectally. For this swallowing he was punished, and during this later period of separate confinement he swallowed a needle, a thimble and two pieces of glass. Again no operation was necessary. In a letter he wrote to his wife about this time he rationalized these ingurgital exercises in the words, " I have attempted to kill myself by swallowing a needle, thimble and two bits of glass unfortunately all these passed right through me, except the needle a part of it came back up my throat a day or two after swallowing it. It appears you can't kill yourself by doing this. You cannot realise what it means to be shut away from everybody day after day. . . . To lose the goodwill of everybody is the thing that is driving me nuts." This letter was, of course, suppressed.

This ostrich-like behaviour was the only occasion on which he has manifested any symptoms of psychiatric disability, and there is no doubt that he is quite sane in the medico-legal use of that term. His only physical disability is hæmorrhoids, for which he has been twice operated on under general anæsthetic during this sentence in Parkhurst.

That, then, is as much as is known of Alan. No better illustration can be found of the difficulty of dealing with such men in the present state of our understanding of them.

CHAPTER SEVEN

THIRTY-TWO PREVENTIVE DETAINEES

THIS chapter will be divided into three sections. In the first we shall analyse the records of the preventive detainees; in the second, consider the degree to which they severally and collectively concentrate on specific offences—the specificity of their recidivism—and the sequence of types of crime in the development of their careers—criminal maturation; and in the third, discuss the deterrent effect of punishment on this group. The second and third sections will be of interest both as a detailed analysis of a limited class of offenders (even though the findings will be of little scientific validity for application to a wider category of offenders) and as an introduction to the similar techniques which will be applied in Chapter VIII to the consideration of the records of 270 confirmed recidivists.

For purposes of comparison, certain statistics relating to Belgian[1] and Finnish[2] preventive detainees will be presented in footnotes.

The inquiry here undertaken must not be regarded as purely, or even primarily, historical; for the preventive detention of the future will have similar problems to solve.

1. ANALYSIS OF THE GROUP

During the week ending October 16th, 1948, there were thirty-two men undergoing preventive detention in England and Wales. Against a general population exceeding forty-eight million and a prison population then exceeding twenty thousand, the number of thirty-two provokes inquiry. What particular and peculiar characteristics had a man to possess before he was included in this group ?

---

[1] H. Bekaert, " L'application de la loi de Défense Sociale du 9 avril 1930, aux récidivistes et délinquants d'habitude," Louvain, 1936. This article also appeared in the *Revue de Droit Pénal et de Criminologie*, 1936, pp. 837 and 1019.

[2] *Recueil de Documents en Matière Pénale et Pénitentiaire*, Vol. XIII, Bk. 1, September 1947, pp. 5-14 : an article by A. P. Arvelo, Director-General of Penal Administration, Helsinki.

We shall seek to answer this question by considering the characteristics of our group of preventive detainees ; and by applying the same analytic methods to both we shall prepare the ground for the comparison of that group with the confirmed recidivists next to be considered.

For both groups, the following information is presented in this and the succeeding chapter[1] under the heading " Analysis of the Group ":

Last offences and their means of commission
All offences in respect of which they have been convicted
Previous sentences
Age :
    (1) When last sentenced
    (2) When first sentenced
    (3) When first sentenced to Borstal
    (4) When first sentenced to prison
    (5) When first sentenced to penal servitude
Place of birth
International criminals
Early environment
Industrial history
    (a) Skilled, semi-skilled or unskilled
    (b) Longest period in any one employment since 1930
    (c) Employed or unemployed when last crime committed
    (d) Own description of trade or occupation (and its accuracy)
    (e) Employment on leaving school
Military record
Home conditions immediately before this sentence
Marital status : Disposition of children
Honesty : Sobriety : Companions and associates
Physical condition
Mental condition and intellectual ability
Prison behaviour and escaping
Religious persuasion and conversions
Tattooing
Aliases
Summary

Last Offences and their Means of Commission

The following are the last offences committed by our thirty-two

---

[1] Information regarding the present sentences and prison employment of the confined recidivist group is also presented in Chapter VIII ; it has already been given for the preventive detainees in Chapter II.

criminals—the offences which led to their preventive detention in October 1948:

Burglary and housebreaking		19
False pretences and larceny by a trick :		
Based on : False cheques	1	
Housing shortage	2	
Presents to relatives overseas	2	
Whisky shortage	1	
		— 6
Larceny from telephone kiosks		1
Larceny from dwelling-houses, lodgings, hotels, etc. ..		4
Larceny of bicycles from the street		1
Forgery of Post Office money orders		1
		— 32

Twenty-seven committed their offences alone; five in company with others, as follows:

    2 co-operated in one larceny from a dwelling-house
    1 was assisted by an ex-convict
    1 was assisted by a woman with whom he was living
    1 was helped by a young naval rating with no previous convictions

Accordingly, only two could be said to have led anyone astray in the commission of their last offences.

All the false pretences, larcenies by tricks and forgery offences relate to property of negligible value, though some of the false pretences and larcenies by tricks were perpetrated at the expense of people who could ill afford the loss which ensued.

In all the above list, only thirteen relate to property of any appreciable value, viz.:

    9 were convicted of quite ordinary housebreakings or burglaries in which whatever was lying about the premises broken into was taken
    1 was convicted of three housebreakings in which £700 worth of property was taken
    1 was convicted of thirty-six larcenies of property to the total value of £800, and
    1 was convicted of extensive larcenies from telephone booths

Thus, three of our group were convicted of offences involving property of considerable value; nine of offences involving property of some value; and twenty of offences involving property of very little value—a maximum of £5.

Nor did their last arrests occasion the police any great difficulty.

They are all well known—many almost affectionately—to the police, and there was rarely any trouble involved in catching them once they reverted to crime. Indeed, several members of our group made very little attempt to avoid arrest—for example, one prisoner entered an open window of a dwelling-house, picked up some articles of clothing, chanced to disturb the occupier of the premises, and said to him, " All right, mister, I don't mean any harm ", and having calmed him awaited the arrival of the police, making no attempt to escape (though this would have been easy); another attended his sister's funeral (his last surviving relative) well knowing that the police would meet him there, and cheerfully submitted to arrest, the police kindly waiting until the ceremonies were concluded. In both these cases, and in many others, one feels that for these men extra-mural life has become too much of a strain, and that prison is the only life to which they have been trained, and in which they find security. Consciously or unconsciously they desire it. But are they " dangerous ", " professional " criminals ?

Considering only their last offences, we can say that our preventive detainees did not threaten society with any offence of a public nature nor with any offences to the person. Their crimes all related to property, and, except in the cases of three of them, did not involve property of any great value. In short, they were nuisances rather than serious dangers to society.[1] Let us see if this is true of all

---

[1] For comparative purposes, here are some Finnish figures relating to the same question, and taken from p. 10 of A. P. Arvelo's article cited above. They concern 199 Finnish preventive detainees : " Les dernières infractions des internées, celles qui les conduisirent dans la maison de sûreté, étaient :

le vol	dans 158 cas
le vol et le vol avec violence	,, 4 ,,
le vol et le vol avec effraction	,, 3 ,,
le vol et l'escroquerie	,, 1 ,,
le vol, le vol avec effraction, le vol avec violence et les voies de fait	,, 2 ,,
le vol et les voies de fait	,, 3 ,,
l'effraction	,, 2 ,,
le vol avec violence	,, 8 ,,
le vol avec violence et les voies de fait	,, 1 ,,
les voies de fait .. .. .. ┬.	,, 10 ,,
le meurtre	,, 4 ,,
l'attentat à la pudeur	,, 3 ,,
	199

Thus specialisation on less serious property offences is also a characteristic of Finnish preventive detainees ; though in Finland proportionately more prisoners whose offences involve violence to the person find themselves in preventive detention than do similar criminals in England.

their offences, and not only of those committed prior to their last sentences.

All Offences in respect of which they have been convicted

Our thirty-two preventive detainees have been convicted in the course of their careers of a total of 1,085 crimes. These do not include the 1,984 offences which were " taken into consideration " when they were sentenced.

As we shall use Table A (see pages 298-299) in other contexts, and for other purposes, the offences committed are shown for each detainee separately. Table A classifies all their offences in accordance with the classification adopted in the Annual Criminal Statistics, and the numbers in the first column which precede the brief description of the type of offence refer to that classification.

It will be seen that the totality of the offences of our " 32 " reveals no more serious a pattern of crime than did the last offences they committed, the concentration of offences still being on burglary, housebreaking and minor larcenies. Again, though this does not appear from Table A, offences in which property of much value was involved were exceptional.

Having considered their offences, let us advert to their previous sentences, not including their present sentences to penal servitude and preventive detention.

Previous Sentences

We shall consider only those sentences imposed pursuant to conviction for indictable offences and for " non-indictable offences akin to indictable offences " (as listed in the Annual Criminal Statistics). Thus we will exclude sentences pursuant to vagrancy-type and other minor offences.[1]

[1] Fourteen of the " 32 " have been previously convicted of " other non-indictable offences ", as follows :

once	..	..	..	..	3 prisoners
twice	..	..	..	..	1 prisoner
three times	..	..	..	..	4 prisoners
five times	,.	..	..	..	2 ,,
six times	..	..	..	..	2 ,,
seven times	..	..	..	..	1 prisoner
nine times	..	..	..	..	1 ,,

This gives a total of 55 such convictions.

	1	2	3	4	5	6	7	8	9	10	11	12
INDICTABLE OFFENCES												
5 Wounding				1								
16 Unnatural offences												
17 Indecent assault on boy												
Importuning male person												
27-33 Burglary, housebreaking, etc.	16	1	1	18	6	17	7	10	2	10	2	5
37-43 Aggravated larcenies		3			35	1	2	2	9	1	3	
44-9 Simple and minor larcenies	6	3	22	10	27	3	2	14	10	9	19	17
50 Obtaining by false pretences		7			16			1	6		2	
51-3 & 55 Other frauds		3										
54 Receiving stolen goods		1	2	1								
57 Other malicious injuries to property												
58 & 59 Forgery												
60 & 61 Coining												
NON-INDICTABLE OFFENCES AKIN TO INDICTABLE OFFENCES												
103-5 Assaults												
109 Cruelty to children												
139 Indecent exposure												
149 Malicious damage						1						
167 Prevention of Crimes Act			4		1	4		2	1		1	
176-80 & 183 Stealing, unlawful possession, etc.									1			
188, 189 Frequenting, on enclosed premises	1					2	1	4				1
OTHER NON-INDICTABLE OFFENCES												
122-38 Highway Acts												
140-1 Intoxicating liquor laws			5							6		
163-6 Poor Law						1						
171 Railway offences												
185 Begging			1						5			1
186 Sleeping out	4					2						
191 Other vagrancy offences	1											
201, etc. Other offences											3	
TOTAL	28	18	35	30	85	31	12	38	35	20	30	24
Offences " taken into consideration "	50	14	—	27	100	56	26	111	77	33	12	74
GRAND TOTAL	78	32	35	57	185	87	38	149	112	53	42	98

The offence of " being an habitual

Foreign offences are fitted as nearly as possible into the above classification. 201, etc., " Other

A

13	14	15	16	17	18	19	20	21	22	23	24	25	26	27	28	29	30	31	32	Totals	No. of offenders involved
																				1	1
																				1	1
					1															1	1
															1					1	1
6	7			19		7		7		13		16		28	1		1	16	11	241	24
1	8			2		3		7	3	7	22	1	2			6	15	7	2	116	20 ⎫
8	8	19	141	2	17	4	11	17	9	3	12		3	5	2	11	3	1	3	274	31 ⎬ 31
4					7	2	10		1		5		21		3	13	12			268	17
1		6			2	7			8	1			3			15	1			50	10
			2	2									2							10	7
						9			2									2		13	3
		1															1			2	2
	1																			1	1
	1																			1	1
											1									2	2
2			1							2			3		2		1	4		28	13
																				1	1
							1						1							11	7
						2														2	1
																				11	2
	8																			9	2
													8							9	2
																		1		8	4
																	1			6	2
										1							2	1		5	4
	1					1	1		2	1			2					2		13	8
22	26	26	143	26	26	17	40	33	25	28	40	33	29	37	24	35	37	36	16	1,085	32
95	51	294	57	17	58	22	59	70	46	56	108	3	256	—	12	143	21	9	27	1,984	
117	77	320	200	43	84	39	99	103	71	84	148	36	285	37	36	178	58	45	43	3,069	

criminal " is not included above.

offences " include " summary convictions " of which details are not given in the criminal's record.

The number of such sentences for our " 32 " is as follows:

Probation, Bound over, Probation of Offenders Act	28
Approved school	8
Borstal detention	7
Imprisonment	326
Penal servitude	92
Preventive detention	13[1]
Fined	3
A total of	477

From this table it appears that the average previous penal record of the members of our group (incurred subsequent to the commission of criminal offences of a more serious nature) is as follows

	Number of Previous Sentences
Probation, bound over, Probation of Offenders Act	·875
Approved school	·25
Borstal detention	·22
Imprisonment	10·19
Penal servitude	2·875
Preventive detention	·41
Fined	·09
A total of	14·91

Also, this mythical average member of our group has been sentenced 1·72 times pursuant to " other non-indictable offences ".

Later we shall compare the above average record with the average penal record of the members of our confirmed recidivist group. For the present purpose, the most significant features to note in the above record are the relatively low figure for previous sentences of Borstal detention, and the relatively high figure for previous sentences of preventive detention. The former demonstrates society's failure to make adequate efforts to reform these prisoners ; the latter reflects the greater facility of securing a conviction as an habitual criminal on one who had previously been sentenced to preventive detention. This figure (·41) does not include two detainees whose previous

---

[1] There were also two other sentences of preventive detention imposed which were quashed by the Court of Criminal Appeal.

sentences of preventive detention were quashed on appeal to the Court of Criminal Appeal. Apportioning the previous sentences of preventive detention to the respective members of our group we find that :

9 of them had been previously so sentenced once
2 ,, ,, ,, ,, ,, ,, ,, twice (and that
2 of them after having been so sentenced had their sentences quashed by the Court of Criminal Appeal)

Accordingly, thirteen of the " 32 " had been previously sentenced as habitual criminals, and eleven had previously served terms of preventive detention.

Age

Computing their respective ages on October 16th, 1948, to the nearest month, I found a range of from 37 years to 65 years 10 months. The average was 50 years 9 months, with a standard deviation of 8 years 1 month. Such a range and such a standard deviation leads to the conclusion that providing a criminal was over 40 years of age, his age, *per se*, was not of great relevance to the likelihood of his receiving a sentence of preventive detention.

Age when first sentenced [1]

Here the range was from 13 to 44 years; the average being 20 years 8 months, and the standard deviation from this average 7 years 2 months. No significant conclusion can be drawn from such figures, though they do cast some slight doubt on the oft-suggested criminal precocity of habitual criminals.[2] But, on the

---

[1] Including truancy and " care and protection " cases.

[2] Similar information is given concerning the Belgian preventive detainees by M. H. Bekaert on pp. 10 and 11 of the article cited above. From the data he presents I have calculated the range, average and standard deviation of ages at which his 181 Belgian detainees were first sentenced by a criminal court, the results being :

range	10 years to 59 years
average	21 years
standard deviation from that average ..	7·96 years

Thus the Belgian experience tends to confirm our doubts as to the precocity of habitual criminality—the close relationship between these figures and those of our group being very striking.

The Finnish data is not sufficiently complete for comparison on this point ; but on p. 9 of the Finnish report it is stated that " environ 80 per cent. de ces récidivistes avaient commis leur première infraction avant d'avoir accompli leur vingtième année." This would indicate an earlier confirmed criminal record on the part of the Finnish habitual criminals.

other hand, as we shall see later, our group is not truly representative of habitual criminals defined in any way except as
under the Prevention of Crime Act, 1908 ; and therefore we
must, until we have considered the confirmed recidivist group,
defer judgment on this question of the criminal precocity of
habitual criminals.[1]

Age when first sentenced to Prison or Borstal

The range was from 15 to 44 years ; the average age at the time
of the first sentence of this type being 22 years, the standard deviation
from this average 6 years 3 months. Again, no significant conclusions can be drawn from these figures.

Only seven of the " 32 " had been sentenced to Borstal
detention; four before they received sentences involving imprisonment, and three after they had been discharged from
a prison. Two of the latter were committed to Borstal at the
same age as when sentenced to imprisonment; and the third
youth had been to prison twice—once at seventeen years, once
at eighteen years—before he was sent to Borstal at the age of
nineteen years.[2]

Age when first sentenced to Penal Servitude

Here we are considering the age when members of our group
received, as adults, their first substantial term of detentive punishment; for the new Act a comparable inquiry will be the age of
preventive detainees when they were first sentenced to corrective
training.

All " 32 " detainees had served at least one such term before a
sentence of preventive detention was imposed on them. The range
of the ages when such previous sentences were imposed is from 22
years to 50 years, the average age being 30 years and 7½ months, with
a standard deviation of 6 years 8 months.

Thus, the average member of our group did not receive a
sentence of sufficient length for any constructive training to be

---

[1] Obviously neither the Belgian nor the English figures take into consideration
undetected criminal precocity. Perhaps—and it seems probable—success in avoiding
detection during the formative years is an ætiological factor in the development of
habitual criminality and explains the figures here presented concerning English and
Belgian preventive detainees.
[2] Such a prisoner is all too often referred to as a " Borstal failure "—he is surely
equally a " prison failure " and even more strongly a " court failure ".

given to him until he was beyond the age (30 years) when, according to the Criminal Justice Act, 1948, his criminal ways may be so settled that it is, practically speaking, impossible to move him from them.

Place of Birth

London	9
Other English cities	7
Remainder of England	14
Scottish cities	1
Eire	1

International Criminals

All the offences of our " 32 " were committed in England or Wales except those of five[1] of them, of whom—

2 have also been convicted by courts in Scotland
1 by courts in Scotland and Australia
1 by courts in Eire, and
1 by courts in Rhodesia and U.S.A.

Early Environment

There is, most unfortunately, no information on which to base any evaluation of the true quality of their early family relationships. Occasionally the reports of Probation Officers or the information collected in the files relating to a Borstal detainee do throw some light on this matter; but such information is too scattered and fortuitous for inclusion in this study.

One need not, nowadays, dwell on the great difficulties that such a lack of information places in the way of the development of an enlightened sentencing policy—its lack is widely felt, and gradually steps are being taken to remedy it as far as concerns juvenile offenders.[2]

All that is here presented is an estimation of the economic status of the detainee's parental home, the classification being into

---

[1] This number does not include those who, whilst serving in the army, were convicted by courts martial sitting out of England.

[2] The continuing tendency for some departments to destroy penal records, after an interval of ten years during which the individual to which they relate is not sentenced to detentive punishment, is most regrettable. Further, where such information does exist, we statutorily deny it to courts before whom prisoners appear later in life—perhaps " deny " is the wrong word, as in a " price-list " system of punishment the need for such information is not always obvious.

those that are "dependent", those that are "marginal", and those
that are " comfortable ":[1]

Dependent	..	..	..	9
Marginal	..	..	..	11
Comfortable	..	..	..	6
Not known	..	..	..	5
				31

The member of our " 32 " not included above was reared in an
orphanage: two who are included above were adopted children.

Industrial History

Under this sub-heading we shall consider:

(a) whether the detainee is or has ever been a " skilled " or
  " semi-skilled " worker;

(b) the longest period he had remained in any one employment
  since 1930;

(c) whether he was employed or unemployed when last crime
  (or series of crimes) committed;

(d) his own description of his trade or occupation; and

(e) his employment upon leaving school.

(a) " Skilled ", " semi-skilled ", or " unskilled "

The classification in accordance with these terms[2] taking each

[1] " Dependent " : receiving aid continuously from public funds or from persons outside
the immediate family circle—chronic dependency.
  " Marginal " : living on daily earnings but accumulating little or nothing ; being in
the margin of self-support and dependency. Also includes cases which are occasionally
" dependent ".
  " Comfortable " : having accumulated resources sufficient to maintain the family for
at least four months.
  These three terms are used in the Gluecks' studies (see p. 113 of Five Hundred Criminal
Careers) and were taken by them from the Statistical Manual for the Use of Hospitals for
Mental Diseases, New York.
  [2] The definition of the terms here used is that given in the Gluecks' Five Hundred
Criminal Careers (p. 114, note 8), and used throughout all their follow-up studies. These
definitions were originally furnished by Professor John M. Brewer, of Harvard University,
and read : " The unskilled labourer does any kind of rough work to which he can be sent
without any training whatever. Mere strength of hand or keenness of eye, untutored
through any course of apprenticeship or training, would serve him. The semi-skilled
worker uses tools and processes requiring learning. He cannot take up the kind of work
unless he has had a period of experience under guidance or study. The processes,
however, are not greatly complicated and the period of training is likely to be short
(three days to three months perhaps). The skilled worker uses tools and processes
which are usable only by one who has given a long period of time " (over three months
in this study) " to the acquiring of the skill. Furthermore, he is quite likely to make use of
scientific methods, such as blueprints in his work."

prisoner at the very best period of his life in this respect (for example, one prisoner though previously " unskilled " has recently and in prison become an efficient wireless mechanic, and is shown as " skilled "; and another prisoner who years ago had some engineering knowledge which he has now totally forgotten is also classed as " skilled ") is as follows:

Skilled ..	..	..	..	..	3
Semi-skilled	..	..	..	..	7
Unskilled	..	..	..	..	22

Considering the generosity of definition of these terms, no comment is necessary on the poor showing of our " 32 " in this respect.

(b) Longest period in any one employment since 1930

Excluding military service (and service in the Merchant Navy) we can state these periods as follows:

No employment	..	..	..	6
" Odd jobs "[1] ..	..	..	..	2
Up to one month	..	..	..	7
One to two months	..	..	..	3
Two to three months	..	..	..	4
Three to six months	..	..	..	6
Six months to one year ..	..	..	2
Over one year ..	..	..	..	2

There is, in fact, not one of the " 32 " who has a reasonable working record since 1930. The most pathetic are those, such as the athetotic prisoner, who repeatedly try to get or hold down employment but who are prevented by their physical condition from doing so. Of the six who have done no work whatsoever during this period, four quite frankly state that they do not like work, while two cannot and could not work for a living owing to their poor health.

One must not forget, in considering the employment record of these preventive detainees, that though none of them seems to regard prison existence as a shameful thing nearly all of them have a profound horror of the workhouse and a contempt for its inmates. The exceptional prisoner in this respect is one who repeatedly and sincerely contends that he spent " the happiest years of his life in Rotherham Workhouse."

---

[1] This concurs with these two prisoners' own account of their activities.

The above statistics are sufficient to establish the extremely poor employment records of the group. Let us consider a few of those who did make some effort to find and hold employment during these years since 1930. Archy and Angus have already been mentioned in this context, and three other prisoners—"X", "Y", and "Z"— deserve notice:

Until 1938, when out of prison, " X " worked for various short periods, never over four months, as a hotel porter and kitchen hand in London hotels. He was regarded as a satisfactory worker and was in employment on both occasions when he was arrested between 1930 and 1938. When discharged from prison in 1940 he took several brief labouring jobs, and then settled down to regular work with a constructional firm, remaining in this employment for nine months, and eventually leaving of his own accord. Lack of employment was, therefore, not an ætiological factor in his recent criminality.

Although formerly " Y " made no genuine effort to find employment or to keep any work found for him by the aftercare societies, on his discharge from prison in December 1942 he obtained employment as a porter at a club in Curzon Street for three weeks, then at an hotel in Queen's Gate for one week, and then at an hotel in Oxford Street for one month. During this period he committed no criminal offences. He forcibly contends that he made a genuine effort, and that each time he was discharged it was owing to dissension with other members of the staff when it became known that he was an ex-convict. Ex-convicts frequently make this allegation ; but in this case it seems, from his employers' reports, to have been true. After this third attempt he reverted wholeheartedly to crime—in his own words, " it was a mess-up all round," he had, when working, " a dog's life of it," and he was " fed up with the outside world."

The recent employment record of " Z ", which follows, denotes a genuine tragedy :

May 5th, '44, until May 25th, '44	odd-job man—left own accord
June 3rd, '44, „ June 24th, '44	waiter at hotel—left own accord
July 4th, '44, „ July 17th, '44	porter at club—left own accord
July 19th, '44, „ Aug. 28th, '44	porter at club—left own accord
Aug. 30th, '44, „ Sept. 13th, '44	railway porter—gave satisfaction but put off as unfit for heavy work.
Sept. 19th, '44, „ Oct. 2nd, '44	stoker and cleaner at club—left own accord

He was forced by ill health to leave each of the above employments ; he then reverted to housebreaking, taking goods of little value.

(*c*) Employed or unemployed when last crime (or series of crimes) committed

Employed	2
Unemployed	30

Amongst the "unemployed" are included those who were "working for themselves" or "doing odd jobs".

(*d*) The Detainee's own description of his trade or occupation

On each occasion that a prisoner is admitted into prison he is required to state the trade or occupation he follows when free. The following table records the statements of our group, dividing those statements into the probably true and the almost certainly false, the benefit of any doubt being given to the prisoner.

	True	False
Labourer	9	
Seaman	3	
Chef, cook		1
Street trader	1	
Painter		2
Bookmaker	1	
Baker		1
Bootmaker	1	
Hotel porter	1	
Mechanical engineer ..	1	2
Journalist	2	
Hairdresser	1	
Miner	2	
Cook-baker		1
Wireless mechanic .. .	1	
Basket maker		1
Tailor		1

In the above table, if the stated occupation was followed for any time, however brief, during the detainee's career it is shown as true. Most of the false statements are made by experienced prisoners who have more regard for the desirable prison tasks than for the reality of their past life—the "painters", "cooks" and "bakers" being typical, and the "cook-baker" simply an optimist. Strangely enough, though the subterfuge is fully realised by all the prison staff, it is a definite advantage to a prisoner desiring employment in the kitchens at Parkhurst (where the preventive detainee well knew that he would pass much of his term of penal servitude) to have such a statement on his penal record.

Of them all, only two have any present pretensions to occupational skill—the bootmaker and the wireless mechanic.

(e) Employment on leaving school

Taught a "skilled" or "semi-skilled" occupation	9
Army and then no vocational training	7
Labouring or "unskilled" occupation	11
"Dead-end jobs"	5

Military Record

No service in armed forces[1]	12
Served in peace-time only	3
Served during 1914-18 war	11
May have served in 1914-18 war (doubtful)	2
Served in 1939-45 war[2]	1
Served in both wars	2
Not known	1

Of the seventeen who have certainly seen military, naval, merchant navy, or air force service:

1 was posted as a deserter when last arrested

6 were last discharged with "very bad" or "bad" characters

1 was last discharged with a "fair" character

8 were last discharged with "exemplary" or "good" characters, and

1 was last discharged when his criminal record became known to the army authorities

Of those who served in the 1914-1918 war, four were wounded in action.

Home Conditions immediately before this Sentence

Using their own terminology, all thirty-two were "on the run". None of them was happily married or living in settled conditions. According to their financial position so they used common lodging houses, lodgings, furnished rooms or cheap hotels.

Three of them were known to have been living with women to whom they were not married; but none of these liaisons had any quality of permanency.

Marital Status: Disposition of Children

Bachelors	17
Divorced	3
Widowers[3]	—
Married[4]	12

[1] Including Merchant Navy.

[2] Only for a matter of weeks in the army before he deserted, committed a crime, was sent to prison, handed to army escort, again deserted, and eventually discharged.

[3] Here appear only those who know they are widowers.

[4] Here are included those who do not know whether or not they are widowers or divorced.

Of the twelve who are married, the position of their marriage is as follows:

Live with their wife when out of prison	—
Not living together and not writing ..	7
Separated	5

These seven marriages in which the husband and wife are not living together when he is out of prison probably include several where the wife is dead and the husband does not know about it. They also may well include one or two in which the wife has divorced the husband or been legally separated from him, about which occurrences the husband professes to be ignorant.

The three divorced prisoners and four of the married ones had no children. The remaining eight men who have been married are the fathers of a total of fifteen children. (There is no record of any illegitimate children of the unmarried men.) Of these fifteen children, twelve are adult and three are living with their mothers.

It would be hard to find a more lamentable pattern of mis-directed sexual energy and marital discord.[1]

Eleven of our group stated upon their last reception to prison that they had no "next of kin". This may or may not be true; certainly fourteen of them are completely out of touch with their family. However, two of our " 32 " write to their children, and five of them write occasionally to their parents.

Honesty: Sobriety: Companions and Associates

When the detainee is received into prison the police report on the prisoner, which is forwarded to the Governor of the prison, makes mention, *inter alia*, of the prisoner's honesty, his sobriety, and his companions and associates. Let us tabulate such reports on the members of our group.

(a) Honesty

All were stated, most emphatically, to be dishonest.

[1] The marital status of the Belgian preventive detainees is strikingly similar to that of our group. Of M. H. Bekaert's 181 detainees (see p. 8 of his article) : 108 were bachelors and 73 had been married. Of these 73, 51 were divorced and 10 were widowers. Accordingly, 12 (under 7 per cent.) had possible marital relationships, and 169 (over 93 per cent.) were without such relationships—and this at the time of their last reception to prison ; at the conclusion of their sentences even the figure 12 will have dwindled appreciably.

(*b*)   Sobriety

Using the terms of the police reports, we have :

Teetotaller	1
Sober, sober habits	15
Temperate habits, fairly temperate ..	2
Moderate drinker	4
Not of drunken habits	2
Not a heavy (excessive) drinker ..	3
Intemperate	2
Drinks very heavily, a heavy drinker ..	2
Addicted to drink	1

Thus, for only five of the " 32 " could drink be regarded as a possibly significant causative factor of their present criminality.

(*c*)   Companions and Associates

Again using the phraseology of the police reports:

Thieves and prostitutes	2
Thieves, convicted thieves	8
Prostitutes	1
Not known, no regular companions ..	7
No regular companions	3
Not an associate of criminals	2
No companions or associates	6
Solitary habits	2
Associate of labourers	1

Thus, just as our " 32 " do not nowadays lead people astray, most also avoided undesirable associations when out of prison—they knew that such associations increased the likelihood of their conviction as habitual criminals.

Physical Condition

Six of the " 32 " are *precluded* by their physical condition from living for more than a short time outside an institution—hospital, prison or charitable home. These six are:

" Barmy "—see p. 275.
" Alfred "—see p. 272.
One (who has a pronounced cast in his right eye) had pneumonia when 16 years of age followed by double empyæma for which he was operated on. Since then he has had numerous operations for recurrence of empyæma and removal of tubercular portions of his ribs. He had pulmonary tuberculosis in 1920 and for a few years thereafter (it is now quiescent) ; pneumonia

and pleurisy in 1944. He suffers also with bronchial catarrh, and with post-operative tuberculosis of the lower abdomen. He reacted positively to a Wasserman Test in 1945.

Another who is nearly stone deaf and has been deaf for seventeen years (recently issued with a hearing aid under the National Health Scheme) has a hernia, chronic bronchitis, and, in 1932, gonorrhœa. As a result of a childhood accident the fingers of the left hand and the left hand itself have wasted and are now quite useless.

Another prematurely senile detainee, who though only 60 years of age gives 70 as his age so as to be employed in the " old-age party " whilst in prison (this party do virtually nothing—the Parkhurst authorities, recognising his premature senility, kindly accepted his false statement of age and put him in the old-age party). He had pleurisy at the age of 55. Chronic dyspepsia. Left inguinal hernia. Right bubonocele. Eyes very poor indeed —corneal opacity.

Another who is athetotic—who jitters about wildly, his shoulders and arms jerking violently even during sleep. Left inguinal hernia. Left varicocele.

Of the remaining twenty-six members of our group, the following six are seriously *hindered* by their physical condition from pursuing extra-mural occupations suitable to their mental abilities:

" Arthur "—see p. 268.
" Archy "—see p. 286.
One who has chronic inflamed hæmorrhoids, which have twice been removed by operation. Also severe bilateral varicose veins with varicose ulcer medial side of left foot—Trendelenburg operation scar right side (done in 1927).

Another who has an operative scar on his right groin, and whose right testicle is missing. He has a very troublesome right inguinal hernia. Further, has had several attacks of confusional insanity, and is developing into an involutional melancholic.

Another who had diphtheria and croup in 1900 ; enteric fever in 1909 ; fractured both tibia in 1913 ; has an enlarged prostate ; and suffers with a hydrocele and inguinal hernia. He has to be catheterised regularly owing to a long-standing stricture. He is somewhat unstable, but shows no signs of mental disorder or defect.

Another who, since an attack of rheumatic fever in 1923, has had a pronounced and troublesome cardiovascular deficiency.

The remaining twenty are physically capable of holding employment suitable to their mental abilities; that is, though not necessarily good specimens physically, they are not in need of very frequent medical attention. Indeed, as a group they are physically pitiable, being far less healthy than a group of similar age distribution taken from the general population. Amongst them are three men with chronic bronchitis ; three with severe hernia; one who has undergone frequent operations for hæmorrhoids; one with a history of mild epileptic fits; one with a history of hysterical fits; one who has suffered from rheumatic fever, scarlet fever and jaundice; one who is blind in one eye; one who fractured his skull and both wrists in the 1914-1918 war and whose wrists are still slightly deformed and imperfectly articulated; and one who has had intermittent bouts of rheumatic fever; and finally one who, at the age of twenty-five, caught Blackwater fever, has also suffered three attacks of rheumatic fever, was gassed in 1915, and has a chronic enlargement of the glands on the left side of his neck. The medical histories of the remaining seven members of the group are not mentioned in this depressing list since there is nothing particular to report about them.

Here, then, is perhaps the most noticeable quality of our " 32 ". Many are totally or partially incapable of facing the rigours of non-institutional life,[1] and few of them are not appreciably inconvenienced by their physical condition.

Mental Condition and Intellectual Ability

It is not easy, lacking special psychiatric research and in the absence of mental tests, to describe the mental conditions and intellectual abilities of our " 32 " with any accuracy. However, the syndrome " institutionalised " is fairly well defined—intellectually atrophied, emotionally starved, trained for years to rely on others for daily needs, denied steady employment or the incentive to grow in vocational skill, sexual energy misdirected

---

[1] The experience in the Union of South Africa is interesting in this regard : there the boards of visitors to certain prisons have to determine the date of release of preventive detainees who are held under an indefinite sentence ; and their task is complicated by the poor physical condition of many of the habitual criminals, especially the native detainees. In the *Annual Report of the Director of Prisons (Union of South Africa) for the Year 1946*, at p. 2, the following statement appears : " The board is impelled to invite attention to delays in releasing some aged and medically unfit convicts owing to the serious lack of provision for accommodating some of these in other than prison institutions. A number have earned their release from prison by length of detention and good behaviour, but, owing to their having become detribalised, having lost touch with all relatives and friends and their complete inability to do anything more than the lightest labour, the board is unable to recommend their release on probation. Some are senile, others are tuberculotic and in need of some further medical attention, a few are deformed, and a few are feeble-minded. They would become destitute if released without being placed in homes or medical institutions. The board urges that definite provision be made . . . to house and care for them upon their release from prison." The analogy here with many of our " 32 " is not far-fetched. Most of our " 32 " are " detribalised " and many need constant medical supervision—certainly twelve of our group require habitual hospitalisation rather than habitual penalisation.

to onanism or other perversions, and quite incapable of coping with life outside of an institution. Affirming roundly and emphatically that such a pattern is the norm for our "32", one can best describe the group from this point of view by mentioning those who vary from that norm to any appreciable extent.[1] Thus, we must mention:

"Arthur" (see p. 268), who is unstable emotionally, who falls into fits of depression with suicidal desires and considerable distress.

"Albert" (see p. 283), who though emotionally unstable has manifested during this term of imprisonment an ability to master a technical subject—radio engineering.

"Barmy" (see p. 275), a hypomaniac who has already been certified insane once during his life.

"Alan" (see p. 289), a "swallower".

One who in 1941 at Dartmoor swallowed some pieces of razor blade.

In 1937 he was placed under observation, being very depressed and allegedly suffering hallucinations.

Another who when received into prison in 1940 had an attack of confusional insanity which cleared up before he could be certified. He gradually improved, though a fine tremor of the hand remained. In 1943, again in prison, he had another attack—confusion, amnesia, apprehension, hallucinations—which again slowly and imperfectly left him. He is now developing into an involutional type of melancholic.

Another of rather superior intelligence to the rest who in his youth received training as an engineer.

Another who has a history of epilepsy.

Another whom we have already mentioned as being athetotic. His brother is also athetotic. In 1938 this prisoner was operated on at Wormwood Scrubs (a left Bassini's operation), and whilst recovering from the anæsthetic showed extraordinary violence, behaving in a way suggestive of confusional insanity.

And finally one who has occasional hysterical fits which he pretends are epileptic. Scholastically he is rather above the average, having been taught by his father, a country parson, and having worked for some time as a journalist.

The above ten members of our group are the most noticeable variations from the norm; the other twenty-two can be accurately lumped together as "institutionalised" as we have defined it.[2]

---

[1] Two not mentioned might be regarded as borderline mental defectives, the diagnosis of this condition being obscured by their protracted penal conditioning.

[2] Dr. G. K. Stürup, chief of the Herstedvester Prison for Psychopaths, in Denmark, having examined a group of Danish preventive detainees, wrote : " It seems to me that many preventive detainees are more clear-cut psychopaths than those in my charge as psychopathic detainees." *Report on the Eighth Congress of Scandinavian Psychiatrists*, p. 32.

Prison Behaviour and Escaping

I have classified the prison behaviour of members of our group as "bad", "indifferent", "good", or "very good".[1] The result was as follows:

Bad	..	..	..	..	5
Indifferent	..	..	..	..	8
Good	..	..	..	..	10
Very good	..	..	..	..	9

Thus, the behaviour of the twenty-seven of our " 32 " during their recent sentences has caused the prison authorities very little concern. That fact accords with their protracted conditioning to the penal régime; and as the Departmental Committee on Persistent Offenders reported:[2]

> " Compliance with prison routine is no evidence of a change of attitude or of any reform of character. It is common to find that men who persistently revert to crime when at liberty are well behaved in prison. Discipline among the preventive detention men is usually maintained without difficulty and misconduct is rare."

Only two members of our group have ever attempted to escape from custody:

> One has made four attempts to escape, as follows :
> In February 1941 escaped from police station by removing bricks from his cell—recaptured later the same day ;
> In July 1941 was discovered tampering with his cell in an effort to escape ;
> In October 1943 made a ladder and hid it in his cell. It was discovered before he executed his plan.
> In April 1944 a hacksaw, a rope and razor blades were found hidden in his cell.
> Another in January 1921 slipped his handcuffs and escaped from his escort at Liverpool Street railway station when being taken from Essex Quarter Sessions to Pentonville Prison. He was recaptured three days later.

---

[1] These terms are defined by reference to conduct during the current and penultimate prison sentences, as follows : Bad : a large number of minor offences, or one serious offence ; Indifferent : a few offences of a not very serious character ; Good : one or two contraband or gossiping offences only ; Very Good : no prison offences.

[2] P. 56 of their report.

Religious Persuasion and Conversions

The following table shows the last statements of members of our group as to their religious persuasion:

Church of England	..	..	..	17
Roman Catholic	..	..	..	3
Wesleyan	..	..	..	2
Christian Scientist	..	..	..	1
Salvationist	..	..	..	1
Methodist	..	..	..	2
Unitarian	..	..	..	1
None	..	..	..	5

Sixteen of these men have changed the denominations to which they have nominally adhered throughout their prison careers:

5 of them have made one change
9 of them have made two changes
1 of them has changed three times, and
1 of them four times

Is one being sceptical in seeing in these frequent un-Pauline conversions a recognition of the social and humanitarian function of the chaplain rather than of his spiritual mission? To this point, and the contentions that spring from it, we shall return when similar changes have been investigated for the confirmed recidivist group.

Tattooing

Solely out of courtesy to Lombroso I note the fact that of our " 32 ":

14 are tattooed, and
18 are not tattooed

Aliases

Finally,[1] let us consider the number of previous names under which members of our group have been received into prison:

Name has not varied		..	..	..		..	..	9
1 previous name different from present name					..		..	4
2 „	names	„	„	„	„	..	..	5
3 „	„	„	„	„	„	..	..	6
4 „	„	„	„	„	„	..	..	5
5 „	„	„	„	„	„	..	..	1
6 „	„	„	„	„	„	..	..	1
11 „	„	„	„	„	„	..	..	1

[1] We shall not consider any inferences arising from the comments of governors and chaplains on each detainee. For many years, such are the criminal records of our " 32 ", neither governor nor chaplain could possibly predict the prisoner's reformation. He might hold out vague and ephemeral hope of it, and trust that age had brought wisdom to the prisoner, but he could hardly predict such reformation in individual cases. The list of unhappy and inaccurate predictions is not, therefore, worth recounting.

These aliases occur for three reasons: first, names are changed
in the hope (vain for such well-known criminals) of confusing the
police; secondly, they are changed in the knowledge that thus
some minor administrative inconvenience will be created; and thirdly, sometimes merely because the prisoner prefers the new name he
has invented or copied. An object lesson in such changes is given by
one of our group, who has been received into prison with the following
names:

BC
ABC
AB Alfonso C
AB Alfonsus C

(in each case, A, B and C remaining constant), the aim being
to create confusion between the courts and the prison administration.

Summary

More light will be shed on our " 32 " preventive detainees
when we have analysed the confirmed recidivists, and are able to
compare the qualities of the two groups. In the meantime we may
mention some significant factors which have already been revealed.

First, our group is physically far below the public norm, and
many of them are precluded by their physical condition from a
normal life. Equally, they are far below standard mentally, and
disturbed emotionally—though whether this has been a cause of
their criminality or whether their lengthy prison sentences have been
a cause of their many neuroses cannot be answered for the group;
normally each has reacted unhappily on the other.

Secondly, our group is unskilled at any trade or occupation.
Again the ætiology of this condition is complicated and largely
irrelevant to the present existence of the problem.

Thirdly, their crimes are predominantly of the type that are a
nuisance rather than a danger to society; and very few of them are
the " dangerous " " professional " criminals at which the 1908
Act was aimed.

Accordingly, we can, without exaggeration, regard our group
as composed of men who are either not quite sick enough for permanent treatment at public expense in hospitals or sanatoria, or not
quite sufficiently psychotic for confinement under our present law
in an asylum for the insane ; and who are possessed of a distorted
pride which sees shame in being an inmate of a workhouse or similar

institution, but not in being a prisoner (and certainly not in being a prison aristocrat).[1]

The new Act will not eliminate such men—to treat them as we have done does not diminish the nuisance they present to society, and increases the expense of maintaining them. It is, moreover, unkind. The Prison Commissioners did their best for many of them —as they say, preventive detainees " are generally harmless and elderly men whose sole aim is to lead a quiet life, and this the present system of preventive detention effectively provides "[2]; but surely prison is not the place for the near-invalid and the near-certifiable.

2. THE SPECIFICITY OF RECIDIVISM AND CRIMINAL MATURATION

In this section we shall seek the answers to two questions concerning our " 32 "; to what extent did they concentrate during their criminal careers on any type or types of crime; and, presuming changes in the types of offences committed, do these changes follow any regular pattern measured by age or by a process of criminal and penal experience ? The former we shall call " the specificity of recidivism "; the latter, " criminal maturation ".

It may be argued that these two inquiries are too subtle in dealing with so limited a number. This must be admitted, for no scientifically valid deductions can be drawn from such a small group; however, as we shall make similar inquiries for the confirmed recidivist group it has been thought best to apply the same techniques throughout. Also, though not leading to scientifically valid conclusions about other criminals, the results of our inquiries will give us considerable information about the group we are considering, and will assist in the construction of fruitful hypotheses for future research.

(a) The Specificity of Recidivism

An examination of the degree of concentration on specific types of crime necessarily requires the adoption of some typology of offences; but the classification of crimes into types which are even

---

[1] To the same effect is Sir Norwood East's contention that some of the preventive detention prisoners "although not insane or mentally defective, belong to the constitutional psychic inferior group of psychopathic personalities who cannot stand alone, and whose habit of committing crime frequently and returning to prison may be the best adaptation to social life they are able to make." *Society and the Criminal*, p. 115.

[2] *Report of the Commissioners of Prisons and Directors of Convict Prisons for the Year 1945*, p. 71.

empirically satisfying has proved to be a problem of transcendent difficulty. The difficulty lies in the fact that it is usually sought to combine two different elements in such classifications—an objective estimation of the social dangerousness of a crime, and a subjective consideration of the crime in accordance with the motive actuating the criminal. There is thus a confusion between objective classification of offences and psychological classification of offenders. But to avoid this confusion and realising that identical motives can actuate the theft of a bicycle in the street and the crime of arson—indeed, any two offences—let us concentrate solely on the task of creating an objective classification of crimes.

Here, then, we are concerned only with the observer's estimation of the gravity of a crime, and of the kinship between one crime and another. From the maximum and minimum punishments statutorily prescribed for different crimes we may receive some guidance in constructing such an objective classification of offences; but we shall find that in the actual application of such punishments the courts have greatly altered the sequence of gravity that we would have deduced from the statutes. Further, between one court and another, and between one criminologist and another, there are profound differences in their respective estimations of the social dangerousness of various offences and of the relationships between them. One reason for this is that it is impossible completely to exclude the conception of motive, and, once admitted, that conception is likely to have a great influence on any classification by dangerousness of offence. Another reason is that we frequently react with the greatest horror to those offences to which we are subconsciously most tempted, and are not greatly moved by those whose attractions we have not been compelled to repress—and such subconscious attractions will vary with each individual. There are many other reasons for these variations of opinion; but we need not labour them for their existence is undoubted, and can be seen most clearly in regard to sexual offences such as homosexuality, incest or bigamy. For example, some Benches consider bigamy as striking at the root of the social structure, as threatening the sanctity and stability of English family life as a whole, and therefore regard it as their duty to inflict heavy punishments on such offenders so as to deter other potential bigamists: other Benches, conscious of the difficult position in which many persons are placed by the inflexibility and expense of the divorce laws, do not impose severe punishments on bigamists unless there are other circumstances aggravating the harm they have done.

We are therefore forced to the conclusion that there is no scientifically satisfying objective classification of crimes; and that only a psychological classification of the motives of offenders—which would require concentrated and individual attention to each offender —could be of universal application. But, as we have seen, our system of punishment is predominantly regulated by a tariff of punishments for a list of offences (modified by the previous criminal record of the offender), and with such a system of condign punishment as a point of departure it is possible to create a pragmatic classification of offences which, though not completely satisfying, will receive an appreciable measure of agreement.

In this section (and later for the confirmed recidivist group) we shall consider the crimes of our group in the light of two different classifications of offences—first, that adopted by Dr. H. Mannheim in Chapter XII of his *Social Aspects of Crime in England between the Wars*; and secondly, our own modification of the classification adopted in the annual volumes of Criminal Statistics, which we used in Table A.

Dr. Mannheim's classification, and the code he used to designate the different types of crimes, is as follows:

I =Larceny
II =Breaking
III =Robbery
IV =False pretences, fraud, etc.
V =Receiving
VI =Crimes against person (not sexual)
VII =Sexual crimes (including bigamy)
VIII=Forgery
IX =Coining
X =Malicious damage and arson
XI =Vagrancy
XII =Prostitution and living on earnings of prostitutes
XIII=Drunkenness
XIV=Prevention of Crime Act
XV =Highway offences
XVI=Others

This classification has been applied to the 3,069 crimes of our " 32 " habitual criminals (including, it will be seen from a reference to Table A, those offences which were " taken into consideration " and for which sufficient data exists for their objective classification) with the following results.

No member of our group has specialised on only one type of offence, though " 15 "[1] in committing a total of 320 offences in respect of which he has been sentenced has only twice departed from offences of type IV; and both were chance drunken assaults of no great consequence. Also " 16 " can be regarded as a specialist, for in the 200 offences for which he has been sentenced there are again only two which vary from type IV; and both were larcenies from the person in which he stole £1 and 3s. 6d. respectively. It is worth remarking that the only two members of our group who can be regarded as "specialists", under this classification of offences, have both concentrated on obtaining money by false pretences.

There are seven records (including " 15 " and " 16 ") with only two different types of offence, the combinations being:

$$
\begin{array}{ll}
\text{I} \quad \text{and II} & =2 \\
\text{I} \quad \text{and IV} & =4 \\
\text{IV and VI} & =1
\end{array}
$$

There are four records with only three different types of offence:

$$
\begin{array}{ll}
\text{I and II and XIV} & =2 \\
\text{I and IV and VIII} & =1 \\
\text{I and IV and X} & =1
\end{array}
$$

There are twelve records with only four different types of offence:

$$
\begin{array}{llll}
\text{I and II} & \text{and IV} & \text{and V} & =1 \\
\text{I and II} & \text{and IV} & \text{and VII} & =1 \\
\text{I and II} & \text{and IV} & \text{and XIII} & =1 \\
\text{I and II} & \text{and IV} & \text{and XIV} & =3 \\
\text{I and II} & \text{and V} & \text{and VI} & =1 \\
\text{I and II} & \text{and V} & \text{and XIV} & =1 \\
\text{I and II} & \text{and XI} & \text{and XIV} & =2 \\
\text{I and II} & \text{and XIV} & \text{and XVI} & =1 \\
\text{I and IV} & \text{and VII} & \text{and XVI} & =1
\end{array}
$$

There are seven records with only five different types of offence:

$$
\begin{array}{lllll}
\text{I and II and III} & \text{and XI} & \text{and XIV} & =1 \\
\text{I and II and IV} & \text{and XI} & \text{and XIV} & =1 \\
\text{I and II and IV} & \text{and V} & \text{and XVI} & =1 \\
\text{I and II and IV} & \text{and XIV} & \text{and XVI} & =1 \\
\text{I and II and VII} & \text{and XI} & \text{and XIV} & =1 \\
\text{I and II and VII} & \text{and XI} & \text{and XVI} & =1 \\
\text{I and II and X} & \text{and XI} & \text{and XIV} & =1
\end{array}
$$

---

[1] References to individual preventive detainees will be made in accordance with their position in Table A.

There is one record with six different types of offence: I and II and V and XI and XIII and XIV.

There is one record with seven different types of offence—I and II and IV and VIII and XI and XIV and XVI—and no member of our " 32 " has diffused his criminal talents any more widely than this.

Dr. Mannheim tabulates the offences of those members of his group[1] who have been sentenced in respect of more than three types of offence. Amongst our group there are twenty-one members who have been so sentenced, and their offences can be grouped as follows:

$$\text{I and II and . . . and . . .} = 20$$
$$\text{I and IV and . . . and . . .} = 1$$

Only six of our " 32 " have combined crimes against property (I to V) with crimes against the person (VI and VII), and in the histories of five of these the crime against the person has been the sole variation from an otherwise regular routine of crimes against property, whilst one offender ("30") has once importuned a male person for immoral purposes and once assaulted the police.[2]

Thus our " 32 " concentrate on crimes against property, but not on any specific type of such crime. In their active phases they commit larceny, housebreaking, false pretences and other frauds. At other times they are convicted under the Prevention of Crimes Acts or for vagrancy offences. In this respect they differ appreciably from the 183 criminals whose records Dr. Mannheim investigated, concerning whom he reported:

" These figures show that the variety of offences amongst this sample of our records is much greater than that found in previous investigations, and the general impression gathered from a close study of the whole material in our possession strongly confirms this result. The average recidivist, although mainly concerned with crime against property, also, more often than not, tries his hand in other spheres of the criminal law."[3]

[1] *Social Aspects of Crime in England between the Wars*, p. 361.

[2] " 30's " importuning of a male person for immoral purposes occurred when he was seventeen years of age and after he had been convicted twice of being found wandering abroad. From that he graduated immediately to property offences passing through the larceny stage to housebreaking and burglary.

" 28 " also began his criminal career at the age of 29 with an indecent assault on a boy—since when he has confined himself to property offences.

" 19 " is also worth noting—his criminal career began at the age of 21 with a simple larceny, and he is now (aged 45) an accomplished housebreaker. At the age of 37 years he was sentenced to five years' penal servitude for his only offence against the person—an offence of buggery committed on a woman (he still contends that he did not know it was a criminal offence).

[3] *Social Aspects of Crime in England between the Wars*, p. 361.

For the time being we must merely note this variation, leaving any conclusions to be drawn until we have subjected the records of our 270 confirmed recidivists to a similar analysis.

Let us now reclassify the offences of our " 32 " in accordance with the classification adopted in the annual volumes of Criminal Statistics and in Table A. In this context, however, we shall amalgamate some of those classificatory headings and exclude the following offences:

> Cruelty to children ; intoxicating liquor laws ; Poor Law ; railway offences ; begging ; sleeping out ; other vagrancy offences ; other offences ; offences against the Highway Acts ; Prevention of Crime Act ; frequenting ; and on enclosed premises.

Also we shall include only those offences in respect of which the prisoner has been convicted (not those which were taken into consideration when he was sentenced). We are left, then, with the following classification of the offences of our "32", which represents their more serious proved crimes:

Number in Criminal Statistics	Type of Offence	Total Offences	Offenders Involved
	Against the person		
5 & 6	Wounding	1	1
16 & 17	Unnatural offences, sexual assaults, importuning male person	3	3
103-5	Assaults	2	2
139	Indecent exposure	1	1
	Against property		
27-33	Burglaries, housebreaking, etc.	241	24
37-49 & 54	Larcenies and receiving[1]	400	31
51-3 & 55	False pretences and other frauds	318	18
58 & 59	Forgery (and uttering)	13	3
149	Malicious damage	2	2

This classification—which we shall also apply to the two hundred and seventy confirmed recidivists—reveals the degree to which our " 32 " preventive detainees have concentrated on offences against property.

[1] Receiving is most frequently charged against such criminals as we are here considering only when there is insufficient evidence to found a charge of larceny, though it is well known that the criminal so charged with receiving the stolen property was in fact responsible for stealing it. There is no professional receiver amongst our " 32 ". Hence the grouping of larceny and receiving.

(b) Criminal Maturation

Whether, for this type of criminal, there is a relationship between type of offence and age has not been explored. Again difficulties of classification obtrude—difficulties which we shall solve pragmatically and objectively, and with no pretence to psychological or universal accuracy. For our "32", and using a classification of proved offences based on Table A (in turn based on the Annual Criminal Statistics), we can reach a conclusion on this age-offence relationship by the following method. First, let us exclude from consideration those types of offences which occur less than twelve times in Table A (and which cannot logically be grouped with other kindred types of offence) and cannot therefore serve as a basis for statistically accurate conclusions. Secondly, exclude "other offences" from consideration because they constitute a group lacking homogeneity. Thirdly, classify the remaining offences in Table A as follows:

Number in Criminal Statistics	Type of Offence	Total Offences	Offenders Involved
27-33	Burglary, housebreaking, etc.	241	24
37-49 & 54	Larcenies and receiving	400	31
50-3 & 55	False pretences and other frauds ..	318	18
58 & 59	Forgery	13	3
167, 188, 189	Prevention of Crime Act, frequenting, on enclosed premises, etc.	39	17
163-6, 185 186 & 191	Poor Law, begging, sleeping out, and other vagrancy offences	28	9
		1,039	

We have dwelt on the difficulties of classification, and for this grouping no greater degree of validity is claimed than that it represents the statistically and logically necessary classification for our immediate purpose.

The "age-type of offence" relationship for those 1,039 offences and 32 offenders can be discovered by averaging the age of offenders when they committed these offences. This is an average based on offences and not on offenders; but to prevent any undue statistical emphasis being given to the number of offences each offender commits at any one time, or over any one period of liberty, each type of offence committed before he comes before the court is counted once only on each such separate occasion. It is an average based on offences but corrected for variations in criminal activity of offenders, and does therefore give a true picture of this age-offence relationship:

	Average Age at which Committed Years
Burglary, housebreaking, etc.	34·7
Larceny and receiving	29·6
False pretences and fraud	32·4
Forgery	37
Prevention of Crime Act, frequenting, on enclosed premises, etc.	34·4
Poor Law offences, begging, sleeping out, and other vagrancy offences	26·6

These averages would be of greater significance if the ages at which the members of our group commenced their (known) criminal careers were not spread over such a wide range—thirteen to forty-four years. As it is they may tend to give too much emphasis to the chronological age of each particular offender. In some way it is desirable, therefore, to fix the normal position of a type of offence in a criminal career as such; whether that career began in the offender's youth or maturity. Thus we should investigate the "criminal maturity-type of offence" relationship; predicating that a criminal career can have an ebb and flow independent of the age of its onset in the particular offender. By fixing the average position of each type of offence both in the chronological age and in the criminal careers of various types of criminals, we should gain information of the greatest interest, and of considerable diagnostic and prognostic value. This we shall seek to achieve for the two types of criminals we are investigating.

The method of inquiring into the "criminal maturation-type of offence" relationship developed for this purpose (and applied to preventive detainees and confirmed recidivists) is as follows: the list of each offender's crimes is divided into four quarters, these quarters being based on the number of sentences, and each quarter is given a value from 1 to 4. Accordingly, for a criminal who has been sentenced sixteen times, the quarter-lines will be drawn thus :

					Value
Sentences	1 to	4 inclusive		..	1
,,	5 ,,	8	,,	..	2
,,	9 ,,	12	,,	..	3
,,	13 ,,	16	,,	..	4

And for a criminal who has been sentenced fifteen times they will be drawn thus:

			Value
Sentences	1 to 3 inclusive ..	..	1
Sentence	4	..	1·5
Sentences	5 „ 7 inclusive ..	..	2
Sentence	8	..	2·5
Sentences	9 „ 11 inclusive ..	..	3
Sentence	12	..	3·5
Sentences	13 „ 15 inclusive ..	..	4

A similar method of drawing the quarter-lines was followed whatever the number of sentences in the offender's career. Using these values, each type of offence preceding each sentence was given a value for all offences of the members of our group, and then these values were averaged.[1]

Concerning the 1,039 aforementioned offences of our group of preventive detainees, the result of this investigation into the " criminal maturity-type of offence " relationship was as follows:

Burglary, housebreaking, etc.	3·04
Larceny and receiving	2·29
False pretences and other frauds	2·64
Forgery •.	2·92
Prevention of Crime Act, frequenting, on enclosed premises, etc.	2·36
Poor Law, begging, sleeping out, and other vagrancy offences ..	1·98

By grouping these two relationships—age and criminal maturity with type of offence—and rearranging them in rough sequence, we reach the following table:

	Age	Criminal Maturity
Poor Law, begging, sleeping out, other vagrancy offences ..	26·6	1·98
Larceny and receiving	29·6	2·29
False pretences and other frauds	32·4	2·64
Prevention of Crime Act, frequenting, on enclosed premises, etc. .. .. ·	34·4	2·36
Burglary and housebreaking	34·7	3·04
Forgery	37	2·92

[1] In the statistical and mathematical work in Chapters VII and VIII I have been given the very great benefit of the advice of Dr. Y. P. Seng, research assistant in the Economic Research Division of the London School of Economics. In fairness to him it must be mentioned that though he approved of the use of all the other statistical methods in these chapters, and verified the accuracy of their application, he would not commit himself concerning this quartering technique, which being an idea of one possessed of no comprehension of statistical theory must be regarded with scepticism until it has proved its worth. However, it would appear to be of some use and validity for the purpose to which we have applied it.

There is thus much similarity between the results of our two methods of searching for a relationship between the average age at which a type of offence is committed and the degree of criminal maturation that must be associated with it. Let us defer our deductions from these figures until we have before us the results of applying similar techniques to the offences of the confirmed recidivist group.

3. THE DETERRENT EFFECT OF PUNISHMENT ON THIS GROUP

In the introduction to this work we saw that deterrence is supposed to function both in the macrocosm of society and in the microcosm of criminals who have endured punishment; and we concluded that at present little is known of the deterrent operation of punishment in that macrocosm. We can, however, to a certain extent investigate its operation in the microcosm amongst convicted criminals—though here any exact evaluation is complicated by the numerous other factors that are involved in a criminal's relapse or reformation.

The deterrent effect of past punishments on an individual may be regarded as something inherent in conviction and sentence, or something which varies with the severity or type of sentence inflicted. The second is the almost universal view, and it is that hypothesis on which our investigation is based. We shall test if the duration of one type of punishment—absolute loss of liberty (imprisonment or penal servitude)—has any differential deterrent effect. To decide this for members of our group will be of considerable value; for it is undoubted that in deciding on the punishments they impose many Benches have in the forefront of their minds this idea of the differential deterrent effect of various periods of imprisonment which they might impose—an effect not only on other members of society (potential criminals), but also on the convicted criminal before them.

It must be realised that working with two narrowly defined types of prisoners we reach conclusions rigidly circumscribed by the definitions of our groups, and that it is unsafe to extend these conclusions to other types of criminals. However, we must start somewhere, and conclusions drawn from a study of our group may assist in the investigation of other types of offenders. Further, our groups, especially the confirmed recidivist group, are of considerable importance to the entire penal system and are certainly representative of a type of criminal numerous enough to merit concentrated and separate attention.

In the subsequent inquiry into the deterrent effect of punishment, the chief limitation on the applicability of our conclusions, even to all habitual criminals, is that all the records we consider refer, by definition, to men who have not yet reformed—who have as yet not been deterred. This limitation can be removed by adequate follow-up studies, and these will be discussed later in this work.

The exact question to which we shall now address ourselves is: *has the length of the period of imprisonment had any effect on the duration of the subsequent period of freedom ?* For the members of our group this question can be answered with mathematical precision.

The method which has been applied is the following: for every sentence imposed two periods were calculated—the number of days spent in prison, and the number of days between discharge from prison and a subsequent conviction.[1] These periods having been noted, a product-moment correlation coefficient was calculated by which the relationship between these periods spent in prison and the subsequent periods of freedom was deduced.

From the totality of their sentences, the following were excluded:

(a) sentences not involving detention in prison;

(b) sentences pursuant to " other non-indictable offences " (that is, the less serious non-indictable offences);

(c) sentences imposed before the offenders attained the age of twenty-one years;

(d) sentences followed by military service on discharge from prison;

(e) sentences followed by emigration to another country on discharge from prison; and

(f) two very minor offences and short sentences of imprisonment (11 days and 56 days) which commenced the criminal careers of two men and were followed by several years before their next offences.[2]

Neither the period " in " nor the period " out " following such sentences was included in the calculations. There remained 348

---

[1] In calculating these periods the number of days shown as spent in prison was not a mere reflection of the sentence imposed, but took account of the actual date of release (which is sentence imposed minus remission plus remission lost through misbehaviour in prison). On the other hand, in the calculation of the period of freedom—the number of days " out "—except prior to the last conviction in respect of which a sentence of penal servitude was inflicted, the time between arrest and conviction, even where bail was not granted, was included ; for it was thought best not to introduce a third and usually brief period of time into the sequence of days " in " and days " out ".

[2] (d), (e) and (f) were thought to be so exceptional as not to be rightly included.

sentences of imprisonment or penal servitude in respect of more serious offences committed by adults—sentences which were not followed by emigration or military service.

The correlation between these 348 intervals of imprisonment and the subsequent 348 intervals of freedom was found to be " ·03 ". There is therefore no significant correlation between them.

Accordingly, we can conclude that for the members of our group of preventive detainees the duration of penal detention subsequent to such sentences had no bearing on the ensuing interval between discharge and reconviction.

CHAPTER EIGHT

TWO HUNDRED AND SEVENTY CONFIRMED RECIDIVISTS

IT is of the first importance to the validity and significance of this
chapter that the means of selecting the criminals to be investigated
as confirmed recidivists should be precise and clear. Though in
Chapter VI their qualifications were outlined, and their relationship
to Section 21 of the Criminal Justice Act, 1948, explained, it will be
advisable to recapitulate these qualifications before analysing the
qualities, traits, characteristics and environmental background of the
" 270 " qualificants.

For inclusion in the confirmed recidivist group a criminal had to be:

(a) at least thirty years of age when
(b) sentenced to a minimum of three years' penal servitude
(c) pursuant to conviction for an indictable offence, and
(d) received into Wandsworth Prison between July 1st, 1946,
and September 30th, 1948.[1]

Further, he must have been previously, and since attaining the
age of seventeen years:

(a) convicted of indictable offences punishable with imprisonment
for two or more years on *six* or more separate occasions, and
(b) committed to Borstal detention or imprisonment on *four* or
more of such previous occasions.

There were 270 criminals who so qualified.[2]

Though we have called them "confirmed recidivists", they can
all be regarded as potentially either preventive detainees or corrective trainees under the provisions of Section 21 of the Criminal
Justice Act, 1948.

[1] Though received into Wandsworth Prison—the London recidivist prison—between
July 1st, 1946, and September 30th, 1948, the members of our group were, when their
records were seen, distributed over the following prisons, having been transferred from
Wandsworth : Winchester, Parkhurst, Dartmoor, Maidstone, Wakefield, Oxford, Leeds,
Canterbury, Manchester, Birmingham, Bristol, Norwich, Wormwood Scrubs, Pentonville
and Lewes. The majority, however, were held in Wandsworth and Parkhurst.

[2] Two prisoners who were certified insane and transferred to mental institutions
shortly after their reception to Wandsworth, though qualifying as above, were not included
in our "270". One who was so certified much later in his sentence was included, and
has remained in our group.

In analysing these men and their offences, we shall use the terms defined and follow the method applied when the preventive detainee group was investigated. This will facilitate comparison between the two groups, and avoid the necessity of redefining our methodological instruments.

1. ANALYSIS OF THE GROUP

Present Sentences[1]

3 years' penal servitude			..	..	166
3½ ,,	,,	,,	..	..	1
4 ,,	,,	,,	..	..	50
5 ,,	,,	,,	..	..	18
6 ,,	,,	,,	..	..	3
7 ,,	,,	,,	..	..	8
8 ,,	,,	,,	..	..	4
9 ,,	,,	,,	..	..	1
10 ,,	,,	,,	..	..	2
11 ,,	,,	,,	..	..	2
12 ,,	,,	,,	..	..	1
15 ,,	,,	,,	..	..	1
Penal servitude and preventive detention			..	..	13[2]

Last Offences and their Means of Commission

Here we will follow the classification adopted in the annual Criminal Statistics for England and Wales.[3]

Where a prisoner was last sentenced in respect of two different types of property offences, he will appear only opposite the most serious of his offences; where he was last sentenced in respect of a property offence and a different type of offence, both will be shown.[4]

[1] Remanets of previous penal servitude sentences to be served during these sentences are not included. The sentences here listed are those as varied or confirmed by the Court of Criminal Appeal where an appeal has been made to that court. For example, C. J. (initials here as elsewhere are fictitious), who was sentenced to three years' penal servitude and five years' preventive detention, appealed to the Court of Criminal Appeal, his sentence of preventive detention being quashed. He appears amongst the 166 sentenced to three years' penal servitude.

[2] The thirteen convicted and sentenced as habitual criminals received the following sentences :

3 years P.S. and 5 years' P.D.						..	8
4 ,,	,,	,,	5	,,	,,	..	1
4 ,,	,,	,,	6	,,	,,	..	1
5 ,,	,,	,,	5	,,	,,	..	1
5 ,,	,,	,,	8	,,	,,	..	1
10 ,,	,,	,,	5	,,	,,	..	1

[3] The details of this classification appeared in the pre-war volumes of Criminal Statistics, Appendices A and B. Since it covers forty pages, this classification has been omitted from the more recent volumes.

[4] Hence the total of 279 in the third column (see page 331).

Number	Type of Offence	Number of Offenders Sentenced
2	Attempted murder	1
3	Sending letter threatening to murder	1
5-8	Wounding	4
6, 7, 9-15	Other offences of violence	5
16-18	Unnatural offences (and attempts), etc.	3
19-25	Rape and other offences against females	1
26	Bigamy	5
27-33	Burglary, housebreaking, etc.	115
34-6	Robbery and extortion	19
37-43	Aggravated larcenies	26
44-9	Simple and minor larcenies	29
50-3, 55	False pretences and other frauds	36
54	Receiving stolen goods	25
56	Arson	1
58 & 59	Forgery (and uttering)	4
60 & 61	Coining (and uttering)	2
62-6, 68 & 70	Other indictable offences	2
		279

Let us consider some of the above types of offence in greater detail. The twenty-nine simple and minor larcenies can be grouped according to the type of articles stolen as follows:

Motor vehicles 7
Pedal cycles 3
Suitcases 7
Coats, etc., from restaurants, hotels or clubs 3
Articles displayed in shops (shoplifting) 3
Articles left in unattended motor vehicles 3
Other minor larcenies 3

The twenty-six aggravated larcenies can be classified as follows:

Larceny in a dwelling-house 15
Larceny as a servant 6
Larceny of articles in the course of transmission by post .. 5

The thirty-six false pretences and other frauds represent offences of great diversity, many of which are of some subtlety. They defy any straightforward classification, frequently being attuned to the particular susceptibilities of each victim. Broadly speaking, however, there are three main types practised by members of our group —those based on worthless cheques, those involving the marital desires of spinsters, and those based on offering extra-legal advantages to the prospective victim. The latter two are of such a nature that the criminal will normally commit many more offences than are reported to the police, the victims of their pretences being reluctant to report the crime. An offence of one prisoner deserves to be mentioned : during a previous sentence of imprisonment for false pretences he persuaded a fellow-prisoner that he was the proprietor of a flourishing French wine company, but that he would need money to extend its operation throughout England. On discharge from prison, his fellow-prisoner invested nearly £600 in this fictitious business.[1] For this, and six other offences of a similar nature, he was sentenced to five years' penal servitude.

Many of the false pretenders show great ability and extreme cunning in their criminal technique, suiting the story to the victim with considerable psychological insight. There is room for a study of the ætiology of false pretences as a separate and clearly distinguishable type of crime; for until more is known of offenders of this type, of their persistent criminality, and of their eventual life of phantasy in which they clearly believe much that they falsely allege, any discussion of this type of crime is not likely to be fruitful.[2]

Of the twenty-five sentenced for receiving stolen goods, only eleven can be regarded as genuine " receivers " (i.e. they were not convicted of receiving merely because evidence was lacking to connect them with a housebreaking or larceny which they had in fact committed).

One hundred and eighty committed their offences alone; ninety in company with others, as follows:

With one other :

With preconvictions	..	..	..	.. 33
Without preconvictions	..	..	..	.. 6
Not captured and not known		..	..	.. 2
				— 41

---

[1] There is an interesting story, possibly apocryphal, of a prisoner who whilst in prison obtained by false pretences large sums from a visiting magistrate ! Certainly, after a previous term of imprisonment one of our group obtained a " loan " of £1,000 from a prison visitor.

[2] Such a study should be conducted on three planes : psychological, statistical and by means of case histories. In particular it would be interesting to know whether the pattern of false pretences reveals itself in the child-parent relationship, and if so, in what form.

With two others :
With preconvictions	..	..	..	.. 31
Without preconvictions	..	..	..	.. 2
Not captured and not known	..	..	..	1

$-$ 34

With more than two others :
With preconvictions .. .. 15[1]

Thirty-four used violence or the threat of violence in the commission of their last offences.   Eight others violently resisted arrest.

For the property offences, the value of the property taken is shown in the following table.[2]   All property offences committed since the prisoner's last release from prison in respect of which he was sentenced are included.

Inchoate—nothing set aside for taking	37
Up to £5	19
£5 to £99	91
£100 to £1,000	60
Over £1,000[3]	48

The gravity of their last offences revealed in the above tables is the pattern of serious crime in this country.

From our analysis of the preventive detainees in Parkhurst Prison in 1948 we deduced that they presented no great danger to society—that they were predominantly nuisances.   Now, when we consider the last offences of confirmed recidivists—potential preventive detainees—we find that we are facing the kernel of the problem of present criminality.   This contrast is the measure both of the failure of the 1908 Act, and of the great importance that must be attached to the habitual criminal provisions of the 1948 Act.

All Offences in respect of which they have been convicted

Our 270 confirmed recidivists have been convicted in the course of their careers of a total of 6,501 crimes.   These do not include the 6,379 offences which were " taken into consideration " at various

---

[1] Included in this table are eight prisoners, each of whom committed his last offence in company with his wife or mistress.   One prisoner had an original use for an accomplice : he committed a housebreaking in company with another criminal, was chased by the occupier of the house, and stopped by two policemen.   He managed to persuade them that he was the occupier of the premises chasing the housebreaker, his accomplice, who being fleeter of foot was some hundred yards ahead.   He was arrested two days later.

[2] The offences of the two prisoners convicted for coining are not included in this table.

[3] Two of these involved property of value exceeding £20,000, which has not been recovered.

times when they were sentenced. For reasons of space we cannot construct for this group a table comparable with Table A which would reveal all the offences of each of our prisoners. Table B[1] which follows is, therefore, confined to the total number of proved offences (i.e. not including those offences " taken into consideration ") of each type committed by the confirmed recidivists, and the number of offenders who were involved in them.

TABLE B

Number	Offence Type	Number of Offences Committed	Number of Offenders Involved
	Indictable Offences		
1	Murder[2]	1	1
2	Attempted murder	1	1
3	Sending letter threatening to murder ..	3	1
5	Wounding	17	15
8-10	Other offences of violence	33	21
16-18	Unnatural offences	44	11
19-22	Rape and other offences against women	7	6
26	Bigamy (and attempted bigamy) ..	22	15
27-33	Burglary, housebreaking, etc.	1,306	206
34-6	Robbery and extortion	54	35

[1] In 1938 the Canadian Royal Commission on the Penal System considered certain statistics relating to those prisoners confined in Canadian penitentiaries (Federal prisons) on January 1st, 1938, who had been convicted more than ten times. The following table is reproduced for comparative purposes from Appendix III of their report, and shows the crimes for which the 188 who so qualified had been convicted. It will be seen that a very similar pattern of crime is revealed here as in Table B :

Theft	1,057
Breaking, entering and theft	454
Drunkenness and liquor offences	415
Vagrancy, loitering, etc.	383
False pretences	265
Miscellaneous offences from breach of Railway Act to perjury and robbery while armed	301
Assault, disorderly, damage to property	215
Receiving and possessing stolen property	113
Escaping	60
Possession of drugs	47
Indecent act, indecent exposure, buggery	44
Carrying offensive weapons	38
Forgery, counterfeiting and uttering	35
Carnal knowledge, rape, etc.	7
	3,434

[2] This was a murder committed whilst on active service. The sentence of death was commuted to twenty years' penal servitude, the prisoner eventually being released during the sixth year of his detention. Since then he has been a persistent housebreaker.

TABLE B—*continued*

Number	Offence Type	Number of Offences Committed	Number of Offenders Involved
37-43	Aggravated larcenies	621	169
44-9	Simple and minor larcenies	1,801	264
50-3, 55	False pretences and other frauds ..	892	120
54	Receiving stolen goods	359	130
56	Arson	2	2
57	Other malicious injuries to property ..	16	13
58 & 59	Forgery (and uttering)	118	37
60 & 61	Coining (and uttering)	17	3
	Other indictable offences	63	28
	Non-Indictable Offences akin to Indictable Offences		
103-5	Assaults	180	74
107	Brothel keeping	5	3
109	Cruelty to Children	1	1
139	Indecent exposure	9	6
149	Malicious damage	44	28
167, 176-80, 183, 188, 189	Prevention of Crime Act, stealing, unlawful possession, frequenting, on enclosed premises, etc.	390	168
	Other Non-Indictable Offences		
106	Betting and gaming	25	10
108	Cruelty to animals	4	1
112	Education Acts (including truancy) ..	2	2
122-34	Highway Acts—motoring offences ..	117	44
140-3	Intoxicating liquor laws	101	38
150-3	Merchant Shipping Acts, Army, Navy and Air Force offenders[1]	69	44
163-6	Poor Law	19	13
171	Railway offences	15	10
185-7 & 191	Begging, sleeping out, other vagrancy offences	42	18
	Other offences dealt with summarily ..	101	49
	Total proved offences	6,501	(270)
	Offences " taken into consideration " ..	6,379	183
	GRAND TOTAL	12,880	270

[1] Most desertions and other military offences are *not* shown in the prisoner's record. Thus the figure of 69, since it includes only those noted in the penal records, grossly underestimates the actual number of such offences committed.

The following frequency distribution table complements Table B by showing the number of offences committed by each member of our group in respect of which they have been sentenced:

Number of offences Committed				Individuals
6- 10	..	..	..	2
11- 15	..	..	..	20
16- 20	..	..	..	39
21- 25	..	..	..	24
26- 30	..	..	..	27
31- 35	..	..	..	31
36- 40	..	..	..	28
41- 50	..	..	..	22
51- 60	..	..	..	13
61- 70	..	..	..	18
71- 80	..	..	..	7
81- 90	..	..	..	5
91-100	..	..	..	7
101-110	..	..	..	3
111-120	..	..	..	6
121-130	..	..	..	5
131-140	..	..	..	4
141-150	..	..	..	1
151-160	..	..	..	3
Over 160[1]	..	..	..	5
				270

Accordingly, each member of our group has committed and been sentenced for an average of 47·7 offences, with a standard deviation from this mean of 41·7 offences.[2]

Thus our confirmed recidivists, as a group, as well as having recently committed offences of appreciable danger to society, have a criminal record including a considerable number of such offences.

[1] These five are 164, 199, 224, 276 and 326 respectively. We may note in passing that eleven members of our group have devoted themselves almost exclusively to crime for periods exceeding forty years. One, now aged 70, began his career of habitual petty delinquency at the age of 11 years.

[2] From the Canadian statistics on the prisoners in penitentiaries on January 1st, 1938, who had been convicted more than ten times, the following has been calculated : The average number of offences committed by each member of that group was 18·4, with a standard deviation of 8 offences. The Canadian figures do not include offences " taken into consideration ", and therefore are comparable with the distribution of offences amongst our confirmed recidivists only when corrected for this fact. The English average, excluding offences " taken into consideration ", is 24·1, with a standard deviation of 12·6 offences.

Previous Sentences

Having considered all their offences and their present sentences, let us advert to their previous sentences imposed pursuant to conviction for indictable offences or for non-indictable offences akin to indictable offences[1]—that is to say, for the more serious types of crime.

The number and types of such sentences imposed on our " 270 " are as follows:

	Total Sentences	Offenders Involved
Probation, bound over, Probation of Offenders Act	402	212
Approved school	60	48
Borstal detention	103	95
Imprisonment	2,488[2]	270
Penal servitude	298	145
Preventive detention	18	15
Fined	116	78
	3,485	270

From this table we can deduce the average previous penal record of the members of our group (incurred subsequent to the commission of criminal offences of a more serious nature) :[3]

Probation, bound over, Probation of Offenders Act	..	1·48
Approved school	..	·2
Borstal detention	..	·38
Imprisonment	..	9·21
Penal servitude	..	1·10
Preventive detention	..	·07
Fined	..	·43

This mythical average member of our group had also been sentenced once pursuant to "other non-indictable offences".

The comparison of the above average previous penal record with that of the preventive detainee group (see page 300) reveals that the most significant difference between them is that the average preventive detainee has been previously sentenced to preventive

[1] Seventy-nine of the " 270 " have been previously convicted of " other non-indictable offences " as follows :

once ..	..	..	30	five times.	..	..	5	ten times	..	..	4
twice ..	..	..	13	six times	..	..	1	eleven times	..	..	1
three times	..	..	11	seven times	..	..	1	twenty times	..	..	1
four times	..	..	9	eight times	..	..	1	twenty-one times	..	1
				nine times	..	..	1				

This gives a total of 272 such convictions.

[2] The range of such sentences previously imposed is from three to thirty-one.

[3] These are averages based on all 270 offenders, and not on the number of offenders who had actually previously been sentenced to each type of punishment.

detention more frequently than the average confirmed recidivist —·41 as contrasted with ·07. The other differences between their previous penal records may well be a function of the different age compositions of the two groups,[1] courts hesitating to impose penal servitude on younger men and more freely imposing sentences under the Probation of Offenders Act, 1907.

Eleven of our confirmed recidivists have been subjected to corporal punishment—three have suffered the " cat " and eight have been birched. Two of the three sentences of the " cat " were imposed pursuant to robberies with violence, the third being ordered by the Board of Visitors for an assault on a prison officer: all three later committed crimes of violence, the first two being subsequently convicted of wounding with the intention of inflicting grievous bodily harm, the third of robbery with violence. The later histories of the eight who were birched[2] are similar. The six who were birched by order of a court all later committed crimes of violence—two being convicted of robbery with violence; two of aggravated assaults; one of three aggravated assaults, of arson,[3] and of malicious damage; and one is the sole member of our group who has been convicted of rape (at the same time he was found guilty of robbery with violence, and of attempting to suffocate his victim). The remaining two prisoners, both of whom were birched for prison offences, have less violent later histories—however, one was implicated in the Dartmoor Mutiny of 1932, and the other has turned his wrath upon himself, twice having attempted suicide and frequently suffering minor self-inflicted injuries.[4]

Let us now turn from the objective details of the offences committed by members of this group, and the punishments inflicted

[1] This is particularly true of the higher ratio of Borstal detention amongst the confirmed recidivists, for by the time the Borstal system was functioning many of the preventive detainees were beyond the age at which such a sentence could be imposed on them.

[2] Six of these birchings were judicially imposed, the remaining two being punishments for prison offences. One of the six, as a youth, was ordered on two separate occasions to be birched for minor larceny offences.

[3] The offence of arson committed by this prisoner is of some interest. At 10.35 p.m. he called at a police station seeking accommodation for the night, was told that he could not be allowed to sleep there, and left the station immediately. At 11.30 p.m., after a complaint of a hayrick fire had been received, he walked into the police station and asked: " Is the b—— burning ? " He was arrested and sentenced to three years' penal servitude.

[4] From this presentation of the later histories of the eleven of our " 270 " subjected to corporal punishment, one cannot allege that the corporal punishment imposed was a contributory cause of the later violent conduct, for the number involved is too small, and by definition a propensity to violence antedated the corporal punishment. But, on the other hand, our figures do cast considerable doubt on the deterrent quality of this form of punishment.

on them, to a consideration of some of their personal qualities, and of their environmental background.

Age when last sentenced

Computing their respective ages on the date of their last conviction, I found a range of from 30[1] to 70 years. The average was 41 years 6 months, with a standard deviation of 8 years 6 months.

Age when first sentenced[2]

Here the range was from 8 to 42 years; the average being 19 years 2 months, and the standard deviation 3 years 3 months.[3]

For the preventive detainee group, as for the confirmed recidivists, our figures indicate a later onset of proved criminality than might have been expected, and is often suggested. Further research will be needed to decide whether habitual criminals do in fact commence crime at an average age of nineteen to twenty years, or whether our figures merely indicate that many of the criminals whose records we are analysing had considerable preliminary success in avoiding the detection of their crimes, at least by the police.[4] This preliminary success in avoiding arrest might well prove to be a causative factor in habitual criminality—causative in the sense that it confirms and strengthens a pre-existing condition.

Of our "270", 29 per cent. were first convicted between the ages of eight and sixteen years, and 32 per cent. between the ages of seventeen and twenty years, making a total of 61 per cent. who were first convicted before attaining their majority.[5]

---

[1] The qualifying minimum for a " confirmed recidivist."

[2] Including truancy and " care and protection " cases.

[3] The age at which the 188 Canadian recidivists committed their first offences can be computed from the report of the Royal Commission, as follows :

range	..	..	.. 8 to 51 years
average	..	..	.. 21 years 1 month
standard deviation		..	8 years 1 month

[4] In *English Juvenile Courts*, by W. A. Elkin, p. 201, the idea was advanced that this later incidence of proved criminality amongst this type of criminal can be attributed to the fact that until the Children's Courts were established and functioning adequately there was frequent hesitancy in charging youthful offenders. To some few of our prisoners this might apply, but its effect cannot account for the relative lateness of the appearance of our confirmed recidivists in the courts, bearing in mind that their present average age is 41 years.

[5] Comparable figures for the Canadian recidivists were :

eight to sixteen years	..	32 per cent.
seventeen to twenty years	..	30 ,,
		62 ,,

At the other end of the age range there are thirteen confirmed recidivists who were first convicted between the ages of thirty and forty-two years. All thirteen specialise in offences against property (four in larceny; four housebreaking and ;burglary; and five in false pretences). Given as an hypothesis that all thirteen were imbued with personality defects tending towards criminality, it is interesting to inquire what environmental conditions precipitated the commission of their first crimes. What was the spark which set fire to their incipient criminality ?

With regard to ten, the position is:

Four committed their first crimes during their first protracted period of unemployment (one of them having also taken to drink during this period) ;

Five committed their first crimes shortly after serious disturbances in their marital relationships (two—their wives dying ; one—his wife deserting him ; another deserting his wife ; another after a serious argument and fight with the prostitute with whom he was living). Of these five, three became addicted to drink in the period between the marital disturbance and the commission of the crime.

One committed his first crime pursuant to discharge from the police force for drunkenness.

The remaining three were subject to no apparent environmental change shortly preceding their first conviction.

Age when first sentenced to Borstal detention

Ninety-five of our group have been sentenced to Borstal detention. This occurred at the following ages:

15 years	3[1]
16 „	13
17 „	17
18 „	22
19 „	24
20 „	13
21 „	3

Ignoring periods of up to three days' imprisonment, and periods of remand in prison awaiting trial, fifty-four of these ninety-five were sentenced to Borstal detention before being sentenced to periods of imprisonment. The remaining forty-one

---

[1] According to their age as stated in their existing penal records.

had been committed to prison before their period of Borstal training, as follows:

1 previous sentence of imprisonment	..	..	30
2 „ sentences „	„	..	..	9
3 „ „ „	„	..	..	1
4 „ „ „	„	..	..	1

The provisions of Section 18 of the Criminal Justice Act, 1948, by which courts may sentence youthful offenders to be detained for up to three months in a detention centre, may provide a new outlet for the popular desire for a " short sharp punishment" for young offenders. It was possibly this idea that led to the premature imprisonment of many of these forty-one confirmed recidivists.

Age when first sentenced to prison

The range is from 15 to 42 years; the average age at the time of the first sentence of imprisonment[1] being 21 years 7 months, with a standard deviation of 4 years 4 months.

We have now revealed an important characteristic of our group: though of average age of 41 years when last convicted, and 19 years when first sentenced, the average age at which they were first sentenced to imprisonment was 21 years. One hundred and six of them—almost 40 per cent.—had been committed to prison before attaining their majority. It would therefore seem valuable to investigate to what extent the early application of imprisonment has deprived that punishment of any deterrent quality it might possess, and has habituated youths to a criminal career, to criminal associations, and to a criminal standard of values. Considering the above figures, it is surely not too bold an hypothesis to regard the extensive application of imprisonment to youthful offenders not only as a non-deterrent but as a causative factor in confirmed recidivism.

There are some gross examples of the premature imposition of imprisonment on members of our group. Twelve were so sentenced when sixteen years of age, and three when only fifteen. Of these three, one was sentenced to imprisonment once, another four times, and the third five times (four times to imprisonment, and once to penal servitude) before the age of twenty-one years.[2] Five other

---

[1] Periods of up to three days are not here considered. Nor are periods spent in prison on remand for trial.

[2] This last sequence of sentences was imposed in Australia ; the others mentioned are all sentences by English courts.

members of our group were committed to prison on four occasions before they became adults.

Age when first sentenced to penal servitude

One hundred and forty-five of our confirmed recidivists have been previously sentenced to penal servitude, as follows:

Once previously	63
Twice „	42
Three times previously	20
Four „ „	13
Five „ „	4
Six „ „	2
Seven „ „	1

Also, fifteen of the above have been previously sentenced[1] to preventive detention as follows:

Once previously	12
Twice „	3

The range of ages at which these 145 prisoners were first sentenced to penal servitude is from 17 to 55 years;[2] the average being 30 years 3 months, with a standard deviation of 6 years 5 months.

Place of Birth

London	128	⎫
Other English cities :		
Liverpool	6	
Sheffield	3	
Birmingham	3	
Newcastle	2	
Southampton	2	⎬ England : 226
Leeds	2	
Oxford	1	
Reading	1	
Hull	1	
Portsmouth	1	
	— 22	
Remainder of England	76	⎭

[1] Not including those whose convictions as habitual criminals or sentences of preventive detention were quashed on appeal.

[2] There were four sentences of penal servitude imposed on offenders under the age of 21 years :
   one in Eire, aged 17 ;
   one in Canada, aged 18 ;
   one in Australia, aged 18 ; and
   one in England, on a youth aged 19, convicted of manslaughter.

Scottish Cities :

Glasgow	..	..	6	
Edinburgh	..	..	2	
Dundee ..	..	..	1	
Aberdeen	..	..	1	
			—	10
Remainder of Scotland	..		8	
Wales : Cardiff	..	..	1	
Remainder of Wales	..		8	
Eire	..	..	6	
Northern Ireland ..	..		3	
Australia	..	..	3	
Canada	..	..	1	
South Africa	..	..	1	
Russia	..	..	1	
Malta	..	..	1	
Spain	..	..	1	

This information is not of any great assistance in the determination of the urban or rural quality of habitual criminality, for the large proportion of our confirmed recidivists born in London may merely reflect the means by which we selected our group—taking all those with certain qualifications admitted to Wandsworth Prison, a London convict prison. However, we can deduce to what extent this predominantly English body of men have exercised their talents in other countries.

International Criminals

Hereunder we shall exclude those civil or military offences committed by members of our group when serving overseas in the armed forces, and those offences committed in foreign ports by merchant seamen.

Forty-three of our " 270 " have been convicted outside England and Wales, as follows:

In Scotland	..	..	..	..	..	..	19
In Scotland and U.S.A.	..	..	..	..		1	
In Scotland and France	..	..	..	..		1	
In Scotland and Switzerland ..	..	..	..		1		
In Ireland (N. Ireland and Eire)	..	..	..		6		
In Australia	..	..	..	..	..	3	
In South Africa	..	..	..	..		3	
In Canada	..	..	..	..	..	3	
In Canada, U.S.A. and Eire ..	..	..	..		1		
In U.S.A.	..	..	..	..	..	1	
In U.S.A. and Nassau	..	..	..		1		
In France	..	..	..	..	..	1	
In Spain and Belgium	..	..	..		1		
In Belgium, Bermuda, Canada, Eire and France	..		1				

Thus only eighteen of the confirmed recidivists have committed offences in countries outside the British Isles; and the European criminal rarely crosses the Channel.

Early Environment

The terms "dependent", "marginal" and "comfortable", were defined in Chapter VII (see page 304), and we shall adhere to those definitions in this chapter. It will be recalled that they gave a very wide meaning to "comfortable", including therein any family which had accumulated resources sufficient to maintain itself for four months.

Many problems arose in deciding on the classification of any particular family under these terms, and no complete accuracy is claimed for the grouping finally adopted which, owing to the incomplete and irregular information available, must inevitably vary with the opinions and deductions of the person reading the evidence.[1] However, where any substantial doubt remained, the prisoner's early economic environment was classed as "not known".

The economic status of their parental homes was, then :

Institution or orphanage	15[2]
Dependent	56
Marginal	62
Comfortable	48
Not known	89

On the question of the "broken home", a matter of first importance in the ætiology of juvenile delinquency and criminality, some information is available concerning our "270". The following classification was made on the basis of the major portion of the first ten years of the prisoner's life—for example, Y.E.'s father deserted his mother twelve months after Y.E.'s birth. A few months later he was sent to an orphanage where he remained until the age of eleven, when he returned to his mother. He therefore appears hereunder amongst the group in "Institution or orphanage", and not in the

---

[1] The decisions on this point concerning the preventive detainees are more reliable in that these prisoners were consulted where there was any doubt. Even so, five were marked as "not known", the statements of the prisoners, or deductions made from their conversation, not being accepted in the absence of some corroboration in the penal, Borstal or probation records.

[2] Included here when more than five of the first ten years were spent in an orphanage.

" Mother only " group. Similarly a prisoner who is adopted before he is five years of age is classed as " adopted ".

Both parents	73
Mother only	21
Father only	18
Mother and stepfather	22
Father and stepmother	11
Grandparents	5
Other relatives	14
Adopted	10
Institution or orphanage	22
Not known	74

Accordingly, of the 196 of whom we know, 123—nearly 70 per cent.—come from " broken homes ".

Twenty-four of our confirmed recidivists are known to be illegitimate.

It must be stressed that the above information as to the economic status of their parental homes and the number that emanated from " broken homes " provides only a clue to the understanding of the true quality of their early family relationships. Many that came from " comfortable " homes where both their parents lived had the seeds of their criminality sown by their affectionless and amoral family environment; and, of course, the contrary pattern frequently occurred, the members of the " dependent " and " broken homes " loving the child and devotedly endeavouring to guide him.

It is a matter of regret that only in a few cases is any information available in these records—and to the courts which sentence these prisoners—as to inherited constitutional or psychological defects ; and also that what information there is, is of an irregular and often psychologically unenlightened quality. How can sentences be rationally calculated in ignorance of such matters ?

When reading through these records for purposes of the above groupings, note was taken of those prisoners who were subjected to extreme psychological stresses during their infancy and early youth—illegitimate, unwanted and rejected children; obviously " affectionless characters ",[1] alcoholic, insane, grossly immoral or criminal parents; and so on. There were forty-eight such cases.[2]

---

[1] As defined by Dr. John Bowlby in *Forty-four Juvenile Thieves*.
[2] In this analysis of a group no purpose would be served by presenting these forty-eight exceptional cases at length—exceptional not in the sense of their unhappy family relationships but in that information was available about those relationships.

Industrial History

(a) " Skilled ", " Semi-skilled ", or " Unskilled "[1]

Considering each prisoner at the very best period of his life in this respect, and giving him the benefit of any doubt:

Skilled 46
Semi-skilled 96
Unskilled 128

Many shown as " skilled " and " semi-skilled " were trained in their crafts—often as carpenters, fitters, bootmakers or sheet metal workers[2]—in Borstal or prison.

(b) Longest period in any one employment since 1930

Excluding service in the armed forces, but including service in the Merchant Navy, we can state these periods as follows:

No employment 10
" Odd jobs "[3] 21
Self-employed[4] 37
Up to one month 11
One to two months 19
Two to three months 32
Three to six months 33
Six months to one year 27
Over one year 80

These periods of employment over a span of eighteen years, though not as brief as those of the preventive detainees, clearly indicate the particularly poor working record of the confirmed recidivists.

[1] See p. 304 for definitions of these terms.
[2] One prisoner trained as a sheet-metal worker at Chelmsford Borstal Institution is extremely grateful for this training, and when out of prison is an efficient and reliable worker, having no difficulty in obtaining employment. He also uses his training by occasionally turning his hand to coining !
[3] Here appear those who would give no information that could be verified to the police concerning their employment but who alleged that they did odd gardening or labouring jobs for private individuals. One prisoner who has in the last thirty-four years been employed for only nine days—as a window-cleaner—appears in the " up to one month " group.
[4] " Self-employed " includes street-trading, bookmaking, working as a jobbing gardener, selling glasses in hotels or elastic on the side-walk, and so on. Where a man has worked in some employment and has also been self-employed he is shown under " self-employed " only when he has been working on his own for a longer single period than he has worked for any employer.

(*c*) Employed or unemployed when last crime (or series of crimes) committed

Employed[1]	75
Unemployed	195

Thus, in a time of full employment, over 72 per cent. of our confirmed recidivists were unemployed the last time they recommenced their criminal activities.[2]

We cannot tell, in all cases, whether the unemployment led to the commission of the crime, or the intention to commit the crime led to the abandonment of the employment. However, with many prisoners unemployment would seem to be a causative factor in their relapse to crime. By a causative factor I here mean a condition which, though it may not canalise or modify an existing asocial tendency, at least controls the occasion on which this tendency shall express itself. It is ætiological in the sense that it conditions the selection of the occasion for crime.

(*d*) The Prisoner's own description of his trade or occupation.

As was done for the preventive detainees, a table was prepared showing each prisoner's statement of his trade or occupation, and dividing the true from the false statements. The resulting table appears as Appendix D, and covers some seventy-four occupations varying from labourer to research chemist.

(*e*) Employment on leaving school

Taught a " skilled " or " semi-skilled " occupation	88
Army (including I.R.A.)	25
Labouring or " unskilled " occupation	70
" Dead-end jobs "[3]	36
Self-employed (street-trading, etc.)	10
No regular work—predominantly crime	8
Not known	33

---

[1] Includes " self-employed " as widely defined in (*b*) above, and also service in the armed forces or in the Merchant Navy from which the prisoner had not deserted.

[2] Of the 188 Canadian recidivists only thirty-seven—under 20 per cent.—were employed when last arrested. Of course, the time between the commission of the offence and arrest could well account for their even poorer showing in this regard than our group.

[3] H. K. is an example of the cloying effect of " dead-end jobs ". Between 1932 (aged 15) and 1937 (aged 20) he was employed as an errand boy by twelve different firms. There were appreciable intervals of unemployment between one employment and the next. In 1935 he stole from a motor van and was placed on probation. In 1938 he committed a similar offence and was sentenced to three months' imprisonment. Since then he has almost confined his activities to crime.

(f) Prison employment

Before concluding our investigation of their industrial histories, mention should be made of their employment in prison when their records were consulted. Their prison tasks were, at that time, as follows:

Mailbags	 78	Builders	 3
Tailor's shop	 84	Matmaking	 3
Carpenter's shop	 13	Officers' mess orderly	.. 2
Sack shop	 12	Hospital cleaners	 2
Gardens	 9	Clerks ..	 2
Kitchen ..	 6	Cleaners	 2
Laundry	 6	Old-age party	 2
Tinshop	 5	Hospital orderly	 2
Painters ..	 5	Barber	 1
Shoe shop	 5	Bookbinding ..	 1
Brush shop	 4	Library	 1
Bakehouse	 3	Electrician	 1
Inside works	 3	Weaver	 1
Farm party	 3	Bricklayer's course ..	.. 1
Miscellaneous stores	 3	Engineer's fitter's course	.. 1

In hospital, 6

There was rarely any connection between prison employment and the individual's trade or vocation when at liberty. Exceptions were the carpenters—most of whom were employed in the carpenter's shop where as a rule they were diligent work-men—and a few other more skilled prisoners whose talents were put to use by the prison authorities. In all, there were seventeen who thus found an outlet for their industrial skills whilst in prison.

To summarise our inquiry into the industrial history of confirmed recidivists—though not particularly lacking in industrial skill, and though drawn from those following many different trades and occupations, they tend not to settle down to any one employment for any appreciable length of time, and generally are unemployed on those occasions when they turn to crime.

Military Record

No service in armed forces[1] 93
Served in peace-time only 11

[1] Including the Merchant Navy, but not including the I.R.A.

Served in Boer War and 1914-18 war   1
Served during 1914-18 war   34
May have served in 1914-18 war (doubtful)   5
Served in 1939-45 war   112
Served in 1914-18 and 1939-45 wars   7
Permanent soldier   3
Not known   4

Of the 168 who have certainly seen military, naval, merchant navy or air force service:

Deserters when last arrested   29
Discharged with " very bad " or " bad " characters[1]   42
Discharged with " fair " or " indifferent " characters   19
Discharged with " exemplary ", " very good " or " good " characters[2]   31
Discharged on medical grounds, character " good " or not assessed   29
Merchant Navy ; no information *re* discharge   10
" Services no longer required "—character not assessed   ..   7
No information regarding the discharge   1

Thus, at least 40 per cent. of those who have served in the armed forces did so in an unsatisfactory manner.

Home Conditions immediately before this Sentence

No fixed abode[3]   131
In army   4
Better hotels, flats or over three months in lodgings   21
Living at place of employment (butlers, etc.)   2
With parents or relatives in homes :
  (a) Clean or reasonably good conditions   14
  (b) Dirty or very poor conditions   7
                                                              —   21
With wife or *de facto* wife in home :
  (a) Clean or reasonably good conditions   50
  (b) Dirty or very poor conditions   19
  (c) Condition not known   21
                                                              —   90
In home of a friend—good conditions   1

[1] Or because of civil offences.
[2] Frequently the military authorities were generous in giving these " good " characters, men who had deserted several times during their period of service often being so classed. Two of the thirty-one were mentioned in despatches—one whilst a prisoner of war, the other for his meritorious conduct in the North African campaign.
[3] Includes hostels, common lodging houses, cheap hotels and sleeping out.

Marital Status

Bachelors[1]	88
Divorced	31
Widowers[2]	10
Married[3]	141

Of the 141 who are married, the present position of their marriages is:

Living with wife when out of prison	57
Not living together, but writing to one another..	11
Not living together and not writing	46
Separated	25
Doubtful[4]	2

Of our "270", fifty were known to be living, when they were last arrested, with women who were not their wives.

The position of these liaisons is:

	Bachelors and Divorcees	Married and Widowers
Transient	8	11
Was semi-permanent, now finished ..	9	12
Still lasting	2	8

Our confirmed recidivists, married and unmarried, have a total of 285 living children (not including step-children, adopted children and several children born to prisoners' wives, the husband known not to be the putative father). These 285 children, twenty-eight of whom are illegitimate, are living as follows :

Self-supporting			50
With mother and father (when he is " out ")			73
With mother and not with father[5]			91
With mother—father's return doubtful			9
Deserted by mother and father :[6]			
In orphanage or other non-penal institution		25	
With relatives		24	
Adopted or with foster-parents		9	
Whereabouts not known to prisoner		4	
			— 62

[1] Including one whose marriage was annulled.

[2] Here appear only those who know they are widowers.

[3] Here are included those who do not know whether or not they are widowers or divorced.

[4] In these two cases the effect of the present sentences of penal servitude on the cohesion of the marriages is not known.

[5] Including cases in which the mother has remarried, or is living with another man, or with her parents or other relatives. Unmarried mothers are also included.

[6] This includes cases where the mother is dead or in prison.

Only six of these children are known to be in Borstal or Approved Schools, but since there is no need for prisoners to reveal this fact and no practical way of ascertaining it from the prisoners' records, it is certain that there are many more than six delinquents among these 285 children. Unhappily, crime is in this sense self-propagating and our " 270 " have imposed intense environmental and some hereditary stresses on their children.

The marital pattern revealed is not as bad as that we found amongst our preventive detainees, but it is an abnormally confused one in which, not surprisingly, a stable home life is quite exceptional.[1]

The ætiological significance of the disturbed marital relationships of members of our group can only be surmised. Certainly, many cases were found—some of which we have already mentioned —where the death of a wife or other breach in the cohesion of the marriage was a precipitating cause of the individual's relapse to or commencement of a criminal life.

One of the effects of the undue proportion of broken homes reveals itself in the lack of correspondents and visitors for many of these confirmed recidivists while they are in prison. The ensuing feeling of remoteness from the outside world tends to confirm their acceptance of criminal and penal standards.[2] There are forty-five members of our group who have no next-of-kin.

In reading through the records note was taken of those confirmed recidivists whose marital relationships were extraordinarily complicated or confused, and clearly linked with the prisoner's criminal way of life: there were thirty-two such cases. Also, there are at least six other prisoners who are happily married to women who are themselves active criminals. This latter is a rather different pattern and argues the complete " professionality " of their criminality, and their acceptance of a penal and criminal existence.

---

[1] The comparable figures for the 188 Canadian recidivists are :

Married	65
Widowers	12
Bachelors	111
Number with dependants ..	47
Number of dependants	100

Here, as in our group, there is an abnormally high percentage of bachelors.

[2] To the same effect is a statement by D. Clemmer : " Forty per cent. of our population had broken homes, as defined. As to whether or not this is a causative factor in crime no opinion is ventured. It is definitely asserted, however, that this fact affects the prison culture. About one-third of our prisoners have almost no visits and receive almost no mail. This condition makes for the most lonely and deadening of existences."—*The Prison Community*, p. 48.

Such women are always admirable "prisoners' wives", visiting and writing frequently, and knowing exactly what they can and cannot bring or send to their husbands whilst they are in prison.[1]

But apart from these criminal wives, and the few others who, though not themselves active in crime, cheerfully live on the proceeds of their husbands' crimes (there are eight members of our group deeply attached to their families which they manage to support largely by their criminal activities),[2] the wives of sixteen of these prisoners must be mentioned—they are the breadwinners of their families, holding their homes together, and by dint of their own hard work providing a relatively secure background for their children to which their husbands are admitted. The punishment these men inflict on their wives is infinitely in excess of that imposed on the men by the courts. The decision facing a woman with children whose husband has several times previously been committed to prison is an extremely difficult one. Let us take a typical example— J. J., aged 30, is a married man who lived with his wife and one child, aged nine years, in a prefabricated bungalow. Their living conditions were clean and comfortable, and they were all on good terms. When they married the wife was ignorant of his four previous criminal offences and his sequence of sentences of probation, imprisonment, Borstal detention and imprisonment. Since the marriage he has been three times convicted and sentenced to prison. After the first two periods of imprisonment, during which she maintained the home by domestic work, they were reunited. Now he has been sentenced to three years' penal servitude, and she is considering seeking a separation order. To hold the marriage together will condemn her, she has no doubt, to a life of drudgery; to break it and cut herself adrift from a man to whom she and her child are deeply attached is also undesirable, but if she is to do so the break must be made now while she is still young. At least sixteen

---

[1] In *Walls Have Mouths* W. F. R. Macartney makes this point : " The professional crook who comes from a criminal family is seldom let down in this respect . . . he can be almost certain that his wife or girl, no matter what she does while he is away, maybe for years, will write to him, will visit him, and will be waiting for him when he comes out "—p. 61.

[2] One prisoner, a receiver, keeps his wife and family in comfort by his legal and extra-legal business transactions. When he is in prison his father comes out of retirement and manages the business, supporting both families. The father was, until his " retirement ", conducting the business in a similarly shady way to that which he has taught his son.

wives of members of our group have followed the first course and have sacrificed their lives to their children and to their usually worthless husbands.

The above side-wind has blown us temporarily off the course of our analysis of the confirmed recidivists. As a group, we found their marital relationships most unsettled, and that an undue proportion of their children were condemned to a permanently disrupted home life.

Before leaving these problems arising from their sexual relationships it must be mentioned that at least eighteen of them are absolute or amphigenic inverts. There are undoubtedly many more than eighteen homosexuals amongst our group, and this number represents only those who have revealed this condition in crimes committed in or out of prison, and by other strong evidence in their medical and prison records. It does not include contingent inverts whose homosexuality is conditioned by the extraordinary circumstances of their imprisonment, and of whom there is a very large number in the prison community. The proportion of this type of homosexual is particularly high amongst our group, all of whom have considerable institutional experience and are detained for protracted periods.

To summarise: though the sexual energies of the confirmed recidivists are not so misdirected, nor the marital relationships so disturbed, as those of the preventive detainees, with the increasing institutionalisation of the former group the differences between them are tending to diminish.

Honesty : Sobriety : Companions and associates

The police reports on the honesty, sobriety, companions and associates of the confirmed recidivists can be summarised briefly, the exact terminology used being presented in Appendix E.

Honesty.—All except two, who have committed no property offences, were stated to be dishonest.

Sobriety.—One hundred and fifty-seven are reasonably sober. Concerning eighteen the police have no knowledge on this point. It is difficult to estimate the extent to which the insobriety of the remaining ninety-five is connected with their criminality. In some cases it is clear that bouts of alcoholism and crime occur together, and there are five such cases amongst our records, two of which relate to serious crimes of violence (attempted murder and rape). There is also one other case of a prisoner who though he takes relatively little alcohol is extremely susceptible to it, and whose larceny offences are usually committed after alcohol has been taken.

Three of our group are known to be or to have been drug addicts

Companions and associates.—The police do not adversely describe the companions and associates of one hundred and ten of the confirmed recidivists (including in this number those who are of a solitary disposition and who have no associates). Concerning the remaining one hundred and sixty, the police express varying shades of disapproval (see Appendix E), from " companions are of doubtful character " to " associates with convicted thieves, prostitutes, deserters and undesirable people in low-class cafés." The ætiological significance of these associations is doubtful, but certainly they help to perpetuate and condition the way of life of a confirmed recidivist.

Physical Condition

When a prisoner is admitted, the medical officer, as well as noting on his record the details of his previous maladies, injuries, scars and present physical condition, gives a brief statement of his general state of health. For our " 270 " these were:

Good	..	..	.. 132
Fair	..	..	.. 78
Indifferent	..	..	.. 31
Poor	..	..	.. 29

It was found that fifty-one members of our group are either precluded by their physical condition from living for more than a short time outside an institution (hospital, prison or charitable home) or are seriously hindered from pursuing extra-mural occupations suitable to their mental abilities.[1]

---

[1] These fifty-one include the badly deformed, those with amputated limbs, those with limbs wasted by disease or paralysed, those with pronounced cardiovascular deficiency and other heart defects, the tubercular, the diabetic, those whose vision is very defective and who are hindered by severe squints, and so on ; but in no case was the disadvantage exaggerated, and all fifty-one are undoubtedly " seriously hindered " by their physical condition.

The frequency with which several particular physical defects occur is:

Asthma 8
Arthritis or chronic rheumatism 17
Chronic bronchitis 25
Hæmorrhoids (requiring operation) 14
Varicose veins (requiring regular attention or operation) .. 30
Troublesome hernias 28

Twenty-five have been concussed or suffered some serious injury to the head.

The incidence of venereal disease is certainly underestimated by the following figures, which represent only those prisoners whose syphilis or gonorrhœa has been diagnosed and treated in prison, or who have informed the medical officer that they have so suffered:

Syphilis 23
Gonorrhœa 45

The general picture of the health of the confirmed recidivists is then of an appreciably lower standard than that of a cross-section of the general population; but who do not constitute as pathetic a group as the preventive detainees.

Mental condition and intellectual ability

No reliable information is shown on the prisoner's record as to his educational standard or intellectual ability,[1] nor has it been found possible to submit any of them to mental or scholastic tests.

The position is only slightly more satisfactory concerning their mental condition. Outstanding psychopathological defects are noted on the medical history sheets, and the results of any special mental observations to which they are subjected; but 269 of them are shown to have " no psychiatric disability ", or to be " not certifiable and not M.D.", or have not been considered from this point of view. The other member of our group was certified during this sentence and committed to Broadmoor.[2] But despite this formal

[1] In the penal records there is a space to note the prisoner's standard of education in reading, writing and arithmetic. In this space, for all " 270 ", appears either of the following legends—" RWM " or " RWA ". They both have no connection with reality, and the difference is a result of clerical confusion between " Reading and Writing, Moderate ", and " Reading, Writing, Arithmetic ". Nor is there any variation from these formulæ for highly intelligent, well-educated prisoners, or for the six illiterate, borderline mental defectives in our group.

[2] Six other members of our group have at one time or another been certified and committed to asylums.

pattern of sanity appearing from the records, there are forty-nine requiring special mention. Nine are borderline mental defectives. Forty can be classed as "non-sane, non-insane offenders" as that phrase has been defined by Sir Norwood East[1] and others, or alternatively as "psychic inferior personalities", as "psychopathic personalities", or as possessed of serious "personality defects".[2] Whatever the exact psychiatric classification and terminology used, it is certain that these forty-nine[3] are suitable inhabitants for that type of special institution envisaged in the East—de Hubert Report on the Psychological Treatment of Crime.

From our investigation of the two groups of habitual criminals it is clear that for at least 20 per cent. of them "a special penal institution is required, combining the features of a prison and a mental hospital, where the non-sane, non-insane offender can receive training and specialised medical care."[4] It is understood that the eventual establishment of such an institution is likely ; the effect on the prison population in general will be most salutary.

One problem that should be investigated in such an institution is that of the "swallower". Amongst our confirmed recidivists there are nine prisoners who have on several occasions swallowed foreign objects, sometimes thus attempting suicide but usually for more obscure motives. There are several explanations advanced for these strange deglutitional exercises, but on examination none of them constitutes a rational and satisfactory explanation of what appears to be predominantly a prison phenomenon.

Thus, though the confirmed recidivists include a lesser proportion of near-certifiable offenders or borderline mental defectives

[1] See the Galton Lecture, *Eugenics Review*, April 1947, and *Society and the Criminal*, p. 229.
[2] "Psychopathic Personality Traits—Terminological Considerations," by Jan Sachs, *Acta Psychiatrica et Neurologica*, Vol. XXL, p. 1.
[3] There are several others in our group who would be included were exact diagnosis and classification undertaken.
[4] *Society and the Criminal*, Sir Norwood East, p. 240. At p. 15 of the same work this idea, as it had been presented in the East—de Hubert Report on the Psychological Treatment of Crime, is summarised : "In the institution selected cases could live under special conditions of training and treatment. . . . Its aims would be to amend behaviour by the application of psychiatric experience. The institution would also serve as a colony in which a further type of offender could live who had proved unable to adapt himself to ordinary social conditions, but for whom reformative measures, however specialised, seemed useless and the inflexibility and restrictions of ordinary prison life inappropriate."

than do the preventive detainees, twenty per cent. so far vary from the normal as to require special psychiatric attention.[1]

Prison behaviour and escaping

Their conduct during their current and penultimate prison sentences was:

Bad[2]	..	..	..	.. 47
Indifferent..	..	..	.. 36
Good	..	..	..	.. 77
Very good[3]	..	..	.. 110

Thus they are a very well-behaved group.

In a study of two hundred Dartmoor convicts, Dr. J. J. Landers[4] classified their reactions to imprisonment as follows:

Passive indifference	..	..	27 per cent.
Adaptation	..	..	43 „ „
Mild hostility	..	..	30 „ „

The showing of our confirmed recidivists accords well with these findings, the differences between them being explained by the longer habituation of the confirmed recidivists to penal conditions, and their higher average age.

It seems strange, at first sight, that though the habitual criminal finds it impossible when at liberty to conform to the conduct society demands of him, he does not express his revolt against authority whilst in prison. If our group did not include psychopaths, their prison conduct would conform even more completely to the requirements of the prison authorities.[5]

Four of our group took part in the Dartmoor Mutiny of 1932, receiving sentences of twenty-one months' imprisonment, three

---

[1] It is very likely, owing to the irregular and meagre quality of the information at present available, that this figure of 20 per cent. grossly underestimates the true position. Dr. G. K. Stürup, chief of the Herstedvester Prison for Psychopaths in Denmark, having conducted a diagnostic investigation of a randomly selected group of prisoners in the ordinary Danish prisons (from which psychopaths are potentially excluded) reported that " out of 335 prisoners examined psychopathy was found only in 5 per cent. of the ' first-timers ', while the figure for habitual criminals was 37 per cent."—*Report on the Eighth Congress of Scandinavian Psychiatrists*, p. 32.

[2] A high proportion of those whose conduct is " bad " belong to the non-sane group we have mentioned, several being aggressive psychopaths.

[3] For definitions of these terms see p. 314.

[4] *Journal of Mental Science*, November 1938.

[5] Mention should be made of one prisoner, aged 45, who has spent the greater part of his life since the age of 8 years in penal institutions and has never lost a day's remission of sentence owing to misconduct.

years', three years', and four years' penal servitude respectively. Several others, though in Dartmoor at the time, were not involved in the mutiny.[1]

Four prisoners, though committing no prison offences, are great nuisances to the administration by maintaining a flow of trivial petitions and applications. This they do either to relieve the monotony, or because they have come to believe some of their own wildly untruthful allegations.

Twenty-four confirmed recidivists have at one time or another during their penal careers attempted, with varying success, to escape:

From Approved school or Borstal	7
Prison	12
Cells at various law courts	3
Military custody	1
A mental institution	1

Only three could be regarded as determined escapers, and these had good physique and keen intelligence to help them in their frequent, and occasionally successful, attempts to escape. All three have considerable standing in the eyes of the other prisoners.

Religious persuasion and conversions

The following table shows the last statements of members of our group as to their religious persuasion:

Church of England	143
Roman Catholic	39
Wesleyan	18
Christian Scientist	16
Salvationist	13
Jewish	10
Methodist	8
Presbyterian	6
Unitarian	1
Quaker	1
Atheist, none, nil	15

---

[1] One of them was of some assistance to the penal authorities for, as he says, he " was the man that blowed the organ and saved an officer." The chaplain who was at Dartmoor in 1932 informs me that this man certainly did stick to his post, as organ-blower, while the chaplain endeavoured to calm the prisoners.

During their prison careers eighty of these men have changed the denominations to which they nominally adhered:

Once	43
Twice	22
Three times	8
Four times..	3
Five times	2
Six times	1
Seven times	1

It is submitted that these conversions, the majority of which are unlikely to have sprung from any spiritual conviction, support the suggestion that there should be a trained social worker attached to each prison, who could concentrate on the legitimate need of the prisoners for social advice and guidance, especially in their relations with their families. This work is at present performed by the various chaplains, and tends to distract them from their many other necessary functions in the prison community. Such a social worker should not concern himself with aftercare but would have a full-time occupation, not as assistant to any chaplain but relieving all of them of much of the work which they now do and for which they have no specific training. For example, a knowledge of the recent social security legislation would be indispensable to such a social worker, and this knowledge is lacking in many of the chaplains to whom prisoners turn for such advice.

Such conversions are also occasionally made with the idea of obtaining the company of a chaplain less busy than the representative of the Established Church. The steadily increasing number of unofficial prison visitors is to some extent supplying this need to the unqualified advantage both of the prisoner and of the community.

Tattooing

Again, out of respect to the memory of Lombroso, be it noted that sixty-three of our confirmed recidivists are tattooed.

Aliases

Name has not varied	102
One previous name different from present name	47
Two ,, names ,, ,, ,, ,, ...	32
Three ,, ,, ,, ,, ,, ,, ...	28
Four ,, ,, ,, ,, ,, ,, ...	19
Five ,, ,, ,, ,, ,, ,, ...	11
Six ,, ,, ,, ,, ,, ,, ...	17
Seven ,, ,, ,, ,, ,, ,, ...	5
Eight to fourteen ,, ,, ,, ,, ,, ...	9

Summary

The true significance of those qualities of the confirmed recidivists which we have analysed can only be elucidated by a series of follow-up studies, the technique for which we shall consider in Chapter IX. Let us now recapitulate some of their outstanding characteristics.

These confirmed recidivists have considerable penal and criminal experience, and their activities constitute an appreciable danger to society—they form the hard core of crime. Though not convicted when very young, they suffered imprisonment early in their careers. They are predominantly of British birth, and emanate from homes rather poorer than average, a large proportion of which are " broken homes ". Though not particularly lacking in industrial skill, and though drawn from many different trades and occupations, they tend not to settle down to any one employment and generally are unemployed when they turn to crime. They do not make useful soldiers. Their home conditions and marital relationships are very unsettled, and their children are often condemned to a permanently disrupted home-life. Though physically and mentally below the standard of the general population, this does not incapacitate them from leading useful and happy lives. As prisoners they are well-behaved.

2. THE SPECIFICITY OF RECIDIVISM AND CRIMINAL MATURATION

(a) *Specificity of recidivism*

In Chapter VII we dealt with the problem inherent in any typology of offences, and adopted, for a similar inquiry to that undertaken here, a classification of crimes used by Dr. Mannheim, setting against it a modified form of that classification used in the annual volumes of Criminal Statistics. In respect of the 12,880 crimes for which our 270 confirmed recidivists have been sentenced we shall again use these methods to ascertain to what extent they have concentrated on any type or types of crime. As Dr. Mannheim's classification has been slightly modified for our present purposes—the headings being amplified and explained—it is set out here in this changed form to avoid ambiguity in its application to the offences of this group.

Code Number	Type of Offence
I	Larceny
II	Breaking
III	Robbery and extortion
IV	False pretences, fraud (includes embezzlement, larceny by trick, and larceny as a bailee)[1]
V	Receiving
VI	Crimes against the person (not sexual)
VII	Sexual crimes (including bigamy)
VIII	Forgery (and uttering)
IX	Coining (and uttering)
X	Malicious or wilful damage and arson
XI	Vagrancy (including begging)
XII	Prostitution or living on earnings of prostitutes
XIII	Drunkenness
XIV	Prevention of Crime Act
XV	Highway offences[2]
XVI	Others[3]

The application of this classification to the offences of the confirmed recidivists revealed that they diffused their criminal talents as follows:

Number of types of crime committed	Number of criminals
One	4
Two	25
Three	58
Four	66
Five	69
Six	26
Seven	14
Eight	6
Nine	2

Accordingly, concentration on any one type of offence was exceptional, as was a diffusion of effort beyond seven types. This

[1] Includes the offence of an undischarged bankrupt obtaining credit.

[2] When a car is stolen, convictions for highway offences such as driving without a licence or without insurance frequently follow. Such offences are not included here, being only incidental to the larceny offence. Where they are independent offences they are included.

[3] Only the more serious " other offences " are included ; and in particular the following are excluded—military offences such as deserting, or unlawfully wearing uniform or military decorations ; fraud or trespass on the railway, or on the London Passenger Transport Board ; gaming offences ; contempt of court ; offences relating to identity cards (except forging an identity card, which appears under VIII) ; truancy ; minor Poor Law offences ; offences against the National Registration Act, 1939 ; unlawful sale of liquor, or drinking out of hours ; prison breaking ; being a stowaway ; poaching ; deserting or failing to maintain family ; and other minor offences.

is clearly shown in the following graphic presentation of the above figures:

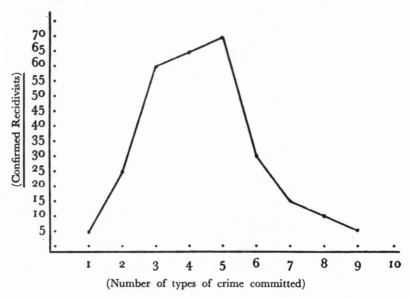

(Number of types of crime committed)

The four confirmed recidivists who completely specialised in one type of offence were all "swindlers", not varying from offences of type IV. There are two others who can be regarded as specialists, their other offences all falling within type XIV. Including these two as absolute specialists, we find that five concentrated on type IV, and one on type I.

The offences of the twenty-five who were sentenced in respect of two types of crime were:

$$
\begin{array}{ll}
\text{I} \quad \text{and II} & = 4 \\
\text{I} \quad \text{and IV} & = 17 \\
\text{I} \quad \text{and XIV} & = 1 \\
\text{II and XV} & = 1 \\
\text{IV and VIII} & = 1 \\
\text{IV and XIV} & = 1
\end{array}
$$

Amongst the seventeen convicted of types I and IV are several who are near-specialists in fraud and false pretences and whose cases will be considered later. Ten others were convicted of two

types of crime and also under the Prevention of Crime Act.[1] If these
are included, we find that only thirty-nine of our prisoners—14·4
per cent.—have confined themselves to the commission of one or
two types of crime.

The offences of the fifty-eight who were sentenced in respect
of three different types of crime were:

$$
\begin{array}{llr}
\text{I, II and III} & = & 1 \\
\text{I, II and IV} & = & 9 \\
\text{I, II and V} & = & 9 \\
\text{I, II and ...[2]} & = & 18 \\
\text{I, IV and ...} & & 16 \\
\text{I or II, ... and ...} & & 5
\end{array}
$$

The offences of the remaining one hundred and eighty-three who
were sentenced in respect of more than three different types of crime
were as follows:[3]

$$
\begin{array}{lllr}
\text{I} & \text{and II} & \text{and ... and ...} & = & 150 \\
\text{I} & \text{and III} & \text{and ... and ...} & = & 6 \\
\text{I or II} & \text{and IV} & \text{and ... and ...} & = & 15 \\
\text{I or II} & \text{and V} & \text{and ... and ...} & = & 4 \\
\text{I or II or III} & \text{and VI} & \text{and ... and ...} & = & 5 \\
\text{I or II or III} & \text{and VII} & \text{and ... and ...} & = & 2 \\
\text{I or II or III} & \text{and VIII or IX} & \text{and ... and ...} & = & 1
\end{array}
$$

Regarding types I to V, VIII and IX as crimes against property,
and entirely excluding offences of type XIV, we find that:

107 (40 per cent.) have committed crimes against property only, not one
has committed other types of crime only.

163 (60 per cent.) have committed crimes against property, and other
types of crime.

Of these 163, 102 combine crimes against property (I to V
only) with crimes against the person (VI) or sexual crimes (VII).
Dr. Mannheim found that this particular combination of crimes

---

[1] Including these ten in those who have committed only two types of crime, and
excluding the two we previously counted with the absolute specialists, the following
pattern emerges :

$$
\begin{array}{llr}
\text{I} & \text{and II} & = & 11 \\
\text{I} & \text{and IV} & = & 19 \\
\text{II} & \text{and V} & = & 1 \\
\text{II} & \text{and XV} & = & 1 \\
\text{IV} & \text{and VIII} & = & 1
\end{array}
$$

[2] That is I, II and another except III, IV or V.

[3] This table is presented in the above form so as to be readily comparable with that
on p. 361 of Dr. Mannheim's *Social Aspects of Crime in England Between the Wars*.

occurred in twenty-three per cent. of his cases; it occurs amongst nearly thirty-eight per cent. of our confirmed recidivists.

The investigation into the crimes of our group shows that their increasing criminal and penal experience has brought with it an even greater variation in the types of crimes they commit, and constitutes an accentuation and proof of Dr. Mannheim's statement that " the average recidivist although mainly concerned with crime against property, also, more often than not, tries his hand in other spheres of the criminal law."[1]

Further, we have found that though nearly forty per cent. of the confirmed recidivists have committed offences against the person, and sexual offences (including bigamy), none specialises in these types of crime.

The contrast between these findings and those that resulted from our analysis of the offences of the preventive detainees strengthens our contention that many of the latter must be regarded as habitual petty delinquents.

As a final confirmation of the pattern of crime that we have traced, the following table is presented. The classification used and the method followed is that which was described on page 322.

Number in Criminal Statistics	Type of Offence	Total Offences	Offenders Involved
	Against the person :		
1-5	Murder, manslaughter, etc.	22	17
8-10	Wounding and serious assaults	33	21
16-22	Unnatural offences, sexual assaults, importuning male person, rape, etc.	51	15
26	Bigamy	22	15
103-5	Assaults	180	74
139	Indecent exposure	9	6
	Against property :		
27-33	Burglaries, housebreaking, etc.	1,306	206
34-49, 54	Robberies, larceny, receiving	2,835	264
50-3	False pretences, frauds, etc.	892	120
56 & 57	Arson and malicious injuries to property ..	18	14
58-61	Forgery, coining (and uttering)	125	37
149	Malicious damage	44	28

Having thus established that the overwhelming majority of the confirmed recidivists diffuse their criminal efforts over several types

[1] *Ibid.*, p. 361

of crime, let us consider the exceptions to this rule—those who show a greater specificity in their recidivism.

The largest group of specialists and near-specialists (i.e. those with only one or two exceptions which are incidental to the type of crime they commit) are the swindlers, who concentrate on false pretences and similar frauds. There are fifteen of these amongst the confirmed recidivists.

There are four who are near-specialists in larceny,[1] one in house-breaking, two in coining, and one who has only exceptionally varied from receiving stolen property.

One prisoner, in addition to several swindling offences, has committed bigamy no less than five times, such marriage ceremonies being, of course, a part of his false pretences.[2] Another, though occasionally turning to offences against property, has committed bigamy once, and unnatural offences of an aggravated nature against young children on five separate occasions.[3]

There are five who concentrate almost exclusively on taking a particular type of article—one on wireless sets, two on bicycles, one graduated from bicycles through motor cycles to motor cars, and the fifth—perhaps the strangest of them all—throughout a long criminal career has by means of larceny, shopbreaking and false pretences stolen ice-cream, sweets or milk, and nothing else.[4]

We must mention finally the prisoner who has, in the last thirty years, been convicted and sentenced on twenty-two occasions for a total of 121 offences and has on seventeen of these occasions and in respect of 102 of these offences followed the same *modus operandi*. He feigns illness, collapsing in the street or whilst travelling on public transport, and thus obtains sympathy and charity. For several years his father shielded him from the legal consequences of his conduct; then for twenty years he was sentenced to periods of imprisonment of up to six months, being charged on each occasion with obtaining food and sometimes hospital treatment by false pretences. During the last ten years the indictments have been changed to allege a public mischief, and the sentences increased

---

[1] One of whom has concentrated on shoplifting.

[2] On one occasion he arranged to meet two of his " wives " simultaneously in different parts of the same railway station. He handled the situation with ease.

[3] He continues to be released from prison, if only infrequently, despite the extreme danger that he presents to young children.

[4] Dr. John Bowlby fits the larceny of this type of article into the psychopathology of the affectionless character—*Forty-Four Juvenile Thieves*, p. 49.

so as to vary between nine months' imprisonment and five years' penal servitude (his present sentence).[1]

But these specialists and near-specialists are exceptions to the general pattern we have traced: the confirmed recidivists diffused their criminal activities over a variety of offences against property; sixty per cent. also committed other types of crime; and thirty-eight per cent. committed offences both against property and against the person.

(b) Criminal Maturation

In Chapter VII we described a method of investigating the relationships between the type of offence committed, the criminal's age, and " criminal maturity " values. Let us apply this technique to the offences of the confirmed recidivists, basing our calculations on the following classification[2] of 5,998 of their proved offences:

Number in Criminal Statistics	Type of Offence	Total Offences	Offenders Involved
1-10, 103-5	Crimes of violence (non-sexual)	235	81
16-22, 26, 139	Sexual offences (including bigamy)	82	33
27-33	Burglary, housebreaking, etc.	1,306	206
34-36	Robbery and extortion	54	35
37-49, 54	Larcenies and receiving	2,781	264
50-3, 55	False pretences and other frauds	892	120
56, 57, 149	Arson, malicious injury to property, malicious damage	62	38
58, 59	Forgery (and uttering)	118	37
60, 61	Coining (and uttering)	17	3
167, 176-80, 183, 188, 189	Prevention of Crimes Acts, unlawful possession, frequenting, etc.	390	168
163-6, 185-7, 191	Poor law and vagrancy offences	61	26
		5,998	270

[1] His nineteen other offences are : Assault, attempted suicide, offences under the Prevention of Crime Act, and inflicting grievous bodily harm. The stick he carries as an adjunct to his hypochondriac false pretences becomes, in certain circumstances, a weapon of offence. He gave his age as 78 years, though actually he is only 58. Three times he has been submitted to mental observation, but in no case has any psychiatric disability been diagnosed.

[2] Certain " other non-indictable offences " have been omitted in this context. These were of a type which have no relationship to the problem of criminal maturation. Reference to Table B on pages 334-5 will show that of " other non-indictable offences " only those numbered 163-6, 185-7 and 191 have been included in this investigation.

The result of these lengthy calculations can be stated briefly, as follows: the average age at which each type of crime was committed, was (in chronological sequence):

Poor Law and vagrancy offences	.. 24·5 years
Larcenies and receiving	.. 28·7 years
Crimes of violence (non-sexual)	.. 30·5 years
Sexual offences (including bigamy)	.. 31·3 years
Coining[1]	.. 31·6 years
Prevention of Crimes Acts, etc. ..	.. 31·7 years
Burglary, housebreaking, etc. ..	.. 31·7 years
False pretences and other frauds	.. 33·2 years
Arson, malicious damage and injury	.. 33·4 years
Forgery	.. 34·7 years
Robbery and extortion	.. 34·9 years

The criminal maturity value (from 1 to 4) which must be allocated to each type of offence is:[2]

Poor Law and vagrancy offences ..	.. 1·88
Larcenies and receiving ..	.. 2·27
Prevention of Crimes Acts, etc.	.. 2·52
Sexual offences (including bigamy) ..	.. 2·56
Crimes of violence (non-sexual) ..	.. 2·66
False pretences and other frauds ..	.. 2·67
Coining[3]	.. 2·75
Arson, malicious damage and injury ..	.. 2·77
Forgery	.. 2·82
Burglary, housebreaking, etc.	.. 2·87
Robbery and extortion	.. 3·36

It is necessary to stress that, though the results of this inquiry into the criminal careers of the confirmed recidivists accord well with our findings concerning the crimes of the preventive detainees,[4] we have not progressed very far towards an outline of the sequence of types of crime and their relative positions in the normal career of the habitual criminal. Until further research has been conducted into other similarly selected groups of habitual criminals it would be

---

[1] As there are only seventeen offences of coining committed by only three members of our group, this average cannot be regarded as significant.

[2] It will be appreciated that this quadrant method of deducing a criminal maturity value does *not* give the true average position of each type of offence in the criminal career of a confirmed recidivist : what it does reveal is the order of each type of offence relative to other types of crime. The results of the quadrant method and of the average age of commission method of investigating this problem conform well with one another : the rank correlation coefficient of the two being " + .85 ".

[3] Again the figure for coining cannot be regarded as reliable.

[4] See p. 325.

unwise to draw many conclusions on this subject. Certainly, it is clear that Poor Law and vagrancy types of crime, larcenies, and receiving tend to occur early both in the criminal's life-span and in his criminal career; also that forgery, robbery and extortion occur late in both these respects. But between these poles is an important and incompletely charted territory.[1]

3. THE DETERRENT EFFECT OF PUNISHMENT ON THIS GROUP

The preceding inquiry into the "criminal maturation—type of offence" relationship was more exploratory than conclusive; but in the present section it has been found possible to reach some certainty on a question of considerable importance. The problem investigated was—*has the length of the periods of imprisonment imposed on the confirmed recidivists had any effect on the duration of their subsequent periods of freedom?*

The method explained in Chapter VII[2] was applied; but periods spent out of prison in hospitals, in sanatoria, in asylums for the insane, or serving overseas in the Armed Forces or with the Merchant Navy were not included in the calculations. Similarly, periods spent "at large", the prisoner having escaped from custody, were counted neither with "days in" nor with "days out". Finally, interruptions by "other non-indictable offences" were not included in our calculations and appear amongst the "days out".[3]

For the 270 confirmed recidivists there were 2,372 periods of imprisonment and 2,372 subsequent periods of freedom to be calculated. This having been done, a product-moment correlation was computed, the resulting coefficient of correlation being "·02". There is, therefore, no significant correlation between them.

The investigation into the deterrent effect of imprisonment on the confirmed recidivists corroborates the similar inquiry conducted into the sentences inflicted on the preventive detainees, the co-efficients of correlation being "·02" and "·03" respectively. Together, these co-efficients represent a correlation between 2,721

---

[1] One might perhaps draw conclusions like the following : False pretences and other frauds, though generally committed by the more mature offenders, occupy a median position in the normal sequence of crimes committed. This, and similar hypotheses, must be tested by further investigation before they can be propounded with confidence.

[2] See pp. 326 to 328.

[3] All too often a large number of " days out " implies only successful and undetected criminal activities ; but we cannot take cognisance of this, and as this condition is statistically as likely to occur after a short as a long sentence of imprisonment it can be ignored.

pairs of observations, and establish conclusively that, for our two groups of habitual criminals, the length of each period of penal confinement had no effect on the subsequent interval between discharge and reconviction. It is submitted that recognition of this fact could be of much assistance to courts faced with the problem of sentencing this type of criminal.

During the above calculations, certain interesting subsidiary figures emerged. The average duration of the 2,372 periods spent in prison by the confirmed recidivists was *322* days, with a standard deviation of 360 days (standard error, 7·6 days): the average duration of the subsequent periods of freedom was *318* days, with a standard deviation of 434 days (standard error, 9 days). For purposes of comparison with these figures, the average duration of the periods of freedom following non-penal sentences (fine, probation, bound over, dismissed under the Probation of Offenders Act, 1907, admonished, etc.) was computed. There were 223 such sentences, and the intervals before the next conviction for a criminal offence[1] averaged *491* days, with a standard deviation of 541 days (standard error 36 ·2 days).[2] Thus, the deterrent effect of the non-penal sentences was certainly no less than that of the penal sentences imposed. Non-penal sentences did not, however, protect the community for as long as did the penal sentences—491 days as contrasted with 640 days (322 " in " plus 318 " out ").

---

[1] Not including " other non-indictable offences ".

[2] As was done for penal sentences, periods spent in hospital, in the armed services overseas, etc., were not counted towards this average of 491 days.

CHAPTER IX

FOLLOW-UP STUDIES AND PREDICTION TABLES

THE purpose of punishment and the consequent development of a coherent sentencing policy are important and highly contentious issues. On one point, however, there is unanimity: more information is required of the actual operation and effectiveness of various punishments. This requirement is parallel and complementary to the other widely appreciated need for a greater knowledge of each individual offender before sentence is passed on him.

Facilities available to courts for obtaining information on each offender, particularly the juvenile offender, are steadily increasing ; but, as yet in this country, little has been done to follow-up the effects of each type of sentence on various groups of criminals.[1] Such follow-up studies would be of assistance in many ways, and it is the purpose of this chapter to mention some of the advantages that will accrue from them, and to suggest a method of pursuing this type of research.

The first and obvious advantage can be related to our study of habitual criminals—if we could know the later histories of the three hundred criminals whose records we have investigated, and then distinguish the analysed traits and qualities of those who conform to society's minimum behaviour requirements from those who fail to do so, we would have taken the first step necessary to evaluate the characteristics and environmental circumstances that are of significance to their reformation. Further testing of the tentative and hypothetical conclusions thus reached would gradually develop a greater understanding both of the type of criminal under investigation and of the efficiency of various punishments.

Only by knowing the group, by comprehending the norm, can we correctly diagnose the individual offender. Enlightened individualization of punishment depends necessarily on understanding the qualities of the group to which the individual most nearly conforms, and the various effects of punishments on members of that

---

[1] See L. Radzinowicz's article, " The After-Conduct of Discharged Offenders ", in *The Modern Approach to Criminal Law*, p. 142.

group; for then the potentialities of the weapons in the hands of the court can more easily be adjusted to those qualities of the individual that differentiate him from the group. The Gluecks[1] call this process the " objectification of experience ". There is no doubt that in the absence of a frame of reference it is hard to evaluate any phenomenon, and this is especially true of such a psychologically complex phenomenon as a criminal. By discovering the later histories of criminals and distinguishing between those who succeed and those who fail to adapt themselves tolerably to society, we shall establish such frames of reference for different types of offenders and greatly increase the value of whatever information is given to a court on each particular criminal.

An equally important result that can be expected from such follow-up studies is an increasing knowledge of the effects of various punishments on different types of offenders.

Some of the difficulties that hinder the development of an enlightened sentencing policy are attributable to the lack of information which follow-up studies would supply. Before we address ourselves to the problem of method, let us consider some of these difficulties.

In *The Sentence of the Court*, Sir Leo Page made a spirited attack on sentencing policy. Few men have more experience in this field than Sir Leo, and yet throughout his work one feels an obvious and ever-present need for further information—for scientific fact to reinforce his informed speculation which relies on selected cases for proof. The whole idea of criticising judicial sentences purely by considering the prisoner's criminal record is fraught with grave difficulties, and an error of sentencing must be indeed gross if it is to be discernible on the face of the record. Amongst the great majority of the sentences passed on the habitual criminals we have investigated, provided one bears in mind the diverse purposes being sought by the courts, such manifest errors do not appear. Nevertheless, the case histories Sir Leo presents are not dissimilar from several of those in our group.[2]

Such apparent errors in sentencing as can be detected have not been catalogued because they inevitably reflect little more than the critic's approach to punishment, and because in the present state

[1] A bibliography of some follow-up studies and works on prediction tables is given at the end of this chapter.

[2] The most frequent error of this nature found in our material has already been mentioned—the too early and repeated application of imprisonment to youthful offenders.

of our knowledge it is impossible to build up any sound rules of sentencing policy. It is not only the type of sentence, nor the duration of the period of imprisonment, nor even what is done during that period, but the relationship between those factors and the different types of criminal that is significant to this problem. This relationship can only be revealed by empirical research in which classifications of criminals are gradually adapted to classifications of punishments. The need for both aspects of this research is revealed in Sir Leo Page's book.

First, classifications of criminals: considering persistent offenders he adopts the distinction (accepted also by the Gladstone Committee in 1894) between " those who are unable to resist " and those who choose to be criminals," and asserts that " nothing is more certain than that this division exists."[1] Such a distinction, though perfectly legitimate, must be evaluated in the light of its criminological or penological utility. It is a subjective psychological classification of persistent offenders, which suffers from the drawback that criminals are to be allocated into one or the other category on the basis of the objective circumstances of their offences, and on their criminal records. It is submitted that it is quite impossible by such impersonal means to make an accurate psychological diagnosis of a question of volition—for that is what is involved; and that it is therefore probable that if a purely objective classification of persistent offenders proves to be of use to the development of a rational sentencing or penal policy, some such division as that between " habitual petty delinquents " and " habitual criminals " will be drawn. In our study of preventive detainees we noted the need for such a purely objective classification drawn on the basis of the dangerousness of the offender's crimes and the value of the property involved in them. But such a discussion of various possibly fruitful classifications of persistent offenders cannot be effectively conducted until we follow-up their careers, making use of various classifications and gradually refining those which prove to be of the greatest value.

Secondly, classifications of punishments : Sir Leo's support for the long sentence as contrasted with a series of short or relatively short sentences is plausible in the present state of our knowledge of the effect of different periods of imprisonment. Nevertheless, it is easy to exaggerate its advantages. He states, for example, " I

---

[1] P. 102.

have no doubt at all that the long sentence deters more powerfully than any other legal sanction."[1] Yet, as we have proved, our 302 habitual criminals were not deterred any more effectively by long than by short sentences, there being no significant correlation between the duration of their sentences and the subsequent periods of freedom before reconviction. There is the possibility that the relatively long sentence may prove to be the final precursor to their eventual reformation, and in this respect we cannot project our findings into the realms of certainty until we have further information, which can only come from effective follow-up studies. However, it is surely neither the " long " nor the " short " sentence that must be applied, but rather the " appropriate " sentence for each type of criminal, and the appropriate treatment during that sentence.

The use of follow-up studies in the development of an enlightened sentencing policy carries with it the danger that the effect of the sentence on the offender's later career may be notionally isolated. There are, of course, many other factors which will have tremendous influence on his later conduct—the process of " ageing " to which we have referred, the existence of full employment when he is discharged, and so on—but since the sentence is the most obvious variable, there is a tendency to over-emphasise its effect, and unless care is taken to avoid this the value of the statistical examination of criminal's later careers can be vitiated.

Let us now consider a technique to be followed in a series of follow-up studies based on the information analysed in this work. Undoubtedly the most exhaustive method of examining the information that would be collected by such studies is that of constructing Prediction Tables by which the statistical probability of later conduct is correlated with pre-existing qualities, traits, circumstances and punishments. The philosophy behind this application of actuarial techniques to criminology has been succinctly explained by the Gluecks in their *After-Conduct of Discharged Offenders* and emphasised by Dr. H. Mannheim in *Juvenile Delinquency in an English Middletown*,[2] and here it need only be affirmed that at present these tables constitute the only known reliable method of estimating the probability of reforming various types of criminals by various types of punishments, and consequently are essential if judicial sentences are to be better adapted to their function. They have, too,

[1] P. 178.   [2] Pp. 87-9. See also the bibliography at the end of this chapter.

the great advantage that they can be statistically tested and validated, refined and proved, so that eventually the help that they would provide for the courts would be undeniable.

Prediction Tables can be significantly computed only from follow-up studies into the careers of an appreciable number of criminals,[1] and the later careers of our 300 prisoners can serve only as a pilot study by which the significant variables for a larger study are assessed—that is to say, as a basis for propounding preliminary hypotheses. Two alternative courses can then be followed: either these hypotheses can be tested on a sufficiently large number of cases to reach statistical significance for the prognostic instruments that will be fashioned, or alternatively a relatively small-scale investigation into a further 300 offenders can be conducted, the hypotheses formed from the later careers of the first 300 being tested on the second group, and modified and redefined to accord with the correlations between the attributes tested for all 600. Then a third, and then a fourth small follow-up study, applying the same procedure, and so on, the refinement and checking continuing with each step, and with them the accuracy of the Prediction Tables.

The former course, the investigation of the careers of, say, 1,500 prisoners, would involve considerable expense, and the labours of a specialist team of research workers. In this there are dangers—it is likely that even on the basis of a preliminary pilot study the variables selected to correlate with reformation—the predictive factors—would not be those that prove on further research to be the most significant or accurately phrased. To take an example: suppose a high correlation is found in the pilot study between success in avoiding reconviction and a stable marriage. Prediction Tables might be constructed using the attribute of " stable marriage " as one of the variables to be quantitatively assessed. Later it may be discovered that it is not the stability of the marriage, but its cohesion in relation to some other factor or factors, such as the age when the prisoner was married and the recentness of the marriage, that is significant, and not the present stability of the marriage *per se*. In a large and expensive research undertaking this discovery of the necessity to reformulate a predictive variable may

---

[1] On the question of the optimum number, see *Mathematical and Tabulation Techniques,* Supplementary Study B, by Louis Guttman in *The Prediction of Personal Adjustment,* by Paul Horst.

well be most embarrassing. If the smaller sequence of follow-up studies is undertaken, such changes can more easily be made.

Even when a large research undertaking of this nature has been completed, and the criminologist, statistician and sociologists have agreed on their Prediction Tables, these must still be tested on a new group of prisoners. This validation is of the utmost importance, for it constitutes the proof of the efficacy of the prognostic instrument devised, a proof that must be rigidly made before such techniques are utilised by the courts. On the other hand, with the sequence of smaller follow-up studies, the process of proof is contemporaneous with the redefinition and reweighting of the prognostic attributes, until, as the tables are gradually refined, " successful " prediction is established.

It is important that the " success " of Prediction Tables be measured from two points of view—inclusive and exclusive. That is to say, the prognosis must *include* as many as possible of those who later conform to society's minimum standard of tolerable conduct, and as few others as possible; and secondly, it must *exclude* as few as possible of those who do later conform whilst excluding as many as possible of those who do not. These are two very different measures of " success "; but no Prediction Tables should be regarded as satisfactory until they are validated in both respects to a high standard of accuracy.

Such Prediction Tables can be developed either from the large research undertaking, or from the series of less imposing follow-up studies. Tactically, it would seem wise to press for the sequence of smaller studies involving the co-operation of a criminologist and a statistician, and concentrating on no more than 300 criminals; for though considerably less expeditious, it is equally satisfactory from the scientific point of view. For this purpose, or indeed for any other similar undertaking, the data that has been collected for this book is available and will be given to any person approved by the London School of Economics and by the Prison Commissioners. If follow-up studies are to be conducted in this country, advantage could well be taken of the opportunity presented by the existence of this analysed information and of its adaptability to that purpose.[1]

---

[1] The statistical problems involved in the construction of prediction tables are treated in *The Prediction of Personal Adjustment*, Paul Horst, Social Science Research Council New York, 1941. The works of Sheldon and Eleanor Glueck constitute the best practical illustration of the sociological and criminological problems involved in follow-up studies.

The following bibliography, though by no means exhaustive, covers the most important writings in the English language on follow-up studies and prediction tables.

BURGESS, E. W., " Factors Determining Success or Failure on Parole ", in *The Workings of the Indeterminate Sentence Law and the Parole System in Illinois* ", by A. A. Bruce, *et al.*
" Parole and the Indeterminate Sentence ", in Annual Report of the Department of Public Welfare, Illinois, 1937.

GLUECK, SH. and E., *500 Criminal Careers ; 1,000 Juvenile Delinquents ; 500 Delinquent Women ; Later Criminal Careers ; Juvenile Delinquents Grown Up ; Criminal Careers in Retrospect ; After-Conduct of Discharged Offenders.*

HAKEEM, M., article in *Federal Probation*, July-September 1945.

HORST, PAUL, *et al.*, *The Prediction of Personal Adjustment*, New York, 1941.

Journal of Mental Hygiene, July 1944, " Predicting the Behaviour of Civilian Delinquents in the Armed Forces."

MANNHEIM, H., *Modern Law Review*, Vol. V, July 1942, p. 273 ; *The Sociological Review*, Vol. XXXIV, July-October 1942, p. 226 ; *Juvenile Delinquency in an English Middletown*, p. 87.

MONACHESI, E. D., *Prediction Factors in Probation*, Minneapolis, 1932.

RECKLESS, W. C., *Criminal Behaviour*, pp. 390-4.

SANDERS, B. S., "Testing Parole Prediction", Proceedings of American Prison Association, 1935 ; " Consistency of Recording Statistical Data from Prison Files ", *Journal of American Statistical Association*, 1937.

VOLD, G. B., *Prediction Methods and Parole*, Hanover, U.S.A., 1931 ; " Do Parole Prediction Tables Work in Practice ? " *American Sociological Review*, 1931.

Also the following articles in the *Journal of Criminal Law and Criminology* :

1931, Vol. 22, p. 11 : C. Tibbitts, " Success or Failure on Parole can be Predicted : A Study of 3,000 Youth Paroled from Illinois State Reformatory."

1932, Vol. 22, p. 844 : C. Tibbitts, " Reliability of Factors Used in Predicting Success or Failure on Parole."

1934, Vol. 25, p. 10 : E. H. Sutherland, *et al.*, " The Reliability of Criminal Statistics."

1935, Vol. 26, p. 202 : G. B. Vold, " Prediction Methods Applied to Problems of Classification within Institutions."

1935, Vol. 26, p. 377 : W. F. Lanne, " Parole Prediction as a Science."

1936, Vol. 26, p. 561 : W. W. Argow, " Criminal-Liability Index for Predicting Possibility of Rehabilitation."

1941, Vol. 31, p. 693 : H. L. Long, " A Proposed Rating Scale for Measuring Parolee Adjustment."

APPENDICES

APPENDICES

APPENDIX A

Part II of the Prevention of Crime Act, 1908 (8 Edw. 7. Ch. 59)

10.—(1) Where a person is convicted on indictment of a crime, committed after the passing of this Act, and subsequently the offender admits that he is or is found by the jury to be an habitual criminal, and the court passes a sentence of penal servitude, the court, if of opinion that by reason of his criminal habits and mode of life, it is expedient for the protection of the public that the offender should be kept in detention for a lengthened period of years, may pass a further sentence ordering that on the determination of the sentence of penal servitude he be detained for such time not exceeding ten nor less than five years, as the court may determine, and such detention is hereinafter referred to as preventive detention, and a person on whom such a sentence is passed shall, whilst undergoing both the sentence of penal servitude and the sentence of preventive detention, be deemed for the purposes of the Forfeiture Act, 1870, and for all other purposes, to be a person convicted of felony.

(2) A person shall not be found to be an habitual criminal unless the jury finds on evidence :

    (a) that since attaining the age of 16 years he has at least three times previously to the conviction of the crime charged in the said indictment been convicted of a crime, whether any such previous conviction was before or after the passing of this Act, and that he is leading persistently a dishonest or criminal life; or

    (b) that he has on such a previous conviction been found to be an habitual criminal and sentenced to preventive detention.

(3) In any indictment under this section it shall be sufficient, after charging the crime, to state that the offender is an habitual criminal.[1]

(4) In the proceedings on the indictment the offender shall in the first instance be arraigned on so much only of the indictment as charges the crime, and if on arraignment he pleads guilty or is found guilty by the jury, the jury shall, unless he pleads guilty to being an habitual criminal, be charged to inquire

---

[1] Rule 11 of the Indictments Act, 1915, provided that " Any charge of a previous conviction of an offence or of being an habitual criminal . . . shall be charged at the end of the indictment by means of a statement— . . . in the case of an habitual criminal . . . that the offender is an habitual criminal ". This mandatory rule displaced s. 10 (3) of the Prevention of Crime Act, which was permissive —" shall be sufficient "—and so s. 10 (3) ceased to be of any effect.

whether he is an habitual criminal, and in that case it shall not be necessary to swear the jury again :

Provided that a charge of being an habitual criminal shall not be inserted in an indictment—

    (*a*) without the consent of the Director of Public Prosecutions; and

    (*b*) unless not less than seven days' notice has been given to the proper officer of the court by which the offender is to be tried, and to the offender, that it is intended to insert such a charge;

and the notice to the offender shall specify the previous convictions and the other grounds upon which it is intended to found the charge.

(5) Without prejudice to any right of the accused to tender evidence as to his character and repute, evidence of character and repute may, if the court thinks fit, be admitted as evidence on the question whether the accused is or is not leading persistently a dishonest or criminal life.

(6) For the purposes of this section the expression " crime " has the same meaning as in the Prevention of Crimes Act, 1871, and the definition of " crime " in that Act, set out in the schedule to this Act, shall apply accordingly.

11.—A person sentenced to preventive detention may, notwithstanding anything in the Criminal Appeal Act, 1907, appeal against the sentence without the leave of the Court of Criminal Appeal.

12.—Where a person has been sentenced, whether before or after passing of this Act, to penal servitude for a term of five years or upwards, and he appears to the Secretary of State to have been an habitual criminal within the meaning of this Act, the Secretary of State may, if he thinks fit, at any time after three years of the term of penal servitude have expired, commute the whole or any part of the residue of the sentence to a sentence of preventive detention, so, however, that the total term of the sentence when so commuted shall not exceed the term of penal servitude originally awarded.

13.—(1) The sentence of preventive detention shall take effect immediately on the determination of the sentence of penal servitude, whether that sentence is determined by effluxion of time or by order of the Secretary of State at such earlier date as the Secretary of State, having regard to the circumstances of the case and in particular to the time at which the convict, if sentenced to penal servitude alone, would ordinarily have been licensed to be at large, may direct.

(2) Persons undergoing preventive detention shall be confined in any prison or part of a prison which the Secretary of State may set apart for the purpose, and shall (save as otherwise provided by this Act) be subject to the law for the time being in force with respect to penal servitude as if they were undergoing penal servitude:

Provided that the rules applicable to convicts and convict prisons shall apply to persons undergoing preventive detention, and to the prisons or parts of prisons in which they are detained, subject to such modifications in the direction of a less rigorous treatment as the Secretary of State may prescribe by prison rules within the meaning of the Prison Act, 1898.

(3) Persons undergoing preventive detention shall be subjected to such disciplinary and reformative influences, and shall be employed on such work as may be best fitted to make them able and willing to earn an honest livelihood on discharge.

(4) The Secretary of State shall appoint for every such prison or part of a prison so set apart a board of visitors, of whom no less than two shall be justices of the peace, with such powers and duties as he may prescribe by such prison rules as aforesaid.

14.—(1) The Secretary of State shall, once at least in every three years during which a person is detained in custody under a sentence of preventive detention, take into consideration the condition, history and circumstances of that person with a view to determining whether he shall be placed out on licence, and, if so, on what conditions.

(2) The Secretary of State may at any time discharge on licence a person undergoing preventive detention if satisfied that there is a reasonable probability that he will abstain from crime and lead a useful and industrious life or that he is no longer capable of engaging in crime, or that for any other reason it is desirable to release him from confinement in prison.

(3) A person so discharged on licence may be discharged on probation, and on condition that he be placed under the supervision or authority of any society or person named in the licence who may be willing to take charge of the case, or on such other conditions as may be specified in the licence.

(4) The directors of convict prisons shall report periodically to the Secretary of State on the conduct and industry of persons undergoing preventive detention, and their prospects and probable behaviour on release, and for this purpose shall be assisted by a committee at each prison in which such persons are detained, consisting of such members of the board of visitors and such other persons of either sex as the Secretary of State may from time to time appoint.

(5) Every such committee shall hold meetings, at such intervals of not more than six months as may be prescribed, for the purpose of personally interviewing persons undergoing preventive detention in the prison and preparing reports embodying such information respecting them as may be necessary for the assistance of the directors, and may at any other times hold such other meetings, and make such special reports respecting particular cases, as they may think necessary.

(6) A licence under this section may be in such form and may contain such conditions as may be prescribed by the Secretary of State.

(7) The provisions relating to licences to be at large granted to persons undergoing penal servitude shall not apply to persons undergoing preventive detention.

15.—(1) The society or person under whose supervision or authority a person is so placed shall periodically, in accordance with regulations made by the Secretary of State, report to the Secretary of State on the conduct and circumstances of that person.

(2) A licence under this part of this Act may be revoked at any time by the Secretary of State, and where a licence has been revoked the person to whom the licence related shall return to the prison, and, if he fails to do so, may be apprehended without warrant and taken to prison.

(3) If a person absent from prison under such a licence escapes from the supervision of the society or person in whose charge he is placed, or commits any breach of the conditions contained in the licence, he shall be considered thereby to have forfeited the licence, and shall be taken back to prison.

(4) A court of summary jurisdiction for the place where the prison from which a person has been discharged on licence is situate, or where such a person is found, may, on information on oath that the licence has been forfeited under this section, issue a warrant for his apprehension, and he shall, on apprehension, be brought before a court of summary jurisdiction, which, if satisfied that the licence has been forfeited, shall order him to be remitted to preventive detention, and may commit him to any prison within the jurisdiction of the court until he can conveniently be removed to a prison or part of a prison set apart for the purpose of the confinement of persons undergoing preventive detention.

(5) The time during which a person is absent from prison under such a licence shall be treated as part of the term of preventive detention:

Provided that, where such person has failed to return on the licence being forfeited or revoked, the time which elapses after his failure so to return shall be excluded in computing the unexpired residue of the term of preventive detention.

16.—Without prejudice to any other powers of discharge, the Secretary of State may at any time discharge absolutely any person discharged conditionally on licence under this part of this Act, and shall so discharge him at the expiration of five years from the time when he was first discharged on licence if satisfied that he has been observing the conditions of his licence and abstaining from crime.

APPENDIX B

" Other Grounds "—See Section 10 (4) of the Act—Commonly Alleged in the Notice to the Offender of the Intention to Charge him as an Habitual Criminal

(*a*) THAT you are an associate of thieves and persons of bad character.

(*b*) THAT between the   day of   and the   day of you have been almost continuously in prison for various offences.

(*c*) THAT at the date of your apprehension upon the charge for which you now stand committed for trial you were a convict on licence which had not expired.

(*d*) THAT since the   day of   you have been convicted on occasions on   charges of   and sentenced on   occasions to imprisonment and on   to penal servitude, and you have now been committed for trial for

(*e*) THAT between   and   (the date of the commission of the crime for which you now stand committed for trial) you were in honest employment at   in which you could have remained, but on the   you of your own will abandoned that employment and, after that date, resumed your dishonest or criminal life.

(*f*) THAT having been discharged from prison on the   day of 19   , on the   day of   19   , you committed the crime for which you are now awaiting your trial.

(*g*) THAT since the   day of   19   , the date of your last release from prison, you have, as admitted by you since you have been in custody upon the charges upon which you are now awaiting your trial, in addition to the offences the subject of those charges, committed the following offences, viz.:—

(*h*) THAT at the date (of your apprehension upon the charges upon) (of the commission of the offences for) which you now stand committed for trial you were a convict on licence from the said sentence of preventive detention, which had not expired.

(*j*) *For insertion after the list of convictions.*

AND FURTHER TAKE NOTICE that evidence may be given against you to prove that when you were asked to give some account of yourself, in order that you might have an opportunity of showing that you had since the date of your last release from prison been following some honest employment, you (declined to give any information on the subject which could be verified) (or) (replied " ——— ").

APPENDIX C

Rules for Preventive Detention made pursuant to the Prevention of Crime Act, 1908

177.—The arrangements prescribed or approved by the Prison Commissioners under these Rules shall be such that the treatment of a prisoner (other than a prisoner in the penal grade) shall be in no way less favourable than under the rules applying to him while serving his sentence of penal servitude.

Privileges

178.—Arrangements shall be made by the Commissioners, under which every prisoner may become eligible, subject to such conditions and limitations as the Commissioners may prescribe, to earn all or any of the following privileges:

(*a*) A money credit for work done, at such rates as the Commissioners may from time to time prescribe;

(*b*) Facilities for using any money credit to such extent and in the purchase of commodities of such kinds as the Commissioners may from time to time approve;

(*c*) Opportunities for association, not only during working hours but at other times, with suitable facilities for education and recreation;

(*d*) Facilities for reading newspapers and other periodical publications;

(*e*) Facilities for smoking;

(*f*) Additional facilities for writing and receiving letters and for receiving visits.

Diet

179.—Subject to the provisions of Rule 177, the diet shall be such as the Commissioners may from time to time prescribe.

Penal Grade

180.—A prisoner who is idle or careless in his work, misconducts himself, or is known to be exercising a bad influence on other prisoners or to be making himself objectionable to them, may be placed in a special grade to be known as the Penal Grade, and while he remains in that grade he shall not be eligible for any privileges under Rule 178.

181.—Prisoners in the Penal Grade may be located in a separate part of the prison, but shall not be excluded from association at labour unless this is necessary for preserving discipline and order.

Offences Against Discipline

182.—(1) All or any of the following awards may be made, in addition to those allowed by the General Rules, by the Board of Visitors or any one of them, or by a Commissioner:

(a) Transfer to the Penal Grade for such period as may be considered necessary;

(b) Forfeiture of money that may have been credited to him under Rule 178 (a);

(c) Forfeiture, restriction or postponement of other privileges obtainable under Rule 178.

(2) All or any of the foregoing awards may be imposed on a prisoner by the Governor, subject to such limits as may be prescribed by the Commissioners:

Provided that no prisoner shall by order of the Governor be kept in the Penal Grade for more than three months unless such order has been confirmed by the Board of Visitors or by a Commissioner.

183.—Any award made under Rule 182 may be terminated at any time by the authority by whom it was made.

Advisory Committee

184.—The Advisory Committee appointed under Section 14 (4) of the Prevention of Crime Act, 1908, shall meet at the prison at least once a quarter; and as occasion arises shall make such individual reports on prisoners as will assist the Commissioners in advising the Secretary of State in regard to the discharge of such prisoners on licence.

Discharge

185.—On a prisoner's discharge any money which has been awarded to him under these rules and is standing to his credit shall, unless the Commissioners otherwise decide, be transferred to the society or person under whose supervision he is placed to be expended or to be held for his benefit at the discretion of such society or person.

Return to Preventive Detention

186.—Any prisoner whose licence is revoked or forfeited shall, on his return to Preventive Detention be placed in the Penal Grade and kept therein for such length of time as the Advisory Committee shall consider necessary.

Earnings

225.—(A) (1) Every prisoner not in the Penal Grade shall be eligible for earnings, and on the commencement of his sentence of preventive detention will receive 1s.

(2) The payment of earnings, provided that a prisoner is medically fit for work, will be made in accordance with (a) a basic rate, and (b) a party rate.

(3) Basic rates will be as follows:

During the first year	1s. 3d. per week
During the second year	1s. 8d. per week
During the third and subsequent years ..	2s. 0d. per week

Time spent in the Penal Grade will not count.

(4) Party rates will vary according to the party and the amount of work performed. The minimum party rate will be 3d. per week, and the maximum 1s. per week (now altered to 1s. 6d. per week in accordance with a recent prison-wide 50 per cent. increase of earnings).

(5) (Relates to payment when ill.)

Association, Recreation and Newspapers

225.—(B) (1) Prisoners not in the Penal Grade may be permitted to associate at meals and in the evening. They will be eligible for classes and lectures. Games, as approved by the Commissioners, will be permitted.

(2) In addition to the newspapers provided out of public funds for the use of prisoners in association, prisoners not in the Penal Grade will be allowed to purchase any periodical approved by the Commissioners, provided that after a prisoner has been in possession of such periodical for a reasonable time, it will be at the disposal of the prison authorities.

(3) It is within the discretion of the governor to allow papers to be taken into cells or to be left in the association rooms.

Visits and Communications

225.—(D) (1) Every prisoner not in the Penal Grade shall be entitled, after the first four weeks of his sentence, to write and receive a letter, and to receive a visit, once a week.

(2) A prisoner in the Penal Grade shall be entitled, after two months in the grade, to write and receive a letter and to receive a visit once in two months.

(3) Subject, in the case of visits, to the convenience of the prison administration, a prisoner shall be entitled to write and receive a letter, and to receive a visit on any day in the period applicable to his case, irrespective of the date of the last letter or visit.

(4)' In lieu of a visit in any period, a prisoner shall be entitled to write a letter and to receive a reply, or to receive a letter and write a reply to it.

Special Store

225.—(E) (1) The Governor will submit to the Commissioners a list of commodities to be sold at the store, together with tenders for the supply, in order that the prices to be charged to the prisoners may be fixed and approved. Purchases will be effected by means of demands filled in and signed by prisoners which will be retained and recorded at the store.

(2) Prisoners not in the Penal Grade may be allowed to purchase pipes, tobacco and other approved articles in the store.

APPENDIX D

Statements by the Confirmed Recidivists as to the Trades and Occupations Followed

	True	False
Accountant		1
Baker	2	4
Barber	1	
Boilermaker	1	
Bookmaker	2	
Bookseller	1	
Bootmaker	4	
Bricklayer	5	
Bricklayer and plasterer	1	
Builder	4	2
Cabinet maker, carpenter, joiner	12	3
Car-hirer	1	
Carrier, transport contractor	3	
Caterer	1	1
Chef, cook, storekeeper-cook	6	8
Chemist, help in shop		1
Chemist, Research, B.Sc.	1	
Cinema attendant	1	
Clerk	8	
Coachbuilder	1	
Cook and baker		1
Electrical engineer	4	1
Electrician	1	2
Electrical mechanical engineer	1	
Engineer	3	6
Estate Agent	1	
Farmer	1	
Fish porter	2	
Fitter and fitter's mate	6	
Flat and club porter	3	
Foreign correspondent	1	
Fruiterer and greengrocer	2	
Hairdresser	1	
Hotel keeper	1	
Horsebreaker	1	
Indoor servant—butler	1	
Jobbing gardener	1	
Journalist		1
Kitchen porter	2	1
Labourer (coal porter, etc.)	31	
Laundry hand	1	1
Lorry driver (coach, motor drivers)	14	
Machine setter	1	

	True	False
Masseur, qualified	1	
Mill hand	1	
Miner	5	
Motor-car dealer	2	1
Motor engineer (qualified or trained)	3	
Motor-car mechanic	3	1
Musician	2	
" None "	1	
Painter (glazier and painter, painter and decorator)	13	
Plasterer	5	
Plumber, plumber's mate	2	
Printer	1	
Radio engineer	2	
Reporter		1
Salesman	3	
Seaman (stoker, steward)	11	
Sewing-machine mechanic	1	
Sheet-metal worker	1	
Sign-writer	2	
Slater	1	
Soldier	7	
Solicitor's clerk	1	
Steel-hardener	1	
Street trader and general dealer (elastic, laces, almost anything)	13	
Tailor	1	
Timekeeper[1]	1	
Toolmaker	3	
Waiter	1	
Watchmaker		1
Watchman, night-watchman	11	

APPENDIX E

Police Reports as to the Sobriety and Companions and Associates of Confirmed Recidivists

Sobriety

Teetotaller (or total abstainer)	6
Sober or of sober habits	73
Temperate habits	18
Moderate drinker	25
Not addicted to drink	10
Not addicted to alcohol	7
Not a heavy drinker	8

[1] It was not easy to decide whether the prisoner who stated he was a " timekeeper " had in fact ever followed this as a non-institutional occupation. Probably he had not ; but as he has received sentences totalling 51½ years of imprisonment, I had no doubt that he would make an excellent " time keeper " and, honouring his wit, classed his statement as true.

Fairly sober	10
Moderate sobriety	5
Intemperate (habits)	6
Fairly heavy drinker	3
Fond of drink(ing)	7
Frequents public houses	10
Not (of) sober (habits)	5
Drunken habits	7
Drinks heavily	9
A heavy drinker	18
A very heavy drinker	5
A drunkard	1
Habitual drinker	2
Addicted to drink	12
Frequently drunk	1
Drinks to excess	1
Often found drunk	1
Confirmed alcoholic	1
Methylated spirits addict	1
No answers or not known	18

Companions and Associates

Associates with { persons of good character / a good class of people }	10
No regular companions, or no known associates	30
Associates with no one } Solitary disposition }	16
No known male associates	14
Fond of female company, no known male associates	16
Associates with persons of the dealer type	2
Companions are of doubtful character	9
His companions are undesirable/not good types	3
Only companions are young boys	1
Most of his companions are men of effeminate type	2
Associates with women of loose type	1
Fond of company of young males	1
An associate of deserters and other doubtful characters	2
Associates with people (persons) of bad character	2
An associate of known thieves	13
,, ,, ,, convicted thieves	37
,, ,, ,, ,, ,, and doubtful (undesirable) characters	4
,, ,, ,, ,, ,, ,, coiners	1
,, ,, ,, ,, ,, ,, race gangs	2
Associates with convicted housebreakers and thieves	7
An associate of persons convicted of crime and others with inebriate habits	3
An associate of criminals (convicted persons)	23
Companions are persons with criminal records	6

Associates with convicted thieves and women of immoral character .. 7
Associates with (convicted) thieves and prostitutes 23
Associates with (convicted) thieves and (sodomites) male prostitutes .. 6
Senior member of an active gang 1
Associates with convicted thieves, prostitutes, deserters, and undesirable
    people in low-class cafés 1
Not known to police and no answer 27

APPENDIX F

THE PRISON RULES, 1949 (S.I. 1949, No. 1073)

Special Rules for Prisoners Sentenced to Preventive Detention

160.—A sentence of preventive detention shall be served in three stages in accordance with the eight following rules.

First Stage

161.—(1) The first stage shall be served either in a regional prison . . . or in a local prison, and shall be for not less than one year nor more than two years.

(2) A prisoner in the first stage shall be treated in all respects under the rules applicable to prisoners serving a sentence of imprisonment.

162.—The Governor of the regional or local prison shall report to the Commissioners on the expiration of the first twelve months of the sentence, and thereafter at such intervals not exceeding three months as the Commissioners determine, on the suitability of the prisoner for removal to the second stage.

Second Stage

163.—The second stage shall be served in a central prison and the arrangements in this stage shall be such that the treatment of a prisoner (other than a prisoner in the penal grade) shall be not less favourable than that of a prisoner serving a sentence of imprisonment in a central prison.

164.—Prisoners serving sentences of preventive detention in a central prison shall so far as practicable be accommodated in a separate part of the prison and shall not be allowed to associate with prisoners serving sentences of imprisonment except in the course of industrial or agricultural employment.

165.—Arrangements shall be made under which a prisoner who has passed into the second stage may become eligible to earn privileges over and above those allowed to a prisoner serving a sentence of imprisonment, including:

    (a) payment for work done at a higher rate,
    (b) facilities for spending money earned in prison either at a prison store
        or on such articles, including newspapers and periodicals, purchased
        outside the prison as may be approved,
    (c) the cultivation of garden allotments and the use or sale of the produce
        in such manner as may be approved,

(d) the practice in the prisoner's own time of arts or crafts of such kinds and in such a manner as may be approved,

(e) additional letters and visits,

(f) association in common rooms for meals and recreation.

Third Stage

166.—(1) The question whether a prisoner in the second stage shall be admitted to the third stage, and the date of his admission, shall be decided by the advisory board established under Rule 171:

Provided that the date of admission of any prisoner to the third stage shall not be more than twelve months before the date on which he will have served two-thirds of his sentence.

(2) The advisory board, when a prisoner is brought before them under paragraph (1), shall consider not only his conduct in the second stage, but whether they expect to be able, within the period to be served in the third stage, to recommend his release on licence.

(3) Where the advisory board defer their decision under paragraph (2), the case shall be reconsidered at intervals of not less than three months.

167.—The period to be served in the third stage shall not in any case be less than six months and shall not normally exceed twelve months.

168.—(1) The third stage shall be designed both to fit the prisoner for release and to test his fitness therefor, and may be served in such conditions of modified security as are available for the purpose, whether in connexion with a central prison or elsewhere.

(2) During this stage every effort shall be made, by special industrial and social training and otherwise, to fit a prisoner to take his place in normal social life on discharge.

(3) As and when suitable arrangements can be made, prisoners in this stage, or in the latter part thereof, may be permitted to live in conditions of modified security designed to form a transition from prison life to freedom.

(4) The advisory board may at any time order the return of a prisoner to the second stage if it appears to them to be in the interests of himself or of others to do so, and the Governor, if he considers it necessary, may so order in his discretion subject to confirmation by the board at its next meeting.

(5) The intention of paragraph (2) of this Rule shall so far as practicable be carried out for prisoners who are not selected for the third stage during the last period of six to twelve months before their date of release on licence under Rule 172.

169 and 170.—Provisions as to Discipline, and the Penal Grade as a punishment for prison offences.

Release on Licence

171.—(1) The board of visitors shall consider the character, conduct, and prospects of every prisoner serving a sentence of preventive detention, and shall report to the Commissioners on the advisability of his release on licence.

(2) For this purpose the board of visitors shall be assisted by an advisory board consisting of three members of the board of visitors approved by the Secretary of State, and such other persons not exceeding four, of whom one may be a Commissioner or Assistant-Commissioner, as the Secretary of State may appoint. The chairman of the advisory board shall be appointed by the Secretary of State.

(3) The advisory board shall meet at the prison at least once a quarter.

172.—(1) Every prisoner, whether or not he is admitted to the third stage, shall be eligible for release on licence when he has served five-sixths of his sentence of preventive detention.

(2) A prisoner admitted to the third stage shall be eligible for release on licence, subject to the provisions of this Rule, when he has served two-thirds of his sentence of preventive detention.

(3) The advisory board shall at each quarterly meeting consider the case of every prisoner who has served three months or more in the third stage, with a view to recommending his release on licence within three months thereafter if they are satisfied, having regard to his conduct in the third stage and his prospects on release, that there is a reasonable probability that he will not revert to a criminal life.

(4) Where a prisoner has under paragraph (4) of Rule 168 been returned to the second stage, and has again been placed by the advisory board in the third stage, he shall be considered for the purpose of release on licence as if he had entered the third stage for the first time.

(5) The Governor shall at once report to the Commissioners any circumstances arising in the case of a prisoner in whose favour a recommendation has been made which may affect their decision on that recommendation, and may if necessary remove the prisoner to the second stage pending the Commissioners' decision.

Orders of Recall

173.—(1) A prisoner who has been recalled from release on licence shall on his return to prison in consequence of such recall be placed in the first stage, and may at the discretion of the Commissioners be removed to the second stage within a period of twelve months from his return to prison as aforesaid :

Provided that if the unexpired period of the sentence is less than two years, the whole of it may be served in the first stage.

(2) A prisoner who has been recalled shall not again be eligible for release on licence before he has served five-sixths of the unexpired portion of his sentence and, if that period is completed in the first stage, the question whether he shall be released on licence shall be decided by the Commissioners on a recommendation of the Governor of the local prison.

INDEX

A

Akers-Douglas, A., 35, 36, 37
Alcohol, 310, 353-4
Aldington Camp, 241
American National Prison Congress, 1870, 22
Archambault, Mr. Justice, 137 ; Archambault Report, 140, 143
Aristotle, on moral accountability, 17
Arson, 338 n.
Arvelo, A. P., 208-9, 220-1
Auckland prison, 154
Australia, habitual criminal law in, 86 ff.
Avory, Mr. Justice, 57

B

Barberton prison, 163, 164
Barnes and Teeters : *New Horizons in Criminology*, 21 n.
Beauchamp, Earl, 54
Beechworth reformatory prison, 101, 102, 103, 105, 106
Bekaert, Hermann, 206-7, 220, 293, 301 n., 309 n.
Belgium, habitual criminal law in, 184, 190-1, 193, 194-5, 206-7; statistics of habitual criminals, 219-20 ; preventive detainees in, 301 n., 302 n.
Bigamy, 318-19, 365
Borstal Institutions and training, 4, 12, 21, 302, 340 ff.; records, 67 n.
Botsfengslet prison, 210
Bowlby, Dr. John, 15, 281, 365 n.
Brewer, John M., 304 n.
Bridge, Nigel, 15
Brisbane prison, 111-12
Broadmoor, 21, 355

C

California, castration in, 24
Camp Hill, 70 and n.
Canada, habitual criminal law in, 137-44 ; recidivists in, 347 n.;
Canadian Royal Commission on Penal System, 334 n., 336 n.
Cape, the, habitual criminal law in, 161 ff.
Capital punishment, 23, 219 n., 222, 245, 263
Case histories, 268-92, 306, 310-15
Castlemaine reformatory prison, 101
Castration, 24
Cecil, Lord Robert, 37, 54
Channel, Mr. Justice, 45, 52-3

Chelmsford Borstal Institution, 346 n.
Cinderella prison, 163, 164
Clemmer, D.: *The Prison Community*, 4 n., 351 n.
Corporal punishment, 338
Craig, R. W., 138
Criminal Appeal Act, 1907, 41
Criminal Appeal, Court of, 42 ff.
Criminal Justice Act, 1925, 249 ; 1948, 13, 266, 303
Criminology, Classical School of, 17-19
Criminology, Positivist School of, 19
Crofton, Sir Walter, 21
Czechoslovakia, habitual criminal law in, 187, 203

D

Dartmoor Mutiny, 1932, 338, 357-8
Delaquis, Ernest, 209
Denmark, indeterminate sentences in, 23 ; castration in, 24 ; habitual criminal law in, 190, 195, 201, 203, 207, 214 and n., 215 ; preventive detainees in, 313 n.
Drug addicts, 354
Dual-track system of preventive detention, 39 and n., 80, 102, 109, 114, 126, 153, 178, 201-2, 251, 257

E

East, Sir Norwood, 317 n., 356 and n.
Efford, Lincoln, 158 n.
Elkin, W. A. : *English Juvenile Courts*, 339 n.
Ellis, Havelock, 1
Ewing, A. C.: *The Morality of Punishment*, 16 n.

F

Ferri, Enrico, 1, 224
Feuerbach, 235
Finland, habitual criminal law in, 188, 190-1, 193, 195, 198-200, 208-9, 214 and n., 215, 217, 219 and n.; statistics, 220-1 ; preventive detainees in, 301 n.
Foster, F. A. P., 70 n., 229
France, Penal Code in, 4 ; and transportation, 24 ; habitual criminal law in, 86, 175-83, 185, 193 ; and principle of *nulla poena*, 235
Fremantle prison, 124, 129, 131
French Guiana, habitual criminal law in, 179, 180
French Island reformatory prison, 101

393